NATION FORMATION

Politics and Culture
A Theory, Culture & Society series

Politics and Culture analyses the complex relationships between civil society, identities and contemporary states. Individual books will draw on the major theoretical paradigms in politics, international relations, history and philosophy within which citizenship, rights and social justice can be understood. The series will focus attention on the implications of globalization, the information revolution and postmodernism for the study of politics and society. It will relate these advanced theoretical issues to conventional approaches to welfare, participation and democracy.

SERIES EDITOR: Bryan S. Turner, *Deakin University*

Also in this series

Welfare and Citizenship
Beyond the Crisis of the Welfare State?
Ian Culpitt

Citizenship and Social Theory
edited by Bryan S. Turner

Citizenship and Social Rights
The Interdependence of Self and Society
Fred Twine

The Condition of Citizenship
edited by Bart von Steenbergen

NATION FORMATION

Towards a Theory of Abstract Community

Paul James

SAGE Publications
London • Thousand Oaks • New Delhi

320.5401

JAM

© Paul James 1996

First published 1996

SAGE Publications Ltd
6 Bonhill Street
London EC2A 4PU

SAGE Publications Inc
2455 Teller Road
Thousand Oaks, California 91320

SAGE Publications India Pvt Ltd
32, M-Block Market
Greater Kailash – I
New Delhi 110 048

British Library Cataloguing in Publication data

A catalogue record for this book is
available from the British Library

    ISBN 0 7619 5072 9
    ISBN 0 7619 5073 7 (pbk)

Library of Congress catalog card number 96–068420

Typeset by M Rules
Printed in Great Britain at the University Press, Cambridge

For comrades and friends associated with *Arena*,
particularly for Gerry and Geoff

Contents

Acknowledgements

The approach of *Nation Formation* is profoundly influenced by the theoretical arguments of Geoff Sharp. It is difficult to convey this debt through academic conventions such as footnoting for it derives from over a decade of ongoing discussion. On the national question more specifically I need to mention the influence of Benedict Anderson's slim but important volume, *Imagined Communities*. It remains the most insightful book written in the area. I have learned much about conceptual method and issues of historical transformation in working my way through the writings of Karl Marx, Anthony Giddens, Ernest Gellner and Tom Nairn, as well as Max Weber and Emile Durkheim. At the same time, my ideas were formulated in the context of a long-time association with a group of people perhaps best known through reference to the Melbourne-based journal *Arena*, people for whom practical and engaged politics is as important to their lives as intellectual enquiry.

Given the scope of this study I have been extraordinarily fortunate to have been criticized and helped by many people with specialized knowledges ranging across a diversity of areas. There are numerous people whom I need to thank. They include those with whom I have discussed back and forth across the national question; friends and colleagues who have read the manuscript in whole or part and commented upon various drafts; people who have made critical suggestions about the direction of its central themes; as well as those who have contributed to its research and production. In particular I would like to thank Steve Alomes, Ben Anderson, Tony Ayers, Verity Burgmann, Peter Cotton, Phillip Darby, Gloria Davies, Lindsay Fitzclarence, Anthony Giddens, Gerry Gill, John Hinkson, Rod Home, Kim Humphery, Rita Hutchison, Graeme James, Jean James, Henry Krips, Bruno Letour, Vicki Lukins, Stuart Macintyre, Jim MacLaughlin, Julie McLeod, Marion Merkel, Michael Muetzelfeldt, Eleni Naoumidis, Ephraim Nimni, Alison Ravenscroft, Edna Ravenscroft, Harry Redner, Alan Roberts, Gary Shapcott, Geoff Sharp, Charles Tilly, Stephanie Trigg, Bryan Turner, Helen Watson, Doug White and others.

I need to thank the editors of various journals for their support in criticizing and publishing research in progress and earlier versions of sections of this book: *Arena, Philosophy of the Social Sciences, Canadian Review of Studies in Nationalism, Arena Journal* and the *Melbourne Journal of Politics*. I want also to thank colleagues and students, past and present, in the Politics Department at Monash University, in particular Freya Carkeek, Hugh Emy,

Michael Janover, Peter Lawler (now at Manchester), Andrew Linklater (now at Keele), Darren Lynch, Paul Muldoon, Harry Redner and Chris Ziguras. At Sage Publications, Robert Rojek has been the most efficient and enthusiastic editor one might hope to have. He was a pleasure to work with, as was Pascale Carrington, the book's production editor.

Amongst all these critics, there are five persons that have to be singled out for special appreciation and thanks. Geoff Sharp was extraordinarily generous with his time, offering support, responding at length to draft chapters, and opening up lines of approach which fundamentally shaped my thinking; Rita Hutchison worked painstakingly through successive drafts never demurring at yet another set of changes to read; Ben Anderson commented extensively on an early manuscript of *Nation Formation* making numerous helpful suggestions; discussions with Gerry Gill served to crystallize some intuitions on method and theory; and Alison Ravenscroft helped me in numerous ways with her careful reading and insightful comments.

Introduction

In the late twentieth century, nationality is lived as a series of remarkable contradictions. We are living through a time when the nation-state continues to be one of the central constituents of international relations, yet its slow death is constantly proclaimed. The call of nationalism resounds stronger than ever as people grapple with social change and the fragmentation of social identity. It is a time when the processes of globalism have brought to bear new emphases on the local, a time when the fragility of identity has highlighted our relationship to place and people. Certainly there are cosmopolites who regard themselves as floating free of national attachments, but for most of us the nation-state continues to frame our lives. And it does so at different and contradictory levels.

The nation is at once assumed to be a rich and inalienable relationship of specifiable compatriots; at the same time it connects anonymous strangers most of whom will probably never even pass each other in the street. It is lived as a 'concrete' relationship which each individual takes to his or her grave, and yet it is abstracted across time and space in ways that leave us culturally oblivious to the particular deaths of any other than those persons who are our immediate associates or who in some way have publicly walked the national stage. National community is subjectively experienced as a 'primordial' relation which, except for a few late arrivals who have to be *naturalized*, is said to be traceable deep into the past as a complex though specific genealogy. Yet the bounding of such ties by the nation-state is objectively quite modern: most of us in the contemporary nation-state must now self-consciously rediscover our own personal genealogies – our roots back into the dead generations.

Such contradictions, themselves historically specific, form the background to my attempt to characterize the nation as a changing but distinctive kind of abstract community.[1] Since this entails something of a new departure, or at

---

1. The argument draws heavily upon a perspective developed by Geoff Sharp and others called, for want of a less elaborate name, the 'constitutive abstraction argument'. Specific concepts written within this approach are footnoted where appropriate. The argument has been developing in the pages of the journal *Arena*. Its fullest early expression can be found in Geoff Sharp, 'Constitutive Abstraction and Social Practice', 1985. See also, for example, Gerry Gill, 'Post-Structuralism as Ideology', 1984; John Hinkson, 'Postmodern Economy: Value, Self-Formation and Intellectual Practice', 1993; and Geoff Sharp, 'Extended Forms of the Social', 1993. The journal began in 1963 as a forum for the Australian Left. In 1993 two new publications emerged out of the old: *Arena Magazine* and *Arena Journal*, the latter being an international journal of social theory and ethically concerned discussion of contemporary social practice. Both publications are produced collectively as part of a broader co-operative project of research and cultural politics. While the project is still developing, it is in a very real sense emerging as a school of social enquiry.

least a new emphasis in method, the book begins by outlining a theoretical approach for describing the changing dominant social forms of the national community. It argues that the commonly acknowledged failure of commentators to theorize the nation adequately is partly due to an inattention to the complications ensuing from the necessarily abstracting nature of theorizing as an intellectual technique. More broadly, it is due to an inattention to the implications of contradictions arising out of the wider, *material* abstractions of social relations. How can the nation be experienced as a concrete, gut-felt relation to common souls and a shared landscape, and nevertheless be based upon abstract connections to largely unknown strangers and unvisited places? As part of the 'nation of strangers' we live its connectedness much more through the abstracting mediations of mass communications and the commodity market than we do at the level of the face-to-face, but we continue to use the metaphors of the face-to-face to explain its cultural power.

If the central argument holds that it is important to consider the contradictory intersection of more abstract with more concrete forms of association in grounding the emergence of the nation, then its corollary is that in either failing to recognize this process or treating abstraction as only relevant to the realm of ideas, social theorists have substantially limited the depth of their theorizing. In other words, *Nation Formation* is an exploratory examination of the socially grounding (*ontological*) conditions which make the changing forms of national association possible. Since the concept of ontology is liable to misinterpretation it is worth defining even before the argument begins to be elaborated. The concept is used in the sense of the modes of being-in-the-world, the forms of culturally grounded conditions, historically constituted in the structures (recurrent practices) of human inter-relations. Thus the concept does not fall back upon a sense of the 'human essence' except in so far as the changing nature of being human is always taken to be historically constituted. The concept is not confined to the sphere of selfhood except insofar as the self is always defined in interrelation with the 'other'.

The book asks why is it that this area of examination, the ontology of national formation, has been a relatively untheorized shadow-area, traversed in the main either by idealists who imbue it with the force of a primordial essence or by historians who seem resigned to documenting its outer reaches. Although the book discusses what are argued to be *necessary* grounding conditions and contextualizes these in history, it makes no sustained attempt to answer such questions as why the nation came into existence, or what are the *sufficient* conditions for such a development. Its aim is to explore in theory and practice what Slavoj Žižek calls 'the ambiguous and contradictory nature' of the nation:

> On the one hand, 'nation' of course designates modern community delivered of the traditional 'organic' ties, a community in which the pre-modern links tying down the individual to a particular estate, family, religious group, and so on, are broken – the traditional corporate community is replaced by the modern nation-state whose constituents are 'citizens': people as abstract individuals, not as members of particular estates, and so forth. On the other hand, 'nation' can never be reduced to a

network of purely symbolic ties: there is always a kind of 'surplus of the Real' that sticks to it – to define itself, 'national identity' must appeal to the contingent materiality of the 'common roots', of 'blood and soil', and so on. In short, 'nation' designates at one and the same time the instance by means of reference to which traditional 'organic' links are dissolved *and* the 'remainder of the pre-modern in modernity': the form 'organic inveteracy' acquires within the modern, post-traditional universe; the form organic substance acquires within the universe of the substanceless Cartesian subjectivity. The crucial point is again to conceive both aspects in their interconnection: it is precisely the new 'suture' effected by the Nation which renders possible the 'de-suturing', the disengagement from traditional organic ties. 'Nation' is a pre-modern leftover which functions as an inner condition of modernity itself, as an inherent impetus of its progress.[2]

The most illuminating contributions to the national question are those which have attempted to develop a social-theoretical framework sensitive to historical research, philosophies of ideas and political interpretations, those which show an active awareness of the relevance of work done in a breadth of disciplines, from literary studies to anthropology and from linguistics to political geography. Along with Benedict Anderson's work which has this quality, we must include the diverse contributions of Ernest Gellner and Anthony Smith, Tom Nairn and Anthony Giddens. These, in turn, stand upon the shoulders of traditions which go back to the classical social theorists: Emile Durkheim, Max Weber and Karl Marx. Hence the book is structured around an examination of 'stages' of theorizing of the nation. It is critical of all these writers, though acutely aware that the critique itself is made possible only by building upon and reworking the insights they opened to consideration. The discussion tries to make sense of the strengths and limitations of the theorists in terms of their own grounding assumptions, the historical period in which they are writing, and the form of the nation which they face in that period. In other words, it takes a social-theoretical approach to the history of method: it is not intended to be a comprehensive survey of theory or history.

The book's structure is very simple. The first two chapters summarize my methodological and definitional assumptions, attempting to evoke what is meant by the notion of the abstract community. Following this introduction, Part Two examines the classical theorists: Chapter 3 looks at Marx, the nineteenth-century theorist who spent the most time on the national question; Chapter 4 discusses the writings of Durkheim and Weber. By situating these writers in historical context it attempts a reconnaissance of the question, 'why, in the period of the late-nineteenth, early twentieth centuries, when national formation was assuming an ontological predominance, were theoretical responses to this consolidation so limited?'

In the second main section, Part Three, some contemporary theories of the nation are critically assessed. Taking Tom Nairn (Chapter 5), Ernest Gellner (Chapter 6) and Anthony Giddens (Chapter 7) as key, representative figures within variant debates and traditions, it asks to what extent have these recent writers moved to strengthen and deepen our understanding of the national

2. Slavoj Žižek, *For They Know Not What They Do*, 1991, p. 20.

formation. The structure of this section mirrors that of Part Two, beginning with the contribution of a prominent marxist and going on to discuss the work of a well-known writer coming out of the Weberian–Durkheimian tradition. It is suggested that while each of these theorists makes an important contribution, each is fundamentally limited by his largely one-dimensional theory of social formations. This leads on to the chapter on Anthony Giddens, a theorist who has attempted to synthesize both of these traditions into a coherent alternative. However, it is argued that ultimately a similar problem of developing theory on 'one plane' is also found in Giddens' work.[3] As with Part Two on the classical theorists, Part Three considers some of the historically conditioned assumptions which give rise to and frame contemporary approaches to the national question. In contrast to the early chapters, the stronger concern here is to assess the detail and structure of their theories, to evaluate how comprehensive they are, how internally coherent, and how they stand up against the wealth of material elucidated by recent empirical and social research.

Throughout the book, the discussion attempts to draw out the implications of the continuing theoretical weaknesses in our general understanding of the nation, but rather than just being a general exposition of theory, this is located first in extensive reference to salient historical periods through which national formations emerged and changed; and secondly in discussion of particular theories. In discussing historical change, *Nation Formation* concentrates upon the structural subjectivities which ground national formation: three categories of human existence and social relations – the body, space and time – provide focusing sub-themes. They were chosen because of their obvious bearing upon the national question. The body relates to the nationalist emphasis upon organic metaphors such as the 'blood of the people'; space is relevant to the emphasis on territoriality; and time is important to the cultural themes of historicity, tradition and primordial roots.

History is not treated as a continuous, evolving narrative. Nor is it possible to confine the study, as in the conventional sense, to a neat, specifiable time-frame, nor to a particular country or region. That would be to assume the logic of an assumption that is being questioned, namely, the ideology that particular nation-states have internally coherent histories able to be traced on a single-level time-line, and that they are the culmination of progressive development with an essentially continuous form of social relations. Neither, as will soon become apparent, do I uncritically accept the revisionist (often postmodernist) claims that there are no such things as social boundaries, social systems (closed or open); no totalities and therefore no 'sub-systems', 'dimensions' or 'levels' of such a society. In the same vein, I reject the bald version of the revisionist assertion that the nation is a recently contrived, cultural *invention*.

A continuing concern of the book is to place theory in history. All the

---

3. The concept of theory on 'one plane' cannot be more than hinted at here but it is crucial to later discussion. For a detailed definition see Sharp, 'Constitutive Abstraction', 1985.

while, my overriding interest is to work through the possibilities of the argument that the nation is a particular kind of abstract community, to probe its relevance for a theory of national formations and national subjectivities, and indirectly, implicitly, to canvass its implications for rethinking directions in political practice. The nation and nation-state have become extraordinarily important in framing the practices and subjectivities of contemporary social life from the individual's sense of identity to the 'collective' activity of fighting wars. At the same time, the increasing permeability of nation-state boundaries to waves of culture, capital and emigrants has provided the context for contradictory responses: on the one hand, new and more febrile nationalisms such as in Bougainville and Bosnia, Russia and Rwanda; and on the other hand, denials of the continuing significance of the national frame as the nation itself comes to be reconstituted by the structures of postmodern capitalism and the processes of globalization. As the national form undergoes new changes it becomes all the more pressing that we critically examine old and new lines of understanding.

PART ONE: OLD AND NEW LINES OF UNDERSTANDING

1

The Nation as an Abstract Community

> [The nation] is imagined as a *community*, because, regardless of the actual inequality and exploitation that may prevail in each, the nation is always conceived as a deep, horizontal comradeship. Ultimately it is this fraternity that makes it possible, over the past two centuries, for so many millions of people, not so much to kill, as willingly to die for such limited imaginings.
>
> These deaths bring us abruptly face to face with the central problem posed by nationalism: what makes the shrunken imaginings of recent history (scarcely more than two centuries) generate such colossal sacrifices? I believe that the beginnings of an answer lie in the cultural roots of nationalism.
>
> Benedict Anderson, *Imagined Communities*, 1991

Understanding the nation-state has gained a renewed urgency as across the world we watch grotesque and continuing wars, bloody conflicts fought either in the name of national independence or of national integrity. Everywhere the call of the nation continues to be invoked: in the old Yugoslavia with the horrors of ethnic cleansing; in post-communist Russia as Yeltsin's oppressive stance on national integrity creates new counter-nationalisms across the Caucasus; in Rwanda as an ethnic civil war creates the conditions for the largest scale refugee movement in human history; and in Indonesia as military-cultural solutions are sought to the 'problems' of East Timor and Irian Jaya. Enough has been written about the immediacy of the national conflict to suggest however that it is sometimes important to step back from the fray and to reflect comparatively, historically and theoretically. Despite all the work we have done the nation remains 'the one most untheorized concept of the modern world'.[1]

This first chapter begins to establish the ground-work for making sense of the argument that the nation is a particular kind of abstract community,

---

1. Partha Chatterjee, *The Nation and its Fragments*, 1993, p. xi.

abstract in the dominant level of its integration, in the mode of its subjectivities as well as in the symbolic representation of that relationship. It is an
abstract community but one which always, subjectively and ideologically,
reaches back to more concrete ways of living and representation. This makes
it the best and worst kind of human associations, beset by contradictions,
open to self-conscious cultural management, yet embedded deeply within
our taken-for-granted histories. In working its way through this argument the
book tends to accent questions relating to the nation as a material form of
social relation. However, given the usual philosophical and commonsense
meaning of abstraction as a process pertaining only to ideas, it is easier to
begin with a comparison which puts its emphasis on modes of representation.
This opening is no more than an overture. Instead of referring to one of the
many issues of the day – the hoisting of the tri-colour Russian flag over the
blackened and bombed-out city of Grozny, or the flying of the swastika in
street marches through Berlin – we begin with a different flag and with some
representations of identity which are often discussed in the literature and
somewhat less contested in practice.

It is fairly uncontroversial to suggest that French citizens have a more
abstract relation to each other as represented through the industrially manufactured piece of calico they call the *tricolore* than the Aranda tribe of central
Australia have embodied in the particular animal or plant of their totemic
identity.[2] However, the basis for any proposed qualitative difference between
these two modes of representation cannot adequately be located in the material character of the objects themselves, piece of cloth or natural totem.
Neither can it be assumed that intensity of identification is necessarily relevant to such a comparison. Reverence for the *tricolore* or, to take an example
from a different national setting, the Warsaw cenotaph fragment, is undoubtedly intense. The Warsaw stone was once part of the Polish Tomb of the
Unknown Warrior, almost totally destroyed by a Nazi bomb attack during
World War II, and now is concreted into the facing of the foundation of
Victory Square. Notwithstanding this rich overlay of reference, a condensa-
tion of meaning which redoubled over the course of recent history and
intensified its subjective hold, the fragment signifies a more abstract (though
not necessarily more complex) relation to others as strangers-yet-compatriots
than the skull of a dead relative holds for a Trobriand Islander.

2. Reading through *The Elementary Forms of Religious Life*, (1912) 1976, pp. 219–239, examples can be found where Durkheim treats the totem and the flag as homologous signs standing
in for a social reality – 'the totem', he says, 'is the flag of the clan' (p. 220). However, given the
overall thrust of his theory of social forms he would have to agree that there is *something* different about them. I will argue that there are substantial differences between the social forms which
give meaning to such 'signs', but approaches which posit ideal-type distinctions such as that
between the 'traditional' and the 'modern' give us very limited insight into these differences.
Equally, positing a theory of forms does not entail homogenizing all the different ways of living
that are possible within the broad, common structures and ontologies of such forms. For example, that the Pintupi people put a greater emphasis upon identity as bound up in the 'concrete'
place to which they 'belong' than they do upon identity as bound in living totems, confirms
rather than qualifies the present thesis (Fred Myers, *Pintupi Country, Pintupi Self*, 1986).

The source of the difference is fundamentally to be found in the social relational setting. A tribal, reciprocal-exchange society provides a qualitative contrast with a Western nation-state: the problem is to find a way of describing the difference without implying a dichotomous Great Divide. The cenotaph is set in a focal urban location, existing as a symbolic evocation of long-since-forgotten compatriots who died in the course of Polish history. It is thus symbolically stretched across extended reaches of time and space. Whereas the deceased Trobriander's skull is, over a ritually significant number of years, passed from hand to hand, *known* person to *known* person, before being given over to his or her matrilineal relatives to take to a final place of rest. This is to say that the skull is set within a more concrete relation and the cenotaph a more abstract relation. However, rather than to set up a dichotomy between the concrete and the abstract, it is to begin an argument about different dominant, materially constituted levels of abstraction.

Perhaps the key point which brings home the more abstract quality of the cenotaph is that by definition a cenotaph is always empty of human remains. Its dominant meaning signifies the death of no one in particular. This would not be possible in a tribal burial site. Like the national flag, the cenotaph is constructed (often self-consciously) as signifying the abstract representatives of the national community – national heroes in general rather than known persons. The suggestion that the cenotaph is an abstract sign does not infer that its meaning is merely an arbitrary or culturally empty construction. Nor does it suggest that its abstraction denies the possibility of particularized connections. A cenotaph is a place invested with a specific and macabre richness, a place of national remembrance for a history of generations, who, as the forward projection of linear time would have it, 'shall not have died in vain'. Placed here are the generations 'who shall not grow old'. Thus a superordinate sense of place overlays, connects, and abstracts from particular deaths; but it does so without precluding the possibility that an individual mourner will give the empty tomb particular, direct, and more concrete significance. In other words, in attempting to understand the cenotaph we are faced with an overlaying of levels of abstraction.

With this overlay of levels, such apparently direct symbols as the skull are complicated. It is indicative that I *can* call it a symbol. By contrast, it can never be an empty symbol for the traditional Trobriander. It first of all signifies a particular relation and at its most abstract remains an embodied symbol. In contemporary, Westernized society the skull continues to be a highly condensed symbol of death: witness the mass-media depictions of the fields of nationalist-inspired killing in Pol Pot's Kampuchea. Recently the cover of *Time* magazine used a dirt-encrusted skull to illustrate the words: 'Unburied Sins: From Cambodia to Rwanda, the world struggles to avenge the victims of atrocity and genocide'.[3] However, what are we to make of the fact that the skull was reduced to a macabre illustration without reference

3. *Time*, 22 May 1995.

point.[4] The photo credit simply read: 'Photograph by Scott Peterson – Gamma Liaison'. It seems that it is now more important to acknowledge the photographer's corporate agency than to locate the place or even country in which the person died. In the same vein, what are we to make of the laughter that often ensues when contemporary Western theatre-goers first hear Hamlet bitterly say: 'Alas, poor Yorick! – I knew him . . .'? (*Hamlet*, [c.1602] V.i) For the contemporary sensibility, the attenuation of association from decaying skull back to particular human being is in most circumstances incongruously distant. This is not to presume that the modern person cannot make such a connection, but it is to say that the connection is not brought to the fore by our assumed habitus. The mixed humour and pathos in Fazil Iskander's poem 'Memory of a School Lesson' depends upon us knowing that the language of the sacred is no longer sacrosanct:

> Prince Svyatoslav drinks from a skull.
> And, of course, in this he is at fault,
> For the skull is a sacred vessel,
> Which, luckily, is not drunk from.[5]

Different forms of representation are integral with different forms of association, and the history of these forms of human association can similarly be theorized as a complex overlaying of levels of abstraction. The roots of the modern nation, while being overlaid by more abstract levels of integration, are continuous with 'prior' dominant forms of social integration. They range from kinship ties predominant in reciprocal-exchange societies to institutionally mediated extensions of social connection, such as carried by the monarchical state and the Church. Continuation of the *forms* which structure more concretely constituted societies (as well as the continuation of aspects of their content) is not precluded by the setting which conditions the rise of the national formation.[6] However, as is exemplified by comparing different 'ways of seeing' burial sites and human skulls, more embodied forms of integration tend either to be reframed in terms of the new dominant level, such as has happened to monarchy, or marginalized in pockets of 'backwoods arcadia' as happened to many peasant groupings.[7] An example of the reconstitutive process is the way the language of kinship and blood-ties, abstracted to name the relation to '*Our* Father who art in heaven' (Matthew, 6: 9), was later used

4. See Philippe Ariès, *The Hour of Our Death*, 1981, pp. 328–332, on the early modern roots of the rendering of the skull as 'abstract symbol'.

5. In Daniel Weissbort, ed., *Post-War Russian Poetry*, 1974.

6. Gerd Baumann's work on the Miri (*National Integration and Local Integrity*, 1987) shows how it is possible for tribal face-to-face communities to find ways of 'local redintegration' (his term for a particular kind of re-integration) despite the penetration of the nation-state. For some quite different examples see Jonathon Wylie, 'The Sense of Time, the Social Construction of Reality, and the Foundations of Nationhood in Dominica and the Faroe Islands', 1982.

7. Eugen Weber's research (*Peasants into Frenchmen*, 1976) attests that under the overbracing level in dominance that makes possible the national community, 'unclaimed' enclaves can exist long after national boundaries are secured. People could, in particular until the late nineteenth century, live for generations in the largely unreconstituted interstices of the emergent nation-state.

to describe aspects of national solidarity: mother-tongue; patriot; fatherland; in Japanese, family-state (*kazoku kokka*); or as the Italian term *la madre Patria* would have it, the mother-Fatherland. All the while, however, kinship is subordinated to, or at least overlaid by, the new forms of solidarity from city-state and kingdom to nation. Etienne Balibar forcefully articulates the difficulty of theorizing this when he says:

> That is why the representation of nationalism as 'tribalism' – the sociologists' grand alternative to representing it as a religion – is both mystificatory and revealing. Mystificatory because it imagines nationalism as a regression to archaic forms of community which are in reality incompatible with the nation-state (this can be seen from the incompleteness of the formation of a nation whenever powerful lineal or tribal solidarities still exist). But it is also revealing of the substitution of one imaginary of kinship for another, a substitution which the nation effects and which underpins the transformation of the family itself.[8]

In short, I want to argue that modern national association only becomes possible within a social formation constituted in the dominance of a level of integration (described in the next chapter as disembodied integration). This involves an abstraction from people's more particularistic relations with others.

There is a long way to go to even establish the terms of this argument. But having fired off a single flare, it is advisable to begin its elaboration from a less direct point of entry. By the end of the next chapter it is intended that we will arrive back at a clearer and more useful restatement of the opening assertion.

The 'imagined community' as an abstract community

The argument that the nation is an abstract community has considerable descriptive resonance with Benedict Anderson's representation of the nation as an imagined, political community – 'imagined as both inherently limited and sovereign':

> It is *imagined* [we might translate imagining as one among the many possible processes of abstraction] because the members of even the smallest nation will never know most of their fellow-members, meet them, or even hear them, yet in the minds of each lives the image of their communion.[9]

While the argument that the nation is a particular kind of abstract community does not draw directly on Benedict Anderson's theoretical underpinnings – in part because his theory and methodology are left implicit – there is nevertheless much to be learnt from Anderson's historical insights. His is a powerful and elegantly presented treatise. In summary, he argues that the transition from religious communities and dynastic realms to the new, imagined national communities entailed a fundamental (ontological) change in the mode of apprehending and being in the world. It was made possible by a 'half-fortuitous, but explosive interaction between a system of

8. Etienne Balibar and Immanuel Wallerstein, *Race, Nation, Class*, 1991, p. 102.

9. Anderson, *Imagined Communities*, 1991, p. 6 (cf. fn. 9 on the same page). Insertions into quotations which are bound by square brackets are my additions to the original text.

production and productive relations (capitalism), a technology of communications (print), and the fatality of human linguistic diversity'.[10] The core
insight that I want to draw upon is that for the nation to become a predominant organizational and cultural form there had to occur changes in the
framing categories and practices of being.

Anderson uses the example of time. The medieval sacred community was
bound as a simultaneity-along-time. This connection was not lived as if it
were the reflexive result of human practice, but as a manifestation of something else, something which has always been, something universal and
omnitemporal – God in 'Messianic time'. Past, present and future were held
together by the omnitemporal Reality of the Word. Even genealogies were
ultimately connected by the sacred as much as by blood. By contrast, the idea
of the nation posits a community of strangers moving simultaneously through
'homogenous, empty time', time which is measured by the calendar, 'empty'
time which people fill with their own history. The connection between past,
present and future can be provided by something as apparently banal as the
date which heads a newspaper.

Imagined Communities is developed with exciting perspicacity. However, by
so prominently centring the concept of imagination as the organizing principle, Anderson limits the reach of his argument. This is not just a quibble over
word choice. The concept is both too central and not sufficiently developed.
The solution does not necessarily lie in elaborating this highly evocative term.
Anderson acknowledges that 'all communities larger than primordial villages of face-to-face contact (and perhaps even these) are imagined'. In the
same way, I have already noted that both tribal and national communities are,
at different dominant levels, constituted abstractly. Anderson follows this up
by saying, quite rightly, that forms of communities can be distinguished by
the style of their imagining. Javanese villagers, he says, 'have always known
that they are connected to people they have never seen, but these ties were
once imagined particularistically – as indefinitely stretchable nets of kinship
and clientship'.[11] It is an important distinction to make, but it leaves the ful-
crum of his analysis, the concept of imagination, doing almost no theoretical
work. The notion of particularity here marks the line of differentiation, but as
we have already seen in comparing a Trobriand burial and a Polish cenotaph,
such a conception very quickly becomes complicated. Something like a
metaphor of constitutive levels is, I will argue, helpful for teasing this out.

The subsidiary point is that even if imagination is conceived of as lived and
materially framed (Anderson analyses ways of thinking, not just the content
of ideas), the concept overly emphasizes the world as being made up of systems of signification. Writers such as Cornelius Castoriadis and Claude
Lefort have already entered into the labyrinthine pursuit of a theory of the
social imaginary. However, an excursion into the category of the imaginary

10. Ibid., pp. 42–43. The body of Anderson's analysis focuses on the latter two dimensions of
the 'interaction'.
11. Ibid., p. 6.

suggests that this is not particularly helpful in extending our understanding of the imagined community substantially beyond what Anderson has already achieved. Castoriadis writes: 'The imaginary of which I am speaking is not an image *of*. It is the unceasing and essentially *undetermined* (social-historical and psychical) creation of figures/forms/images, on the basis of which alone there can ever be a question *of* "something". What we call "reality" and "rationality" are its works.' His entire book is consequently spent opening up a space in materialist social theory for this category 'that constitutes history as such', that, for example, allows 'us' to name ourselves as a particular association.[12] This present book, by contrast, is more concerned with the conditions which frame different ontologies. It takes it as given that persons can act creatively and imaginatively, but is concerned to emphasize the constitution of different forms of social practice. It thus rejects the notion that the imaginary is undetermined.

By beginning from the concept of the imagined, Anderson inadvertently makes the way of thinking, or the form of consciousness, primary in defining the national formation.[13] His concept (as opposed to his analysis) of imagination puts misleading emphasis on the mode of subjectivity. One of the basic challenges still confronting theories of the nation is to bring together the subjective with the objective, that is, to synthesize an understanding of national consciousness, nationality and nationalism as entailing certain forms of subjectivity, with an approach to the nation, the nation-state, and the nationalist movement as objective forms of social relations. *Nation Formation* attempts to build upon Benedict Anderson's historical insights by developing an approach which cuts across familiar conceptions of the relation between social conditions and social consciousness.

Any criticism of *Imagined Communities* is heavily qualified. It is not being suggested that Anderson's theory is idealist.[14] His theory cannot be considered to fall within the standard expression of the idealist/materialist dichotomy still assumed by writers as sophisticated as Liah Greenfeld and Michael Mann.[15] The substance of *Imagined Communities* brilliantly develops

12. The concept is worked through in Castoriadis' *The Imaginary Institution of Society*, 1987 (quotes are from pp. 3, 161, 148) and is discussed by John Thompson ('Ideology and the Social Imaginary', 1982).

13. It can quickly be acknowledged that the concept of 'abstraction' has a similar problem in commonsense language of being confined to the realm of ideas, but as I will discuss at various points throughout, this usage can be dislodged. Marx's work on the commodity and labour abstractions (see for example, *Capital*, vol. 1, (1867) 1977, part 1, ch. 1) shows how abstraction occurs in the *practice* of exchange relations. See also Sharp, 'Constitutive Abstraction', 1985; Alfred Sohn-Rethel, *Intellectual and Manual Labour*, 1978; and José Maria Ripalda, *The Divided Nation*, 1977. See also for example the section entitled 'The material abstraction of social relations' in Chapter 7 below.

14. Cf. Jim MacLaughlin, 'Reflections on Nations as "Imagined Communities"', 1988, and Balibar and Wallerstein, *Race, Nation, Class*, 1991, p. 106 fn. 11.

15. When, for example, Liah Greenfeld attempts to 'allow for the causal primacy of ideas, without denying it to structures' (*Nationalism*, 1992, p. 21) she is still working within an old-style dichotomous divide. Michael Mann's division of the bases of social power into four substantive

the historically grounded position that the national formation can only be theorized 'by aligning it not with self-consciously held political ideologies, but with the large cultural systems that preceded it, out of which – as well as against which – it came into being'.[16] However, the centrality of the concept imagined works against the theory being grounded in this way. When Anderson comes to explain the spread of the national formation as being possible because of its 'modular', capable-of-being-transplanted quality, we are back to an emphasis on ideas, even though much of the substance of his analysis implies the relationship between the content of ideas, the form of subjectivity and the changing social relations. In the language of the present text, ideologies such as nationalism are, through their abstract form, available to be elaborated beyond their original formative context. However (and this is a fundamental qualification consistent with a reworked theory of historical materialism), such ideologies can only take root in the consciousness and practice of individuals or people(s), whose relationships to each other are already in the process of being reconstituted at a more abstract level. If the vanguard nationalists of Latin America were 'marginalized vernacular-based coalitions of the educated' it was, as Anderson himself says, not *just* because self-interest, or practical exigency, or even an understanding of Enlightenment ideas moved them.[17] It was that the mode of their activities, as for example state functionaries or provincial printers and publishers, was part of the re-forming of their own subjectivities and of the larger social relations. This helps to make sense of the issue that although the concepts associated with nations and nationalism were European in derivation, nationalism as a political movement was already taking hold in the New World well before the *peuple* of the oft-proclaimed 'first nation-state' took to the streets of Paris to storm the Bastille (the symbolic beginning of the French Revolution in 1789).

The idea of nationalism never *in itself* moved anyone. This is to say that ideas only take hold in a constitutive medium in which they have meaning, not that ideas cannot be profoundly influential. In the words of Miroslav Hroch:

> The diffusion of national ideas could only occur in specific social settings. Nation-building was never a mere project of ambitious or narcissistic intellectuals . . . Intellectuals can invent national communities only if certain objective preconditions for the formation of a nation already exist.[18]

In order to proceed to a clarification of the argument that the nation is an abstract community, its central concepts still need to be laid out and defined, as, first of all, does the concept of 'nation' and its cognates.

---

sources – ideological, economic, military and political – still carries the notion that because these are analytically distinguishable categories they sit *behind* social life offering four 'distinct potentially powerful organizational means to humans pursuing their goals' (*The Sources of Social Power*, vol. 2, 1993, p. 10). Ideas (ideologies) become things to take off the shelf, sometimes to good effect, sometimes not.

16. Anderson, *Imagined Communities*, 1991, p. 12.

17. Ibid., ch. 4.

18. Hroch, 'From National Movement to Fully Formed Nation', 1993, p. 4.

Some definitions: from *natio* to nation

Thus far, I have tried to use the term 'nation', and the cluster of associated concepts – nation-state, national community, national consciousness, nationality and nationalism – with some care about their differentiation. However, they are vague, elusive and historically changing concepts. We should be aware of this and its implications for social theory, seeking workable clarity rather than striving for an uncompromisingly precise lexicon.

Johan Huizinga suggests that the Latin terms *patria* and *natio* (plural, *nationes*) should be taken as a way into this area for it was in Latin writings that these concepts were formed.[19] It raises the interesting point that Latin, the language of the cleric and intellectual (the truth language, in Benedict Anderson's phrase, of European religion and scholarship) should be the medium of conceptualizing what was to become the means of its own undermining. This occurred particularly through the assertion in Latin of the richness and relativity of the vernacular languages, and hence the marginalizing of the old truth language. A related point, a continuing theme of this book, is that it is intellectuals who, by virtue of the way their work lifts them into an abstract relation to locale and time, become *a* central 'grouping' relevant to the rise of the national formation.[20] It is important to note even at this early stage that it was not just intellectuals and intellectual groupings who were abstracted in relation to locale and time. The merchant, trader of commodities and money-changer were all drawn into a wider ambit than the local and the face-to-face. Their relation to customers and competitors quickly lost the particularity of association concomitant with gift exchange and even feudal bartering. A further, very interesting example is the case of the professional soldier. The division of soldiers fighting for the same sovereign into separate *nationes* parallels the case of university scholars. The distinctiveness of the intellectuals derives from the way in which their work is carried beyond them, not only by the abstraction of language but also on the wings of abstract media such as writing – scripted, printed and most recently digitalized. We will return to this theme towards the end of this chapter and throughout the discussion, but for the moment there is only the need to introduce it empirically and in relation to the problems of definition.

19. Johan Huizinga, *Men and Ideas*, 1959, p. 105.
20. As a working definition the term 'intellectual' will be used to refer to those persons who work critically with ideas, extending or assessing the given frame of knowledge. It includes those persons who work in both the scientific and humanistic branches of the intellectual culture. While all intellectuals are intellectually trained, whether 'self-taught' through the abstract medium of others' writings or tutored in an institutional setting, they are a distinct grouping from the broader category of the 'intellectually trained' (a term taken from Geoff Sharp and Doug White, 'Features of the Intellectually Trained', 1968). The latter term, somewhat akin to Alvin Gouldner's use of the term 'technical intelligentsia', refers to those intellectual (as opposed to manual) workers who in Lewis Coser's Weberian phrase live off rather than for ideas. See Geoff Sharp, 'Intellectuals in Transition', 1983; Ron Eyerman, Lennart G. Svensson and Thomas Sederqvist, eds, *Intellectuals, Universities and the State in Western Modern Societies*, 1987; Alvin Gouldner, *The Future of Intellectuals and the Rise of the New Class*, 1979.

It is indicative that the term *natio* was used in the Middle Ages particularly (though not at all exclusively) to distinguish communities of foreigners at the newly formed universities, in refectories of the great monasteries, and at the reform councils of the Church.[21] The self was here defined through identifying 'the other', and the mode of identification was explicitly lifted into abstracted modality: persons were identified as being part of an aggregate which overlaid the older sense of identity conferred by kinship and place. This new need for self-definition was invoked in communities which were both cosmopolitan *and* face-to-face; communities which came into constant contact with others. Identification occurred through various means of categorical distinction including place of birth and way of speaking, but these distinctions took on a new generality. This helps to explain the paradox that it was in settings where the working language was Latin, and where their pretensions were universalistic, that scholars and clerics almost immediately turned back to more particularistic distinctions, and separated into *nationes*. Around 1220, half a century after the establishing of the University of Paris, four divisions were declared between its scholars: *France*, indicating the native speakers of the Romance languages; *Picardie*, referring to the peoples of the Low Countries; *Normandie*, being those scholars from north-eastern Europe; and *Germanie*, including people whom we now unself-consciously call German and English. At the University of Bologna there were said to be thirty-five *nationes*. They gradually combined into two aggregates, *Citramontanes* and *Ultramontanes* (those from the near- and other-side-of-the-mountain). At Oxford, factions were so intense, with several fatal riots arising out of conflicting observances of the festivals of patron saints, that in 1320 the University officially recognized the existence of two *nationes*: it was decreed that the three guardians of the Rothbury Chest should always include a Northerner and a Southerner. In 1334 the riots, 'dangers, perils, deaths, murders, mayhems and robberies' led the northern masters to secede and set up an alternative university at Stamford.[22]

These few examples should suffice to illustrate some of the various applications and stretchings of the term *natio*, the intersections with religious, regional and language communities, the intensity with which people held to such *nationes* – even at this early stage people were killed in the name of these allegiances. It should also serve to illustrate the distinctiveness of the term from the post-eighteenth-century usage of the words 'nation' and 'nation-state'. The Latin concept of *natio* had a shifting meaning, designating various associations of people:

    21. See amongst others Guido Zernatto, 'Nation: The History of a Word', 1944.
    22. G.G. Coulton, 'Nationalism in the Middle Ages', 1935; Elie Kedourie, *Nationalism*, (1960) 1993, pp. 13–14; John Lawson and Harold Silver, *A Social History of Education in England*, 1973, chs 2–3; Hans Kohn, *The Idea of Nationalism*, 1944, pp. 107–109; Emile Durkheim, *The Evolution of Educational Thought*, (1904–5) 1977, pp. 97ff.; Max Weber, in *From Max Weber* (essays from 1904 to 1920), 1968, p. 179; Philip Caraman, *University of the Nations*, 1981. The quote comes from J.I. Catto, ed., *The History of the University of Oxford*, vol. 1, 1984, p. 186. See also pp. 64–67, 187, 396–399.

Closely linked with *natus* [birth] and *natura* [inborn characteristics], it vaguely indi-cated a larger context than *gens* or *populus*, but without there being any fixed distinction between the three terms. The Vulgate [that is, the authorized Latin ver-sion of the biblical scriptures prepared mainly by Jerome near the end of the *fourth* century] used *gentes*, *populus*, *nationes* interchangeably for the nations [*sic*] of the Old Testament, and that biblical usage determined the significance of *natio* for the time being. It indicated a fairly indefinite interrelationship of tribe, tongue and region, sometimes in a restricted sense, sometimes in a broader one. [In the Middle Ages, the] Burgundians, the Bretons, the Bavarians, and the Swabians were called nations, but so were the French, the English, and the Germans. Unlike *patria*, *natio* did not have an administrative significance, and initially not a political one either. But little by little the various relationships of dependence and community obtain-ing exerted an influence on the restriction and delimitation of the concept *natio*.[23]

If Frederick Hertz and Bernard Guenée[24] are right, we can be a little more precise than the above passage from Huizinga suggests. *Natio*, which had a similar root to 'native', was used before the Middle Ages for 'uncivilized' peoples: *nationes ferae* (Sallust), *natio servituti nata* (Cicero), *innumerabiles et ferocissimae nationes* (Hieronymus). Hence in the Vulgate, *natio* is used to refer to the Gentiles, while the chosen people is the *populus*. However, *natio* came later to refer to all aggregations, or classings, of people with a common 'ethnic' background,[25] including, as we have seen, those most prestigious and 'civilized' of associations, university corporations.

It is a strange twist; the common thread seems to have been that the term marked an association between persons who found it important to distinguish themselves from others, but for whom the distinguishing marks of old were insufficient or no longer available in the same way. After the Middle Ages, *natio* was initially used in Germany and France to designate the ruling classes, in opposition to the *Volk* or *peuple*. Up until this period, the words *communis patria* or *regna*, the latter primarily meaning 'kingdom' but used more broadly as in *civitates et regna*, were the most commonly used means of denoting the highest earthly association of allegiance. As will be discussed in the next chap-ter it was also during the post-medieval period that the concept of *status* (root of the word 'state') changed from being embodied in the person of the prince towards being the abstracted administrative apparatus of the body politic.

The concept of 'nation' took on a more abstract meaning and clearer political ascriptions from the sixteenth century.[26] The use of the word to mean the 'whole people of a country' was in evidence from the early seven-teenth century, though, as Raymond Williams suggests, 'realm', 'kingdom' and 'country' continued to be more common until the late eighteenth century. The English term 'nationalism' (similarly written in French as

23. Huizinga, *Men and Ideas*, 1959, pp. 106-107.

24. Frederick Hertz, *Nationality in History and Politics*, 1944, pp. 5–7, Bernard Guenée, *States and Rulers in Later Medieval Europe*, 1988, Introduction, ch. 3, and Appendix.

25. 'Ethnicity' is placed in inverted commas here because as a twentieth-century term it is anachronistic in this context. Ethnicity, I argue, involves an abstraction from the reciprocal ties of kinship.

26. Philip White, 'What is a Nationality?', 1985.

nationalisme) is even more recent. Rarely found even in the early nineteenth century, it referred to the doctrine that certain nations had been chosen by God.[27] The conjoining of 'nation' with 'state' – the latter term itself only becoming common in the eighteenth century[28] – seems, as does the use of the term 'nationalism', to have been generalized as late as the mid-nineteenth century.

It was during this period that the cluster of terms associated with the notion of 'kingdom' were substantially supplanted by 'nation' and its cognates, referring to an overarching, continuous and abstract community of loyalty. Running on into the nineteenth century, the concept of the 'nation' continued to carry contradictory levels of meaning. It was at once an embodied community based upon ties of genealogy (that is, the racial, linguistic nation) and a disembodied aggregation of 'free individuals' connected by a culturally willed closing of territorial boundaries (the nation, in Renan's words, formed by daily plebiscite).[29] This tension was for example evidenced in a late nineteenth-century commentary on how Adam Smith used the term 'national': 'Edwin Cannan [writing in 1894] thought Adam Smith's "nation" consisted only of the collection of individuals living on the territory of a state and considered whether the fact that in a hundred years' time all these people would be dead, made it impossible to speak of the "nation" as a continuously existing entity.'[30] In the early twentieth century the force of such philosophical conundrums seemed to be comfortably submerged by employing a common caveat about how complex the term is: 'it defies easy definition', as they said. And apart from the hesitations of a few recalcitrants it entered common-sense parlance with little debate. One writer remarks that in 1918 with Wilson's Fourteen Points the quality of being a nation-state was formally made the basic criterion of state legitimacy and of international relations.[31]

At the very least, the historical shifts confront us with extensive problems of establishing definitions. Anthony Giddens, a relatively careful glossarist, defines the nation as a 'collectivity existing within a clearly demarcated territory, which is subject to a unitary [and uniform] administration, reflexively monitored both by the internal state apparatus and those of other states'.[32] The definition is not without (fatal) drawbacks which I will discuss in Chapter

27. Raymond Williams, *Keywords*, 1976, pp. 178–179; Anthony Smith, *Theories of Nationalism*, 1983, p. 167.

28. Kenneth Dyson, *The State Tradition in Western Europe*, 1980, ch. 1.

29. According to Martin Thom ('Tribes within Nations', 1990, p. 23), an inspection of Renan's earlier writings shows that he was less committed to the voluntarism than his famous lecture, 'What is a Nation?' would suggest.

30. Eric Hobsbawm, *Nations and Nationalism since 1780*, 1990, pp. 26–27.

31. Cornelia Navari, 'The Origins of the Nation-State', 1981, p. 14. While overall I agree with the suggestion, a glance at the Fourteen Points speech shows that Wilson never uses the word 'nation-state': 'nation' assumes a coverall meaning. Hence, League of Nations and United Nations.

32. Anthony Giddens, *The Nation-State and Violence*, 1985, p. 116.

7, but it has distinct advantages over the common definitions of the nation as a politically sovereign people or as willed association. It does not have to deal with the issue as to whether a people can be said to be sovereign under an authoritarian or totalitarian state-apparatus. It is a structural definition rather than depending upon an assessment of the strength of national sentiment. Importantly, the definition goes on to recognize that the nation(-state) comes to be sustained only within a complex of other nation(-state)s. And, pregnantly, this world system is said to be formed at a particular conjuncture in 'world time'.[33]

Moreover, the definition emphasizes the relatively uniform administration of state sovereignty over a specific area with a boundary rather than a frontier. Given that even a relative or proclaimed uniformity was not possible under even the most centralized, absolutist state system such as that of Louis XIV (1638–1715) or Frederick William I (1688–1740), it adds to a definitional distinction between the nation-state system and absolutism. The absolutist state, prevailing in Europe during the seventeenth and eighteenth centuries (with concurrent structural parallels in Japan), was a late-feudal social formation where political power was increasingly bureaucratized and depersonalized even as sovereignty was invested in a single ruler. In Europe, it coincided with the entrenchment, particularly for the aristocratic classes, of the abstract concept and practice of 'absolute' private property.[34]

Absolutist power did not fade off at its edges as it tended to do towards the frontiers of the feudal regimes or the earlier empires. However, it was not until *after* the height of absolutism that negotiated, abstract lines on maps were considered to precisely mark states' sovereign boundaries. Maps provide us with an extraordinary example of the process of abstraction of place. As Giddens records, the first boundary drawn as a line of mutually agreed demarcation between states occurred in the 1718 Flanders Treaty.[35] We should keep in mind that along with many conventional geographers Giddens tends to underestimate the concern for precise delimitation of boundaries which existed prior to the nation-state. Nevertheless, his general distinction between frontier and border is useful. John Armstrong gives an example from the fourteenth century of a seventy-eight kilometre straight-line boundary cutting through frozen lakes and open terrain,[36] but this nevertheless would seem to be a case of a precise frontier rather than a boundary demarcation in the sense Giddens uses. By way of definition, a frontier is a particular kind of boundary which marks the end of territory before it transforms or shades off into open space. It is unusual for frontiers to be precise lines of delimitation;

---

33. The concept of 'world time', taken from Wolfram Eberhard, suggests that superficially similar processes may be quite differently constituted depending upon the period of world history in which they are set. See Eberhard, *Conquerors and Rulers*, 1965, pp. 13ff, and Anthony Giddens, *Power, Property and State*, 1981, pp. 167–168.

34. See Gianfranco Poggi, *The Development of the Modern State*, 1978, ch. 4; and Perry Anderson, *Lineages of the Absolutist State*, 1974.

35. Giddens, *Nation-State and Violence*, 1985, p. 90.

36. *Nations before Nationalism*, 1982, p. 27.

however, long before the development of states there were other kinds of boundaries which were culturally maintained as delimiting social life and social movement. (It is tempting here to extend the discussion into an elaboration on how absolutism and boundary demarcation were transformed in the abstraction of the state, making possible the modern conjunction of state and nation. But it is better left until further down the track.)

Unfortunately, however, for all its strengths Anthony Giddens' definition conflates nation and nation-state.[37] It brackets off the complicating actuality of early modern 'nations'. This can be partly handled by distinguishing the existence of 'nations before nation-states' by the use of the original Latin designations *natio, nationes*, as intimated earlier – still, there is a further issue. Giddens' suggestion that a nation 'only exists when a state has a unified administrative reach over territory over which its sovereignty is claimed',[38] is narrowing and exclusive. In one sense it is useful and will be retained as a partial definition of the *modern nation-state* (albeit with the qualification that in theory more than one nation can reside in the territory of an established nation-state). However, the suggestion is too narrowing in that it implies reducing the nation-state and the *nation* to one form of social practice – the institutional – and to one level of social integration, a level which shall be called 'the agency-extended'.[39]

The language of 'levels of integration' used here will carry much more weight later in the discussion, but for current purposes it is sufficient to illustrate the nature of Giddens' delimitation with a few examples. For Giddens, non-state-bounded 'national' associations are merely adherents to the ideology of nationalism, not nations. But definitional neatness has its costs. Do territorially associated 'collectivities' magically become nations when a unified state asserts claims of unified sovereignty? Alternatively, to the extent that a collectivity is a *lived* abstract community, formed beyond the level of the face-to-face, is it not too restrictive to exclude all non-state-bound collectivities from the appellation of 'nation'? What are we to make of the following examples?

Diaspora nations – that is, self-proclaimed but scattered nations, or trans-state networks like the Jews prior to, and even after, the formation of the State of Israel.[40]
Irredentist nations – where the nation is said to extend beyond the boundaries of the existing state, such as in the case of the Somali where at least a third of their population lives in neighbouring Ethiopia, Kenya and Djibouti.[41]

37. On the other hand, Giddens is heedful to distinguish between nation-state and nationalism. At one point, for example, he says 'the advent of the nation-state stimulates divergent and oppositional nationalisms' (*Nation-State and Violence*, 1985, p. 220).

38. Ibid., p. 119.

39. For an expansion of this criticism of Giddens see below, Chapter 7. The concept of 'the agency-extended' is defined in Chapter 2.

40. Gabriel Sheffer, ed., *Modern Diasporas in International Politics*, 1986.

41. I.M. Lewis, ed., *Nationalism and Self-Determination in the Horn of Africa*, 1983.

Sub-state nations – again self-proclaimed 'nations', including the Québécois and the Cree in Canada, the Tamils in Sri Lanka, the Basques and Catalans in Spain and France, and the Irish, Scottish and Welsh in Great Britain.[42]

The fact that the examples above are ambiguous and that some may be open to be challenged as examples of nations does not detract from my purpose of indicating the complexity of the question. Writers like Anthony Smith, John Armstrong and Walker Connor[43] have attempted to deal with such issues by defining the nation as a self-differentiating or politically self-conscious ethnic group. I would be happy enough to accept this nicely unadorned rendering except for two main reservations. Firstly, these writers allow, at least in their explicit pronouncements, the idealistic possibilities of the definition to dominate its meaning. Connor goes furthest in this direction when he says that the 'essence of the nation is a matter of attitude, the tangible manifestations of cultural distinctiveness are significant only to the degree that they contribute to the *sense* of uniqueness'.[44]

The second main reservation is that defining the nation in terms of 'ethnicity' entails elaborating what is meant by this additional, similarly amorphous and contradictorily abstract/concrete term. The three writers just mentioned rightly want to reject the 'primordialist' assumption of a biological or historically unchanging ethnicity, the projection of an essence which has an inherent political destiny. On the other hand, they also want to qualify the quite sophisticated 'modernist' argument that, as Ernest Gellner puts it, 'Nationalism is not the awakening of nations to self-consciousness: it invents nations where they do not exist'.[45] Benedict Anderson, whom we could also place in the modernist camp, criticizes this comment of Gellner's for assimilating '"invention" to "fabrication" and "falsity", rather than "imagining" and "creation"'.[46] There are strong, historically based reasons for qualifying the point even further.

To this end, Smith introduces the French term *ethnie*, meaning ethnic community existent prior to and during the present Age of Nations. For Smith, ethnicity resides not in biology but in culturally transmitted, myth-symbol complexes, particularly what is called – following Armstrong and d'Abadal i de Vinyals[47] – the *mythomoteur*. These are the 'constitutive myths of the

42. For example, on Quebec see Larry Shouldice, ed., *Contemporary Quebec Criticism*, 1979; Dominique Clift, *Quebec Nationalism in Crisis*, 1982, and Michael Ignatieff, *Blood and Belonging*, 1994, ch. 4.

43. Anthony D. Smith, *The Ethnic Revival*, 1981, and his *The Ethnic Origins of Nations*, 1986; John Armstrong, *Nations before Nationalism*, 1982; and Walker Connor, *Ethnonationalism*, 1994.

44. Connor, ibid., p. 43. For a critique of this problem in Smith's *The Ethnic Revival*, 1981, see Jim MacLaughlin's strong but sometimes overstated article, 'Nationalism as an Autonomous Social Force: A Critique', 1987.

45. Ernest Gellner, *Thought and Change*, 1964, p. 168. See also his *Nations and Nationalism*, 1983, p. 55 for a similar argument.

46. Anderson, *Imagined Communities*, 1991, p. 6.

47. Smith, *Ethnic Origins*, 1986, draws on Vinyals' article via Armstrong, *Nations before Nationalism*, 1982, p. 9.

ethnic polity', the myths of common descent. However, the continuing problem of over-emphasizing ideas is still evident. Myths are elevated to both the
motor of early history and its 'cognitive maps', rather than examined in the
context of the forms of social relations which sustain and are in part reproduced by such 'histories' of a shared ancestry.[48] There seems little point in
introducing the exotic term *ethnie* into the present study when 'ethnic community' can be divested of its primordialist and overly biological emphases.

The word 'community' is too rich a concept to ignore. It has a wonderful
complexity which draws into intersection the cultural–ideological sanctifying
of more direct relations of mutuality with the historical revolt against the
bounding implications that such mutuality entails.[49] The term 'abstract community' is an intentional oxymoron, much like the concept 'a nation of
strangers', which extends upon this contradictory history of the concept and
practice of 'community'. 'Ethnic community' is not immune from the same
tensions of meaning. It will be used, overlapping *natio* and nation, to distinguish those associations lived in terms of the *cultural* predominance of
kinship relations and common genealogy. The form taken by ethnic communities has of course changed over history despite the continuing emphasis on
'common genealogy'. The notion of 'ethnicity' is a very modern expression
which came to be asserted self-consciously at the very time that 'ethnically'
connected groupings were fragmented within overbracing nation-states. I
suspect that as we approach the year 2000 we will see a further lexical–
experiential shift. Just as in some quarters 'ethnicity' replaced 'race' as the
ideologically sound signifer of blood ties, in the Age of Self-Definition the
word 'people' will be increasingly used as a catch-all nomenclature, safe to use
by liberals and racists alike.[50]

Though the contemporary national community continues to 'live off' an
ongoing yet subordinate sense of blood ties, and though ethnic communities
often aspire to have their own state, the difference between the national and
ethnic community can nevertheless be defined without too much ambiguity:
a person can be institutionally *naturalized* as a national, whereas one still has
to be born into ethnicity. Even if it is already an abstract relation, ethnicity
continues to be lived as inscribed culturally in one's body, whereas nationality is culturally contradictory, deeply embedded but more and more open to

48. It is indicative of this tendency (though not of Smith's entire approach) that he says;
'Form is *akin to style*, in that, though the symbolic contents and meanings of communal creations may change over time, their characteristic *mode of expression* remains more or less
constant. Of course, over very long time spans, even forms may change (like artistic styles . . .)'
(emphasis added, Smith, *Ethnic Origins*, 1986, p. 14). The distinction between form and content
is vitally important, but to equate form with style is unnecessarily reductive. It gives only the
sense of form as manifest shape or manner; no sense of form as structured and constitutive.

49. See Williams, *Keywords*, 1976, pp. 65-66; Eugene Kamenka, ed., *Community as a Social
Ideal*, 1982; and Robert Nisbet, *The Quest for Community*, 1953. For a recent survey of the
revival of writings on community, see Elizabeth Frazer and Nicola Lacey, *The Politics of
Community*, 1993.

50. For example see Felipe Fernández-Armesto, ed., *The Peoples of Europe*, 1994.

choice. In practice this contradiction between choice and embeddedness is the source of two opposing political possibilities. On the one hand, we see glimmerings of a reflexive sense of embedded identity and place, a critical politics that works towards a renewed sense of community without its old closures and ethnocentrisms.[51] On the other hand, news bulletins are replete with the negative outcomes of a renewed identity politics:

> If the nation's past, contained in an image of racial and cultural difference, is relegated outside its democratic, collective history, then the signifying sign of race and its iterative, interruptive temporalities of archaism and discrimination inform the very moment of the enunciation of the contemporaneity: time and time again, the sign of the complex, unassimilable phenomena and paraphernalia of racial marking emerges with its banal evil . . . Time and time again, the nation's pedagogical claim to a naturalistic beginning with the unchosen things of territory, gender, and parentage – *amor patriae* – turns into those anxious, ferocious moments of metonymic displacement that marks the fetishes of national discrimination and minoritization . . .[52]

As well as indicating definitional problems, the foregoing discussion of 'long durational' shifts has served to highlight several important methodological issues. It will now be useful to spell these out more directly. The following chapter is designed to set up the minimal, broad requirements for sustaining the proposition that the nation is a particular kind of abstract community.

51. This is my political position: the present text however is not the place to defend such 'critical communitarianism' against orthodox internationalists and civic (postmodern) globalists at one end of the spectrum and conservatives and New Right radicals at the other end who want to protect against cultural 'loss' by instituting sets of neo-medieval barriers to social interchange. See, for example, the debates in Michael Keith and Steve Pile, eds, *Place and the Politics of Identity*, 1993.
52. Homi Bhabha, 'Anxious Nations, Nervous States', 1994, p. 208.

2

National Formation in Theory

The momentous nature of the ruptures which characterize politics today is reflected in the inadequacy of our familiar interpretative frameworks. Disorientation, along with a sense of foreboding and even helplessness, has become widespread. Not only does this affect the relatively familiar political discourses of social democracy and socialism, it strikes too at the core of the more basic frameworks of liberalism and marxism. The grounding categories of these different versions of political economy are opened out to questioning as change charts a course into unfamiliar territory.

John Hinkson, 'Postmodern Economy', 1993

When we consider the familiar ideological descriptions of the national past – the invention of tradition, or the instrumentality of national nostalgia – we realize that they do little justice to this discursive movement of the nation's time and being caught in the act of turning-returning, to the restless hesitation that articulates the contemporaneity of the past: part disavowal, part elliptical idealization, part fetishism, part splitting, part antagonism, part ambivalence.

Homi Bhabha, 'Anxious Nations, Nervous States', 1994

Any discussion of the national question faces the dilemma that the contemporary forms of the nation and nation-state are both objectively modern, and yet at the same time they are rooted in long-run, cultural forms of association. Because a long history of controversy is evoked by even putting the issue in this way let me hastily make some qualifications. It does not entail accepting the nationalist claim for the deep antiquity and continuity-through-history of their own particular nation. It does not necessarily mean assuming that national festivals or symbols recuperated from the past are anything other than recuperations. Nor does recognition of the dilemma involve accepting the primordialist assumption prominent in mainstream theory until the 1960s, that is, that those long-run forms lay essentially unchanged beneath the surface flux of history. But it does suggest the necessity of allowing for the theoretical space in which, firstly, an explanation of the relationship between the modernity but deeply embedded nature of the national formation might at least be attempted; in which, secondly, the evidence concerning pre-modern *nationes* can be incorporated; and thirdly that allows us to understand the continuation even *within* some contemporary postmodern settings of both modern nationalist ideologies and primordialist assumptions as carrying commonsensical force. At the very least, by developing a theory of changing social forms it is intended that we might cut through the debate between the modernists, the primordialists and the perennialists, the latter arguing that, given the need to belong, nations are a perennial feature of post-tribal history.[1]

The dilemma that national formation is both historically deeply embedded and yet distinctively modern is related to an issue of historical methodology, called here the dialectic of continuity-in-discontinuity. This issue, frequently raised during the following discussion, refers to the way in which history – continuous, apparently evolving human history – can be theorized as a discontinuity of forms of social formation. A number of definitions are crucial to this point.

The term 'form' (or 'social form') is used very broadly. 'Form' describes more than the manifest shape or manner: it designates the way in which social relations are structured. It is a synchronic term which refers both to modes of practice and to kinds of society (where even during the heyday of the modern nation-state, 'society' could not necessarily be equated with nation-state boundaries). The concept of 'social formation' is used more diachronically to describe a society uniquely constituted at a particular historical conjuncture. As a way into understanding particular social formations the present approach works across a number of different levels of analysis, each more abstract than the last. These levels of theoretical abstraction are:

1 Empirical generalization
2 Analysis of modes of practice
3 Analysis of modes of integration
4 Categorical analysis[2]

1 **Empirical generalization**   The first level is self-explanatory – any worthwhile theory constantly engages in empirical generalization, drawing first-order conclusions about the recurrence and patterning of social practices, drawing out general descriptions from the details of history and place.

1. For an elaboration of these terms see Anthony D. Smith, *The Ethnic Origins of Nations*, 1986, pp. 7–13. The assumptions of these approaches are to be avoided. Equally, I do not want to be subsumed *within* the categories 'Traditionalist–Culturalist', 'Modernist' or 'Post-modernist' as set up by Jonathan Friedman in 'Culture, Identity, and World Process', 1989. A helpful treatment of some of these issues can be found in John Hutchinson, *Modern Nationalisms*, 1994.

2. See Appendix 1. Also Geoff Sharp, 'Constitutive Abstraction and Social Practice', 1985. The proposition that theories are couched at various levels of *theoretical* abstraction will be important to the later discussion of the relation between levels of *constitutive* abstraction and the history of approaches to theorizing the national question, but it is too distracting to consider developing it in the body of the text at this stage. Though I disagree with the evolutionist direction in which Jürgen Habermas takes the integrationist way of conceiving of society, the problems with the 'mode of production' approach do, as he says, lead one to look 'in the direction of even stronger generalization, namely, the search for highly abstract principles of social organization' (see Jürgen Habermas, *Communication and the Evolution of Society*, 1979, p. 153). Anthony Giddens hints at a comparable methodological distinction to the one suggested here when he asks, 'what levels of abstraction can be distinguished in studying the structural properties of social systems?' (see Anthony Giddens, *The Constitution of Society*, 1984, p. 181, also pp. 180–193 *passim*).

The damning charge that a theory is empiricist is brought to bear only when it works exclusively at this level, when it argues that the gathering of social facts is a value-free process, or when it treats empirical generalization as the most sound analytic way of knowing.

2 **Analysis of modes of practice**   At a second level of theoretical abstraction, the method draws upon a modified version of the neo-marxist reading of social formations. Rather than assuming the primacy of the mode of production (as in orthodox marxism), social formations are understood to be constituted (historically overdetermined) by a complex of *modes of practice* – modes of production, exchange, organization, communication and enquiry. These patterns of practice are enacted within and across variously extended social boundaries. Even when used in this way the concept of 'social formation' is not limited to a society of a particular size. For example, when specified, a social formation can be coextensive with a world system. This is not to imply, as some world systems theorists tend to, that such a system can be equated with a particular mode of *exchange* (in this case capitalist exchange relations), nor that the loosely articulated trade transversals of the sixteenth century made up such an integrated network as to warrant being called a 'world system'. Along these lines, the concept of 'mode of production', always treated as an overlay of various modes of production, continues to be basic to understanding any social formation, but it is not afforded formal determinant predominance in the first, last or in-between instance.[3] In order to understand, for example, the transition from industrial capitalism to information capitalism as the dominant *formation of practice* we have to study each of the changing modes of practice and their uneven intersections.

The phrase 'forms of social formation' used earlier thus partly refers back to the proposition that particular societies at particular historical conjunctures can be compared with regard to their dominant and subordinate forms of production, exchange, organization, communication and enquiry.

3 **Analysis of modes of integration**   At this level the approach examines the intersecting practices of integration and differentiation, expressed here as ranging from face-to-face integration to disembodied integration where technologies and techniques of extension such as digitalized communications and mass media broadcasting come to mediate and abstract from relations of embodied 'presence'. How is this level more abstract than analysis of modes of practice? By comparison with concepts such as 'production'

3. Cf. Louis Althusser, 'Contradiction and Overdetermination' in *For Marx*, (1965) 1979; and Nicos Poulantzas, *Political Power and Social Classes*, (1968) 1973, *passim*. Raymond Williams, 'Base and Superstructure in Marxist Cultural Theory' and 'Means of Communications as Means of Production' in *Problems in Materialism and Culture*, 1980, provides a nice critique of such approaches. Marx's emphasis on the abstract category of 'mode of production' was part of what made classical historical materialism a kind of 'form analysis'. Introducing the notion of 'modes of social integration' into the present work is not to take away from the insights of a 'mode of production' analysis. Neither is it intended to imply the acceptance of the usually conservative implications of integration theory with its usage of 'the cultural' as a relatively untheorized consensual, static or essential category. It is to propose *a more abstract form of form analysis*.

and 'communication' which are recognized by people as things they do, the concept of 'integration' is more removed. It too is analytically derived from a matrix of lived social relations, but people do not self-consciously effect integrative processes, that is, not until recently with the increasingly abstract reflexivity about the means of social regulation and cultural management. Even Machiavelli was not concerned about integrating 'the people'. This immediately takes us into the issue of relationship between social theorizing and social practice, the 'double hermeneutic' of theory as practice.

4 **Categorical analysis**   This level of analysis directly explores the onto-logical categories that people leave in the realm of the commonsensical, the unquestioned foundation of a social formation – categories of social being such as time and space, identity and the body. These categories have been lifted into theoretical vogue surprisingly recently.[4] This is the realm that post-structuralists and cultural materialists have made their own, the former sometimes forgetting that analysis at that level, if not tied back into more concrete political–ethical considerations, is in danger of abstracted irrelevance, utopianism without a subject, or empty spiritualism.

At this level, generalizations can be made about the dominant categorical frame(s) of a social formation or its fields of practice and discourse. In fact it is only at this level that it is possible to generalize beyond categories of being and to talk about *ontological formations*, societies formed in the uneven dominance of, for example, tribalism, traditionalism, modernism, or post-modernism.

The remaining pages of this chapter are used to develop these last two levels of analysis and to distinguish analytically different forms of human association and subjectivity, in particular, different forms of national association.[5] Emphasis is placed upon these means of theoretical understanding only because they are the least familiar.

Integrative levels

The argument – that a form of social formation such as the nation-state is constituted in the changing intersection-in-dominance of levels of abstraction – can be approached through a fairly straightforward and schematic point of entry. It will entail radically departing from the more usual marxist designations of levels as comprising the economic base upon which are built other structural levels, namely, the political–legal and the ideological–cultural. And it will have almost nothing in common with the structural–

---

4. For example, on time see Norbert Elias, *Time: An Essay*, 1992; Christopher Gosden, *Social Being and Time*, 1994; Arno Borst, *The Ordering of Time*, 1993.

5. This is not on the surface a particularly novel suggestion. Peter Berger, for example, distinguishes 'three types of patriotism': direct communal; extended face-to-face; and abstract patriotism (see *Facing up to Modernity*, 1979, ch. 10). The basis of his approach is, however, quite different from that proposed here.

functionalist designation of the cultural, social and personality systems as relatively autonomous levels of social action.[6]

Levels of integration, understood as modes of structured practices of association (and differentiation) between people, can be expressed in various ways. Here they will be delineated in terms of the modes of embodiment pursuant to each level. As mentioned earlier, three categories of human ontology – the body, space and time – provide sub-themes to carry the discussion back and forth between an abstract schema of social forms and examining lived social formations. This text is thus intended as a dialogue between history and theory, a relation which as Fernand Braudel has put it is too often conducted as 'a dialogue of the deaf'.[7] I do not mean to privilege the body, time and space, but they are certainly central to the national question. Régis Debray, for example, says that the assignation of origins in time and the delimitation of space are the 'founding gesture[s] of any society'.[8] The task in which Debray fails is to posit ontological levels without essentializing the primary ('primordial') level and its grounding categories. Conversely, the task in which the critics of such primordialism fail is to ground the nationalist ideologies of blood (body), tradition (time) and soil (space) in long-run historical practices and forms.

The method of 'form analysis' is a heuristic way of engaging with a historical issue which contemporary social theory continues to find mockingly elusive. By eschewing a classical schema of ideal types it is hoped to avoid the tendency of such approaches to drown living detail in dead stereotype (Clifford Geertz's phrase). However, it still entails a continual stepping back from the rich detail of history, and at times it requires apparently arcane abstract excursions into issues of method.

Three levels of integration are analytically distinguished, each of which is abstract in relation to 'prior' levels. It should be stressed, firstly, that no social formation is constituted at one level of integration. Given the proposition that all societies are formed in the uneven intersection of various overlaying levels of integration, levels enacted across various reaches of time and space, the argument is not open to the criticism that any approach which refers to what Michael Mann calls 'levels of social formation' presupposes a view of society as a single unitary whole, geometrically layered across the same overall space.[9] Secondly, it should be recognized that by putting the weight of emphasis on levels of integration the present text is only taking a couple of steps into a fuller theory of constitutive levels. For example, a fuller theory would have to examine the modes of differentiation associated with different forms of integration. Moreover, it would have to examine in much more detail the relationship between modes of integration and modes of practice. Thirdly, it should be said that I have chosen to distinguish three levels only for reasons

6. The metaphor of levels occurs constantly through Talcott Parsons, *The Social System*, 1951.

7. Cited in Peter Burke, *Sociology and History*, 1980, p. 14.

8. 'Marxism and the National Question', 1977, p. 27.

9. Cf. Michael Mann, *The Sources of Social Power*, vol. 1, 1986, ch. 1.

of illustrating the methodology. To have distinguished two levels migh
given the misleading impression of the acceptance of a dichotomous v
history, commonly expressed as the distinction between the traditiona
the modern. To have chosen to distinguish four, or some greater numb
levels, would have been more unwieldy. For present purposes then the three
levels are:

- the face-to-face
- the agency-extended
- the disembodied

Face-to-face integration

Through human history the face is the most condensed metaphor we have for
conveying the meanings of social relations. Pierre Bourdieu records that 'just
as the Kabyles condense their whole system of values into the word *qabel*, to
face, to face the east, the future, so the older peasants in Bearm would say
capbat (literally, head down) to mean not only "down, below" but also
"northwards", . . . and that words like *capbacha*, "to bow the forehead", or
capbach were associated with the idea of shame, humiliation, dishonour or
affront'.[10] The apparently simple phrase 'face to face' has in this way a
remarkably complex cultural–historical depth. When Elizabeth Barrett
Browning (1806–61) writes 'Face to face, silent, drawing nigh and nigher'
(from 'Sonnets from the Portuguese', 1850) it carries a substantial cultural
baggage. Other bodily metaphors of interaction abound: 'They shall see eye
to eye' (Isaiah, 52:8); 'The silver link, the silken tie / Which heart to heart and
mind to mind / in body and in soul can bind' (Sir Walter Scott, 1771–1832,
from 'The Lay of the Last Minstrel', 1805). Together with newer colloqui-
alisms like 'eyeball to eyeball', they are commonly used in the present even for
interactions beyond embodied contact, but none of them has assumed the
generality of meaning that 'face to face' has engendered.

The concept of 'face-to-face integration' draws upon this complexity to
refer to the level of integration at which the modalities of co-presence, the
modalities of being in the presence of the other, are central and predominant
in maintaining a continuing association of persons even in their physical
absence from one another. Understanding the face-to-face as a level of integration entails putting emphasis upon the importance of the modalities of
co-presence rather than the fact of co-presence, the acts of interaction. This
is crucial to the present argument. It is not wrong to say that face-to-face integration is substantiated in the immediacy of any instance of face-to-face
interaction, that is, even in co-presence 'fading away across time and space' in
the sense used by Anthony Giddens and Irving Goffman.[11] However, such a

10. Pierre Bourdieu, *The Logic of Practice*, 1990, p. 19; see also Terry Landau, *About Faces*,
1989.

11. Giddens, *The Constitution of Society*, 1984, p. 36.

statement puts a too heavy emphasis on the particularities of interaction and downplays the social relational setting. Here we can make an analytic distinction between interaction and integration. The distinction allows for the recognition that *interaction* is never simply present to itself: it always occurs in the context of structured *integrative* relations.[12]

In a setting marked by the dominance of face-to-face integration, such as a tribal or peasant society, the limitations and possibilities of fully embodied interaction constitute the boundaries of social existence and thus of social subjectivity. It conditions the way in which people live such apparently pre-given but already abstracted 'natural' categories as the body, space and time. It binds the abstracting practices of myth-telling, long-distance gift exchange and even cross-tribal partnership with unseen others, within the modalities of co-presence. It binds them within the modalities of reciprocity, continuity and concrete otherness. What is being described here then is an ontological framing, not just circles and lines of spatial extension. In this context, integration does not depend upon individuals constantly standing toe-to-toe, nor after a particular interaction does it, in the modern sense, fade away. In this sense the modalities of co-presence bind absence. For example, kinship based on the existential significance of being born of a particular body into lines of extended blood-relation is a key social form of face-to-face integration. In social formations where kinship is fundamental to social integration, a person is always bound by blood or affinity even after the dramatic separation brought by death.

It is only at the point at which a particular grounding practice can no longer be taken for granted that we meet the recurring paradox that its centrality and continuing importance is formally announced: the proverb 'blood is thicker than water' can only be traced back as far as the early seventeenth century.[13] Similarly, any theory of national association confronts the problem that the common nationalistic catchcry, 'for blood and soil', only arises long after the ontological setting of being bound by kinship and locale has been qualitatively reconstituted. This issue leads into a further step in the present argument. Instances of face-to-face *interaction* are constitutively different when set in the context of different *integrative* levels. Neither the act of being in the presence of others, nor the continuation of ties of blood, nor attachment to a particular locale, necessarily suggest a setting in which the face-to-face is the

---

12. Despite some similarities this is not to say that I fully concur with the way in which Jürgen Habermas distinguishes between system integration and social integration (i.e. experiential integration in the lifeworld). See his *Legitimation Crisis*, 1976, ch. 1. Anthony Giddens also distinguishes social integration ('systemness in circumstances of co-presence') from societal or system integration ('reciprocity between actors of collectives across extended time-space, outside conditions of co-presence'). See, for example, Giddens, *Constitution of Society*, 1984, pp. 28, 64–73, 139–144, 282, 376–377. I will argue later (in Chapter 6) that its strengths can be incorporated into a levels argument without taking on accompanying problems and limitations. See also David Lockwood, 'Social Integration and System Integration', 1964; and Ian Craib, *Modern Social Theory*, 1984, pp. 53ff. and 212ff.

13. See also below Chapter 7 on the first appearance of permanent family names.

dominant integrative level. For example, the description that peak-hour subway commuters are squashed cheek by jowl into the Tokyo express by professional passenger loaders says nothing about the relevant structure of relations which holds together these strangers-cum-national compatriots.

Agency-extended integration

With agency-extended integration, social integration is abstracted beyond being based predominantly on the directly embodied and/or particularized mutuality of persons in social contact. At this level, institutions (agencies) such as the church or state, guild or corporation, and structuring practices of extension such as commodity exchange through merchants, traders, pedlars and the like (agents and mediators), come to bind people across larger expanses of space than is possible under face-to-face integration. More importantly, as the processes of agency extension consolidate and overlay ongoing relations of the face-to-face, different ontological formations become possible. Nineteenth-century and early twentieth-century social theorists such as Emile Durkheim, Ferdinand Tönnies, Henry Maine, Fustel de Coulanges and C.H. Cooley, would seem to be drawing parallel lines of distinctions when they divide societies constituted predominantly in the face-to-face from those they respectively refer to as characterized by organic solidarity, the affirmations of *Gesellschaft*, or the bonds of contractual or secular society. A recent theorist like Anton Zijderveld in his description of the *Abstract Society* would also seem to be making parallel suggestions about changing societal forms. However, the levels argument, a form analysis rather than a specification of ideal types, will more obviously part company with such typologies as this discussion proceeds.

The concept of 'agency', despite its breadth of allusion – as an instrumentality or institution, as the office of an agent, or as a state of exerting power or being in action on behalf of another – needs to be conjoined with the concept of 'mediation' to give a fuller sense of this level of integration. A further analytic distinction could be made between agency-extended integration and what might be called 'object-mediated integration', drawing particular attention to the forms of mediation reproduced in the practice of commodity exchange. For reasons of methodological simplicity, early capitalist market exchange will be subsumed within the schema of levels of integration as already delineated. While pedlars, for example, do not usually act as agents in the institutionalized sense used above, they do mediate relations of production in the breakdown of subsistence and feudal agriculture, and as Fernand Braudel documents, they were most often the agents intermediating between the stores of wholesale merchandisers (or even not-so-important shopkeepers) and the widening classes of consumers.[14]

In a social formation where agency extension is in predominance as it began to be in a quasi-regulated way in the polities of feudal Europe or late-

14. *The Wheels of Commerce*, 1985, pp. 75–80.

imperial China, representatives or agents of the central institutions including clerics, soldiers and tax collectors came to minister to geographically separated groups of people who, at the level of the face-to-face, continued to have few points of connection with other groups. Networks of agency-extension overlapped and were often in competition. As part of this process, an abstracted political concept of space was created. It was a concept of space with antecedents in the Roman Empire and developed from the early Middle Ages in Western Europe, a concept 'capable of distinguishing space [territory] from the people who lived in it, people who, hitherto, had charged it with a purely social identity'.[15] The effects of the process varied across social settings. In Europe and across the Byzantine Christian realm it overlay rather than completely re-formed the more parochial sense of *place*,[16] while in the Middle East, quasi-territorial, ethnic-genealogical identity continued to be derived from the mythologies and practices of nomadism.

Going back further, the diverse formations we collate under the heading 'traditional empires', from the Assyrian to the Carolingian empires, from the Han to the Mogul empires, all depended upon administrative and military representation for the continuing domination of their extensions of territory.[17] Up until the Middle Ages the prince was most often there in person on the battlefield or in the counting house; however, this does not mean that face-to-face ties predominated in that setting. As in the example of feudal Europe, the relationships of the princes and their agents were formed in the uneasy intersection of relations of the face-to-face and of agency-extension. The nature of this intersection shifted over time and from locale to locale. The Roman military tradition, for example, emphasized the 'personal' relation between the army and the ruler – ritual oath-taking sanctioned loyalty to the emperor as a 'fellow-soldier' (*commilito*). However, it is obvious, firstly from the importance placed on emoluments and regular wages and secondly from

15. Robert A. Dodgshon, *The European Past*, 1987, p. 139. It should be qualified somewhat: Dodgshon's phrase, 'a purely social identity', gives a sense of the changed meaning of space only by virtue of the context in which the phrase is placed. The new meaning of space is equally 'social', but takes a different form. See also Robert Sack, *Conceptions of Space in Social Thought*, 1980, ch. 7; and Armstrong, *Nations before Nationalism*, 1982, ch. 2.

16. It is important to my argument to distinguish the concepts of 'space' and 'place'. Whereas the concept of 'space' is open and empty – 'space' is derived from the Latin *spatium*, from *spatiari*, meaning 'to wander' – the concept of 'place' is more particular, more concrete in its reference. The concepts overlap, but certainly from the nineteenth century they have tended to be used quite differently. In Abraham Lincoln's Gettysburg Address (1863) the term 'place' is not interchangeable: 'We have come to dedicate a portion of that field [of civil war], as a final resting place for those who here gave their lives that the nation might live.'

17. Marxist theorists need to take seriously Michael Mann's argument that it was neither class structure nor mode of production that made this territorial extension possible: 'I am not arguing that classes did not exist or that one cannot *describe* Roman or Chinese modes of production: rather that such concepts cannot be used to give an explanation of why these societies were so large in extent and had states of a particular "Imperial" form.' See his *States, War and Capitalism*, 1988, p. 57. Even if Mann is right that the military structure had crucial repercussions for the forces and relations of production, this is not to say that the relevance of the mode of production as making possible the exacting of surplus resources is to be down-played.

the lack of evidence of a flow-on of loyalty to the *res publica* (the republic itself), that this was an uneasy relation, now strong, now weak.[18]

The power of the early empires over their dominions was effected by military coercion, and though it was often religiously sanctioned it was dependent on the beginnings of an agency-regulated exaction of surplus production from subservient, often ethnically differentiated, populations. (As will be discussed in the next section it was also increasingly dependent upon the development of disembodied administrative mechanisms such as basic systems of writing and accounting, record keeping and organization of agency networks.) At the same time, relations between the ruling factions still were based commonly upon face-to-face modalities such as extended-kinship or reciprocal loyalties. In other words, ruling power was still substantially founded upon patrimonial or traditional authority as opposed to the more abstract, bureaucratic and relatively impersonal power of legal authority.[19] However, this too was changing. Patrimony was itself part of the reconstitution of face-to-face relations across all classes. With patrimony, reciprocity became a skewed and hierarchical relationship of fragile, constantly negotiated alliances. In other words, the mode of organization was being recast at a more abstract level of integration. Concomitantly, through the Middle Ages in Europe and elsewhere, the reciprocal ties carried by the subsistence-based barter economy and by vestiges of gift exchange (Mauss) were gradually being subsumed under the over-bracing reaches of trade and more abstract market exchange: that is, the mode of exchange was being recast. As Norbert Elias suggests, the transformation from a barter economy to a money economy connects with a multitude of other processes in conditioning the form of integration.[20]

The development of an intersection between face-to-face and agency-extended relations should not be seen as part of an uncontradictory, consensual, unidirectional or continuous evolutionary pathway. At the height of the Carolingian Empire, Charlemagne (–814)[21] ruled through the appointments of *comites* (locally based agents) and *missi dominici* (circulating agents) and through reliance on bishoprics and abbeys. But as Gianfranco Poggi describes them,[22] such offices were qualified and complemented by understanding derived from *Gefolgschaft*: highly personal, face-to-face bonds of followership between a warrior chief and his retinue of near-peers. In a twist of influences, *Gefolgschaft* became institutionalized in the later feudal system of rule (late eighth to early fourteenth centuries), in turn being qualified by legal principles revived from an *earlier* polity, the Roman empire.

---

18. J.B. Campbell, *The Emperor and the Roman Army*, 1984.

19. For definitions of 'traditional' and 'legal authority' see Max Weber, *The Theory of Social and Economic Organization*, (1910–20) 1945, pp. 329–336, 341–346.

20. Norbert Elias, *State Formation and Civilization*, (1939) 1982, ch. 1.

21. Bernard Guenée, *States and Rulers in Later Medieval Europe*, 1988, pp. 61ff. discusses the competing claims of Capetian and Valois France and, later, of Habsburg Germany to Charlemagne as 'national' precursor and legitimator of monarchical legitimacy. The history of legitimation by ascension of blood-lines is certainly a discontinuous story.

22. Gianfranco Poggi, *The Development of the Modern State*, 1978, p. 20 and pp. 19–25.

As well as the problem of discontinuity in history, the issue of emergent contradiction in historical practices is brought to the fore by the metaphor of levels. (The term 'cultural contradiction'[23] or what I prefer to call 'ontological contradiction' will be used here to designate contradictions arising out of the intersection of constitutive levels.) For example, contradictions between the respective modalities characteristic of face-to-face and agency-extended relations are shown up in the subjective identity of medieval office-bearers. Considerable cultural confusion, generating philosophical and legal debate, had to be resolved in trying to understand the double ontology of the person-as-'office bearer'. Their identity was founded on the one hand upon the limitations and possibilities of being embodied and private, and yet on the other hand on being the bearer of a 'higher' identity through embodying an official or sacred agency with transcendent meaning, abstract in relation to the particularities of its incumbent. Thomas Hobbes (1588–1679) is one example among many writers who found it necessary to distinguish between the '*Naturall Person*' and the '*Feigned or Artificiall person*'.[24] Perhaps the most graphic illustration, relevant to the sub-theme of modes of embodiment, is the feudal conception of the king's body.[25]

Kingship first evolved not as the individual exertion of power but as the expressed authority of a kinship grouping within an extended face-to-face setting: 'king' and 'kindred' have the same etymology.[26] However, while, as we have just discussed, genealogy and other face-to-face ties such as *Gefolgschaft* remained important to the identity of the sovereign through the period of Charlemagne, this came to be overlaid by a more abstract level of identity conferral. The body of the *mon*arch, singular, came to be seen as also the embodiment of an ongoing administrative structure, as the incarnation of a relation between the City of Man and the City of God, and, most pertinently for the present discussion, it became the *corpus repraesentatum* of the relatively new *territorial* concept of the *patria* (the fatherland). The levels of integration were, in effect, set against each other.

In the sixteenth century and after – but with a wealth of antecedents including the *corpus Christi* conception of the early Church councils and the entombing practices of ancient Egypt[27] – the contradiction between the person and the office of the sovereign was resolved by convolutedly projecting a

23. Sharp, 'Constitutive Abstraction', 1985, pp. 72ff.

24. Thomas Hobbes, *Leviathan*, (1651) 1976, pp. 1, 83–86. For a more general discussion of the transformations of 'role' and 'character', and the distinguishing of 'the skin from the shirt' (Pierre Charron's phrase), see Agnes Heller, *Renaissance Man*, 1967.

25. Ernst Kantorowicz, *The King's Two Bodies*, 1957; also Andrew Vincent, *Theories of the State*, 1987, ch. 2; and Otto von Gierke, *Political Theories of the Middle Ages*, 1900.

26. Writers who argue this proposition include: Reinhard Bendix, *Kings or People*, 1978, ch. 2, particularly p. 25; and Friedrich Engels, *The Origin of the Family, Private Property and the State*, (1884) 1985, p. 140 and chs iv–viii, *passim*.

27. Kantorowicz, *King's Two Bodies*, 1957, notes the occasionally observed Egyptian custom 'of entombing two statues of a dead officer: one, attired with a wig and loincloth, in his capacity of a royal officer; and the other one, bald and in a long garment, as the "man" that the dead was' (pp. 497–98, also ch. 9).

unity-in-the-distinction between the natural body and the body politic.[28] The latter body was believed to be of a higher though now increasingly secularized realm. Thus for legal purposes the *abstract king*, Henry VIII, was still alive, though Henry Tudor was long dead. Jurists of the Tudor period in England, simultaneously talking in the medium of the face-to-face and the agency-extended, expressed this unity/distinction as the doctrine of the King's Two Bodies: 'His Body natural (*if it can be considered in itself*) is a Body mortal . . . But his Body politic is a Body that cannot be seen or handled, consisting of Policy and Government, and constituted for the Direction of the People'[29] (emphasis added).

The theme of monarchy will surface time and again. However, before leaving this particular illustration I would like to reformulate earlier characterizations of *natio* and *patria* in terms of the levels argument. During the late feudal period, *patria*, the root of the later term 'patriotism', referred at one level to a person's birthplace or homeland. It paralleled the French *pays* or German *heimat*. But this meaning was held in place by a new, superordinate form of association, the kingdom as *communis patria*, overarchingly held together through relations of agency-extension. Allegiance was owed to *the abstract person* who embodied this territorially expressed extension of space, not to the person conceived through the modalities of the face-to-face. Hence the confused concept of the King's Two Bodies. Centuries later we still find strong expressions of personally held authority – such as the everywhere-quoted statement apocryphally attributed to Louis XIV (1638–1715), 'L'État c'est moi'. However, the abstraction of sovereignty, and the transition from a bureaucracy of monarchical servants to servants of the state,[30] marked the beginning of the end of patrimonially exercised power:

> Power ceases to be conceived as a collection of discrete rights and prerogatives, as it had been under the Ständestaat, and becomes instead more unitary and abstract, more *potential*, as it were. As such, it begins to detach itself conceptually from the physical person of the ruler; we might put it another way and say that it subsumes the ruler within itself.[31]

The more abstract meaning of the *patria* was associated with an ethic which exemplified the reconstitution of the ontological significance of the face-to-face: *pro patria mori*, or death for the glory of the fatherland.[32] Jurists drew on antecedents in Roman law to assert that a person acting in the name of the *patria* could legitimately kill his (or her) *pater*. Some

28. Through this distinction the gender of the monarch could be overlooked. Although, in France, the *Leges Imperii* contained the Salic Law forbidding female succession to the throne.

29. Kantorowicz, *King's Two Bodies*, 1957, p. 7.

30. These phrases allude to G.E. Aylmer's thesis of a transition from *The King's Servants: The Civil Service of Charles I, 1625–1642*, 1961 to *The State's Servants: The Civil Service of the English Republic, 1649–1660*, 1973.

31. Poggi, *Modern State*, 1978, p. 74. For a discussion of the political metaphors drawn upon during the period of Louis XIV's reign see George Armstrong Kelly, 'Mortal Man, Immortal Society?', 1986.

32. Ernst Kantorowicz, '*Pro Patria Mori* in Medieval Thought', 1951.

Humanist intellectuals got carried away and took the ethic to grotesque extremes:

> Thou knowest not how sweet is the *amor patriae*: if such would be expedient for the fatherland's protection or enlargement, it would seem neither burdensome and difficult nor a crime to thrust the axe into one's father's head, to crush one's brothers, to deliver from the womb of one's wife the premature child with the sword.[33]

If feudal patriotism drew upon and yet changed the meaning of the face-to-face, the same could be said of allegiance to the *natio*. These allegiances were formed in the context of face-to-face *interaction*, in such places as universities, monasteries and military barracks. But they were felt by people who had been lifted out of many of the constraints of face-to-face integration. These were people who had, *at one level of their being*, ascended into the disembodied realm of the written Word,[34] or at least who had in practice been 'liberated' from the parochial boundaries of village and kinship-related life. There is no evidence, until we come to a much later period, of the villager experiencing sentiments of incipient nationalism. And by then, the relationship of the village to the outside world had fundamentally changed. By then, the outside world had irrupted to haunt the most parochial hamlet, penetrating at a level which, paradoxically, its inhabitants most often came to actively embrace, even as in many cases they strove against its particular manifestations to maintain the face-to-face boundaries of old. As Jim MacLaughlin reminds us, national formation may have been constitutive but it certainly was not consensual.[35]

The development of the institutional continuity of the body politic and the *patria* beyond the limitations of directly embodied interactions depended upon – among many other conditions – the possibility of storing and transmitting information across time and space in a way that stretched the capacities of personal or word-of-mouth memory. The full significance of writing as a *disembodied* medium of extension is in this respect profound.[36] Writing, literacy and, later, print as means (this marxist term is used intentionally) of information organization, storage and communication, beginning

---

33. Coluccio Salutati, cited in Kantorowicz, *King's Two Bodies*, 1957, p. 245. See also pp. 232–272. Salutati (1331–1406) was a fourteenth-century Florentine 'civic humanist'.

34. M.T. Clanchy, *From Memory to Written Record: England 1066–1307*, 1979.

35. On the importance of recognizing the uneven constitution of national identity across class and from urban to rural settings see Jim MacLaughlin, 'The Political Geography of "Nation-Building" and Nationalism in Social Sciences', 1986; as well as MacLaughlin, 'Reflections on Nations as "Imagined Communities"', 1988.

36. Geoff Sharp, 'A Revolutionary Culture', 1968. This insight is only just beginning to be structurally incorporated into theoretical and historical studies. See Gerry Gill, PhD thesis, forthcoming; Jack Goody, *The Domestication of the Savage Mind*, Cambridge, 1977; Elizabeth Eisenstein, *The Printing Revolution in Early Modern Europe*, 1983; as well as Benedict Anderson, *Imagined Communities*, 1991 and Anthony Giddens, *The Nation-State and Violence*, 1985. Though Max Weber is sometimes credited with the full force of recognizing the significance of writing, it is actually only given sparse or passing attention in his work. See for example Weber, *The Theory of Social and Economic Organization*, (1910–1920) 1945, p. 332.

with the earliest lists of pictograms in Mesopotamia, became basic to the sta-
bilization of the varied forms of centrally administered, agency extension.
Moreover, as Jack Goody and others have convincingly argued, the development of writing and the acquisition of literary skills, as well as affecting the
nature of political systems, contributed to transforming the nature of human
cognitive processes.

Until relatively recently, this medium, which at least within the practices of
intellectually related groupings carried the possibility of more abstract,
decontextualized and disembodied extensions of social interaction/integra-
tion than are engendered by face-to-face or agency-extended communication,
was limited in its constitutive generality. It was bound by the means of production of written texts (the industrial printing press began operating in the
fifteenth century); by the hand-to-hand delivery of written communication
(the telegraph was a product of the nineteenth century); by the separation
between vernacular and administrative or written languages, persisting in
some cases into the twentieth century; by low levels of literacy; and so on. As
a methodological aside it should be noted here how the analysis, working
across levels of *theoretical* abstraction, ties together (a) empirical generalizations, (b) form analyses of modes of production and communication etc., and
(c) form analyses of particular levels of integration, to show how they qualify each other.

The example of writing[37] and the fundamental break that occurred with
printing technologies has been admitted into the discussion here because it
provides a bridge into talking about the 'third' level of social integration, the
disembodied. It is also integral to the phenomenon of the newspaper, raised
here to introduce the process which, in Benedict Anderson's words, 'quietly
and continuously . . . [helps to create] that remarkable confidence of community in anonymity which is the hallmark of modern nations'.[38]

Disembodied integration

The phrase 'disembodied integration' is used to refer to a level at which
people are part of a network of connections where the full modalities of
face-to-face interaction and the continuing practices of intermediating agency
are not the salient features of the social relation. At this level the social relation transcends time and space quite apart from any personal intermediation.
It is an *analytically* distinguishable level at which the constraints on communication, exchange, organization and production entailed in the deceptively
complex fact that human beings have bodies, are qualitatively attenuated. As
has already been stressed in relation to the intersection of the face-to-face and
agency-extended, this is not to say that in a particular social formation

37. While I think Paul Hirst and Penny Woolley underplay the dramatic innovation of writing, certainly I agree that print was in a much more generalized way 'the enabling condition of
an entirely different level of culture' (to use their words). See their *Social Relations and Human
Attributes*, 1982, p. 33.

38. Anderson, *Imagined Communities*, 1991, p. 36.

marked by the emergent dominance of processes of disembodied integration the more concrete levels dissolve. Rather, historical hindsight suggests that they tend, unevenly and beset by contradiction, to be reconstituted in terms of the dominance of the more abstract level.[39] For example, as Goody says:

> The written word does not replace speech, any more than speech replaces gesture. But it adds an important dimension to much social action. This is especially true of the politico-legal domain, for the growth of bureaucracy clearly depends to a considerable degree upon the ability to control 'secondary group' relationships by means of written communications . . . The relation with both ruler and ruled becomes more impersonal, involving greater appeal to abstract 'rules' listed in written code and leading to a clear-cut separation between official duties and personal concerns. I do not wish to suggest that such a separation is totally absent from non-literate societies . . . But it is clear that the adoption of written modes of communication was intrinsic to the development of more wide-ranging, more depersonalized and *more abstract systems* of government; at the same time, the shift from oral intercourse meant assigning less importance to face-to-face situations.[40]

The present approach provides a way of lending some precision to the recent emerging dominance and generalization of a new form in the late twentieth century, one which has commonly been characterized by the appellation, 'the information society'.[41] The approach is also intended to broaden Benedict Anderson's focus on print culture with a much wider emphasis on the manifold of processes which contribute to the abstraction of social being.

The means of disembodied extension are multifarious. Examples taken just from the sphere of communication (though they cannot be divorced from their uses in exchange, production and organization) range from the illuminated manuscript to the daily newspaper, from the telegraph wire to the national and international 'telecom' system, the satellite-connected television grid, and the network which bleeps the passage of capital across the globe to on-line personal computers.[42] None of these media rely upon either their one-to-one communicants or the individuals who make up their mass audiences having a prior face-to-face relationship with each other. Even the newspaper which is distributed by agents – newsagents – does not *in principle* depend upon the people it addresses being interconnected by ongoing networks of agency-extension, although in practice they are thoroughly so-connected.

39. Cf. the interesting but confused argument by Eric Leed, '"Voice" and "Print": Master Symbols in the History of Communication', 1980. He concludes that the present revolution in communications provides the possibility for consolidating an *enriched* version of the 'old', the 'traditional'.

40. Goody, *Savage Mind*, 1977, pp. 15–16. See also Jack Goody, *The Logic of Writing and the Organization of Society*, 1986; and his *The Interface Between the Written and the Oral*, 1987.

41. See Hinkson, 'Postmodern Economy', 1993 and his 'Post Lyotard: A Critique of the Information Society', 1987; Jean Chesneaux, 'Information Society as Civic Mutation', 1987; and Mark Poster, *Foucault, Marxism and History*, 1984; and his *The Mode of Information*, 1990.

42. Technological apparatuses are the easiest way of exemplifying the changed level of integration, but this should not be taken to mean that they in themselves usher in a new age. For a critique of such reductionist determinism see Raymond Williams, *Television: Technology and Cultural Form*, 1974, ch. 1.

At the same time it is important to note that even the electronic media depend, both for the meaning of their content and for the depth of their constitutive hold, upon the assumption of an ontological continuity from the embodied to the disembodied. Examples can be taken from across the twentieth century. One inter-war British writer proclaimed: 'There is a grumble and a cause of complaining if the crofter of the North of Scotland or the agricultural labourer in the West of England has been unable to hear the King [now effectively (dis)embodied by a further level] *speak* on some great national occasion'[43] (emphasis added). The Scottish crofter is no different from any of his or her compatriots in being able to conceive of the reconstituted relationship to a *national* monarchy in face-to-face terms. The Queen Mother can by this process be said to be the most loved person in Britain, as if the technologically mediated relationship via the press and broadcasting networks affords a personal relationship to her.[44]

A person's relationship to their unseen, unheard, 'massified' national fellows is similarly abstract, yet conducted as if it *could* be consummated concretely.[45] Raymond Williams gives the phenomenal meaning of the masses as people we don't know yet. By contrast, Paul Virilio misses out on the contradictory nature of this when he says, 'The masses are not a population, a society, but a multitude of passers-by.'[46] Similarly Zygmunt Bauman misrepresents the dialectic between living in a nation and confronting strangers when he says that 'strangerhood is the waste of nation-state building. They are waste, as they defy classification and explode the tidiness of the grid.'[47] National community, despite being formed within the modern concern for distinguishing and classifying compatriots and foreigners, is replete with strangers. One of the tasks of the state becomes to administer the difference between strangers for inclusion and strangers for exclusion. Each of the media contributes in specifiable ways to this sense of concrete consummation, to the sense that strange compatriots, people on the street, are not merely passers-by. A newspaper is consumed by readers who may at one level presuppose an abstract community of readership, a common community simultaneously moving through calendrical time. All the while, in observing replicas of their own paper being read by their 'subway, barbershop, or residential neighbours, [people are] continually reassured that the imagined world is visibly rooted in everyday life'.[48]

43. John Reith, *Broadcast over Britain*, cited in David Cardiff and Paddy Scannell, 'Broadcasting and National Unity', 1987, p. 157. They go on to talk of the explicit concern 'in the earliest years of broadcasting, to employ radio to forge a link between the dispersed and disparate listeners and the symbolic heartland of national life'.

44. See Tom Nairn, *The Enchanted Glass*, 1988.

45. Although it should be obvious by now, it is worth emphasizing that 'concreteness' and 'abstraction' are treated as descriptive terms, not as dichotomous polarities.

46. Paul Virilio, *Speed and Politics*, 1986, p. 3.

47. Zygmunt Bauman, *Modernity and Ambivalence*, 1991, p. 15.

48. Anderson, *Imagined Communities*, 1991, pp. 35–36. See also Colin Mercer, 'Regular Imaginings: The Newspaper and the Nation', 1992.

The intersection of the emergent level of disembodied extension with 'prior' levels ('prior' is used here to emphasize a formal and ontological ordering, as distinct from a chronological sequence) brings new ontological contradictions. In relation to the national question, the media of disembodied extension radically lift the surveillance, monitoring, administrative and cultural management possibilities of the modern nation-*state*.[49] Out of the same structural processes, though in contradiction with the consolidation of the old national form, the mass media facilitate the over-reaching of national boundaries by meta-national capital, commodities, and cultural values and practices. In old Czechoslovakia, for example, the ultra-Stalinist daily of the Austrian Communist Party, *Volkstimme*, was, until recently, readily bought by Czechs and Slovaks for its listing of Austrian television programmes. Long before the dismantling of the Berlin Wall these programmes crossed the national/political divide. In Belgium, the state controls a national television monopoly, except, that is, for the satellite border-hopping of more than a dozen competing foreign channels. In Australia and New Zealand, the high-profile, nationalistic governments of Hawke to Keating and Lange to Bolger have been in the forefront of renovating their national economies to deregulate the flow of international capital across their borders. In short, the very processes of integration which further the bases for the integrity of the national boundary and for the power of the state (an institution of agency extension), also carry the possibilities for its 'dissolution' from without.

The older form of the nation-state, held together in the intersection of reconstituted face-to-face relations and the still politically ascendant institutions of agency-extension, is with current developments simultaneously prone to be hollowed out from within.[50] The emergent dominance and generalization of disembodied relations provides the conditions for the re-formation of what (somewhat ironically) can be called the classical nation-state.[51]

Anthony Smith expresses the experiential dimension of this when he says, 'We are probably never so aware of phenomena and objects as when we are about to gain or lose them'. He continues: 'In the mid-twentieth century, whatever our attitudes to national*ism*, there was a very widespread assumption in the public mind, echoed in much of the scholarly community, that the nation was something as 'natural' as the family, speech or the human body itself.'[52]

49. This is what Anthony Giddens is referring to when he argues that 'electronic communication for the first time in history separates "immediate" communication from presence, thereby initiating developments in modern culture that . . . are basic to the emergence and consolidation of the nation-state' (*Nation-State and Violence*, 1985 p. 14). See also Habermas, 'Legitimation Problems in the Modern State', in *Communication*, 1979, ch. 5; and Christopher Dandeker, *Surveillance, Power and Modernity*, 1994.

50. This apt phrase is taken from Geoff Sharp, 'Hollowed Out from Within', 1983.

51. 'Classical' is used here ironically because, as discussed in Chapter 3, even in the nineteenth century when commonsense and theoretical views were beginning to take the national and nation-state formation relatively for granted, the nation-state had not consolidated and was already beset by the processes of dissolution.

52. Smith, *Ethnic Origins*, 1986, p. 7. See as an example Esmé Wingfield-Stratford, *The Foundations of British Patriotism*, 1940.

By the late twentieth century, particularly in the West, the given-ness of the national form has become less secure, though, again, this is contradictory. In the capitalist Westernized states (and for different but related reasons in the Third World states) the assertions of national sentiment are becoming more pronounced than has been generally the case in the post-war period. In other words, the national formation is being strengthened at one level, while the prior levels which gave historical national forms their hold are being gradually and unevenly attenuated. The classical modern nation is being reconstituted and in some settings is giving way to what we might call the postmodern nation.[53] That is, postmodern subjectivities and practices are coming to overlay and reframe the (continuing) condition of modernity. This needs some elaboration.

A number of grand (though always contested) narratives were relevant to the modern nation-state: the notions of boundedness and sovereignty; assumptions about the virtues of both high-cultural homogeneity and genealogical integrity; and claims to the civilizing value of assimilating 'backward' ways of life; and pretensions to the progressive necessity of comprehensively regulating the civic culture and national economy. Described in categorical terms, the modern nation was imagined as being bound within particular conceptions of time, space and embodiment. What then characterizes the postmodern nation? If the modern nation-state was experienced as both publicly and intimately structuring one's lifeworld, then the postmodern *nation* (even when it is not named as such) is increasingly *experienced* as an unstructured, and at times even optional, background choice: for example the distinctions between race, ethnicity and nationality have become even further stretched with nationality becoming less and less inscribed in one's body. Simultaneously, under conditions of postmodernity the *state* is most often viewed either as a baleful institution to be minimized and deregulated or as a necessary, if intrusive, organ of public administration, a provider of last-resort services for the vulnerable.

At the heart of the postmodern nation is a fragile and contradictory immediacy. On the one hand, the media of disembodied extension link distant, privatized (or even still-localized) strangers into an abstract national community by paradoxically giving a new immediacy to national occasions and events. When our sporting heroes cover the nation with reflected glory at the Barcelona Olympics, or when our defence forces carry the flag into the Gulf war, we can all 'be there', on the wings of the television. Over the past few decades this media of immediacy has underscored a *new nationalism*.[54] It has

53. The term 'postmodern nation' is used with reference to the way Jean-François Lyotard and others talk of the postmodern condition as the replacement of the old grand narratives by flexible networks of information. However, it should not be taken to imply a concurrence with either the methodology or the politics of such writers. See Lyotard's *The Postmodern Condition*, 1984.

54. It seems to have caught social theorists unawares. It is only possible to find isolated chapters, journal articles and newspaper sketches of instances of the phenomenon. For a discussion of the new nationalism in Australia see Stephen Alomes, *A Nation at Last?*, 1988; cf. Stephen Castles et al., *Mistaken Identity: Multiculturalism and the Demise of Nationalism in Australia*, 1988; Tony Bennett et al., eds, *Celebrating the Nation*, 1992; and Wayne Hudson and David Carter, eds, *The Republicanism Debate*, 1993.

been evident particularly in the late-capitalist countries, from the United States to New Zealand, from Japan to France. Apparently archaic and residual cultural practices (Raymond Williams' terms), including conducting Royal Marriages, sailing Tall Ships, competing before the Gods of Olympus and committing ritual *hara-kiri*, have been given a new level of meaning, thin as it is. National symbols are drawn together as pastiche. Public actors, from political leaders and television evangelists to transnational corporations, have been advised on the basis of computer-analysed opinion polls that it is advantageous to speak in the name of the nation. They speak in the name of the content of prior levels – traditional values and modern nation-building practices – while effectively acting to displace those levels.

The new nationalism is thus continuous with modern nationalism but conducted with a new reflexivity. In this way it is increasingly open to self-conscious cultural management. On the other hand, the new nationalism has a febrile fragility. Because our distance from the past (over time) and from our compatriots (across space) is 'overcome' in the accentuation of a single level of integration (the disembodied), the ontological depth of the contemporary nation-state is 'thinned out'. In the abstraction of time, tradition comes to be a largely self-consciously upheld and selected set of practices. But the more fervent this becomes the more the once taken-for-granted authenticity of tradition is revealed as no longer inscribed in itself, 'no longer written in the stars'. The more our sense of history is managed, 'invented', the more our attention is drawn to the processes of cultural management. In the abstraction of space a constant tension also exists. At least four incongruent developments can be listed: firstly, a nation's territory is thoroughly homogenized in terms of its cultural significance; secondly, some places, such as Uluru (Ayers Rock) in Australia or Mount Fuji in Japan, are conferred with symbolic meaning over and above, although representative of, the whole;[55] thirdly, one's everyday locale is emptied of such meaning – at least in any binding sense – as an increasingly socially mobile population searches for the optimal location to put down roots. And fourthly, certain corporate and state centres, such as stock exchanges and bureaucratic departments, became focal points for global networks of information and capital exchange which both centralize space and dissolve it into what Manuel Castells calls 'flows and channels' or Fredric Jameson calls 'hyperspace'. Anthony Giddens describes aspects of this process in a passage notable for its broad connections:

> The dissolution of the foundation of society in relations of presence substantially replaces the grounding of those primordial sentiments in tradition and kinship by a more routinised, habitual round of 'everyday life'. This is one point of intersection, I have argued, between notions of 'mass society' and the theory of the commodification of time and space deriving from Marx. In the spheres of 'everyday life' created by the expansion of capitalism the areas of 'meaningful' existence retreat – to the intimacy of personal and sexual relations on one side – and to the

55. For a discussion of the fusion of nation and territory, the historicizing of natural sites and the naturalizing of built objects, see Smith, *Ethnic Origins*, 1986, pp. 183ff.

arenas of 'mass ritual' on the other (as in spectator sports and in political ceremonial). In such conditions of social life the ontological security of the individual in day-to-day life is more fragile than in societies dominated by tradition and the meshings of kinship across space and time.[56]

There is a further complication. The long-term, uneven thinning out of day-to-day life has, in conjunction with other factors sharpened by the late-capitalist mode of production and exchange, such as regional economic disparities and cultural divisions of labour,[57] contributed to a renewed emphasis on ethnicity, local culture, regional difference and the existence of hitherto politically 'unrealized nations' *within* the hinterlands of existing nation-states. Along with examples earlier listed under the heading of sub-state nations, others can be added: ethnic groups such as the Alsatians/Lotharingians, Bretons and Corsicans in France, the Kurds in Turkey and the Frisians in the Netherlands. This *neo-nationalism*[58] is then distinct from, in some ways oppositional to, what I have been calling the new nationalism, though both are heightened by the same process. Neo-nationalism is clothed in the garments of the modern nationalist movements of the nineteenth century. Yet in existing at a different point in world time, in being set in the context of a changed intersection of integrative levels, neo-nationalism, like the new nationalism, is part of and a response to a more general transformation of the older national form. The nation-state will not wither away in the foreseeable future, but it can certainly be described as having entered a new stage in the way it bears upon human subjectivity and social relations.

Integrative levels as levels of abstraction

The previous section in setting up a three-level schema of forms of integration drew upon the illustrative point of entry of modes of embodiment. It was suggested that at each successive (that is, *formally* successive) level of integration, the limitations and possibilities of embodied co-presence were progressively abstracted. In practice, integrative relations were not only extended across time and space, but the categories of being-in-the-world, including time and

56. Anthony Giddens, *Power, Property and State*, 1981, pp. 193–194.
57. See for example Michael Hechter, *Internal Colonialism*, 1975 (for a critique of Hechter's assertion of the *centrality* of cultural divisions of labour see Phillip Rawkins, 'Nationalist Movements within the Advanced Industrial State', 1983; and Colin Williams, 'Ethnic Resurgence in the Periphery', 1979); and also, Etienne Balibar and Immanuel Wallerstein, *Race, Nation, Class*, 1991.
58. The term comes from Tom Nairn, *The Break-up of Britain: Crisis and Neo-Nationalism*, 1981. See also Walker Connor, *Ethnonationalism*, 1994, and his 'The Politics of Ethnonationalism', 1973; Joseph Rudolph, 'Ethnic Sub-States and the Emergent Politics of Tri-Level Interaction in Western Europe', 1977; Anthony H. Birch, 'Minority Nationalist Movements and Theories of Political Integration', 1978; Peter Gourevitch, 'The Re-emergence of "Peripheral Nationalisms"', 1979; Franjo Tudjman, *Nationalism in Contemporary Europe*, 1981; Anthony D. Smith, *The Ethnic Revival*, 1981; and Edward Tiryakian and Ronald Rogowski, eds, *New Nationalisms of the Developed West*, 1985.

space themselves, became lived in a more abstract way. The overlay of levels used in this sense was not intended, then, to be understood simply as levels of extension, as mental maps,[59] or as a political geography of time-space distantiation.[60] To do so would be to conceive of the different levels, treated here as levels constitutive of ontological being, as if they merely extend across a single *plane*.[61] (This point is crucial to later discussion.) It would be, in other words, to treat the levels of the face-to-face, agency-extended and disembodied-extended as if they were progressively larger circles of demarcated social activity able to be marked on a map, without recognizing how the more abstract extensions of social relations are part of the overlay or reconstitution even of the form of one's circle of day-to-day associations.

In short, to talk of constitutive levels is not the same as talking of degrees of time–space distantiation. Neither, as mentioned earlier, can the position being developed here be understood as setting up a series of ideal types. The phrase used earlier, intersections-in-dominance, encapsulates the proposition that given the intricate complexity of any specific social formation a society can only be conditionally summarized in terms of its dominant level(s) of integration. The same point has to be made in relation to describing the categorical formations of tradition, modernity and postmodernity. (Just to formalize the use of terms, the concept of 'intersection' is used throughout more abstractly than that of 'conjunction' even though they have parallel meanings.[62]) There is the ever-present proviso that any analysis remain sensitive to the contradictory processes of that level-in-dominance and to the complicating intersections of forms of social practice, however they may be framed: whether it be forms of identity grounded in face-to-face relations such as gender and the embodied differences of race, or other more abstract forms of association such as class. To do otherwise is (again making the point in short-hand) to reduce the complexities of social life to an analysis couched on one plane.

With regard to the national question, the key emphasis then is not just that the processes of extension allow an institutionalized association of people to colonize and administer larger expanses of territory in a relatively even way. The more far-reaching proposition is that the 'stages' of national formation

59. Peter Gould and Rodney White, *Mental Maps*, 1986.

60. Anthony Giddens defines time–space distantiation as the stretching and integration of social systems across time and space. Writings even in critical political geography tend to leave aside the issue of ontological levels of space and time. For example in Derek Gregory and John Urry, eds, *Social Relations and Spatial Structures*, 1985, at the only point at which the question of ontological depth is raised it is said that it 'simply means that the world is conceived as a *multidimensional structure* and not "squashed into a flat surface"' (p. 328). Derek Gregory develops this further in his sensitively written 'Presences and Absences', 1989, but it is elaborated more as a critique of Giddens than the development of an alternative.

61. For a more detailed explanation of this term, see Sharp, 'Constitutive Abstraction', 1985.

62. 'Intersection' tends, for example, to be used with reference to a description of social formations theorized as 'levels of social integration': 'conjunction' is used with reference to the more usual (conjunctural) analyses of social formations.

have been based upon the uneasy intersection of levels of social being, constituted in the emerging dominance and widening generality of the forces and relations of disembodied extension. It is suggested that although the modern (and to a lesser extent the postmodern) nation continues to be experienced as a concrete, historically condensed relation between people, it is only through a constitutive lift in the level of abstraction that it is possible to feel comradeship with a national mass who, except for one's personally known network of associations, will largely remain anonymous strangers.[63]

The materiality of abstraction

Running through the present discussion has been the assumption that the processes of abstraction occur in practice as well as in thought. To round off this chapter I would now like to spell this out further, firstly in relation to the early developments of the modern abstract community, and secondly through reference to the ambiguous place of the intellectually related groupings within these developments. In keeping with the spirit of Benedict Anderson's materialism these pages will attempt to stave off any unintended, idealist residuals that inhere in the phrase 'imagined communities'. It is doubtful, for example, that Anderson would be comfortable with Anthony Smith's rendition: 'Benedict Anderson . . . has defined the new nation of our imagination as a sovereign but limited community, an *essentially abstract mental construct*'[64] (emphasis added).

Abstraction quite obviously does occur in thought and, more broadly, in the modes of apprehending and imagining the world. The history of concepts like 'society' or 'state' bears this out.[65] The word 'state' derived from a face-to-face level of reference, the Latin *stare*, meaning 'to stand', and the comparative term, *status*, a standing or condition which related to specific qualities. The basis of status in the medieval period was one's estate, position and property bound up in heredity and kinship, as well as one's occupation or station in life. Monarchy was the highest estate. In the writing of Niccolò Machiavelli (1469–1527) we still find *lo stato* referring most often to the standing of the prince, rarely to the body politic in the more abstract sense. However, by the sixteenth century the highest estate had come to be tentatively connected to

63. This phrase 'anonymous strangers' is an allusion to Vance Packard's *A Nation of Strangers*, 1972, a lamentation to the fragmentation of contemporary social life.

64. Smith, *Ethnic Origins*, 1986, p. 169. That Anderson has unfortunately left himself open to this interpretation can be seen in MacLaughlin, 'Reflections', 1988.

65. Society', the most abstract and generalized term we now have for a 'body' of people living in structured social relations, came into English in the fourteenth century from the Latin word for companionship. Raymond Williams documents the progressively abstract uses of 'society' (*Keywords*, 1976). By the late eighteenth century it came to predominantly mean a system of common life, or 'that to which we all belong, even if it is also very general and impersonal' (ibid., pp. 243–247). On the etymology of 'state', see Vincent, *Theories of the State*, 1987, pp. 16–19; and Kenneth Dyson, *The State Tradition in Western Europe*, 1980, pp. 25–33. Cf. Alexander d'Entrèves, *The Notion of the State*, 1969, ch. 3.

the body politic, the *patria* and a limited version of the public good. By 1595, Pierre Charron (1541–1603) could write of *l'état* as the 'bond within society which cannot exist without it, the vital essence which brings life to human and natural association'.[66] The transition to European absolutism of the seventeenth and eighteenth centuries was accompanied by a tension between the monarch-as-the-state and the state as an impersonal administration abstracted beyond the monarch.[67] In the context of late absolutism, a theory of constitutional sovereignty was argued out which confirmed the modern sense of what is now commonly referred to as the abstract state, that is, a structure of power independent of ruler and ruled. So in part, I can agree with J.H. Shennan when he says: 'The *concept* of the state as abstract above and distinct from both government and governed . . . was coming to be understood in Europe before the end of the eighteenth century, when its alliance with the national *idea* produced a dynamic new force'[68] (emphasis added). However, this idealist emphasis, which is common across the theoretical spectrum,[69] has very limited explanatory force. The conjoining of the abstract state[70] and the national community of strangers – that is, the formation of nation-states – which began to consolidate in the nineteenth century, required much more than the state and the nation becoming abstract *ideas*. They also became abstract in practice. To explain the reconstitution of sovereignty through this period, Shennan has to reach for an obfuscating label – the *matryoshka* syndrome. The abstract state, like the *matryoshka* doll, he says, has 'one replica within another', an 'elusive . . . ultimate source',[71] the abstract *idea*. The dog and its tail chase each other around in circles.

Alfred Sohn-Rethel has indicated how it is possible to conceive of abstraction as a material process, 'abstraction other than by thought'.[72] And as

66. Cited in Dyson, S*tate Tradition*, p. 27.

67. It is interesting to note, given the concern of this book with the rise of the mass media, that in the early nineteenth century the initially derogatory term 'the fourth estate', probably first used by Edmund Burke (1729–97), came into currency to describe the press.

68. J.H. Shennan, *The Origins of the Modern European State, 1450–1725*, 1974, p. 114.

69. For an example of the more conventional argument, see Anton C. Zijderveld, *The Abstract Society*, 1974, ch. 3; and Robert A. Nisbet, *The Sociological Tradition*, 1970, ch. 2, part 3. Nisbet directly relates abstraction to individualization but narrowly treats the process as referring to ideas, 'primarily to moral values': 'Now these values were becoming – through processes of technology, science and political democracy – abstract; removed from the particular and the concrete' (p. 43). He then runs into the difficulty of resolving the contradiction of individualism and nationalism (p. 44). For an example from the marxist tradition, see Derek Sayer, *The Violence of Abstraction*, 1987. However, Sayer *partly* recognizes the limitations of treating abstraction as only an ideational process when he says: '"Simple abstractions", in short, are neither so simple nor so abstract as they at first sight appear. They always articulate, even as they obscure, some more concrete "substratum" – dare I say it, some material basis?' (pp. 140–141).

70. The 'abstract state' is a commonly used concept. See for example Nairn, *Break-up of Britain*, 1981, p. 17. It is used here with the reservation that all state forms are abstract, and that the so-called 'abstract state' is in practice only the state form at which the desacralization and depersonalization of power, and the 'separation' between the public and private, are relatively manifest.

71. Shennan, *Modern European State*, 1974, p. 85.

72. Alfred Sohn-Rethel, *Intellectual and Manual Labour*, 1978, ch. 2 and *passim*.

Geoff Sharp has developed, Marx's own excursions into how the commodity and labour abstractions of capitalism can be shown to be relevant to issues pertaining both to consciousness and practice. The arguments of Marx and Sohn-Rethel can be extended as a way into theorizing social relations in general. In the earlier discussion of levels of social integration and forms of national association, it became clear that we were discussing not only the abstraction of ideas but also the abstraction of lived social relations. José Ripalda similarly makes a faltering beginning at distancing himself from the idealist approach to abstraction. The following passage is relevant to his thinking about the process of abstraction and the rise of the modern abstract nation-state. It also confronts us with an issue still to be clarified:

> The Enlightenment itself was not an absolute beginning but one stage in a long tradition. Even its vocabulary refers to a century old theme: Nation, Fatherland, People, Tolerance, Freedom, Skepsis were already the key words in the Europe of Charles V [Holy Roman Emperor, 1500–58]. What separated the Enlightenment from the Renaissance did not concern their theories as much as the different reality which constituted the content of these themes. The inherited concepts win in an easily recognizable development a new sensitivity. It was the force of a new form of productive relations which had been developing an unstoppable forward thrust since the second half of the Middle Ages. And its abstraction is not only derived from abstract Rationality which human relationships acquire in book-keeping, calculation of costs, and the programming of investment.[73]

It is at this point that Ripalda starts to get into trouble. Ironically, it occurs, firstly, because of a residual idealism and, secondly, because of the residual problems of the conventional base–superstructure metaphor. They are problems which grow out of each other. The above passage continues:

> There is a second level of abstraction [Ripalda here uses a quite different metaphor of levels than I employ]: the new relations of production can only slowly attain their new concretion, their new world. The 'New' thus appears as abstract in relation to the concretion of the 'Old', which for its part does not have 'Reason'. However, modern abstraction refers to its concrete world. The abstraction of the modern world is not primarily an operation of thought, but above all a palpable action.[74]

Ripalda is concerned to understand the thought-formation of an eighteenth-century intellectual, Hegel, swept before the onslaught of the double reality of the new world, the divided nation cleaved by the 'loss of ancient social solidarity' and the development of a new form of unity. However, because of the conventional base–superstructure framework which underlies the analysis of *The Divided Nation*, Ripalda overemphasizes changing relations of production as fully determinant of intellectual thought and practice. It restricts the implications of his (partial) insight that societies are constituted in overlaying levels of abstraction.

73. José Ripalda, *The Divided Nation*, 1977, pp. 2–3.
74. Ibid.

The abstraction of intellectual practice

It was said earlier that the limitations of Ripalda's analysis confront us with an issue still requiring clarification. The issue is encapsulated in the question: what is the relation of intellectual thought and practice to the dominant level(s) of integration of any particular social formation. The question is important to us for a number of reasons. Firstly, a substantial section of *Nation Formation* concentrates on the question, why did nineteenth-century intellectuals like Marx and Engels, Durkheim and Weber in effect take the nation for granted as a form of social relations? Secondly, it is important to keep in mind that intellectuals were central in the original formations of *nationes*, *patria* and nations. In the twentieth century they are equally central in neo-nationalist movements and in reproducing and managing the ideologies of the new nationalism.[75] Thirdly, although the conjunction of nation and state was forged in the period of the consolidating of the capitalist mode of production, longer-run (material) processes made it possible for certain groupings, particularly intellectuals, to conceive of the existence of *nationes* well before the generalized onset of capitalist relations of production and exchange. Such conceptions also occurred long before 'the people' to whom they referred had any sense of their more extended associations being anything other than either an occasional, external encroachment. Their extended relationships were certainly not understood in terms of the metaphors of face-to-face ties. For example, the medieval 'Welsh' bishop, Geoffrey of Monmouth (note how he was named in terms of a particularity of place), was able, in writing his legendary *History of the Kings of Britain* (1136), to connect the disparate tribes of the Britons across time and space as a once-great people originating in ancient Troy.[76] Similarly, the unknown author of a vernacular translation of *Cursor Mundi*, made about 1300, could imagine some sort of community of 'Ingland [th]e nacioun'.[77] But whether the 'common people' during the Middle Ages could themselves imagine this abstract commonality, 'Ingland', as a communion of compatriots is doubtful.

This issue can be handled in terms of the levels metaphor. Intellectual practice, by definition, works to transcend the limitations of embodied interaction. Even in oral, tribal societies, interpreters of the passing particulars of social life have to abstract generalized explanations.[78] The practices of reading signs

75. See Anthony D. Smith, *Theories of Nationalism*, 1983, ch. 6; Ernest Gellner, *Nations and Nationalism*, 1983; Nairn, *Break-up of Britain*, 1981, pp. 33ff., 99ff., 117ff. and *passim*; Eric Hobsbawm, 'Some Reflections on Nationalism', 1972; and Peter Worsley, *The Third World*, 1978, ch. 2, who, among many others, testify to the centrality of intellectuals and intellectual groupings for the national question.

76. Hugh MacDougall, *Racial Myth in English History*, 1982, ch. 1.

77. Basil Cottle, *The Triumph of English, 1350–1400*, 1969, pp. 16–17.

78. This is not to question the distinction Lévi-Strauss makes between the 'preliterate intellectual', the bricoleur who works through *signs*, and the intellectual who wrestles with *concepts* (entangled with imagery as such concepts tend to be). See *The Savage Mind*, 1966, ch. 1. It is however to agree with Jack Goody's criticism of Lévi-Strauss for continuing to write of the science of the concrete and the science of the abstract in overly dualistic terms.

from nature, storing memories of seasonal cycles, ritualizing knowledge of things in place, telling stories down the generations, all allow tribal interpreters to 'transcend' the immediacy of what Braudel distinguishes as day-to-day time and life-time. It provides the basis for their understanding of things out of place. (The ambiguous meaning of 'out of place' is interpretatively useful.) This practice of abstraction is lifted to a further stage by the most important technique employed by the post-tribal intellectual, namely writing. As we have already seen, at a time when the intersection of face-to-face and agency-extended relations provided the constitutive setting for philosophical debates over the meaning of sovereignty and the office of the king, writing provided a medium of disembodied interchange held in place by, but abstracting from, those dominant forms of social relations. In short, while all social formations are constituted in the overlay of levels of abstraction, there are groupings of people who by virtue of the form of their practice work at a level more abstract than the dominant mode(s) of integration. It is this capacity that makes intellectuals and the intellectually trained – from the medieval cleric to the contemporary public-opinion pollster and advertising executive – important to any discussion of abstract communities.

Without underestimating their centrality, the *ambiguous* place of intellectuals and the intellectually trained still needs to be stressed. The abstract relations associated with intellectual practices are bound up with a form of subjectivity which generates contradictory yet interlocking ideologies. Traditionalism, nationalism, individualism and cosmopolitanism are related as one such complex meld. This point was first made at the beginning of this century by Friedrich Meinecke (1862–1954) but subsequent theorists have not taken any further Meinecke's descriptions of how the 'nation drank the blood of free personalities'.[79] The problem is to explain how the pre-eminent purveyors of nationalist ideologies, ideologies advocating the importance of cultural boundaries, were born out of universalizing, cosmopolitan thought. At the end of the eighteenth century, intellectuals, from the conservative Edmund Burke (1729–97) writing in the *Vindication of Natural Society* (1756) to the libertarian William Godwin (1756–1836) in *Enquiry Concerning Political Justice* (1793), were advocating various forms of pre- or preternational association. At the same time, other intellectuals no less cosmopolitan in practice, such as the German Romantics, were beginning to praise the nation and its *Volk* as the natural, realized subject of history. In the language of the levels argument, while the process of abstraction allows people to reflect upon the historical grounding of their immediate community in face-to-face relations, at the same time it lifts the person doing the recognizing onto a more abstract level which is just as likely to support internationalism or cosmopolitanism as it is nationalism.

The ambiguous place of the intellectual closely relates to a further issue. The process of intellectual abstraction can lead to an increased focus on the

79. *Cosmopolitanism and the Nation State*, 1907, p. 15.

particular, and on that which is being reconstituted. The reconstitution of more concretely constituted practices often generates a sense of loss or romantic nostalgia for a past way of life.[80] By the same process, and often as part of a contradictory subjectivity, it engenders a sense of liberation and detachment. The past becomes a place to be visited either for verification of contemporary progress or, more recently, as a source of comparative knowledge for humanists, anthropologists and tourists. It is only at a highly abstract and generalized level of historicity that it has meaning to propose the building of a replica of Stonehenge next to the closed-off original site so that tourists can concretely feel its rough slabs.[81] It is only very recently in history, as Benedict Anderson reminds us, that the nationalistic hallowing of the barren cenotaphs of Unknown Soldiers has had any meaning.[82] Because, according to the argument being developed here, the nation is formed in the intersection of constitutive levels, it is fundamental to its subjective hold that the abstract community echoes with the concrete murmurings of the hopes and tragedies of embodied existence, including human mortality. The ongoing irony is that this 'recalling of the concrete' constantly works to undermine itself.

The contradictory nature of the recalling of the concrete can best be illustrated through a brief problem-raising example. Justus Möser (1720–94), a German historian writing at the end of the eighteenth century, abstracted an 'exciting new' thematic unity in German history. The princes, he argued, did not form the body (*Körper*) of the nation but were accidents to it. He singled out the common landed-property owners (*die Echten*) as 'the authentic constituents of the nation'. They were a single, integral agency supplying 'not only the unity, the direction, and the power of an epic . . . but also the origin, the development, and the several proportions of the national character amid all its changes'.[83] Möser thus anticipated the later, more sophisticated *and* more abstract, marxian class analysis.[84] He found a way of theorizing a continuity through the discontinuity of German history. He thus, paradoxically, formulated a way of conceiving of German unity which was more abstract and yet less universalistic than the conceptions of the *Volk* as used by the sixteenth-century German

80. The present argument thus accords with Anthony Smith's discussion of historicity but attempts to explain it more broadly. See Smith, *Ethnic Revival*, 1981, pp. 87ff.

81. Jean Baudrillard gives similar examples, such as the caves of Lascaux in 'The Precession of Simulacra', 1983. For a discussion of this process of 'reviving the past', see E.R. Chamberlin, *Preserving the Past*, 1979; and Patrick Wright, *On Living in an Old Country*, 1985. On the replication of 'reality', see Umberto Eco, *Travels in Hyper-Reality*, 1987.

82. Anderson, *Imagined Communities*, 1983, pp. 17–18.

83. Justus Möser, *Sämtliche Werke*, cited in Leonard Krieger's brilliant essay 'Germany', 1975, pp. 94–95. On Möser's concept of 'property' (*Eigentum*) as allegorically a social quality and only secondarily an economic one, see Mack Walker, *German Home Towns*, 1971, Introduction and pp. 171ff.

84. On the etymology of the concept of 'class' in its development in the modern sense between 1770 and 1840 (the period of the Industrial Revolution), see Williams, *Keywords*, 1976, pp. 51–59. Also, from a different sociological tradition, see Nisbet, *Sociological Tradition*, 1970, ch. 5.

humanists. This paradox can be given a consistent logic: social relations constituted at a more abstract level sustain, indeed generate, a tendency to 'critically' reflect on the terms of prior abstractions of unity and to give that unity a new particularity.[85]

In the course of this discussion, aspects of the argument that the nation is a distinctive kind of abstract community have been briefly outlined, drawing inferences for theorizing national formation over different periods. The proposition baldly laid down at the outset can now be recapitulated with some clearer terms of reference. National formation only becomes possible within a social formation constituted in the emerging dominance of relations of disembodied integration. This level of integration is abstracted from and yet based in a manifold intersection with prior levels – relations formed in and through the limitations and possibilities of relations of the face-to-face and agency-extension.

'National' consciousness was voiced, for the most part by intellectuals and later by the intellectually trained, well before the gradually consolidating and naturalizing conjunction of nation and state gained momentum during the nineteenth century. Even in the earliest settings which conditioned the 'recognition' that one's identity was bound up in the *natio*, for example in the medieval university, the consciousness of this 'compatriotism with strangers' depended upon its articulators being at one level of their existence lifted out, abstracted from, the binding relations of the flesh or what has been called face-to-face integration. Intellectual technique was founded upon disembodied relations of time and place. The earliest and most passionate articulators of a connection between identity and the general place of one's birth tended, paradoxically, to be persons who had not only worked via the abstracting medium of writing but those who had also literally journeyed beyond the boundaries of their *natus*. In the Middle Ages this was not the constitutive medium of the general populace.

In the early modern period, generalized changes began to take effect. Place was framed by new forces and relations of agency-extension, in particular by the administrative apparatuses of the absolutist and abstract state. Thus, while relations of kinship and reciprocity continued to give meaning and structure to social existence, outside the village such relations were reconstituted at a more abstract level and at the same time were drawn upon to give meaning to that level. The social relations and subjectivities associated with the emerging predominance of newer means of disembodied extension from the nineteenth-century newspaper to the twentieth-century satellite-linked television network took this further, speaking to abstract audiences while

85. That Möser was a 'German patriot' (Goethe's word for him) and yet early in life corresponded with his family in French and had a close contact with England through the proximity of Osnabrück and Hanover is also consistent with the present argument. See Hans Kohn, *The Idea of Nationalism*, 1944, pp. 423ff.

addressing people as if the relationship was more concrete. It is from this intersection that the modern nation gets its 'depth'. It is from this intersection that it is possible to argue that the nation-state is both deeply embedded and yet objectively modern. It is simply a contradictory process.

The processes of abstraction in re-forming the ontological setting and over-coming the limitations of prior levels have in the late twentieth century thinned out the basis for the objective and subjective hold of the 'classical' nation; even as the modern nation is afforded new means of social connection it is undermined. To the extent that we are witnessing this process at the moment, particularly in the capitalist West, a further 'stage' of abstract com-munity is developing, a postmodern nation. This setting ushers in new contradictions: the state more and more penetrates into the day-to-day life of its citizens (despite the ideologies of minimal government) while on the other hand the degree of one's commitment to the nation increasingly becomes a question of autonomous choice.

The following chapters do not attempt to prove these propositions. Rather they seek through an examination of the strengths and weaknesses of existing theories of the nation and nation-state to explore the explanatory usefulness of the central thesis that the nation is an abstract community. The foregoing discussion has highlighted a number of issues with which an adequate approach to theorizing the national question has to deal. These will provide an undercurrent of themes for subsequent chapters which first of all examine the limitations of nineteenth-century, classical social theory, and thereafter go on to assess the contributions of various expressions of post-classical social theory. The first theme is the relationship of the subjective and objective, the relation between ideas, ways of imagining the world, and the social-relational setting constitutive of and influenced by such forms of imagining. The second theme is the contradiction between the 'primordial depth' of the national form and the objective modernity and discontinuous history of not only any particular nation-state we might wish to examine but also the form of nation-states as we contemporarily know them. The third theme is the role of intellectuals. Although most commentators recognize the centrality of the intelligentsia and the intellectually trained in the stages of national formation, little has been done explicitly to theorize the grounding conditions which make it possible for them to abstract a community among strangers prior to the generalization of a popular national consciousness, and through subse-quent periods of the reconstitution of national integration.

PART TWO: CLASSICAL THEORY

3

Marx and Engels: 'Seeing through the Veil'?

The bourgeoisie has through its exploitation of the world-market given a cosmopolitan character to production and consumption in every country. To the great chagrin of Reactionists, it has drawn from under the feet of industry the national ground on which it stood . . . In place of the old local and national seclusion and self-sufficiency, we have intercourse in every direction, universal inter-dependence of nations. As in material, so also in intellectual production. The intellectual creations of individual nations become common property. National one-sidedness and narrow-mindedness become more and more impossible, and from the numerous national and local literatures, there arises a world literature.

Karl Marx and Friedrich Engels, *Communist Manifesto*, 1848

The Germanizing trend was negation, abstraction in the Hegelian sense. It created abstract Germans by stripping off everything that had not descended from national roots over sixty-four purely German genera-tions. Even its seemingly positive features were negative, for Germany could only be led towards its ideals by negating a whole century and her development and thus its intention was to push the nation back into the German Middle Ages . . . If this trend had been concretely German, if it had taken the German for what he had become in two thousand years of history, if it had not overlooked the truest element of our destiny, namely to be a pointer on the scales of world history, to watch over the develop-ment of the neighbouring nations, it would have avoided all its mistakes.

Friedrich Engels, 'Ernst Moritz Arndt', 1841

Why, in the historical period that the intersection of nation and state was begin-ning to consolidate, did Marx and Engels appear to dismiss the nation-state as a transitory form of association? And how at the same time could they effec-tively take the nation for granted as a category of social relations? This dilemma should be recognized as basic to understanding the limitations of the marxist theory of the nation, a dilemma with continuing implications. More than a problem of emphases internal to their theory, the question points to the necessity of an explanation couched in terms of the period in which they were writing. Asking why the writers of the period did not embark upon a project of theoretically taking apart the 'nation' is intended here to contribute to an overall understanding of the nation in theory and practice. While the chapter does not touch upon the way in which the spectre of nationalism has, in the context of the break-up of Eastern Europe and the Soviet Union, returned to haunt marxism, this is the unspoken setting for the following retrospective questions.

Why wasn't the nation substantially theorized, as Marx so thoroughly initiated in the sphere of political economy, or as Freud began a few decades later in relation to the person? It was not until the beginning of the twentieth century with the publication of Otto Bauer's controversial *Die Nationalitätenfrage und die Sozialdemokratie* (1907) that the 'first substantial Marxist analysis of nation-states and nationalism in relation to socialism' appeared.[1] In a sentence, Bauer's approach emphasized the way in which the nation, persons 'bound together through a common destiny into a community of character', were formed historically and could not be taken for granted as natural. However, the history of marxist theories of the nation is not the subject of this chapter. After a brief section on contemporary debates over the limitations of marxist theorizing, the chapter will focus on the historical constitution of an elision in nineteenth-century theory. Consistent with the spirit of Marx's own theory, it is argued that the author of the phrase 'social being determines consciousness' was constituted within the determining conditions of his own history.[2] This contextualizing has a double focus. Firstly, arising out of a discussion of the social and historical conditions of the nineteenth century, it is suggested that the social form in which the nation emerged contributed to masking Marx's recognition of what a theory of the nation would entail. The nation emerged as a materially abstracted community formed under the pressures of the globalizing extensions of social relations, but also as a bounded community formed around subjectivities of embodied connection. Marx was never able to reconcile these contradictory modes of being. Secondly, arising out of a discussion of how the methodology can be influenced by the conditions of its writing, it is suggested that in attempting to delve beneath the surface of the dislocations and upheavals of social life Marx fell back upon the abstract explanatory category of class. As important as class analysis is, when reductively seen in terms of the base–superstructure framework, it closed off the possibility of a comprehensive theory of the nation-state.

A poverty of theory?

After the mid-nineteenth century, although still in the shadow of the Enlightenment, the 'obviousness' of the nation changed from being a source

1. Tom Bottomore, 'Sociology', 1983, p. 112.
2. Paraphrase of Karl Marx, 'Preface to A Contribution to the Critique of Political Economy' (1859), in Karl Marx and Frederick Engels, *Selected Works*, vol. 1, 1977, p. 503. Ian Cummins (*Marx, Engels and National Movements*, 1980, p. 11) opens by making a comparable point, positing it as the pivotal concern of his book, but it is only developed in terms of historical events, or 'directly political factors' (p. 179). See also his 'Marx, Engels, and the Springtime of Peoples', 1985.

of its taken-for-grantedness to the ground of a new agitation. Intense debate ensued during the Second International, recasting Marx's view that 'nationality is already dead'.[3] But despite this interchange, marxism still fundamentally failed to develop an adequate theory of the nation. Moreover, if we come forward to the present, even as the fact of this poverty of theory is being more commonly noted, little has been said by way of explanation for the elision.[4] Apart from Tom Nairn's 'thesis of the inevitability of the failure'[5] and other scattered shafts of insight, discussion usually stays at the survey-of-literature level with its often narrowly conceived debates over the political implications of this line or that. In some ways this appears to be merely a change in style – a new, more exuberant archaeology has rediscovered previously unheralded theorists, in particular Otto Bauer and Antonio Gramsci; for others, the task begins with an amending of detail within Lenin's open pragmatism.[6]

Among most contemporary marxist commentators it has become mandatory to clear the ground, and like Nairn, Bottomore, Miliband and Debray, say something to the effect that: 'In a way, [the problem of theorizing the nation] combines all the impasses of a traditional variant of Marxism. In fact, we have to recognize that there is *no Marxist theory of the nation*; and despite the passionate debates on the subject that have taken place within the workers' movement, it would be far too evasive to say that Marxism has underestimated the reality of the nation'[7] (emphasis added).

Arguments against these assertions of a poverty of theory, against this

3. Karl Marx and Frederick Engels, 'The German Ideology' (1846), in *Selected Works*, vol. 1, 1977, p. 62. The context of the phrase reads: 'Generally speaking, big industry created everywhere the same relations between classes of society, and thus destroyed the particular individuality of the various nationalities. And finally, while the bourgeoisie of each nation still retained separate national interests, big industry created a class, which in all nations has the same interest and with which nationality is already dead.'

4. Anthony Giddens is one person who asks 'Why should this be?' (*The Nation-State and Violence*, 1985, p. 22). But he doesn't take an explanation beyond a history of ideas in attributing it to the limitations of the legacy of earlier theoretical thinking: 'Saint Simon in political theory and to the influence of classical political economy' (p. 26). John Ehrenreich has argued that 'The deeper difficulty Marxists of all varieties have had in comprehending nationalism . . . lies in Marx's own conception of the proletariat' ('Socialism, Nationalism and Capitalist Development', 1983, p. 5), but this is still restricted to discussing theoretical logic.

5. Tom Nairn, *The Break-up of Britain: Crisis and Neo-Nationalism*, 1981, pp. 329–331, 337. He says 'Historical development had not at that time produced certain things necessary for such a "theory"'. Unfortunately these 'things' are hardly discussed by Nairn except to say that marxism was unable to 'foresee the real contradictions of Progress' (p. 337).

6. For example, Brian Jenkins and Gunter Minnerup, *Citizens and Comrades*, 1984.

7. The words of Nicos Poulantzas, *State, Power, Socialism*, (1978) 1980, p. 93. See also for example John Ehrenreich, 'The Theory of Nationalism: A Case of Underdevelopment', 1975, pp. 57–61, and Benedict Anderson, *Imagined Communities*, 1983, pp. 13–15; Nairn, *Break-up of Britain*, 1981, 'Sociology', ch. 9; Bottomore, 'Sociology', 1983, p. 140. Ralph Miliband, cited in Horace B. Davis, *Toward a Marxist Theory of Nationalism*, 1978, p. 1; Régis Debray, 'Marxism and the National Question', 1977, p. 30; Michael Dunn, 'Marxism and the National Question', 1975, p. 29; J.L. Talmon, *The Myth of the Nation and the Vision of Revolution*, 1981, p. 64.

'ritual breast-beating',[8] and for a return to orthodoxy continue to be written. But they are a decreasing minority. J.N. Blaut, for example, maintains that, 'Bringing [the marxist theory of nationalism] up to date will not render it perfect or complete.' In this respect he is right.[9] Blaut's next sentence however firmly places him in the neo-orthodox camp: 'At the present juncture,' he says, 'I think it is more important to recognize the strength, and essential adequacy, of our theory of nationalism than worry about its imperfections.'[10] In much the same way that Ernest Gellner is sophisticated in reworking liberal orthodoxy while remaining within its limited terms, Blaut has only rethought the content, not the form, of the proposition that nationalism is a mechanism of class struggle.

Proponents of neo-orthodoxy in the main have very low expectations of what a theory can be expected to explain. Take Pierre Vilar's breakdown of Marx's sentence, 'the workingmen have no country':

> [This] dense sentence [he says] demands a scrupulous analysis: 1. the nation exists; 2. it is a political fact; 3. each dominant class erects itself as a national class; 4. each national class identifies itself with the nation; 5. the bourgeoisie has done as much, and the proletariat must do so; 6. in accordance with the class that assumes power, the national fact can assume new meaning.
>
> In my view that constitutes a theory, and one, moreover, confirmed by practice. The elaboration depends on the historian.[11]

As a sociologist-historian Vilar begs a thousand questions. In particular, many other theorists would disagree with Vilar's view about what makes a theory. Asserting the social (or political) factuality of the nation has a Durkheimian echo; it only provides the barest beginning of an explanation.

Neo-orthodoxy can be distinguished from a further response, post-orthodoxy. I raise this distinction because there are at least two post-orthodox points of partial dissension from the way in which the poverty-of-theory proposition is formulated. From one direction, the claim that there is no marxist theory of the nation is criticized for inadvertently supporting the commonly held assumption that Marx and Engels' contradictory and apparently *ad hoc* conclusions can be explained away by pointing to the conditioning pressures of political exigency. Ephraim Nimni argues that despite the fragmentary nature of their writings on the nation there is an underpinning coherence. This coherence (and thus the 'legacy' of problems bequeathed to subsequent generations of marxist

8. Eric Hobsbawm, 'Some Reflections on "The Break-up of Britain"', 1977, p. 8.

9. Even the natural sciences have entered (what the post-structuralists happily call) the age of indeterminacy: relativity, quantum mechanics and Godel's theorem in mathematics all entail the recognition that theory will always be incomplete.

10. James M. Blaut, 'Nationalism as an Autonomous Force', 1982, p. 20. It should be noted that even this doyen of orthodoxy does acknowledge that 'Marx–Engels' theory of state-viability . . . was, by the way, the closest they came to a theory of nations' (p. 5). See also his *The National Question*, 1987.

11. Pierre Vilar, 'On Nations and Nationalism', 1979, p. 22.

theorists)[12] was sustained within a 'form of economic reductionism combined with a social evolutionary paradigm'.[13] While it would be both circular and idealist to claim that these limitations in themselves explain the poverty of theory, the problems with a reductionist base–superstructure approach have to be tackled as one of the impasses of marxism (Poulantzas' phrase). Other positions or variations offering only new cul-de-sacs which are discussed later in more detail can here be noted only cryptically: they range from Ernest Gellner's ineffective inversion of the base–superstructure metaphor, to Fredric Jameson's category contortions in collapsing substantive changes in the structural–cultural form into changes between the theoretical spheres of structure and culture.[14]

From a second post-orthodox direction, the proposition that there is no marxist theory of the nation is partially questioned by those who might be called the new archaeologists. Ronaldo Munck provides a bridging example. He begins his book, *The Difficult Dialogue: Marxism and Nationalism*, by echoing Poulantzas: 'Essentially,' says Munck, 'Marxism has no theory of nationalism.' But, after running through the myriad of classical to contemporary marxist contributions, he is satisfied to turn back to Bauer and Gramsci, to the socialist-Zionist, Ber Borochov, and the Irish socialist-republican, James Connolly. It remains a rhetorical gesture in that it comes at the conclusion of his book and remains undeveloped. His assessment that these writers provide the material 'to forge some kind of coherent Marxist approach to nationalism'[15] is made on the basis that bits and pieces of their work are relevant to a theory of the nation.

One of the tasks of the sixth chapter will be to assess the extent to which contemporary marxist theorists, in particular Tom Nairn, have contributed to overcoming 'Marxism's great historical failure'. Instead of going over ground covered step by step in the numerous and comprehensive exigetical histories of marxism on the national question,[16] we will take up themes

---

12. The notion of a 'legacy' of problems is put in inverted commas advisedly. A 'legacy' in this sense is only such by virtue of it continuing to be actively adhered to and cannot be in itself an explanation for its continuing theoretical hold.

13. Ephraim Nimni, 'Great Historical Failure: Marxist Theories of Nationalism', 1985, p. 59. See also his *Marxism and Nationalism*, 1991.

14. These will be discussed in Chapter 6: Ernest Gellner, 'Scale and Nation', 1974; Fredric Jameson, 'Postmodernism, or the Cultural Logic of Late Capitalism', 1984, p. 86.

15. Ronaldo Munck, *The Difficult Dialogue: Marxism and Nationalism*, 1986, quotes from pp. 2, 168.

16. See for example: Samad Shaheen, *The Communist (Bolshevik) Theory of National Self-Determination*, 1956; Demetrio Boersner, *The Bolsheviks and the National and Colonial Question*, 1957; Maxime Rodinson, 'Le Marxisme et la Nation', 1968; Michael Löwy, 'Marxists and the National Question', 1976, pp. 81–100; Horace Davis, *Theory of Nationalism*, 1978, and *Nationalism and Socialism*, 1967; Eric Cahm and Vladimir Claude Fisera, *Socialism and Nationalism*, 1978; Dave Holmes, 'Marxism and the National Question', 1979; Jenkins and Minnerup, *Citizens and Comrades*, 1984; Walker Connor, *The National Question in Marxist–Leninist Theory and Strategy*, 1984; Nimni, 'Historical Failure', 1985; Munck, *Difficult Dialogue*, 1986; and Ephraim Nimni, 'Marx, Engels and the National Question', 1989.

already touched upon, themes which have become increasingly important in contemporary social theory: the constitution of and relationship between social forms and subjectivity; the analytical connection between structure and culture, base and superstructure; the problem of bringing the debates about the 'rise of the cultural' and the 'invention of tradition' into contact with discussions of longer-run social forms; the issue of how to take account of the social categories of space and time; and the dilemma of how to understand the work of intellectuals as formed in an historical context and yet pushing at the constitutive edges of that particular context. The present chapter begins by discussing marxism's classical roots.

Marx and Engels in the age of nationalism

Karl Marx (1818–83) and Friedrich Engels (1820–95) lived and worked through the period commonly called the age of nationalism.[17] It was during their lifetimes that the place of their birth, the Rhineland, was incorporated in a unified Germany (the 'Second' *Reich*). They had argued over many years for this outcome, though not for the form that unification eventually took under the Prussian Junker, Otto von Bismarck (1815–98). Their position on German unification expressed a theoretical logic which can neither be called nationalistic nor be glibly criticized as contradictory. Engels may have been a German nationalist in his youth,[18] and Marx a Young Hegelian;[19] however, even their early writings were quite distinct from the directions taken by contemporary German nationalist movements such as Young Germany, the *Burschenschaft* and the *Turnverein*.[20] None the less, the crossovers between the internationalist leanings of Marx and Engels' work and the age of nationalism are striking: the publication of their *Manifesto of the Communist Party* 'occurred quite ironically in the same year made famous by an early manifestation of nationalism's rapid spread, namely the revolutions of 1848. From

17. The preface of Hans Kohn's impressive 'encyclopedic' book *The Idea of Nationalism* (1944, p. vii) begins with the sentence: 'The age of nationalism represents the first period of universal history.'

18. Davis, *Nationalism and Socialism*, 1967, pp. 2–3, 46. Engels wrote regularly for the 'Young Germany' journal *Telegraph für Deutschland*. See Marx and Engels, *Collected Works*, vol. 2, 1976, e.g. p. 149.

19. David McLellan notes that Marx's first contribution to the *Rheinische Zeitung* followed Hegel in seeing the state as an 'expression of Reason and the highest incarnation of morality' (*Karl Marx: Early Texts*, 1972, p. xvii).

20. The *Burschenschaft* was a radical student association founded in 1815 to work for German unity; the *Turnverein* 'Gymnastic Movement' was begun by Friedrich Jahn in 1811 to raise a 'regenerative elite' for the German nation. Engels was critical of Jahn and the Gymnasts as one-sided extremists (see Marx and Engels, *Collected Works*, vol. 2, 1976, pp. 138–141, 166). As we might have expected, more populist nationalistic associations did not emerge until much later (in the 1880s) and even then the most active members of organizations like the Pan-German League were drawn from the academically educated. See Roger Chickering, *We Men Who Feel Most German*, 1984, chs 1 and 5.

this point on, nationalism and Marxism were contemporaries.'[21] For example, Marx was exiled in London at the same time as the Italian nationalist, Giuseppe Mazzini (1805–72). Except for Mazzini's brief returns to the continent, both men lived in London for the remainder of their working lives, arguing for 'opposing' forms of abstract community.[22]

In order to highlight the tenor of the period in which Marx was writing, it is instructive to slice into the nineteenth century at a particular juncture. No overriding methodological pre-eminence is claimed for this approach. It is simply a means of confining the illustrative historical detail described at the level of empirical generalization, while more graphically pointing up the conjunctures, overlapping levels and contradictions in the broader sweep of change. The year 1871 is somewhat arbitrarily chosen; it is symbolic because it was the year of German unification and of the Paris Commune, and pertinent because it is within the most productive period of Marx's writing.

The section about to be embarked upon, 'Contradictions and transformations', will argue that Marx for good reasons overestimated the flattening force of late nineteenth-century internationalization. The subsequent section, 'Intersection of levels', will suggest that despite this he remained ambiguous in his treatment of the historical specificity of the nation-state, both overemphasizing its consolidation in the late nineteenth century and overasserting the potential of the bourgeois revolution to sweep away national difference. Together these points will be used to suggest the beginnings of an explanation for the limitations of his theory of the nation.

1871: contradictions and transformations

In 1871 Marx's writings were readily circulated to an international, or rather, a number of language-bound, reading publics: the Russian translation of *Das Kapital* went to press, the *Communist Manifesto* was published in the feminist New York journal, *Woodhull and Claflin's Weekly*; and the *Civil War in France* (May 1871) was printed as a pamphlet in London and serialized in several countries of Europe, including the German and Belgian journals, ironically called, respectively, *Volksstaat* and *L'Internationale*.[23] The broader point is that 1871 was caught in the midst of the extension of the means of

21. Connor, *The National Question*, 1984, p. 6. Interestingly it was Engels who, long before Connor, first drew attention to this coincidence: 'Preface to the First Italian edition of 1893', in Marx and Engels, *Selected Works*, vol. 1, 1977, p. 106. Engels added that consequent upon the 1848 revolutions 'these two great nations [Italy and Germany] were reconstituted and somehow again put on their own . . . the men who suppressed the Revolution of 1848 were, nevertheless, its testamentary executors in spite of themselves'.

22. From 1868 Mazzini lived at Lugano, only fifteen miles outside Italy, and in 1872 he made his way across the border disguised as an Englishman, to die at Pisa in his 'homeland'. For an introduction to Mazzini's writings, and his advocacy of nationality and the 'holy Fatherland' as the association best moving toward a universal and moral 'Catholicism of Humanity', see his *The Duties of Man and Other Essays*, (1844–70) 1924.

23. Hal Draper, *The Marx–Engels Chronicle*, 1985, pp. 162–173; Thomas Guback and Ronald Bettig, 'Translating the *Manifesto* into English', 1987.

spreading ideas, simultaneously within, across and beyond nation-states. Internationalism and nationalism (as well as, and in cultural contradiction with the processes of internationalism, the 'rediscovery' of the spirit of the village) were facets of the same process of the extension and abstraction of social relations. The rediscovery of prior forms of association had quietly burgeoned with the *Philosophes*, but bloomed in the century that Marx's life was to span. It is not an accident, as they say, that nineteenth-century historiography became exuberant in its research of comparative and nationally couched histories. Examples can be drawn from our chosen year of 1871: Henry Maine (1822–88), English jurist and historian, published *Village Communities*; Pierre Le Play (1806–82), French mining engineer and sociologist, published *The Organization of the Family*; also, between 1868 and 1913 the German jurist Otto von Gierke (1844–1921) wrote his multi-volume *German Law of Associations*. This was the period in which the Great Divide between the 'archaic' and the 'modern' was first given theoretical force.

On the one hand, there was the internationalizing of academic and publishing networks and such developments as the emergence of the concept of world news. In 1870–71 the world was carved up into exclusive news territories by a European cartel headed by Reuters.[24] Marx was still more concerned about the older, rapidly consolidating forms of transport – railways – than the new, more abstract and disembodied means of communication such as the telegraph. He failed to note that the world was for the first time being interconnected in a way that, unlike even the circulation across a world market of abstracted commodities, detached the mode of communication from the various means of embodied transport.[25] For example, in 1871, less than three decades after the construction of the first overland telegraph lines, the furthest interlinking of the British Empire was achieved with an underwater line to Australia. Messages no longer had to be carried by people, either personally or by conveyancing agents.

On the other hand, even these processes were not simply forces of internationalization. The first information revolution, 'begun' at the time of Johann Gutenberg (c.1394–1468) and confirmed in the burgeoning of print-capitalism, was also contributing fundamentally to the process of delimiting national boundaries. This included the establishment of wide-circulation, largely metropolitan-based daily newspapers as well as, at the other end of the literary spectrum, the initially less market-oriented activities of a new profession of intellectuals, the 'vernacularizing lexicographers, grammarians, philologists and litterateurs'.[26] Lexicographers, such as the American Noah Webster, subtly contributed to marking the difference between kindred

24. Jeremy Tunstall, *The Media are American*, 1977, ch. 1.

25. Giddens, *Nation-State and Violence*, 1985, makes something of this point, emphasizing its significance in the consolidation of the nation-state (pp. 172–178).

26. Anderson, *Imagined Communities*, 1991, *passim* and quoted from p. 71. He calls the nineteenth century the 'golden age' of this lexicographic revolution.

national cultures, down to choosing different patterns of spelling,[27] while others, such as those from the Académie Française, acted in not-so-subtle ways to break the hold of the regional dialects.

Marx and Engels emphasized the process of internationalization, the 'breaking down of barriers', and the penetration of and drawing into a world capitalist economy of all that was regional, 'backward', or isolated. But this led to an underestimation of the fact that those same processes which generated internationalism were (in more than an interim way) also reconstituting peasants as national citizens.[28] Secondly, it led to the acceptance of a doctrine which, although logically subsumable within their theory of internationalization, further retarded the possibility of Marx and Engels thinking their way out of the image of Monsieur Capital marching insouciantly across the globe, trailing behind him the increasingly tattered remnants of nationality. I am referring to the Hegelian doctrine of historical and 'historyless peoples', progressive and unprogressive peoples, the latter said to have a future only as ethnographic movements.[29]

> These relics of a nation mercilessly trampled under foot in the course of history, as Hegel says, these *residual fragments of peoples* have always become fanatical standard-bearers of counter-revolution and remain so until their complete extirpation or loss of their national character, just as their whole existence in general is itself a protest against a great historical revolution.[30]

Much can and has been made of Marx and Engels' ethnocentrism and the dominance in their work of an ideology of progress, but neither detailing the doctrine of historyless peoples nor debating whether or not Marx and Engels were latent racists will take us very far in understanding the limitations of their theory of the nation.

Marx and Engels' views on the reach, penetration and historical depth of capitalism have in many ways been confirmed by recent research. Theorists like Immanuel Wallerstein and Eric Wolf have criticized the tendency of social science as it heads in both its universalizing and particularizing directions to underplay the homogenizing force of capitalism and to assume the nation, or people, or state as the basic unit of analysis. They, like Marx and Engels, have argued instead for a world-capitalist system which had its origins prior to the sixteenth century.[31] Leaving aside intense debate over methodology and

27. V.P. Bynack, 'Noah Webster's Linguistic Thought and the Idea of an American National Culture', 1984.

28. Eugen Weber, *Peasants into Frenchmen*, 1976.

29. Engels was more prone to this position than Marx. See Solomon Bloom, *The World of Nations*, 1941, ch. 3; Charles C. Herod, *The Nation in the History of Marxian Thought*, 1976; Anthony D. Smith, *Theories of Nationalism*, 1983, pp. 72–74; Silva Meznaric, 'A Neo-Marxist Approach to the Sociology of Nationalism, Doomed Nations and Doomed Schemes', 1987; Roman Rosdolsky, *Engels and the 'Nonhistoric' Peoples*, 1964.

30. Engels, 'The Magyar Struggle' from the *Neue Rheinische Zeitung*, edited by Marx in *Collected Works*, vol. 8, 1977, p. 234.

31. Immanuel Wallerstein, *The Modern World System*, 1976; and Eric R. Wolf, *Europe and the People Without History*, 1982. See also William N. Parker, writing out of a different tradition, in *Europe, America and the Wider World*, 1984.

details of emphasis, their critique of bounded states as *the* basic analytic unit
has, for the most part, been convincing.[32]

However, concentrating on the homogenizing, internationalizing force of
capitalism can have the effect of treating social life as if it were constituted on
one plane.[33] We have to be careful for example not to overstate the coherent
interconnectedness of the world system (or at least, and this is the crucial
point, not to confuse the levels at which and for whom the connection is
made). The complexity of levels can be illustrated through a brief excursion
into the dominant ontologies of time and space current in the late nineteenth
century. Even at the late point in history now under discussion conceptions of
the globe remained unstable. In 1871 there was for example still no standardization of time within England, France or Germany, let alone across
Europe or the globe. World Standard Time was not introduced until 1884,
and then it came mainly through commercial pressure from North America.
It was not really adopted until after the 1912 conference in Paris. An 1870
pamphlet by Charles Ferdinand Dowd, *A System of National Time for
Railroads*, listed over eighty different time standards in America alone.[34]

Most people certainly did not think of themselves as located in a single,
nationally bound time-frame, or in one time-phase relative to a systematically
graded, global schema. The exceptions were found in the intellectually related
groupings and aristocratic and business classes. Global circumnavigation, as
distinct from transcontinental migration, was in practice restricted to an isolated aristocrat-intellectual such as Sir Charles Wentworth Dilke or an
entrepreneur-adventurer such as the Boston businessman George Francis
Train. For the reading classes, global voyagers had come into literary vogue,
climaxing with Jules Verne's international bestseller, *Around the World in
Eighty Days* (written 1871–2), but the appeal of such novels was based on
their novelty. Verne's books, of which there are more than sixty, were collectively written as *Les Voyages Extraordinaires*, and subtitled 'Known and
Unknown Worlds'. Sir Charles Wentworth Dilke's world-tour memoirs published in 1868 were modestly called *Greater Britain: A Record of Travel in
English-Speaking Countries*; and William Perry Fogg was lashing out when in
1872 he called his book *Round the World*. The aristocratic grand tour was not
displaced by world discovery tourism until the end of the epoch of discovery
at the turn of the century, and most people were only semi-literate and would
not have read their accounts. Even Jules Verne himself remained uncomfort-
able about the emerging concept of global space. His central character,
Phileas Fogg, a fetishist for punctuality, and the personification of Verne's

32. For a useful overview of the debates see Robert S. DuPlessis, 'The Partial Transition to
World Systems Analysis in Early Modern European History', 1987, pp. 11–27.

33. This is not to say that emphasizing the processes of internationalization makes one prone
by definition to 'treating social life as if it were constituted on one plane'. See the section above
in Chapter 2 entitled 'Integrative Levels as Levels of Abstraction'.

34. See Stephen Kern, *The Culture of Time and Space*, 1983, pp. 12–16, 74–75; and Giddens,
Nation-State and Violence, 1985, pp. 172–178.

theme of time-regulated humanity,[35] rounded the world in the specified time and won his bet helped by the 'fact' that by 'journeying toward the east, [he] was going toward the sun, and consequently the days became as many times four minutes less for him as he crossed degrees in that direction'.[36] Obviously it is not possible. Verne (1828–1905) is as confused as the popular conceptions were bemused. None the less, behind the confusion there is here the barest beginnings of the view that time and space are relative, that time can be disembodied. However, for intellectuals of that period, even such as Marx and Engels, the sweeping power and apparently liberatory consequences of 'the breaking down of [spatial] barriers' was self-evident in a way that the ontological relativity of these categories of space and time was not.

A further point needs to be made. The abstraction of time and space involved not only a looking out beyond the limits of the old horizons, but also a closing in, a new means of focusing the meaning of place. Articles published as early as the 1830s spoke of the gradual annihilation of space and time. This is important to the conception of national space. One author wrote of the devastating effect of the railways, saying that 'on the map of the imagination [every house, village, town and territory] would finally be reproduced and reduced down to the infinitely small!' Employing a different hyperbole another said that 'the whole population of the country would, speaking metaphorically, at once advance *en masse*, and place their chairs nearer to the fireside of their metropolis'.[37] This contraction of space and time is experienced simultaneously with (in fact by virtue of) the extension of the means of incorporating more space into an experiential ambit. The contraction of rural areas 'into a metropolis . . . conversely appears as an expansion of the metropolis: by establishing transport lines to ever more outlying areas it tends to incorporate the whole nation'.[38] Thus *writers*, intellectuals, began to reformulate this changing sense of time and space in terms of the intersection of nation and state. In the twenty years prior to 1871, German railroad mileage tripled; it was one, small, self-conscious part of the transfiguration of 'hometown society' (*Natürliche Gemeinschaften*)[39] and the consolidation of the nation-state.[40] By 1871 the same logic was *beginning* to apply to the subjective sense of the globe.

35. Jean Chesneaux comments that the character of Phileas Fogg was the 'man-machine' who in Verne's words functioned 'without friction' (*The Political and Social Ideas of Jules Verne*, 1972, p. 42).

36. Jules Verne, *A Tour of the World in Eighty Days*, (1873) n.d. See Kern, *Culture of Time and Space*, 1983, p. 218.

37. *Economie Sociale*, 1839, and *Quarterly Review*, 1839, cited in Wolfgang Schivelbusch, 'Railroad Space and Railroad Time', 1978, p. 32.

38. Shivelbusch, 'Railroad Space', 1978, p. 33.

39. The hometown lost political relevance and was drawn into an extended setting even though the nostalgic 'recuperation' of *Gemeinschaft* values proceeded apace. Mack Walker, *German Home Towns*, 1971, ch. 12, 'Death and Transfiguration'. Fascism of course brought the 'longings of intellectuals for national community and hometownsmen's parochial values' into a new intersection.

40. For a more extensive discussion of the relation between time and the nation-state see David Gross, 'Space, Time, and Modern Culture', 1981–82, and his 'Temporality and the Modern State', 1985.

Taking just the issue of the sense of space, it can be concluded that by a process of abstraction in thought and practice, contraction *and* extension were being experienced simultaneously. Marshall McLuhan's vision of a shrinking global village was in one sense beginning to be conceivable by the late nineteenth-century intellectual. But imagining, much less producing, the form of that writer's community, with its new level of time-space simultaneity mediated by the computer and satellite-broadcasting was still a long way off.[41]

We have to enter the twentieth century to find the generalization of this quite new subjectivity of time and space. In *Remembrance of Things Past*, a novel by Marcel Proust (born in 1871), telephone operators act as the 'priestesses of the Invisible' bringing the sound of a stark contradiction: 'distance overcome' but through communication with the truncated abstraction of a dying relative.[42] In Proust's work as much as through Einstein's (1879–1955) – touched upon in the next chapter – it is possible to see the dawning of the age of relativity where time and space are self-consciously located on relative and shifting planes. Back in 1871, even though Marx and Engels were able to theoretically take partial hold of the extension and fragmentation of social relations, and despite Marx's paradigm-breaking analysis of the abstraction of time in the production, fetishism and circulation of commodities, they were still nevertheless bound within the same broad ontological view of extension and internationalization as the bourgeois globe-trotter, Jules Verne. That is, extension was conceived of as occurring on one plane.[43] This is basic to understanding the first part of the dilemma with which we began, namely that Marx saw the development of a global class-structure through which 'nationality is already dead'.

In a theory which recognizes the globalizing impact of capitalism but remains set on one plane, however much the dialectic is invoked internationalization and the levelling effect of capitalism will perforce appear *the* dominant, and the *basic*, constitutive logic. It is particularly so given that Marx and Engels, like Darwin (1809–82) and even, in his own way, Nietzsche (1844–1900), were concerned to develop an underlying theoretical explanation and practical synthesis of the process of fragmentation. The subjectivity of the extension of social relations as levelling, continues to be expressed in the present: we can cite equally the contemporary, conservative ideology of

41. Marshall McLuhan, *Understanding Media: The Extensions of Man*, 1964.
42. Discussed by Kern, *Time and Space*, 1983, ch. 8. Compare this to Jules Verne's *The Begum's Fortune* where in his futuristic millennial city, significantly called *France*ville (the Village of France), the town council hold their meetings by telephone. See Kenneth Allott, *Jules Verne*, (n.d.) c.1940, *passim* on science, technics and the themes of time in Verne's work.
43. This is a related but narrower point than that made by Geoff Sharp when he says: 'A general way of stating the limits within which Marx's theory was constrained is to represent his conception of society as set within one constitutive plane. While the theory of the commodity breaks into a further constitutive layer, the image of society as composed of an intersection of constitutive layers is never explicitly generalized.' ('Constitutive Abstraction and Social Practice', 1985, p. 59).

the end of class, as well as a contemporary marxist like Marshall Berman who when describing Marx's era says, 'For the first time in history, all confront themselves and each other on a single plane of being.'[44] It is not that they are wrong, but having a theory of this levelling of subjectivity is a different matter. More of this later.

1871: intersection of levels

Just as we have to be careful about not overstating the interconnectedness of the world system, equally the consolidation of the nation and state, even as late as 1871, should not be exaggerated. Ascribing full significance to this in one sense complicates the problem of explaining Marx's approach. It appears to confound the second part of the dilemma, namely that although nationality is said to be 'already dead', Marx and Engels effectively take the nation for granted, treating it as a long-run, post-tribal form of association. They use the term 'nation' as equally applicable to polities from the Phoenicians to the Germans both before and after unification under Prussia.[45] Connor argues that Marx was 'given to slipshod terminology, often using nation to apply to a state or to an ethnically heterogeneous society'.[46] But whether or not this point is accepted the problem still remains. Why is there such an ambiguity in Marx's writing? To explain this it is helpful to recognize the nation as being a contingent, though logical, outcome of the intersection between a constitutive level of social integration which in 1871 was still far from moving into dominance and prior levels which hold continuing force. This formalistic metaphor of intersecting levels is limited in itself, but here as always it is intended only to open the way to discussing issues that the base–superstructure metaphor closes off. Marx and Engels variously described the nation in terms of these different levels, although not named as such, without having a theory which made sense of, or was even sensitive to, the ambiguity it engendered. For them a nation was at once a tribe of people bound by face-to-face ties of kinship and mutual history, and a community of strangers connected by more abstract means of integration including commodity exchange. In the context of a general culture which had not resolved the definition of the nation, Marx and Engels, understandably then, remained unconcerned about the implications of this ambiguity for the politics of the national question.

Rather than confounding the problem, recognizing the uneven consolidation of the nation-state brings us closer to an explanation of the poverty of theory. The argument about intersection of levels needs expanding but it can be done partly in the context of arguing through the still undemonstrated

44. Marshall Berman, *All that is Solid Melts into Air*, 1983, p. 116.
45. See for example *Selected Works*, vol. 1, 1977, pp. 55, 111, 112, 304, 307, 321.
46. Connor, *The National Question*, 1984, p. xiv. See also the more sympathetic writings of Bloom, 'The Social Conception of the Modern Nation', ch. 2 in *The World of Nations*, 1941; and Roman Rosdolsky, 'Worker and Fatherland', 1965. The ambiguity of the nation as community and as nation-state was prevalent across the world. For example see Erik S. Lunde, 'The Ambiguity of the National Idea: The Presidential Campaign of 1872', 1978.

assertion that even towards the end of the nineteenth century the nation-state was still in transition from the absolutist state and the polyethnic empire. The diverse examples of 'Germany', 'Italy', 'England' and 'Japan' will be used. It is hopefully clear by now that this does not mean I am arguing that the nation is simply an invention of late nineteenth-century Europe and that processes going on outside Europe, or cultural changes going back to the late Middle Ages within Europe such as the vernacularization of literary expression, are irrelevant. In fact, quite the opposite. But those writers who insist on the view that nationalism was a visible force in the medieval world are yet to theorize how it is that such a force is so tentatively established eight centuries later.[47] Perhaps it is no wonder that Marx remained ambiguous on the question.

In 1871, dynastic states and empires, admittedly becoming less absolutist in their control, still made up the large majority of the world's political sovereignties. It has been noted already that it was the year of German national unification. Universal male enfranchisement, excluding the full range of modern 'deviants' such as political exiles like Marx, was announced in that country as well as in France. However, a couple of additional remarks put the German unification and its extension of the rights of citizenship into a different perspective. Germany was not unified as the outcome of its cultural nationalism. We are thus faced with what John Breuilly calls the 'thorny problem of the lack of congruency between "cultural" and "political" nationalism'.[48] A parallel and more paradoxical problem is that unification initially gave the monarchy enormous power while, increasingly, such personally embodied, agency-extended power, sustained in part by force of arms, lost *political* legitimacy with the citizenry who had been given new rights by unification.

It is significant that the Second Reich was formally inaugurated on 18 January 1871 with the crowning of the King of Prussia, Wilhelm I, as the Emperor of Germany; it was conducted on *foreign* soil by the German princes assembled in the Hall of Mirrors of the royal French Palace at Versailles. This was not empty ritual. Wilhelm I received the Imperial German crown without any allusion to the sovereignty of the German people. Germany's newly instituted constitution recognized an autocratic monarch (the *Kaiser*) over a relatively powerless parliament. It was to the *Kaiser* only and not to the parliament or the people that the chancellor was responsible.[49] The first and most powerful chancellor, Bismarck, was able to be dismissed nineteen years later by *Kaiser* Wilhelm II (1859–1941) even though monarchical power was by then beginning to wane.

The details of history disturb the usual, neat sense of progressive change. Anachronistic by some criteria, monarchy persisted even as it was reconstituted in its relationship to sovereignty, political power and to popular culture.

47. See C. Leon Tipton, ed., *Nationalism in the Middle Ages*, 1972; and Halvdan Koht, 'The Dawn of Nationalism in Europe', 1947.

48. See John Breuilly, *Nationalism and the State*, 1994, ch. 2. Quoted from John Breuilly, 'Reflections on Nationalism', 1985, p. 72.

49. Stephen Roberts, *History of Modern Europe*, 1950, pp. 319–321, 343–348.

This poses problems for Marx's proposition that: 'With the change of economic foundation the entire immense superstructure is more or less rapidly transformed.'[50] How would the base–superstructure framework handle the fact that the *Kaiser*, Wilhelm II, who we will see in another connection in a moment, was one of the first 'statesmen' to utilize the management of 'publicity'. Publicity emerged as a new 'necessity' as a relationship developed between the form of diplomacy, still largely conducted among a 'transnational', often blood-related, ruling elite, and the citizenry, a technologically extended, mass electorate increasingly integrated through the popular press?[51] It is an example of the intersection of levels. Even at the end of the nineteenth century, kinship-based, face-to-face relations crossed still-consolidating national boundaries. After Bismarck, 'it was still possible for the Prince Chlodwig zu Hohenlohe-Schillingsfürst to be German Chancellor, for one of his brothers to be a Cardinal of the Roman curia, for one of his nephews to be an Austrian minister, and for another to be an Austrian general and diplomat who later on became Ambassador in Berlin'.[52]

Italy, labelled by Marx and Engels a revolutionary nation, provides a similar picture. In 1871 monarchy was being institutionalized and thus secularized; religion was retreating to the periphery of political power. Italian unity was seen by all except the *Italia irredenta* to be at least on the way to completion. However, the nation was not simply leaving all prior forms in its wake. Seton-Watson makes clear it is 'not a gross distortion to describe "Italy" as a colony of the Piedmontese'.[53] In 1871 Vittorio Emmanuele (1820–78), the erstwhile Piedmontese King of Sardinia, and by this time King of Italy, addressed the first Italian parliament in Rome saying that, 'The work to which we consecrated our life is accomplished . . . our people, after centuries of separation, find themselves for the first time solemnly *reunited in the person of their representative* . . .'[54] (emphasis added). There are in these words two matters of note. There is the implicit reference to an immemorial national existence, if not an unrealized, underlying unity. Secondly, there is the continuation in a more secular-abstract form of the medieval assurance of the king's sacred body as representing the unity of the

50. From the 'Preface to A Critique of Political Economy' (1859), in Marx and Engels, *Selected Works*, vol. 1, 1977, p. 504; cf. Marx and Engels, where they say that 'History is nothing but the succession of separate generations, each of which . . . continues the traditional activity in completely changed circumstances and, on the other [hand] modifies the old circumstances with a completely changed activity' ('The German Ideology' (1846), in *Selected Works*, vol. 1, 1977, p. 38).

51. David Thompson, *Europe Since Napoleon*, 1957, ch. 16, and pp. 374–375; Eric Hobsbawm, 'Mass-Producing Traditions: Europe 1870–1914', 1983. On the limitations of absolutism and the 'myth of the omnipotent ruler' see Walter Hubatsch, *Studies in Medieval and Modern German History*, 1985, ch. 8. Hubatsch cites Friedrich Naumann's 1899 Berlin lecture where, ironically, he said that mass communications had given rise to a nascent third force in politics 'beside Parliament and the Federal Council', namely the *Kaiseramt* (Imperial Office) (p. 154).

52. Hans Morgenthau, *Politics Among Nations*, (1948) 1976, p. 244.

53. Hugh Seton-Watson, *Nations and States*, 1977, p. 108.

54. Document in M. Christine Walsh, ed., *Prologue*, 1968, p. 103.

body politic.[55] Behind those words are further issues: the settlement of 1870 had placed the parliament in Rome, destroying the temporal power of the papacy. It was part of the general world-wide remaking of the sacred–secular relation. (On the other hand, the Law of Guarantees declared the pope's person inviolable: the Vatican for its part refused to recognize the Italian state until the Lateran Treaty of 1929.) Secondly, despite the movement for unification being more populist than its German equivalent, monarchical power rather than power conferred by the people was still predominant. Thirdly, regional self-interest and provincialism was still extremely strong. When Giuseppe Garibaldi (1807–82) handed over the southern half of 'Italy' to his king he was deferring to a fellow Piedmontese. Garibaldi, the 'great Italian nationalist', was himself born at Nice, a French citizen, and christened Joseph Marie. Nice reverted to the kingdom of Piedmont in 1815. Fourthly, *Risorgimento*, a literary term applied to the movement for unification, came to be commonly reserved for those like Cavour (1810–61), who were loyal monarchists, aristocratic, elitist, cynically pragmatic and 'decently nationalist'.[56] Fifthly, though I think this is a case of pushing the thesis of cultural invention to straining point, there was not, according to Eric Hobsbawm, any obvious cultural continuity of symbols and practices that the *Risorgimento* could draw upon to solve the problem summarized by Massimo d'Azeglio (1798–1866) when he said, perhaps apocryphally, that, 'we have made Italy: now we must make Italians'.[57] It is certainly true that at the time of unification from amongst a 'forest of dialects' only 2.5 per cent of 'Italians' spoke 'Italian'.[58]

It might be objected that the previous examples of Germany and Italy are drawn from outside the group of 'old continuous nations' (Seton-Watson's phrase). But, while it should be conceded that the objection has some validity, more significantly for the purposes of the present discussion, Marx and Engels treated those polities as part of their revamped version of the Hegelian category of great historical nations. Though not as unreflectively as the King of Italy, they implicitly wrote in quite untheorized terms of there being a deeper continuous *historical* unity underlying political disunity.[59] Bloom tries

55. Ernst Kantorowicz, *The King's Two Bodies*, 1957; Bryan S. Turner, 'Personhood and Citizenship', 1986, pp. 1–15.

56. Raymond Grew, 'How Success Spoiled the Risorgimento', 1967.

57. Hobsbawm, 'Mass-producing Traditions', 1983, p. 267.

58. Geoff Eley, 'Nationalism and Social History', 1981, p. 91.

59. This is not to say that 'nationality' or 'nation' were conceived in essentialist terms, nor as an unchanging historical fact. Bloom (1941, pp. 14–15) comments that although 'Marx frequently spoke of nations and races as "natural" entities', the 'natural' was not used as a term of fixity. This has a lineage which goes back to Vico's *New Science* where, according to Erich Auerbach's paraphrase, he said that, 'The history of mankind, or the "world of nations" (in contrast to the world of nature, which God created), was made by men themselves; accordingly men themselves can know it' (*Literary Language and its Public*, 1965, p. 7, and 'Introduction', *passim*). If this seems a very early period to be questioning the natural, it is underscored by the fact that Vico (1668–1774) was all but ignored until a century after his death.

to explain this by pointing out that Marx and Engels implicitly distinguished between two categories of human nature, a generic sense (human nature in general) and a historical sense (human nature in continuous transformation).[60] But it just takes us further into the problem rather than offering a way out of it.

Further to this, the objection to the choice of examples can be met by extending their range. Similar points about intersecting levels can be made in relation to England, the so-called first nation.[61]

The land where Marx and Mazzini were exiles had a territorial integrity and a relative continuity of effective, centralized authority, certainly going back to the English Revolution in the seventeenth century. Going back further, in the sixteenth century during the Reformation, Catholic Christendom was subordinated to the authority of the crown and parliament. The Roman Church in England became the Church *of* England. It was also in the 1530s that the state came to be spoken of impersonally as the locus of the political loyalty, and owed 'next to God a natural and humble obedience'.[62] And going back further still, in the fourteenth century Chaucer (1343?–1400), like Dante (1265–1321) and Petrarch (1304–74), was writing in the vernacular. Despite all this, in 1871 the monarchy continued to be politically powerful.[63] In that year the growing republican movement flickered and died back, partly due to the public response to an unsuccessful regicide attempt. Victoria von Saxe-Coburg-Gotha (1819–1901), Queen of Great Britain and Ireland, later *appointed* Empress of India, rose again in one of her many fluctuations of popularity.

Victoria is interesting not just because her title 'represents emblematically the thickened metal of a weld between nation and empire'.[64] Firstly, her blood ties testify to the continuing national bastardy of the European dynasties.

60. Bloom, *World of Nations*, 1941, ch. 1.

61. Nairn says of the *United Kingdom* that it 'was the first state-form of an industrialized nation' (*Break-up of Britain*, 1981, p. 14). 'Because it was the first, the English – later British – experience remained distinct. Because they came second . . . later bourgeois societies could not repeat this early development. Their study and imitation engendered something substantially different: the truly modern doctrine of the abstract or "impersonal" state which because of its abstract nature could be imitated in subsequent history' (p. 17).

62. From the preamble to the 1533 Act of Appeals drafted by Thomas Cromwell (1485?–1540), son of a Putney blacksmith, fuller of cloth, and alehouse keeper, himself a lawyer and intellectual, who rose to be the second most powerful person in England, after Henry VIII, that is, until he was executed for treason. Discussed in Philip Corrigan and Derek Sayer, *The Great Arch*, 1985, ch. 2. See also Alan G.R. Smith, *The Emergence of a Nation-State*, 1984.

63. Between the 1870s and World War I there was a fundamental change in the basis of British and other monarchies: an increase in publicly oriented, ostentatious ritual ironically marked the decline of monarchical power. Similarly the Church *of* England moved towards more ceremonial grandeur. See David Cannadine's documentation of the material changes and dislocations by which 'the "preservation of anachronism", the deliberate, ceremonial presentation of an impotent but venerated monarch as a unifying symbol of permanence and national community became both possible and necessary' ('The Context, Performance and Meaning of Ritual', 1983, quoted from p. 122). See also Tom Nairn, *The Enchanted Glass*, 1988, pp. 327ff.

64. Anderson, *Imagined Communities*, 1991, p. 88.

Secondly, leaving aside the changing response to her husband, Albert, her reign is indicative of the minimal but culturally contradictory concern that the 'common people' had for the nationality of their monarchs.[65] It was important that Victoria be born in the precinct of England – her pregnant Bavarian mother-to-be was rushed across the Channel – but it was irrelevant whether or not she was born of English blood. There was a greater furore over Victoria's class-crossing dalliance with John Brown than her nuptial parading of a German who looked like a swarthy operatic-tenor.[66]

Thirdly, she represents the overlap of levels of integration: despite the previously discussed, more abstract extension of social relations in the mid-to-late nineteenth century (when social integration became mediated by such developments as the railway and telegraph, the press, and an international circulation of commodities), we find embodied in the person of Victoria face-to-face associations and concrete ties of blood stretching across Europe from Balmoral to Belgium, Bavaria and Bulgaria. Victoria was the patrilineal descendant of the (German) House of Hanover. And on her mother's side, she was a daughter of the Bavarian House of Coburg (whence she was related to the kings of Belgium from 1831, of Portugal from 1837 to 1910 and of Bulgaria from 1908 to 1946). Uncle Leopold (1790–1865) was the first king of the Belgians. Wilhelm II, already discussed as one of the first wielders of the power of publicity, was her grandchild, as was Princess Alix of Hesse, the wife of the last Czar of Russia, Nicholas II (1868–1918). Victoria married her cousin, Albert, Crown Prince of Prussia (1819–61). And if she had been a man she might have also been crowned king of Hanover instead of her Uncle Ernest. Moreover, to compound the stretch of associations, Victoria spent an increasing amount of time at Balmoral Castle, where Albert massacred Highland deer and she came to emphasize the thin stream of Scottish blood in her veins. She had the floors of Balmoral carpeted in tartan. In short, calling Queen Victoria 'English' or even 'German' is inappropriate. It is only marginally more appropriate than saying that God is an Englishman. And yet the life of Victoria von Saxe-Coburg-Gotha was in the middle of what Anthony Smith has called the ethnic revival.[67]

65. Cf. the *Constitution of the United States* (Article 2, Section 1): 'No Person except a natural born Citizen, or a Citizen of the United States, at the time of the Adoption of this Constitution, shall be eligible to the office of President' (1787) in Richard B. Morris, *Basic Documents in American History*, 1965.

66. Certainly, we should keep in mind Bernard Guenée's point (*States and Rulers in Later Medieval Europe*, 1988, p. 49) that from the beginning of the fourteenth century the possibility of one king ruling both England and France was negligible. By the nineteenth century this incipient sense of 'national' difference had sharpened so that, in contrast to King George I (1714–27), who never learnt to speak English, Albert was denied the title of king because of his foreignness. Nevertheless my argument in relation to Victoria remains. Birth on British soil was the only sign of her 'Englishness': face-to-face connections were elevated as the dominant source of her identity in a context where face-to-face integration was subordinant.

67. Anthony D. Smith, *The Ethnic Revival*, 1981. Among the many monographs on Victoria see for example Elizabeth Longford, *Victoria R.I.*, 1966.

Using 1871 as the point of reference, examples of still-consolidating nationhood can be drawn from far and wide. It is important that we take an example from outside Europe. In anticipation of the later chapters on contemporary theorists, my argument here is that in a place like Japan it was not simply Western influence which affected the transformation to a nation-state: changes were occurring in social form. In 1871 the Meiji Restoration, consciously following the Hohenzollern Prussian–German model, centralized all local, 'feudal', military units in Japan, giving Tokyo a monopoly over the means of violence.[68] Max Weber (1864–1920) was yet to define this monopoly as basic to the nation-state.[69] Though in quite a distinct setting, some similar processes to those described for Italy, Germany and England were at work: from the dialectic of consolidating nationalization and stretching internationalization to the overlay of levels graphically evidenced in the intersection of the emperor as embodied, sacred representative and yet mediated by a growing bureaucratic apparatus.[70] To conjure this up in an example rich in connections: the overthrow of the Tokugawa Shogunate was a modernizing push from above, certainly influenced in part by Western-educated intellectuals, but which restored the traditional emperor as the essence of the national polity, or *kokutai*. It began as an attempt to expel the European barbarians but ended by effecting an open door to Western influence. It emphasized its traditional basis but imposed national loyalty above clan loyalty. Thus in an event which was indicative of the intersection of levels, the Emperor Meiji, as part of his *ancient* ritual of ascension, read a new oath which included the principle that: 'Knowledge shall be sought among the nations of the world.'[71] This possibility of such an oath entails a relativization of knowledge and a rationalization of the sacred, a changing subjective–objective practice of being-in-the-world.

One last point: it was also in 1871 that the Japanese established a department of education to begin for the first time a compulsory public school system. Japan was in the forefront of change. In July of that year, Bismarck's state policy of cultural–national unification, *Kulturkampf*, had only just begun, paralleling a less self-conscious policy going on throughout Europe of wresting education away from the Church and towards what Ernest Gellner

---

68. Anderson, *Imagined Communities*, 1991, pp. 95–97. While this may have in one sense been a conscious process I tend to agree with John Breuilly's criticism of Anderson for (implicitly) treating the Meiji Restoration as a straightforward case of 'Official Nationalism'. See Breuilly, 'Reflections', 1985, p. 72.

69. Definition from Max Weber, *The Theory of Social and Economic Organization*, (1910–20), 1945, p. 156.

70. Though it recognizes that there are unique features about Japanese 'ultra-nationalism' this argument is thus quite distinct from those positions which categorically distinguish between nationalism of the East and West. For example see John Plamenatz, 'Two Types of Nationalism', 1973.

71. Reproduced in Arthur Tiedemann, *Modern Japan*, 1955, pp. 99–100. See also: Bernard Eccleston, 'The State and Modernisation in Japan', 1986; Kazuta Kurauchi, 'Durkheim's Influence on Japanese Sociology', 1964; and Carol Gluck, *Japan's Modern Myths*, 1985.

(Chapter 6 below) argues is the basis of the nation-state, namely, centralized 'exo-education' with generalized and generic intellectual training.[72]

All that is solid melts into air

So far, two main issues have been discussed in relation to Marx's relative inattention to developing a theory of the nation. Firstly, I argued that Marx was embroiled in the processes of internationalization; that he conceived of the extension of social relations as if it were occurring only on one plane; and that this led him to theorize capital as completely remaking the world in its own image. Secondly, I stressed that, despite overemphasizing the single-level dominance of internationalization, Marx remained ambiguous in his treatment of the historical specificity of the nation.[73] It was implied that this might have had something to do with the complexity of the nation itself. This can now be put more directly.

Part of the basis of Marx's ambiguity was the fact that on one level the nation appeared as primordial, and yet, in intersection with new levels of integrative extension, it was still in the process of consolidating even as it was being reconstituted. Absolutist monarchy was, as we discussed earlier, an example of a social institution formed in an earlier intersection of face-to-face and agency-mediated relations. While being reconstituted through the sixteenth to nineteenth centuries in terms of new intersections, monarchy was all the while an active rather than archaic, viable rather than residual, contemporary force.[74] Monarchy was as Arno Mayer has argued a centrepiece of the persistence of the *anciens régimes*.[75] This puts into perspective the paradox

72. Ernest Gellner, *Nations and Nationalism*, 1983, ch. 3. On *Kulturkampf* see Geoff Eley, 'State Formation, Nationalism and Political Culture in Nineteenth-Century Germany', 1982. On the relationship between class and intellectual training in Germany see Derek van Abbé, *Image of a People*, 1964, ch. 3. On France see Jonathan Scott, 'Inculcation of Nationalism in French Schools after 1870', 1964. The British had only the year before passed their Education Act (1870), effectively to the same end. See John Lawson and Harold Silver, *A Social History of Education in England*, 1973, ch. IX. In 1871 the British Religious Tests were repealed: they had previously meant that Catholics such as Lord Acton, English baronet, later Regius Professor of History at Cambridge, did his tertiary studies outside England. Acton's kinship ties, like Victoria's, crossed Europe: his mother was a Bavarian countess while his father held office under the King of Naples; an uncle was a Roman cardinal. His maternal grandfather, of Habsburg descent, became a French citizen during the revolution, and his paternal grandfather was an English adventurer who became prime minister of Naples.

73. This explains how writers such as Rosdolsky, '"Nonhistoric" Peoples', 1964 and 'Worker and Fatherland', 1965, and Joseph Petrus, 'Marx and Engels on the National Question', 1971, could differ so fundamentally over whether Marx believed that capitalism and the bourgeois revolution were going to bring the demise of national difference.

74. This is implicitly a way of restating the terms used by Raymond Williams in his discussion of cultural processes while retaining much of the spirit of his analysis (*Marxism and Literature*, 1977, ch. 8). For more historical detail on the 'transition' from monarchy to nationalism see Reinhard Bendix, *Kings or People*, 1978.

75. Arno J. Mayer, *The Persistence of the Old Regime*, 1981, ch. 3. Mayer, however, places more emphasis on the Schumpeterian notion of 'carry-over' than I think is viable.

that the Tudor Revolution, in investing the monarchy with the title Head of the Church *of* England, brought to it vast new power, but that concomitantly this was in England the beginning of the end of absolute monarchism. The change was part of the inauguration of a more abstract sense of national place. To reassert an ongoing theme, this abstraction of an earlier sense of place was restricted largely to the clerisy and intellectual groupings whose outlook paradoxically was most likely to be universalistic.

In the nineteenth century the nation, formed in this setting of overlapping levels, *appeared* as the natural equivalent to society. It was 'there', underlying changing forms of state. It was simply the association in which people lived, an association that according to some writers (like Mazzini) needed politically framing, and for others, such as Lord Acton (1834–1902) who criticized Mazzini's conception, had *become* an oppressive 'fictitious unity'. The nation *became* an artifice, according to Acton, as soon as it was self-consciously theorized that each nationality needed to be politically coextensive with a single state.[76] Thus even the great liberal critic of the nation, like the socialist critic, as well as the fervent nationalist, shared the unquestioned assumption that the nation was a pre-political, historically natural form of association going through stages of development. In Acton's lifetime, and in his own thinking, the assumption of a pre-political, racial, natural *natio* became less secure. Acton assumed and extolled the existence of an English race of Teutonic descent. He tersely dismissed H.T. Buckle's 1857 *History of Civilization in England* for stating that 'the original distinctions of race are altogether hypothetic'. However, Hugh MacDougall points out that in Acton's later private notes there is the recognition that his dearly held Teutonic myth may have been overthrown.[77]

What Marx and Engels offered which went beyond this was a theory of economic (and political) stages. They could quite consistently say that the nation-*state* was, in its present form, a quite modern phenomenon with 'the whole structure of the nation itself [depending] on the stage of development reached by its production and its internal and external intercourse'.[78] But it was this question rather than the nation-state as a form of social integration that remained more central to their theory.

This whole area can be approached from a complementary angle, one through which it is intended to complicate and extend the preceding discussion. Marx and Engels, like their politically distant contemporaries Nietzsche, Baudelaire, Turgenev, Verne, Dostoevsky, Monet, and even Acton and Hardy, experienced this period-in-transition as one of upheaval. Modernity was perceived in varying ways as effecting a dissolution of solidity. It has wide-reaching implications.

The second half of the present chapter develops the argument that Marx and Engels were as intellectuals (and as persons caught in the maelstrom of

76. John Acton, *Essays on Freedom and Power*, 1862.
77. Hugh MacDougall, *Racial Myth in English History*, 1982, ch. vi.
78. Marx and Engels, *The German Ideology*, 1846, in *Selected Works*, vol. 1, 1977, p. 21.

late nineteenth-century capitalism) doubly constituted in a process of dissolution of old certainties and upheaval of prior forms of social life. The chapter
will broaden the abstraction thesis to indicate the complexity of the nexus
between subjectivity and objective social relations, even for those intellectuals who appeared outside it all. Upheaval and dissolution were reflected in
various aspects of their work from Marx's early romantic poetry to their
'mature' discussions of analytic methodology. It involved a process of what
will be called 'lifting out', the materially grounded tendency to abstract from
the particular.[79] This drive to 'discover' abstract categories such as class or
mode of production which provide a new level of unity was common in the
late nineteenth century across a diversity of intellectual fields. After drawing
examples from both literature and science, I suggest that it had the effect of
blinding them to the fact that, though the nation-state had its roots in the
structures of the 'old world', it was very much constituted by the new and
thus would not be so easily dissolved in the undoubted rush to globalize
social and economic interchange.

At the outset it is necessary to insert a word of warning. It should be
remembered that in the mid-to-late nineteenth century there were prominent
movements in art, history, theology, philosophy and science, all apparently
working in a contradictory direction to the one I have been describing. That
is, we find reassertions of continuity, certainty and solidity. In Marx and
Engels' homeland many instances can be found, from the historicism of
Leopold von Ranke (1795–1886) and his ilk which asserted the solidity of historical facts,[80] to the concerns of the famous Meininger theatre troupe to
reproduce the detail and reality of period dramas: actors wearing real suits of
armour exited through stage-prop doors which closed without wobbling.[81]

But these reassertions, I would argue, were beginning to be just that:
reassertions. In the empiricist and positivist social and natural sciences (as in
the theatre) having to assert the verity of facts was in part a continuing consequence of the lifting of factuality out of what Benedict Anderson, following
Walter Benjamin, has called Messianic time, that is, time as carrying a sacred
connection between universal truth and particular historical facts.[82] This lifting out meant that the significance of factual detail was brought starkly into
the limelight. It was subjected to the possibility of contestation. More
far-reachingly, in the *late* nineteenth century it insinuated the possibility that
the grounding of factuality could itself be up for rethinking. Even classical

79. The concept of 'lifting out' is not intended to carry any vestiges of Hegel's concept of
Aufhebung.

80. On Ranke's national sensibility see Friedrich Meinecke, *Cosmopolitanism and the Nation
State*, (1907) 1970, ch. 12.

81. Van Abbé, ('The Breakdown of 19th Century Certainty', ch. 4 in *Image of a People*, 1964.
On the new drive for dramatic authenticity see Richard Sennett, *The Fall of Public Man*, 1977,
pp. 26–27, 174–176, 202–205.

82. Walter Benjamin, *Illuminations*, discussed by Anderson (*Imagined Communities*, 1991), in
an inspiring passage talking about the changing 'apprehensions of time' (pp. 22ff).

secular science had to argue increasingly for the grounding of its understanding of the natural order. Theatre-goers were inadvertently faced with the
self-conscious experience of suspension of belief: previously the play had
largely created its own reality, but now, ironically, the new verisimilitude cast
the (disturbing) shadow that verity could only be the result of careful simu-
lation. So, for many philosophers, scientists, and theatre-goers alike the real
was no longer an absolute certainty. At the very least it could be said that
reality could no longer simply be assumed.[83] Alternatively it could be argued,
and was argued by some intellectuals like Nietzsche, that reality needed to be
re-grounded.

Marx and his readers in this way became open, firstly, to the need to
develop a more secure basis for considering reality, but secondly, they became
caught up in a problematic distinction between the real and the imaginary. As
will be discussed towards the end of this section, ideologies like nationalism
were in Marx's writing often reduced to imaginary or fictitious representations of the really real. Marx was able to use phrases such as the opiate of the
people, the *camera obscura*, the veil before our eyes, phantoms formed in the
human brain, false consciousness, and so on, phrases which even though
associated with significant theoretical problems signalled a completely new
way.[84] Little more than a decade after Marx's death, Emile Durkheim (as
discussed in the next chapter) was able similarly to revolutionize mainstream
social theory. Despite Durkheim's inheritance of Comtean positivism, and
despite (or, in another sense, because of) his intention to 'establish the foundations of science on solid ground and not on shifting sand', Durkheim was
able to write that we are, as individuals, 'victims of the illusion of having ourselves created that which actually forced itself from without'. The exteriority
of social facts consisted according to Durkheim of representations and practices based upon a substratum which 'can be no other than society'.[85] The
Commonsense Philosophers would continue for a long time yet to prove the
existence of reality by holding up a hand and saying that 'here is a physical
object in the external world',[86] but elsewhere that debate had been largely
bypassed. The shell had been cracked. Even by Marx's time the phenomenal
world was at least in many of the predominant streams of intellectual thought
only an apparent dimension of reality, though of course what constituted its

83. For qualifications of this in relation to the third quarter of the nineteenth century see
Robert C. Binkley, *Realism and Nationalism: 1852–1871*, (1935) 1963.

84. Marx completely reworked the concept of ideology from any previous formulations. More
sophisticated in implication than his own metaphors suggest, the concept served to emphasize
that even when the increasing acuteness of contradictions exposed deliberate distortions by the
ruling classes, ideology was always a relationship between the objective and subjective (Jorge
Lorrain, *The Concept of Ideology*, 1979, chs 1–2).

85. Emile Durkheim, *The Rules of Sociological Method*, (1895) 1966, quoted from pp. 46, 5,
and 3.

86. From the much discussed paper by G.E. Moore, 'A Defense of Common Sense', 1925.
More recently see R.E. Tully, 'Moore's Defense of Common Sense: A Reappraisal After Fifty
Years', 1976.

'real foundation' continued to be contested. And for Nietzsche, Schopenhauer, Feuerbach, the older David Strauss, as well as Marx, all quite different bedfellows, these dimensions were no longer held together in time by an Absolute, beyond reality, God. 'God is dead.' Thus, at least, spoke Zarathustra with relief.[87]

Dissolution of phenomenal certainty would, Marx and Engels believed, force people to face a reality unencumbered by such historical constructions as the modern nation-state:

> All fixed, fast-frozen relations, with their train of ancient and venerable prejudices and opinions, are swept away, all new ones become antiquated before they can ossify. All that is solid melts into air, all that is holy is profaned, and man is at last compelled to face with sober senses, his real conditions of life, and his relations with his kind . . .
>
> In place of old local and national seclusion, we have intercourse in every direction, universal interdependence of nations. And as in material, so also in intellectual production.[88]

This passage can be linked to the earlier suggestion I was making about the nation-state as still in a process of consolidation. Across Europe and the world, as we have seen, the nation as part of the changing constitutive form of social integration had barely solidified. While the 'abstract egalitarianism of citizens'[89] was ideologically entrenched in the treatises of intellectuals from John Locke (1632–1704) to contemporaries of Marx and Engels, like Alexis de Tocqueville (1805–59), it was still a radical doctrine. It was always being qualified and only hesitantly enacted in state policy. For Marx and Engels these barely established changes would be consolidated by the bourgeoisie only to be dissolved. Given this socially conditioned, theoretical logic it was unlikely that Marx and Engels would spend time theorizing the reasons why the nation-state continued to frame people's lives. In bald terms, for Marx and Engels the nation-state in its modern form *had become antiquated before it could ossify*.

The passage also evidences the idea of a more fundamental reality: it is unclear whether the connected phrase, 'relations with his kind', refers to a more fundamental national relation or to a relation of humankind. Later references in the *Manifesto* do not give us much help.[90] It is indicative of the ambiguity discussed earlier. Over and above this theme, but in uneasy relation to it, the passage is brimming with the sense of upheaval. It is as frenetic in its description of the 'moving chaos' as is the synaesthesic poetry of Charles-Pierre Baudelaire (1821–67).[91] As Louis Dupré has argued, Marx was the first

87. Friedrich Nietzsche, *Thus Spake Zarathustra*, (1891–92) 1985, p. 125.

88. Marx and Engels, *The Communist Manifesto* (1848), in their *Selected Works*, vol. 1, 1977, pp. 111–112. See the extended discussion of this passage in Marshall Berman, *All that is Solid*, 1983, *passim*.

89. This is Tom Nairn's phrase (*Break-up of Britain*, 1981, p. 24). In Chapter 6 below the way in which he uses it will be questioned.

90. For example, 'Though not in substance, yet in form, the struggle of the proletariat with the bourgeoisie is at first a national struggle' (*The Communist Manifesto*, (1848) 1977, p. 118).

91. On the connection between Marx and Baudelaire see Walter Benjamin, *Charles Baudelaire*, 1973; and Berman, *All that is Solid*, 1983, part III.

major critic of the very processes of cultural development, including the radical subjectification of the real and the fragmented character of modern culture, processes that made his own work possible.[92] I want to concentrate now on this theme of upheaval and the relation between the subjective and objective, filling it out by relating some of the more direct, framing influences upon Marx's thought – 'as in material, so also in intellectual production'. It is intended eventually to tie back into the argument concerning the abstraction of social life and the intersection of levels of integrative extension.[93]

The nineteenth century was a time of unprecedented, generalized dislocation: more than even the earlier upheavals of plague, war and famine, it challenged the sense of attachment to place. Marx and Engels were born in Trier and Barmen, old metropolitan centres within a region which was not only part of the core of the post-feudal economic transformations, but also one which acutely experienced the transprovincial changes and shifts in the form and placement of European political boundaries.[94] The Rhineland, originally part of the Holy Roman Empire of the German Nation,[95] was after the Middle Ages a *Ständestaat*, or 'polity of Estates'.[96] For a time it was incorporated in post-revolutionary Napoleonic France, a state in transition to a nation-state. In 1815 it was ceded to Prussia, part of a form of absolutist *Ständestaat* known as the Holy Alliance of Princes. Finally in 1871, as already discussed, it was drawn by Bismark into a unified Germany with a Prussian king; this was clearly an act of military and monarchical power-pragmatics rather than the logical outcome of the end of a nationalist telos. The new German Chancellor's biography is instructive on this point. Bismarck (1815–98) lived for a time in Leicester and then Scotland; he entertained the idea of enlisting in the British Army in India. In 1862, in response to an invitation from the Czar to enter the Russian diplomatic corps, an offer that in the post World War period would be considered an invitation to national treason, Bismarck *'courteously'* declined.[97]

In the case of Marx's family the experience of 'storm and stress'[98] generated

---

92. Louis Dupré, *Marx's Social Critique of Culture*, 1983.

93. Throughout the discussion it is recognized that social change is always relative: it is those people who, for whatever reason, are lifted into an abstract overview of the *longue durée* who are prone to talk of cultural crisis. For example, Wolfram Eberhard (*Conquerors and Rulers*, 1965, p. 15) records that Chinese intellectuals of the fifteenth century had complained about the pace of change in their lifetime. Nevertheless, broad historical comparisons can still be made.

94. For a discussion of this from a focus on Trier, see Jerrold Seigel, *Marx's Fate*, 1978, ch. 2, part 1. This book exhibits the strengths (and limitations) of the best kind of psychological history.

95. The expression dates from the mid-fifteenth century: *Das heilige römische Reich deutscher Nation*.

96. Here I am drawing upon the typology elaborated by Gianfranco Poggi in *The Development of the Modern State*, 1978.

97. See Edward Crankshaw, *Bismarck*, 1981; and Morgenthau, *Politics Among Nations*, 1948, pp. 244–245.

98. *Sturm und Drang* was the name of a play with themes characteristic of a literary movement in Germany, 1770–82. The phrase increased in its currency during Marx's time.

quite profound responses. With Prussian control in 1815 and the restricting of
civil liberties, Heinrich and Henrietta Marx decided for pragmatic reasons to
'remake' their public identity. They severed their respective rabbinic genealogies and converted from Judaism to Christianity. Henrietta Marx was further
out of place: she was born in Holland and never completely mastered the
German language.

Karl Marx was born into the period of the death and transfiguration of
German hometown society (to again use Mack Walker's phrase). It was the
period of the great German emigrations, the *Auswanderung*. Upheavals of
population occurred across Europe in ways unprecedented prior to the nineteenth century. The Augsburg *Allgemeine Zeitung* (1816) recorded the
following words of alarm: 'In the richest and fairest parts of Europe there
rules such discontent that whole families resolve to quit their fatherland. The
spirit of restlessness and dissatisfaction is so general and so widespread that
it must have a more profound cause than human foolishness.'[99]

As an intellectual, and later an exile, Marx was doubly moved by the
sweeping extensions and reformations of social life. From the vantage point
of knowing his later work it may seem surprising but in his youth Marx wrote
poetry which was influenced by the same motifs as those which intoxicated
early nineteenth-century Romanticism: the Dionysian longing for eternal fluidity; the romantic irony of emancipation of the self by subjection to the
infinite Self.[100] When Romanticism is described with a different focus the
subjective connection between Marx's early poetry and his 'mature' project of
mapping the abstract connections between the fragments of social life
becomes more apparent. As August Wilhelm von Schlegel (1767–1845) put it,
Romanticism involved the desire to 'soar on the wings of poetic reflection . . .
to abstract from every single thing, to grasp hoveringly the general, to survey
a mass, to seize the totality'.[101] Marx's poem 'The Awakening' sets the individual in a fluid state, 'your beaming eye breaks', being lifted upwards,

> Upwards through the veil,
> Of primeval night,
> Then flash from above
> Eternal Stars
> Lovingly inwards[102]

99. Cited in Mack Walker, *Germany and the Emigration, 1816–1885*, 1964, p. xii. Between 1871
and 1885, at least a million-and-a-half Germans emigrated, predominantly to the United States.
Contrary to commonsense, emigration was more pronounced during times of high economic
activity (p. 181).

100. A less respectful Althusser would find a new 'subject' for his ideology in particular/
Ideology in general, subject/Subject distinctions.

101. Leonard P. Wessell, *Karl Marx, Romantic Irony and the Proletariat*, 1979, *passim*;
Schlegel quoted p. 55. While this is a useful book, it is not to say that I want to have anything to
do with his overall thesis that marxism has a mythopoetic basis and is thus a 'Vital Lie'.

102. Reproduced in full in Wessell, ibid., pp. 231–232. See also *Feelings* (p. 259): 'Never can I
carry out in peace / What has seized my soul so intensely, / Never remain comfortably quiet, /
And I storm without rest.' Note the implicit reference to 'Storm and Stress'.

As well as the image of the stars carrying the sense of the Romantic, infinite *Self*, they are depicted as flashing brightly from above a veil. It recalls the metaphors of the older Marx, previously referred to as depicting reality as veiled.[103] Going further into the poem, the third stanza momentarily snuffs out the 'soul's rippling flame', and reflects the crisis of self-aggrandizement/ self-negation which Romanticism was going through at that time:

> Your Awakening
> Is endless rising,
> Your rising,
> Eternal fall.

Marx soon embarked upon a project that would leave behind the clammy, self-negating underside of Romanticism. However, it was by the same rise and fall, the same lifting-in-abstraction that Nietzsche took in the diverging direction of a neo-nationalist nihilism, that Marx and Engels drew upon to seize the totality and to explain it in terms of itself. They set out through a methodology which Marx referred to as a movement from the 'abstract to the concrete'.[104] Derek Sayer in his book *The Violence of Abstraction* argues that:

> Marx persistently relates the abstraction of social phenomena from their historical integument – he speaks of the abstraction of the state, abstract labour, the abstract individual, and so on, in ways that are too consistent and too frequent to be coincidental – to the particular social conditions of capitalist production and the world of fetishized appearances they sustain. Reification is for him a real process. It is, then, the nature of bourgeois reality itself – *the discrepancy between its appearance and its reality, its real and its ideal forms* – which renders a scientific analysis of such forms necessary.[105] (emphasis added)

Part of their aim was to explain in materialist terms the structures and processes of transformation that constituted the experience that, 'Things fall apart; the centre cannot hold'.[106] However, what limited their analysis was a tendency to conceive of the process of abstraction as a process of the reifying of ideas, or, in other words, the lifting of concrete processes into the realm of *fictitious* phenomena. The so-called real ties of the past, according to this

103. For example see Marx, 'Preface' to *Capital,* vol. 1, (1867) 1977, p. 20: 'But they raise the veil just enough to let us catch a glimpse of the Medusa head behind it.'

104. Marx carefully distinguished this method from Hegel's abstract idealism, but as Seigel reminds us, Marx later became uneasy even about the 'abstract to concrete' description (*Marx's Fate,* 1978, p. 371). It was left out of the 1859 'Preface' which replaced the 1857 introduction to 'A Contribution to the Critique of Political Economy'. Marx said 'on closer reflection any anticipation of results still to be proved appears to me disturbing, and the reader who on the whole desires to follow me must be resolved to ascend from the particular to the general' (Marx and Engels, *Selected Works,* vol. 1, 1977, p. 502) The issue remains the same. Note the metaphor of ascension.

105. Derek Sayer, *The Violence of Abstraction,* 1987, pp. 130–131.

106. This phrase was written a generation on. It is from a poem, 'The Second Coming', composed in 1921 by a 'sporadic fascist' from Ireland, W.B. Yeats (1856–1939). Significantly, a generation further on again, Chinua Achebe chose the phrase as the title for his anti-colonialist novel, *Things Fall Apart,* 1958.

view, were being dissolved, and the person was becoming a '*fictitious* phenomenon. In the state . . . he is the imaginary member of an illusory
sovereignty, is deprived of his real individual life and endowed with an unreal
universality.'[107]

Continuity, unity and the abstract avant-garde

This line of discussion on upheaval, dissolution and abstraction could be
taken much further in its own terms, but it is becoming clearer that for a theorist (or a poet) to have a vantage point from which to even describe
upheaval, they have to be *materially* constituted at a level already removed
from that which they conceive as dissolving. It is not just that Marx was a
deracinated individual. And it is not that he was being lifted into a 'fictitious'
realm of reified ideas. The intellectual is always in quite significant ways constituted within the limitations of the present. And yet because intellectual
work is conducted in the main at the level of disembodied extension – that is,
for example, via the medium of the printed word which materially transcends
some of the limitations of time and space – intellectuals, perhaps more than
anyone else, are pushed to find generalized, abstract categories which connect
the vagaries of day-to-day life. This became intensified as the old verities and
the old hierarchies were dismantled. José Ripalda writes:

> The enormous and lucid distance of Marx before the historical epoch in which he
> found himself historically identified is the distance of uprooted individuality. His
> reflection, at the same time that it is the result of this uprooting, reflects the activ-
> ity that produced it dissolving the totalitarian bonds of the old precapitalist
> organism. There is the radical separation of people and the means of production,
> the formal separation between economic society and state, the inversion of social
> relations into impersonal ones and vice-versa, and consequently the transfer of
> human substance to impersonal mechanisms. Marx's radical demystification is the
> same that allowed Adam Smith to identify king and priest with cooks and whores
> in the same category of the unproductive class.[108]

Ripalda places Marx firmly within the bounds of his time, but he also
indicates the level at which Marx steps beyond it. A parallel can be found to
earlier writers like Hegel or Adam Smith (1723–90). Identifying 'king and
priest with cooks and whores', as opposed to locating them on a hierarchy of
being (itself obviously a categorical abstraction), entails a further abstraction.[109] Like calling Queen Victoria von Saxe-Coburg-Gotha 'Mrs Brown', it
is a move not possible within the cultural bounding of an unquestioned and

---

107. From 'On the Jewish Question', 1843, cited in Sayer, *Violence of Abstraction*, 1987, p. 104.
For a more sympathetic reading of Marx on the process of abstraction see Carol Gould's path-
breaking book *Marx's Social Ontology*, 1972, ch. 1.

108. José Maria Ripalda, *The Divided Nation*, 1977, p. 158. The paragraph concludes in a vein
that reflects the spirit of this thesis: 'Marx will belong to the past not when he is refuted . . . but
when others have come to realize what he only anticipated.'

109. Ripalda uses this notion of abstraction to great effect in some instances and in others proceeds with unrealized, loose-but-brilliant assertions.

sacred Great Chain of Being.[110] The process of I referred to earlier as lifting out, and which now is being broadened and referred to as abstraction, is crucial, I suggest, to understanding the experience of upheaval and the nature of intellectual practice; it is fundamental to responding to the dilemma of why there is no nineteenth-century theory of the nation, as well to explaining the quite novel form of social relations which begin to bond a nation of strangers in the first place.

The constitutive abstraction argument allows us to make some sense of the paradox of continuity-in-discontinuity.[111] Earlier I said that Marx and his contemporaries experienced the nineteenth century as a period of upheaval. On the other hand, one of the implications of the foregoing discussion is that through the process of abstraction a level can be 'discovered', and lived, at which a continuity with the past is conceived. How are these propositions connected?

It is true to say that despite the political discontinuities of German history described earlier there was a sense of abstract continuity across time and place being perceived in some quarters of intellectual life such as in German historiography. It was a cultural continuity which went beyond that of the province or borough. This was so as early as the new humanism of the fifteenth and sixteenth centuries. In turn, certainly by the 1500s, intellectuals could refer back to the recently unearthed manuscript by the Roman writer, Publius Tacitus (AD 55–c.120).[112] However, perceiving this continuity which linked some of the tribes of the Roman Empire to the principalities of the Second Reich as a national history entailed a lift in the level of abstraction beyond that of the face-to-face or the agency-extended. I will expand upon this by way of an example in a moment, but the point is that conceiving of such a continuity entailed a mode of apprehending the world, discontinuous with past modes. Moreover there were discontinuous ways of conceiving of continuity: the Renaissance humanists, some of whom began to speak highly of a German character, range from Brant (c.1458–1521), Wimpfeling (1450–1528) and Desiderius Erasmus (1466–1536) to the bathetic chronicler who traced the connection between the Vestal Virgin and the Westphalian nuns,[113] but they can be compared as a group to Hegel or Justus Möser, and contrasted even more starkly with Marx. The linking of cultural with legal and institutional history such as in Möser's proto-historicism (discussed in Chapter 2) required a qualitative intellectual upheaval, a paradigm shift in subjectivity, and Marx took this even further.

---

110. Arthur O. Lovejoy (*The Great Chain of Being*, 1936) shows how the 'idea' stretched from Greek philosophy to the eighteenth century.

111. It is not a new problem. Corrigan and Sayer describe it as the 'dialectic of continuity and change' (*The Great Arch*, 1985, p. 201).

112. *Germania* written c.20. Marx and Engels often refer to Tacitus' writings on the 'ancient tribes of Germany'. See particularly Engels, *The Origin of the Family, Private Property and the State*, (1884), in Marx and Engels, *Selected Works*, vol. 3, 1977, pp. 37, 46, 56, 125, 172–181.

113. A.G. Dickens, *The German Nation and Martin Luther*, 1974, ch. 2, 'Humanism and the National Myth'; Boyd Shafer, *Nationalism: Myth and Reality*, 1955, pp. 87ff.

A further response can be posted which runs parallel with the earlier recognition that upheaval was accompanied by assertions of a new solidity in various quarters from positivism to the performing arts. By the early nineteenth century those who most ardently summoned the continuity of the *Volksgeist* were the self-conscious inheritors of the spirit of discontinuity, that of *Sturm und Drang*. The now commonplace saying, 'the more things change, the more they stay the same', was carefully drafted by a now largely forgotten writer in the months that followed the publication of the *Communist Manifesto*.[114] Similarly, for a significant number of nineteenth-century German intellectuals, anarchic individualism was seen to be complemented by total community.[115]

Hegel provides us with an apposite example of the paradox of continuity-in-discontinuity. The Hegelian dialectic is an attempt to theorize just such a paradox. It does so through a dexterous but inconsistent juggling of the existential and ideal, where all existence is (supposedly) moved by the dialectic of continuous–discontinuous change. Simkhovitch writes that Hegel 'makes chemical processes testify to the "truth" of his conception; he causes stones to cry aloud, and the flowers that bloom in spring crown the dialectic glory'.[116] All existence is moved by the dialectic process, that is, significantly, all existence except the realization of the State. Hegel, official Prussian *Restaurationsphilosoph*, believed that the State is the way of God and the realization of Reason. As Simkhovitch put it, 'The Universal Spirit, which is so dialectically brisk elsewhere, seems to be quiescent in its capacity as *Volksgeist*'.[117]

The nation-state formed in the intersection of levels thus becomes for Hegel the concrete embodiment of the totality of past history and the social order of the present (*Sittlichkeit*). Marx, writing later, is able to find a way of synthesizing the continuity-in-discontinuity at a level which for reasons argued earlier can, paradoxically, by being more abstract than Hegel's idealist universalism, criticize his form of approach as confirming the '*cultus* of abstract man'.[118] But while Marx and Engels dismissed the immanent force of the national *Volksgeist* they took for granted the historical force of the nation-state. The passage about to be quoted from Engels' early writings shows how the continuity is assumed while an idealist way of perceiving that continuity is criticized. Keep in mind that except for the analysis of the commodity and labour abstraction Marx and Engels themselves tended to

114. Alphonse Karr (1808–90), *Les Guêpes*, January 1849, cited in John Bartlett, *Familiar Quotations*, (1882) 1977. Charles Tilly suggests that the writer was Talleyrand (personal communication July 1991).

115. Hans Kohn, *Prelude to Nation-States*, 1967, p. 170.

116. Vladimir G. Simkhovitch, 'Approaches to History: 3', 1932, p. 429. On the internal antinomies of Hegel's work on the *Volksgeist* see Georg Lukács, *History and Class Consciousness*, 1922, pp. 146–149 particularly.

117. Ibid. This is not to say that Hegel was an 'ardent nationalist': see Shlomo Avineri, *Hegel's Theory of the Modern State*, 1972, ch. 3.

118. Marx, *Capital*, (1867) 1977, p. 83.

treat abstraction in the Hegelian sense as a process only occurring in the realms of ideas. Their approach on this issue, however critical, is out of the lineage of Auguste Comte (1798–1857) and his three stages of history: (1) theological or fictitious; (2) metaphysical or abstract; (3) scientific or positive. Engels writes:

> The Germanising trend was negation, abstraction in the Hegelian sense. It created abstract Germans by stripping off everything that had not descended from national roots over sixty-four purely German generations. Even its seemingly positive features were negative, for Germany could only be led towards its ideals by negating a whole century and her development and thus its intention was to push the nation back into the German Middle Ages.[119]

Marx and Engels, at least in their capacity of being intellectuals, worked at a level which was abstract in relation to the practice and discourse of people whose lives were dominated by the *relative* constraints of the day-to-day. Marx and Engels were not even representative of contemporary intellectuals *qua* intellectuals. However, the direction of their work generated a resonance among many of their contemporaries. It was in fact representative of a drive within a diversity of fields to discover abstract categories or categorizations, to theorize a new level of unity which could be said to underlay (or overlay, depending upon the chosen metaphor) the phenomenal world. To indicate the breadth of this drive I would like to cite two examples, one from science and one from literature.

In 1871, Dimitri Mendeleyev (1834–1907) presented a paper which delineated his most developed formulation of what was to be received as the pre-eminent schema of a unitary, abstract totality devised in chemistry up to the end of the nineteenth century. It was an eight-column schema which connected all the elements of the natural world and was called the periodic table of atomic elements.[120] The point being made here as with the other examples is only highlighted by and not dependent upon the fact that it is drawn from the year 1871. This 'invention' was continuous with the past and at the same time part of a specific disjunction from its precursors. Mendeleyev's table took the dominant mode of inquiry, modern science in all its universalizing, regularizing splendour, to its limit. It was a limit which was not anticipated by Isaac Newton (1642–1727) in his exemplary work on the logic of order in the *Principia*. Similarly, the famous Second Law of Thermodynamics – entropy always increases in any closed system not in

119. Engels, 'Ernst Moritz Arndt' (1841) in Marx and Engels, *Collected Works*, vol. 2, p. 140–141. See also Marx, *The German Ideology*, in Marx and Engels, *Selected Works*, vol. 1, 1977, pp. 39, 49, 76.

120. See Geoff Sharp 'Constitutive Abstraction', 1985, where he uses the example of the periodic table to draw attention to the way in which the practical cross-contextuality of the intellectual mode makes possible the building of interpretative models (p. 64 and pp. 48–82 *passim*). Cross-contextuality or the bisociation of different frames of reference is the subject and theoretical base of Arthur Koestler's book *The Act of Creation*, 1964. With much insight, though none of it critical or politically sensitive, Koestler attempts a theory to explain creativity ranging across the basis of laughter and the aesthetic experience to the process of scientific invention.

equilibrium – was a modern law of universalism which was part of the transition to a science abstracting from an already abstract, long-run ideology of
universal regularity.[121]

In literature a similar point can be made, but it is a little more complicated
because the abstract unity of the novel is not one of the foremost intentions
of the author. In George Eliot's *Middlemarch* (published in December 1871),
the textual form is of barely interacting central characters living out their separate lives as described in widely diffused narratives. There is little effort to tie
these characters together: they meet at funerals and marriages. Still there is a
powerful sense of unity. As one critic contends it is a unity not of place, but
of 'moral scene'.[122] The method of writing allows the author and thus the
reader to be everywhere as the 'centred subject of her own decentred fiction'.[123] This depends on a change in the form of subjectivity, and, as Benedict
Anderson has argued relevant to the rise of the nation, this changed subjectivity includes a changed sense of simultaneity. Homogeneous empty time
(Benjamin's phrase) – where simultaneity is 'transverse cross-time, marked not
by prefiguring and fulfilment, but by temporal coincidence and measured by
clock and calendar'[124] – comes to overlay and, in a long-run transformation,
to largely reconstitute what was earlier referred to as Messianic or traditional
time.

Let me restate the proposition with a different slant. Intellectual works, as
apparently unrelated as *Capital*, *Middlemarch* and the Periodic Table of the
Elements, were produced within a common constitutive form, and yet they
were *not necessarily* representative of the overtly dominant ideologies of the
period. This is not to dispute Eagleton's (1978) comment that 'George Eliot
delineates a "space" constituted by the insertion of "pastoral", religious and
Romantic ideological sub-ensembles into an ideological formation dominated by liberalism, scientific rationalism and empiricism'.[125] Quite the
opposite. But it is an attempt to have something to say about the form, and
not just textual form, through which such contradictory ideologies are
brought together. It tries to go further than Eagleton's jumbled conclusion
that 'This contradictory unity of ideological structures provides the productive matrix of her fiction; yet the ideology of her texts is not, of course,
reducible to it. For Eliot's literary production must be situated, not only at the

121. It is interesting to note that Ernest Gellner's theory of the nation 'reflects' the Second
Law of Thermodynamics in arguing that nation-states arise out of 'entropy-resistant traits' as
structure is supposedly replaced by an 'internally random and fluid totality' (*Nations and
Nationalism*, 1983, p. 63, and ch. 6, *passim*). See also the discussion in Zygmunt Bauman's
Culture as Praxis, 1973, pp. 58–67. For marxist examples of drawing explanatory analogies from
science and the Second Law of Thermodynamics see Nikolai Bukharin, *Historical Materialism*,
1921; or more recently Debray, 'Marxism and the National Question', 1977.

122. Mark Schorer, 'The Structure of the Novel', 1967.

123. Terry Eagleton, *Criticism and Ideology*, 1978, p. 120. He indicates that the web, a natural
and organicist metaphor of complex fragility, is one of the central images of the novel.

124. Anderson, *Imagined Communities*, 1991, p. 24.

125. Eagleton, *Criticism and Ideology*, 1978, p. 112.

level of "general" ideology, but also at the *relatively autonomous level of the mutation* of literary forms.'[126] I do not want to return to the orthodox model of determinism, nor reject the constant possibility of contingent outcomes, but on the other hand, though I agree with the *tenor* of Eagleton's final paragraphs, his talk of a 'certain curvature in the ideological space in which texts play'[127] is hardly a great leap forward in literary or social theory. In terms of the present argument, those people, in this case theorists, novelists or scientists, who are trained (always within the terms of their society's dominant configuration of levels of integration) to operate on the boundaries of existing discourse and practice, work on a level which allows them to abstract from that society.[128] This is overdetermined by multifarious processes, some of which have already been discussed, including the extension of social relations sustained by print-capitalism.

It can be linked to the continuity-in-discontinuity proposition. For example, for Rousseau (1712–78) to explain the foundations of his new society and advocating the establishment of self-conscious political nations[129] required that he abstract from the socio-cultural qualities of mankind. In his words, it required that he 'strip this being, thus constituted' to arrive at our 'natural foundations'. Rousseau was able fleetingly to muse that this was a state which 'perhaps never did exist'.[130] Significantly, however, he never explored the implications of such a statement.[131] It is hard to see how, given the cultural conditions of his time, this would have been likely. Even if any such analytic move is made *possible* by the relationship-in-general of intellectuals to their society – it goes back at least to Plato's use of the image of the shadows on the cave wall to argue for philosophers being the keepers of their state – it is however constrained by the particularity of circumstances of the time.

Because the experience of being lifted upwards through the veil is conditioned by material influences with overlapping and long-run cultural histories it is easy to see why it is necessary to talk of continuity-in-discontinuity. From Rousseau's to Marx's century there was the developing and self-conscious

126. Ibid., p. 113, emphasis added.

127. Ibid., p. 180.

128. It is those people who have pushed against boundaries and been able to draw connections between levels of constitutive being from the most concrete to, within contemporary limitations, the most abstract that, alongside the princes of political power, have been given a significant place in what we still conventionally call 'history'. But that is a different story.

129. Anne Cohler, *Rousseau and Nationalism*, 1970.

130. Jean-Jacques Rousseau cited in Irving Zeitland, *Ideology and the Development of Sociological Theory*, 1968, pp. 24–25. See also F.M. Barnard, 'National Culture and Political Legitimacy: Herder and Rousseau', 1983.

131. It would be interesting at another time to trace the history of the notion of the original condition. From the Book of Genesis and the 'Epic of Gilgamesh' through Rousseau's 'Origin of Inequality', to the ambiguous status of Freud's primal-horde myth and then to John Rawls' abstract conception of an 'Original Position' (see his *A Theory of Justice*, 1972) there are striking qualitative changes, with each becoming progressively more abstract.

post-patronage abstraction of the writer, litterateur and artist.[132] For Tocqueville in Marx's time, or Montesquieu (1689–1755) in Rousseau's, it was travel which they singled out as facilitating their sense of 'looking down from above'.[133] Marx and Mazzini, and going back further, Machiavelli (1469–1527), Petrarch and Dante, were all exiles from their native locales. With Marx, as I have argued, the abstraction was further intensified. Marx's century began with the discovery of the Wild Child of Aveyron and by its end was overtaken by various rethinkings of human nature exemplified in Darwinism and Freudianism. Marx's approach as evinced in the concept of 'species being' was in one sense continuous with the limitations and openings of the Rousseauian stripping away of content. But he moved past Rousseau and took the faltering eighteenth-century critique of religious-based essentialism to a new level.[134]

In summary, it has been argued that Marx was pushed by both his constitutive medium and by the form of his intellectual practice to search for 'deeper' or 'higher', more abstract categories of explanation. This proposition I argue adds to an understanding of how the nation could be taken for granted as an historically natural form of association, and, at the same time, be conceived as passing into history, melting into air.[135] In the first chapter I suggested that despite all of its discontinuities the modern nation is *subjectively* experienced as a community of known strangers bound within a specifiable time and space continuity. If it is right to say that the nation is experienced as a concrete and condensed relation between real people (despite the fact that they never meet as-a-community except via materially abstracted, extended relations), then Marx's seeing through the veil of this subjectivity was a profound insight. But it had for Marx the effect of blinding him to the fact that the national subjectivity of the concrete, drawing upon the ontological level of the face-to-face, was integral to the intersection of more abstract levels of social integration. With the realization that this subjectivity could be seen through, the contemporary precariousness of the national form (even before it had solidified) could not help but come to the fore. But without something like a

132. Even the history of such words as 'art' and 'artist' throws light on the change. It was in the late eighteenth century that a generalized distinction was for the first time drawn between artist and artisan - the former said to have a higher 'intellectual' or 'imaginative' purpose. See Raymond Williams, *Keywords*, 1976, pp. 32–35.

133. This is Konrad Burdoch's metaphor summarizing Petrarch's literary sense of '*Italia Mia*'. See Kohn, *Idea of Nationalism*, (1944) 1956, pp. 97–98, 600–601.

134. This is still largely in agreement with Norman Geras in *Marx and Human Nature*, 1983.

135. Keep in mind that Marx's use of the term 'natural' is always ambiguous; it is not an immutable or God-given essence. Marx at one stage was taken with the theories of the French scientist, Pierre Tremaux. In a book published in 1867, Tremaux suggested that racial differences were produced by variations in geological settings. Bloom notes that: 'Without distinguishing between race and nationality, Marx commented that "for certain questions, like nationality, etc., it is here alone that we may find the natural basis"' (*The World of Nations*, 1941, p. 15).

theory of levels it had the double effect of ambiguously leaving the *national* form hanging in its relatively taken-for-granted, relatively untheorized obviousness, and yet highlighting the novel qualities of the modern *state* in which, according to the comment earlier cited from Marx, citizens are 'imaginary member(s) of an illusory sovereignty'.

On the other hand, the nation could not be written off as simply an ideological phantom perpetrated by the leading national class. Marx and Engels were too aware of the vagaries of history and the exigencies of contemporary politics to do that. The doctrine of historyless peoples became an inadequate but logical way of bypassing this tension. From this side of the contradiction the nation was implicitly treated as the post-tribal, transhistorical name for associations between people. 'Nation' and 'society' were interchangeable terms. Either way, the nation disappeared into its own prominence.

Instead of theorizing the constitutive levels which in intersection provide the subjective force of national formations, Marx and Engels – working as I have indicated at a level of abstraction which allowed them to 'strip this being thus constituted' – set themselves in Engels' phrase to 'discover the law of development of human history'.[136] They were able to analyse history in terms of an abstract analytic categorization of the structural relations of persons living and working within the determinations of specific modes of production: namely, class relations. Class provided the missing (abstract) category through which post-tribal history could be both unified and taken apart. Their theory got to the point of alluding to the fact that it was the mode of production and its associated leading class which gave form to the nation in history. But that was the stumbling point. Just as extension was theorized as occurring along a single plane (the flattening out of the constitutive levels of time and associations-with-place were examples discussed earlier), the implications for social being, highlighted by a theory which talks of constitutive levels, were never realized.

Because of the milieu in which Marx and Engels worked, a number of themes dominated their analysis: world history as progressive stages of upheaval, capitalism as the predominant economic form globalizing human existence, and class as the basic (abstract) category of social relations. Thus the extensions and abstractions of social relations were conceived as occurring on one plane. The word 'plane' is used in distinction to the notion of 'levels' to indicate that such a conception involves the collapsing of levels into each other, not simply the forgetting that there are various levels of social existence that can be analytically distinguished. For though Marx was brilliant enough to work beyond the limitations of his own position, it was not a matter of forgetting but of having no realizable way of going a further synthetic step. It was not just, as Nairn has implied, that Marx was

---

136. Engels, 'Speech at the graveside of Karl Marx' (1883), in Marx and Engels, 1977, *Selected Works*, vol. 1, p. 162.

unable to 'foresee the real contradictions of Progress'. The limitations were fundamental and historically framed ones related to the theorizing of social form. They were not simply lack of prescient knowledge of the content of future history. These continuing limitations left marxism, for the most part, stumbling around in the glare of its own insight, unable to conceive of a political practice which could be enacted except on a single constitutive plane.

4
Durkheim and Weber: The Antinomies of Abstract Nationalism

A nationality is a group of human beings, who for ethnica[l], or perhaps merely for historical reasons desire to live under the same laws, and to form a single State, large or small as it may be; and it is now a recognized principle among civilized peoples that, when this common desire has been persistently affirmed, it commands respect, and is indeed the only solid basis of a State.

Emile Durkheim, *'Germany Above All':*
German Mentality and the War, 1915

If the concept of 'nation' can in any way be defined unambiguously, it certainly cannot be stated in terms of empirical qualities common to those who count as members of the nation. In the sense of those using the term at a given time, the concept undoubtedly means, above all, that one may exact from certain groups of men a specific sentiment of solidarity in the face of other groups. Thus, the concept belongs in the sphere of values.

Max Weber, *The Theory of Social and Economic Organization*, 1921

Neither Durkheim nor Weber, nor any of their contemporaries associated with the nascent fields of sociology and political science, Simmel, Tönnies, Pareto, Mosca or Cooley, developed anything approaching what we might call a theory of the nation.[1] This chapter examines some of the reasons why, a generation after Marx and Engels, and at a time when it was clear that in the foreseeable future the nation was not going to fade away, there was a continuing poverty of theory in this area.

Certainly in selected quarters, conceptions of the naturalness and immutability of the nation-state were beginning to be challenged, and many traditions were being pressed by an urgency of debate. Second-International marxism was broadening its terms of enquiry. Through Bauer, Kautsky, Lenin, Stalin and others, it was beginning, even if in problematic ways, to go

---

1. Robert Michels (1876–1936)) might be considered a limited exception to this generalization with the publication in 1917 of *Notes sur les Moyens de Constater la Nationalité* and in 1929 of his study *Der Patriotismus*. However, his theorizing still had the quality of simply enumerating the 'components of the Fatherland concept', with, in the final analysis, a deferent bow to Ernest Renan's (1832–92) concept of a 'community of will' as subordinating all other components. See Michels' *First Lectures in Political Sociology*, (1927) 1965, ch. viii, 'Patriotism'.

beyond treating national formation as on the one hand a historical given and, on the other hand, a narrowly political question.[2] Anarchists such as Kropotkin and Réclus working outside institutional settings were defying the nationalist assumptions of the new academic social sciences, particularly of geography[3] and history.[4] Concurrently, even though many mainstream historical studies continued until well after World War I to be premised on the natural or morally logical basis of the progression from tribe to nation, historians of ideas such as Meinecke, Muir, Oakesmith and Rose were at least beginning to give direct attention to chronicling the complexities of the nation in history.[5] Yet in classical sociology, a discipline which was opening up so many areas of social relations either to the first light of abstract secular enquiry or to the second light of painstaking recension, almost no work was being done on theorizing the processes of national formation. It was not that social theory was being left behind by a handful of insightful historians, but rather that given the work of social theory in other areas it seems strange that social theorists were giving no lead in this one. While they were interested in history, the early social theorists in general did not think highly of the work of historians: in Herbert Spencer's words, 'The highest office which the historian can discharge is that of so narrating the lives of nations, as to furnish materials for Comparative Sociology.'[6]

By comparison with how they treated the question of the nation, the classical social theorists treated religion – the taken-for-granted ethos of an earlier period and still commanding considerable dominion – as one of many social phenomena that 'are covered by a veil that we must first remove if we are to get at them and bring them to light'.[7] On occasion, nationalism came to be called the new religion. And nationality was unveiled as a social fact rather than a social essence. However, there was no analysis of the national form even distantly comparable to Max Weber's or Emile Durkheim's analyses of

2. Ephraim Nimni, 'Great Historical Failure: Marxist Theories of Nationalism', 1985.

3. Jim MacLaughlin, 'State-Centred Social Science and the Anarchist Critique', 1986.

4. On the nationalism of the German neo-Rankeans see John Moses, *The Politics of Illusion*, 1975.

5. Friedrich Meinecke (1862–1954), *Cosmopolitanism and the Nation State*, 1907; Ramsay Muir (1872–1941), *Nationalism and Internationalism*, 1916; John Oakesmith, *Race and Nationality*, 1919; and J. Holland Rose (1855–1942), *Nationality as a Factor in Modern History*, 1916. After a detailed history and a short but convincing critique of the racialist, language-based and Hegelian 'World-Spirit' theories of the nation, Rose however can do no better than to say that nationality 'is an instinct, and cannot be exactly defined; it is the recognition as kinsmen of those who were deemed strangers; it is the apotheosis of family feeling, and begets a resolve never again to separate; it leads to the founding of a polity on a natural basis.' (1916, pp. 152–153). For a sense of the range of studies of the nation written in the pre-war period, see Carlton Hayes' 'Bibliographical Note' at the end of his *Essays on Nationalism*, (1926) 1966.

6. Cited in Peter Burke, *Sociology and History*, 1980, p. 19.

7. Emile Durkheim, *Montesquieu and Rousseau*, (1892) 1965, p. 62. Weber is also fond of the veil metaphor, and recall Marx's use of the same image, quoted and discussed in Chapter 3, pp. 69, 73, 80, above.

religion, respectively in *The Protestant Ethic* (1904–5) and *The Elementary Forms of Religious Life* (1912).

What were the theoretical and material constraints engendering such a continuing limitation of theory? As was discussed in relation to the late nineteenth century, the necessity of theorizing the nation was in part obviated by the very prominence of the category of the nation, but by the beginning of the twentieth century this was complicated by an often intense advocacy for the moral primacy of the national interest. It seems as we look back from the late twentieth century that Hegel's aphorism that the owl of Minerva flies at twilight is still apposite. Examining this question of the continuing limitation of theory is intended to take us through a descriptive history of ideas and beyond the tendency of such a description to over-accentuate the role of theoretical heritage. It entails looking at issues which bear upon the relation between intellectual work across the turn of the century and the form of the nation during that period.[8] In the previous chapter, the focus was the world in which Marx lived, drawing examples from the year 1871. The subject of the present chapter is 'mainstream' social theory during the decades up to and including World War I. The chapter develops lines of examination begun in the earlier chapters, and hence assumes that the various aspects of the constitutive abstraction argument do not require quite as detailed an exposition of their relevance for understanding Durkheim and Weber.

In relation to the continuing poverty of theory it mattered little which overt methodological pathway the classical sociologists took. Emile Durkheim (1858–1917) emphasized the collective basis of subjectivity and social practice, whereas Max Weber (1864–1920) was ultimately a proponent of methodological individualism.[9] Georg Simmel (1858–1918) and Charles Cooley (1864–1929) made their overriding concerns the 'meaningful forms of sociation', centring on relationships in face-to-face interaction and group affiliation rather than on abstract, extended communities such as the nation;[10] whereas Gaetano Mosca (1858–1941) was interested in the theory and practice of larger political structures. None of these theorists spent more than a few paragraphs on theorizing the nation. Likewise, it made little difference which political leanings each of the classical theorists espoused: Weber was a conservative liberal-nationalist and an early member of the Pan German League; Ferdinand Tönnies (1855–1936) was a kind of socialist; Vilfredo Pareto (1848–1923) accepted nomination shortly before his death as a sena-

8. For some beginnings in this area, see Anthony Smith, 'Ethnocentrism, Nationalism and Social Change', 1972; and his 'Nationalism and Classical Social Theory', 1983.

9. J. Agassi, 'Methodological Individualism', 1960.

10. This is not to suggest that they have nothing to say about extended communities. Simmel, for example, writes: 'The characteristics of the large group can, to a considerable extent, be explained as *surrogates* for the personal and immediate cohesion typical of the small group. The large group creates organs which channel and mediate the interactions of its members and thus operate as the vehicles of a societal unity. . . . They are the *abstract* form of group cohesion whose *concrete* form can no longer exist after the group has reached a certain size.' From *The Sociology of Georg Simmel* (1902–7) 1950, p. 96 (emphasis added).

tor in Italy's new Fascist government. None of these theorists who were to be the progenitors of mainstream sociology, social theory and political science was able to pose the question as to why it was nations administered by institutions of state (and empire) that were becoming, at least in the capitalist West, the pre-eminent, extended social form constitutive of cultural identity.

World War I partly changed this lacuna.[11] The classical sociologists were deeply affected by the carnage; it was the first war in history to totalize involvement by the citizenry, dragging in non-combatants including those from the so-called ivory tower. However, although they became involved in the politics of patriotism,[12] the classical theorists were not prompted to follow up substantially the question of why during *this* war, and particularly in its early stages, were so many millions of people willingly prepared to die in the name of their nation. Theorists remained content with continuing the sort of descriptive, ahistorical part-truths that they had forwarded, however presciently, before 1914: 'Wars, in quickening the sense of patriotism, subordinate preoccupation with the self. The image of the threatened fatherland occupies a place in one's consciousness that it does not have in peace time.'[13]

Undeveloped theories of the nation were projected. Simmel in his discovery of the integrative forces of conflict says that 'Essentially, France owes the consciousness of its national unity only to its fight against the English, and only the Moorish war made the Spanish regions into one people'.[14] But, like Tönnies' explanation that 'it is through the merchants that the technical conditions for the national union of independent individuals and for capitalist production are created',[15] such direct comments were usually oddments. They only occasionally surfaced out of analyses that were permeated by the nation as one of their implicit framing categories. Much more relevant to the quandary of the nation of strangers was Simmel's work on the city of strangers. It is tempting then to reduce the problem of preclusion to the limitations of an unacknowledged kind of *methodological nationalism*, that is, to a tendency to equate society with nation.[16] However, we have to be clear about the complexities of this.

It was not that the classical sociologists completely lacked awareness of the increasing centrality of the nation and nation-state in bounding social life. Gaetano Mosca was characteristic in suggesting that nationalism was replacing religion 'as the chief factor of moral and intellectual cohesion within the various countries of Europe'. He says:

    11. However, see Carlton Hayes, 'The War of Nations', 1914, a review essay of the 'pseudo-scientific obscurantism . . . from the minds of the so-called intellectual classes of all nations'.
    12. Durkheim, for example, wrote political pamphlets during the war including, 'Germany Above All', 1915 and (with E. Dennis) *Who Wanted War?*, 1915.
    13. Emile Durkheim, *Moral Education*, (1902–3) 1973, p. 68.
    14. Georg Simmel, *Conflict and the Web of Group-Affiliations*, (1908) 1955, p. 100.
    15. Ferdinand Tönnies, *Community and Society*, (1887) 1963, p. 225.
    16. See Anthony D. Smith, *Theories of Nationalism*, 1983; and Zygmunt Bauman, *Culture as Praxis*, 1973, pp. 78–79.

It satisfies, finally, a yearning of the human soul to love the group to which it belongs above all other groups . . . Unfortunately, love of country, and a natural desire that one's country should make its influence more and more felt in the world, often goes hand in hand with diffidence toward other countries and sometimes with hatred of them. The over-excitation of these patriotic sentiments undoubtedly helped to create the moral and intellectual atmosphere that brought on the World War.[17]

Secondly, it cannot be said that all the classical theorists were oblivious to the limitations of their theorizing. Weber, for example, indicates a partial recognition of his lack of direct attention to theorizing the nation when at one point he writes:

In the face of these value concepts of the 'idea of the nation', which empirically are entirely ambiguous, a sociological typology would have to analyse all sorts of community sentiments of solidarity in their genetic conditions and in the consequences for the concerted action of the participants. This cannot be attempted here.[18]

Weber never did attempt such a project. And it may well be that subsequent attempts to take up his challenge and approach the theory of the nation through typologies, taxonomies and indices of the ideal-type helped carry on the poverty of theory.[19] However, though Weber's comment does not go beyond recognizing the enormity of the task, he clearly was aware that there was more to be done.

Thirdly, we can even find instances when the classical sociologists were partially and momentarily aware of their tendency to treat an untheorized category as the basis of their discussions of society. Mosca is disarmingly candid about it: the theorist, he says, 'has to look objectively upon nationalities . . . treating them merely as a phenomenon of the human mind. But the precept is more easily given to others than applied by one's self.'[20]

Moreover, it is not that it is impossible to reconstruct a theory of the nation from their broader writings. Ernest Gellner's work over the last twenty years (examined in Chapter 6) is a case in point. It developed, with critical

17. Gaetano Mosca, *The Ruling Class*, (1896, 1923 edition) 1965, p. 482.

18. Max Weber, *From Max Weber*, (essays from 1904–20), 1968, pp. 175–176. H.H. Gerth and C. Wright Mills, editors of this selection, suggest that notes written in the margins of the manuscript of *Economy and Society* 'indicate that Weber intended to deal with the idea and development of the national state throughout history' (p. 448).

19. In initiating this tradition we can include Max Sylvius Handman, 'The Sentiment of Nationalism', 1921; and Louis Wirth's seminal essay, 'Types of Nationalism', 1936. I do not mean to be overly critical of these writers. They were doing more than most of their contemporaries.

20. Mosca, *The Ruling Class*, 1965, p. 41. Ironically, in the very next paragraph he implicitly equates 'society' and 'nation'. Similarly, Durkheim and Dennis (*Who Wanted War?*, 1915, p. 5) write that, 'We, and our readers in particular must therefore be on guard against the possible influence of a national partiality, however natural it may be'. They still manage to conclude that their native France was right, Germany wrong: 'The guilt of Germany stands out in strong relief. Everything proves it and nothing either weakens or attenuates it' (p. 60). In this they were no different from Gustave Le Bon, *The Psychology of the Great War*, 1916. Compare the very careful ambiguity in Sigmund Freud, 'Thoughts for the Times on War and Death' (1915).

divergences, out of the Weberian–Durkheimian lineage,[21] as did the work of others such as Anthony Smith and Liah Greenfeld.[22]

In the following discussion, the work and life of two of the most prominent classical social theorists, Durkheim and Weber, provide the dual centres of focus for attempting to take these introductory comments a little further. Durkheim and Weber are singled out both because of their prominence and because they develop general theories of social forms. After a biographical note, written with reference to how they treated national integration as a moral or political imperative, the discussion elaborates the bearing of their respective methodologies upon the national question. In the previous chapter considerable space was given over to exploring the way in which Marx's approach to understanding the nation was limited by a tendency to treat questions of social relations as if they were couched on one plane. While it would be unnecessarily repetitive to show in a detailed way how neither Durkheim nor Weber manage adequately to overcome this problem, that theme nevertheless remains as an undercurrent, surfacing occasionally. Overall, the chapter contextualizes the writings of Durkheim and Weber as two abstracted yet politically engaged intellectuals, attempting to understand a rapidly changing world. It returns to their writings from this angle to draw some conclusions about the ambiguous, untheorized place of the nation in their theories of societal forms.

The differences between Durkheim and Weber are marked. However, I will argue that these differences are set within a common set of assumptions and a common constitutive milieu which crossed the borders of France and Germany, even as those nation-states became increasingly antagonistic.

The imperative of national integration

Emile Durkheim was born in the Vosges, that part of Lorraine not taken over by the Germans when in 1871 they annexed Alsace-Lorraine. This eastern region was an important source of Third-Republic nationalism. Professed cosmopolitan writers such as Gustave Flaubert (1821–80) were deeply affected by the 1871 defeat and annexation. In that year (already discussed in a broader context) Ernest Renan, a cosmopolite who had previously claimed his *patrie* to be the 'human spirit', now embraced the sort of patriotic allegiance he had earlier condemned: 'Those even who are philosophers before

---

21. From his *Thought and Change*, 1964, to his *Encounters with Nationalism*, 1994.

22. Anthony D. Smith, *National Identity*, 1991, and Liah Greenfeld, *Nationalism*, 1992. I stress this point because a couple of my critics in reading the manuscript skipped over this paragraph, suggesting that I mistakenly focus on passages from the classical theorists that are 'beside the point': books which hardly mention the nation-state, such as *The Elementary Forms of Religious Life*, they suggest, have profoundly influenced subsequent generations of commentators on the nation. However, this is precisely my point: when later writers out of the Durkheimian and Weberian traditions construct theories of national formation they rarely refer to Weber's explicit writings on the nation and never to Durkheim's.

being patriots, cannot be insensible to the cry of two million men whom we were obliged to throw in the sea in order to save the rest from drowning, but who were bound to us for life and death. France, therefore, has a point of steel embedded in her flesh which will no longer let her sleep.'[23] Annexation prompted one grouping which included the Vosges *littérateur* Maurice Barrès (1862–1923) towards *revanchisme*, dedicating their lives to restoring the desecrated lost territories.

Another grouping, apparently opposed to the philosophy of revenge, included easterners such as Jules Ferry (1832–93), twice prime minister of France. Their nationalism took a different guise. They moved to emphasize the national-technocratic goal of modernization, particularly, following the manner of Bismarck's *Kulturkampf*, the consolidation of mass, national, secular education. In the 1880s, state funds were offered to scholars to bring back ideas from Germany for effecting educational renovation. One recipient of state sponsorship was Durkheim. Ironically, though born in Lorraine, he felt little of the overt nationalist passion felt by others such as Renan and Flaubert whose connection to those easterners 'thrown into the sea' of German sovereignty was much more tenuous. By the time of his scholarship to Germany, Durkheim had developed a dispassionate though complex relationship to blood and soil: he had for example thoroughly left behind his family's rabbinic tradition and the possibility of following his father as Grand Rabbin des Vosges. His aim was quietly to change the world from a distance through the abstract medium of writing.[24]

Max Weber was similarly born into a changing world, a world of which he became rigorously critical without challenging one of its grounding assumptions. Like Durkheim he was both a cosmopolite and a contradictorily dispassionate nationalist. No doubt it would be possible, along the lines of Arthur Mitzman's psycho-social biography, partly to explain this antinomy in terms of Weber's ambivalent response firstly to his father's subordination of his National Liberalism to the Junker power-state (*Machtstaat*), and secondly to his mother's passive withdrawal from her patriarchal husband into her Calvinist orthodoxy.[25] However, the issue flows wider. In Germany, as in France, there were active political debates over the ideological and practical consequences of the conjunction of the national community and the *Machtstaat*, debates over the nature and importance of tariffs and other economic boundaries, discussions about the fate of the national minorities, and critiques of traditional institutions such as the Church and monarchy. These debates, however, tended not to cut any deeper than immediate policy

23. Renan, *La Réforme Intellectuelle et Morale*, cited in William Buthman, *The Rise of Integral Nationalism in France*, 1970, p. 15. See also Chapter 6 below for a discussion of Renan's 'Qu'est-ce qu'une Nation?'

24. On Durkheim's life see Kenneth Thompson, *Emile Durkheim*, 1982, ch. 1; Edward Tiryakian, 'Emile Durkheim', 1970; and Henri Peyre, 'Durkheim: The Man, His Time and His Intellectual Background', 1964. On the complicated and changing ideologies of nationalism in pre-war France see Eugen Weber, *The Nationalist Revival in France, 1905–1914*, 1968.

25. Arthur Mitzman, *The Iron Cage*, 1969.

considerations. Nation and nation-state were largely taken for granted as forming an unexamined cultural base.

Numerous extra-parliamentary movements in Germany took national considerations as their reason for being. Such groups included the Pan-German League which Weber left, *not* because of its ultra-nationalism, but on the grounds of its sectarian-leaning towards equating the national interest with the interests of the Junker class. All claimed to be above 'mere politics'. The League's aim remained as Weber's ongoing credo – to 'bring together the nationally-minded citizens without considerations of party in the thought that the accomplished fact of the unification of the German race is only the beginning of a larger national development'.[26] The difference was that Weber's theoretical perspective made it possible for him to at least recognize that the issue of national integration was intensely political. For him it was politics carried out at a deeper level than that reached by arguing over the possible institutional arrangements of the means of agency-extension.

Thus from the beginning, the politics of the national question formed the background to Durkheim's and Weber's writing. In Weber's inaugural lecture at Freiburg, 'The National State and Economic Policy' (May 1895), he presented an academic but militant, social-Darwinist argument for the primacy of the nation. He addressed the issue of how Germany, through political education and the 'social unification of the nation', might be led by a maturing bourgeoisie to an even greater epoch of imperial expansion. Germany, he says, 'must remain sensitive to the grand passions nature has placed within us'.[27] He concludes:

> A great nation does not age beneath the burden of a thousand years of glorious history. It remains young if it has the capacity and the courage to keep faith with itself and with the grand instincts it has been given, and when its leading strata are able to raise themselves into the hard and clear atmosphere in which the sober activity of German politics flourishes, an atmosphere which is also pervaded by the solemn splendour of national sentiment.[28]

Just as Durkheim constantly argues for 'a national catechism which will include the elementary teaching of principles which serve as the basis of social organization,'[29] Weber emphasizes that the future rested upon the central role of education in national integration: 'The aim of our socio-political activity is not world happiness but the *social unification* of the nation.'[30] In this they

---

26. Stephen Turner and Regis Factor, *Max Weber and the Dispute over Reason and Value*, 1984, p. 13.

27. Max Weber, Inaugural Lecture, Freiburg, 1895, 'The National State and Economic Policy'. W.G. Runciman notes that, even at the time, the address was received as an 'aggressive and controversial statement of liberal imperialism'. See Max Weber, *Weber: Selections in Translation*, (1895–1920), 1978, p. 211.

28. Weber, Inaugural Lecture, (1895) 1980, p. 448.

29. These are in fact the words Henri de Saint-Simon (1760–1825) cited favourably in Emile Durkheim, *Socialism and Saint-Simon*, (1896) 1959, p. 142. The argument is spelt out in Durkheim, *Moral Education*, (1902–3) 1973.

30. Weber, Inaugural Lecture, p. 447.

reinforced the already existent trends of modernity. Mass, state-funded, primary education was being instituted across Europe; basic intellectual training even for girls and working-class children was increasingly accepted as necessary for instilling the 'scientific' ethic of social solidarity over and above religious obedience.[31] This is not to say that Durkheim and Weber were vacantly mouthing current ideologies. Weber, for example, rejected the incursions made into intellectual liberty by *Kulturkampf*. Both had an avowedly dispassionate, though in their own terms ultimately non-scientific argument, for the 'careful cultivation of national character'.[32] The rationale for their advocacy of the abstract state and for the abstract nation (concepts I initially use here in the sense implied by Durkheim and Weber as more abstract in thought) was in part the logical outcome of their general theories of society and of the methods by which they believed that social relations could be understood.

Different approaches, convergent appreciations

Durkheim begins from the premise that individuals are controlled by coercive external categories of representation and practice which have their source, their 'substratum', in society itself. At the point where these collective manifestations or social facts appear to be natural, we have fallen 'victims to the illusion of having ourselves created that which actually forced itself from without'.[33] Categories as totalizing and ontologically basic as time and space are mutable facts, part of the 'abstract and impersonal frame', intelligible through concrete signs such as the changing of the seasons, and self-consciously accessible through the 'conscience collective'.[34] They originate out of the way in which the social is organized, particularly its demographic volume and density. In attempting to explain the source of social facts, Durkheim departs from the narrow functionalism and explicit teleology of Auguste Comte (1798–1857) and Herbert Spencer (1820–1903). He dismisses the claim that willed actions could *of themselves* bring social facts into being.[35] Nationality is used as a key example. Responding to those such as Gustave Le Bon (1841–1931) who suggest that social phenomena can be explained by the psychology of individuals or groups, Durkheim replies:

> In reality, as far back as one goes in history, the principle of association is the most imperative of all, for it is the source of all other compulsions. As a consequence of

31. Robert Gildea, *Barricades and Borders: Europe 1800–1914*, 1987, ch. 13, 'The Management of Society'. See also J.E.G. de Montmorency, *State Intervention in English Education*, 1902. The preface rings with the urgency of the task. However, this trend was not simply ushered in on a wave of complete change: taking up a university post in Prague, Albert Einstein had to wear a military uniform, avow his belief in God and swear allegiance to the Habsburgs.

32. Weber, Inaugural Lecture, (1895) 1980, p. 438.

33. Emile Durkheim, *The Rules of Sociological Method*, (1895) 1966, p. 5 and ch. 1 *passim*. See also Chapter 3, pp. 69–70 above.

34. Durkheim, *Forms of Religious Life*, (1912) 1976, pp. 10ff., 440ff.

35. For a qualification of the force of this rejection see fn. 44 below.

my birth, I am obliged to associate with a given group. It may be said that later, as an adult, I acquiesce in this obligation by the very fact that I continue to live in my country. But what difference does that make? This 'acquiescence' is still imperative. Pressure accepted and submitted to with good grace is still pressure . . . *For the present*, it is most certainly imposed upon me, for in the vast majority of cases it is materially and morally impossible for us to strip off our nationality.[36] (emphasis added)

Durkheim's conclusion about the impossibility, 'for the present', of stripping away one's nationality is couched here on one plane. That is, while he is well aware that nationality is a socially formed 'imperative', he reduces the ontological depth of national formation to the fact of living within the confines of a particular country in association with others. Nevertheless, it is clear from his premises that for Durkheim the nation is natural only in the sense that it is a social fact determined by preceding social facts.[37] This at least provides the space for a theory of the nation. However, he does not take it any further.[38] Durkheim remains, along with many contemporary writers in other fields and from other places including the heretic English economist John Hobson (1858–1940)[39] or the novelist D.H. Lawrence (1885–1930), a cosmopolitan supporter of the national ideal, critical of his own nation. We can cite again Meinecke's paradoxical comment made in 1907 that the nation drank of the blood of free personalities.

While we are still to place the nation in Durkheim's overall theory of societal forms, at this stage we have sufficient detail to respond to the question as to why Durkheim treats the nation as the repository of the highest ideals, how, given his extolling of the ideals of a generalized humanitarianism, he can justify the more particularizing cultivation of national character. Two points can be made. By his own logic, the fact of humanitarianism must derive from already-given social facts. Therefore they must be embodied in an already-existent social grouping. Secondly, in his words, 'in contrast with the nation, mankind as source and object of morality suffers this deficiency: there is no constituted society'.[40] Thus there is one association that pre-eminently promotes moral conduct, namely the abstract nation, that is, 'the nation – but the nation conceived of as a partial embodiment of the idea of

36. Durkheim, *Sociological Method*, (1895), pp. 104–105.

37. Ibid., pp. 110, 124.

38. It is not surprising then that Marion Mitchell's article, 'Emile Durkheim and the Philosophy of Nationalism', 1931, has no discussion of Durkheim's theory of the nation: her analysis is confined to philosophy and ethics.

39. See the introductory section, 'Nationalism and Imperialism', in John A. Hobson's *Imperialism*, (1902) 1968.

40. Durkheim, *Moral Education*, (1902–3) 1973, p. 76. In the following passage (pp. 77–79) he goes on to show how the ideals of the abstraction, 'humanity', and of the existing society organized as a nation-state can coalesce. In narrow political terms at least, his argument runs in complete opposition to Weber's assertion that what is important for national posterity is 'the amount of elbow-room we conquer for [our nation] and leave behind us' (Inaugural Lecture, (1895) 1980, p. 438).

humanity'.[41] According to Durkheim, through the fact of its increasingly extended form and by what today would be called multiculturalism, the nation 'becomes more abstract, and more general and consequently closer to the human ideal'.[42] Elsewhere he says: 'We must see in the fatherland *in abstracto* the normal and indispensable milieu of human life.'[43]

However, Durkheim runs into problems of consistency here for he is either treating the abstract as materially constituted in the extension of social relations – thus counteracting his tendency to relegate the process of abstraction to the realm of ideas[44] – or, alternatively, he is treating the abstract as unconstituted, thus running counter to his basic premise that even the most abstract laws of morality 'express the nature of concrete reality' founded in actually existing collective practices.[45] Durkheim criticizes Rousseau for a kindred problem:

> Rousseau sees only two poles of human reality, the abstract, general individual who is the agent and objective of social existence, and the concrete empirical individual who is the antagonist of all collective existence. He fails to see that, though in a sense these two poles are irreconcilable, the first without the second is no more than a logical fiction.[46]

Durkheim has a much more acute awareness than Rousseau of the problems to be faced, but this does not resolve his dilemma. I want to expand upon these points, but first let me bring Weber back into contention. Earlier I said that Weber too has a dispassionate argument for supporting the primacy of national interest. However, unlike in Durkheim's approach, the links in Weber's reasoning do not connect as a single chain.

One way into the problem is to note that Weber brackets off the study of

41. Durkheim, *Moral Education*, (1902–3) 1973, p. 80.

42. Ibid., p. 81.

43. Cited by Lewis Coser, 'Durkheim's Conservatism and its Implications for Sociological Theory', 1964, p. 222. Durkheim's general argument for the abstract nation is expanded upon in *Professional Ethics and Civil Morals*, (1890–1900) 1957, ch. 6 and *passim*. Cf. Ferdinand Tönnies, *Community and Society*, (1887) 1963, p. 71 on *Gesellschaft* as 'abstract reason'.

44. For example, see Durkheim and Dennis, *Who Wanted War?*, 1915: German conceptions of national superiority 'sometimes bordering on delirium, did not arise spontaneously, none knowing how or where; they are but expressions of a vital fact. This has justified us in saying that, in spite of its *abstract appearance*, the idea of the State on which Treitschke's doctrine is based masks a concrete and living sentiment; its soul is a certain attitude of will' (p. 44, emphasis added). Durkheim would in substance agree with Vladimir Solovyof (1853–1900) when in 1897 Solovyof wrote: 'At the stage of development now reached by humanity the fact of belonging to a given nationality is to a certain extent confirmed by the individual's self-conscious will. Thus nationality is an inner, inseparable property of the person – is something very dear and close to him. It is impossible to stand in a moral relation to this person without recognizing the existence of what is so important to him. The moral principle does not allow us to transform a concrete person, a living man with his inseparable and essential national characteristics, into an empty abstract subject with all his determining peculiarities left out.' See Solovyof, *The Justification of the Good*, (1897) 1918, p. 297 and ch. 5 *passim*. Also cited in Eugene Kamenka, 'Political Nationalism – The Evolution of the Idea', 1973, p. 9.

45. Durkheim, *Moral Education*, (1902–3) 1973, pp. 111–114, cited from p. 113.

46. Durkheim, *Montesquieu and Rousseau*, (1892) 1965, p. 131.

collective associations and relations. He often writes of collective processes and structures (used in the sense of institutions of agency extension), but his methodological standpoint is the antithesis of Durkheim's. Weber begins with an ahistorical category, the action of '*individual* persons' (his emphasis). When he refers to a state or a nation, or any other social form, he means 'nothing more than a specifically structured outcome of the social actions of individuals either actually performed or constructed as possible'.[47] In other words, collective processes or associations such as the nation-state cannot be treated as sociological facts. They reside in the 'hypothetical and fragmentary' realm of normative representations. They exist as abstractions, real by virtue of being thought to be real. Thus acted upon, they are able to be pieced together by interpretative sociology from an understanding of the motives and actions of 'individual functionaries and members of [the] community' in question.[48] Hence a particular nation can be concretely analysed by a historian, while the form of the nation must be treated as an abstract ideal-type. This has two consequences. The first is methodological: 'The very first step towards a historical judgement is thus . . . ,' Weber says, 'a process of abstraction.'[49] The sociologist 'abstracts himself [or herself] from reality and advances our knowledge of it by elucidating the degree of *approximation* to which a particular historical phenomenon can be classified in terms of one or more of these ["very abstract"] concepts', or ideal types.[50] This confines the process of abstraction to the realm of ideas. The second consequence (extending upon the critique of ideal-type theorizing in Chapter 2) is that collective associations or communal relations are left with only a virtual existence. This has more limiting implications for his study of the nation than it does for his study of the state. If Weber had extended upon his sketchy notes on the 'idea of the nation' his direction would have been thoroughly constrained by treating the nation as a (virtual) object in the sphere of values:

> If the concept of 'nation' can in any way be defined unambiguously, it certainly cannot be stated in terms of empirical qualities common to those who count as members of the nation. In the sense of those using the term at a given time, the concept undoubtedly means above all, that one may exact from certain groups of men a specific sentiment of solidarity in the face of other groups. Thus the concept belongs in the sphere of values.[51]

---

47. Max Weber, 'The Nature of Social Action' in *Weber: Selections*, (1895–1920) 1978, p. 17.

48. Ibid., pp. 16ff. It should be made clear that for Weber, given his definition of an 'association' as a social relationship with exclusionary rules and which 'to "exist" depends entirely on the presence of a head' (p. 33), a nation-state is an association (*Vergesellschaftung*) while the nation is not. The latter, to the extent that it is self-conscious comes under the heading of 'communal relationship' (*Vergemeinschaftung*), based on the 'subjective feeling of the parties'. These are more active versions of Tönnies' *Gesellschaft* and *Gemeinschaft*. See Weber, *Social and Economic Organization*, (1910–20) 1945, pp. 136–139.

49. Weber in *Weber: Selections*, (1895–1920) 1978, p. 118; also pp. 23, 117–119, 128, 130.

50. Ibid., p. 23; also pp. 117–119, 128, 130.

51. Weber, *Essays in Sociology*, 1968, p. 172.

Of course, Weber (following Renan) is right that the nation cannot be defined in terms of empirical qualities, but his subsequent move reduces the nation (a complex objective–subjective relation) to the held-in-common '*subjective* feeling' of individual actors.[52] Coterminous with this methodological–individualist bracketing off of the status of interpretative theorizing is a parallel separation of the status of value judgements. Although Weber agreed with the calls for commitment to the glory of the nation such as espoused by a predecessor at Freiburg, the ex-liberal, anti-semitic historian, Heinrich von Treitschke (1834–96),[53] he was critical of Treitschke as one of the charismatic prophets who confused fact and value. Herein lies a complicated qualification of the statement that Weber has a dispassionate argument for the priority of national interest.

At the centre of his methodology are two overlapping distinctions: one between verifiable fact or logically deduced proposition and interpretative or practical judgements, and the other between the science of culture and the practice of politics. Although not always consistently invoked, they make it possible for him to enunciate the view that the social sciences cannot deduce ultimate values from its findings and, at the same time, to argue (practically) for the nation-state as the ultimate 'power value'.[54] That is, for Weber, it is logically possible within the realm of practical judgements and the practice of politics to argue for the value of the nation-state while separating this issue from the question of how one interprets the constitutive moments of national community or state association. It leads, in summary, to Weber having a logically deduced and dispassionate argument for his conclusion that (his) commitment to the national interest ultimately cannot be reached by verifiable, deductive argument.[55] He says:

> We know of no scientifically demonstrable ideals. To be sure, our labours are now rendered more difficult, since we must create our ideals from within our chests in the very *age of subjectivist culture* . . . it is the stigma of our human dignity that the peace of our souls cannot be as great as the peace of one who dreams of ['a fool's'] paradise.[56] (emphasis added)

This passage also leads us into the familiar theme of upheaval and dissolution (Chapter 3). The contradiction between the rational, self-conscious invention of meaning, creating 'ideals from within our chests' as Weber expresses it, and the attendant loss of traditional meaning in the 'subjectivist culture' was a common theme permeating the writing of avant-garde, turn-of-the-century intellectuals. It can be found in its various manifestations

---

52. (Emphasis added.) This is not to say that he ignores material relations, but rather that they are separated off as factors.

53. See Louis Snyder, *German Nationalism*, (1952) 1969, ch. 6. See also Durkheim and Dennis, *Who Wanted War?*, 1915, for an extensive critique of Treitschke's writings.

54. Weber, 'Value-judgements in Social Science', 1913, in *Weber: Selections*, (1895–1920) 1978, pp. 69–98.

55 See Turner and Factor, *Dispute over Reason*, 1984, pp. 55ff.

56. Weber's 'Viennese declaration' cited in Lawrence Scaff, 'Fleeing the Iron Cage', 1987, p. 738.

in writers from Friedrich Nietzsche (1844–1900) and Henri Bergson (1859–1941) to Thomas Mann (1875–1955) and Lev Nikolayevich Tolstoy (1828–1910).[57] It was, in effect, paralleled by the partial breakdown of the old certainties of positivistic science, evidenced by the work of Albert Einstein (1879–1955) and Max Planck (1858–1947). Although the grand synthesizing projects of science continued on, such as Mendeleyev's periodic table (discussed in the previous chapter) or Bertrand Russell's (1872–1970) and Alfred Whitehead's (1861–1947) *Principia Mathematica*, they tended to become more abstract. Just as the critical positivist Ernst Mach (1838–1916) argued that scientific laws and concepts were perverted by being held up as absolutes,[58] Weber too asserted that any doctrine of ultimate values would founder in contradiction.[59] Thus, for Weber, the only other choice was the affirmation of existing culture, or as Durkheim put it, society as constituted. In words with which Durkheim would agree unqualifiedly, Weber says that the choice entails a preparedness to struggle with its '"antinomies" or "tensions" in order to achieve clarity about the world as it "is"'.[60] The existing arena that Weber thought best served this self-acknowledged, bourgeois struggle against the iron cage of rationalization is a cultural–political arena (an arena itself brought into being by the processes of rationalization) founded upon the conjunction of nation and state.[61]

In short, though using an opposing methodology, Weber is all the time looking through a common cultural–intellectual prism with Durkheim. And from all the refracted possibilities, they both conclude by focusing on the same source of political salvation – national unity.

Where does the 'nation' reside in Durkheim's and Weber's theories of social forms?

Both of these classical theorists posit a basic distinction between traditional and modern societies. This background is important to the discussion in Chapter 6 of the work of Ernest Gellner, a theorist who was influenced by Durkheim and Weber. Durkheim distinguishes between mechanical and organic forms of solidarity, suggesting that with the division of labour and concomitant individuation of social relations, societies formed by mechanical repetition of aggregates inevitably gave way to societies organically coordinated as functionally and morally interdependent bodies (to use his metaphor

57. See William Barrett, *Irrational Man*, 1962.
58. See Michael Biddiss, *The Age of the Masses*, 1978, ch. 2.
59. It is a double contradiction given that such doctrines proclaim consistency. For an exposition of this step, see Weber, 'Politics as Vocation', 1919, in *Weber: Selections*, (1895–1920) 1978.
60. Scaff, 'Fleeing the Iron Cage', 1987, p. 745.
61. This contains a further tension. Neither Weber nor Durkheim loved their native Germany or France as it presently existed.

of society as a living organism).[62] Weber's ideal-type methodology distinguishes three relationships of political organization: traditional, charismatic (always a transitional phase) and rational–legal (the modern side of the Great Divide). Like Durkheim, Weber emphasizes the centrality of the division of labour in the transition from tradition, but he formulates the basis of modern solidarity as much in terms of the process of rationalism, the bureaucratization of the state and the centrality of trained specialists obeying rationally formulated rules and principles, as in terms of a new, individual, moral ethic.[63] Where does the nation fit into these theoretical–historical schemes?

Although in Durkheim's case there is not enough direct discussion of the formation of the nation to allow more than inferences to be drawn, the evidence again tends to point to the ambiguity of his position. The nation is most often projected as an organic society, an association of people tending towards or having their own state. Yet it is implicitly an organic society with a moral homogeneity and an intensity of conscience collective more akin to that generated within traditional (mechanical) society. This carries through into his more straightforward historical description. On the one hand, Durkheim writes of a transformation wrought in Europe during the Renaissance from a generalized religious unity (there is no suggestion of any metaphor of coexistent or intersecting forms in this segment of argument) to a situation where 'each of the groups which had been formed had its own special mode of thought and feeling, its own national temperament':

> By the sixteenth century the great nation states of Europe had been in large measure established. Whereas in the Middle Ages there had been but one Europe, one Christendom which was united and homogenous, there now existed great individual collectivities with their own intellectual and moral characters.[64]

On the other hand, the concepts of nation and nationality are also occasionally used in reference to quite different cultural associations, crossing history from the Hellenic city-states[65] and the 'barbaric nations' which 'could rightly be called monarchies',[66] to the clan 'nations of hunters and fishers'.[67]

The nation is left in a position of comparable ambiguity in Weber's writings

---

62. See Emile Durkheim, *The Division of Labour in Society*, (1893) trans. 1933. This representation of Durkheim's theory is of course overly simplifying, for by the end of *The Division of Labour* he came to see that the institutional stability of organic association depended upon certain continuities of the earlier manifestations of the *conscience collective*.

63. The implicit comparative reference here is to how Weber differs from Durkheim's overriding concern to show that organic solidarity is still a moral order even as the division of labour produces a decline in the relevance of the traditional 'conscience collective'. Rather than attempt to theorize the necessity of a moral basis to societal integration, Weber's *The Protestant Ethic and the Spirit of Capitalism*, (1904–5, trans. 1930) 1958, was a study of the rationalization of religion in connection with the way 'new men' such as Benjamin Franklin were imbued with the capitalist 'ethic'.

64. Emile Durkheim, *The Evolution of Educational Thought*, (1904–5) 1977, p. 171.

65. Durkheim, *Socialism and Saint-Simon*, (1896) 1959, pp. 173, 175.

66. Durkheim, *Montesquieu and Rousseau*, (1892) 1965, p. 9 and pp. 25, 26.

67. Durkheim, *Forms of Religious Life*, (1912) 1976, pp. 233, 415.

on social form, the difference being as already mentioned that Weber writes directly of the 'entirely ambiguous' nature of the concept of the nation. The only hints we get of a pointed theory of national formation are found in Weber's comparative studies of East and West:

> The peculiar character of the Asian intellectual strata essentially prevented the emergence of 'national' political formations, even of the kind which have developed in the West from the later Middle Ages onward – although even in our case, the full conception of the idea of the nation was first elaborated by the modern Western intellectual strata.[68]

The peculiar character of the Asian intellectual strata was not based on their different relation to the process of rationality: intellectuals of both East and West tended toward the rational side of the traditional (charismatic) rational divide. It resided in the manifest separation of Asian intellectuals as a stratum from the mass of the population: 'Only in Japan did the development of feudalism bring with it some hints of a genuinely "national" consciousness, though this was mainly on the basis of the knightly class's sense of status.'[69] Weber's use here of the centrality of status-orientation takes us directly back into the realm of values and ideas. Elsewhere, Weber makes the very interesting point that intellectuals are 'to a specific degree predestined to propagate the "nation ideal"';[70] however, the depth of this proposition is limited by his emphasis on power relations. This issue will come up in different ways in later chapters on Ernest Gellner and Anthony Giddens. The reason for this 'predestination' of the intellectual is reduced to the fact that the power and prestige interests of intellectuals, amongst others, are bound up with the preservation of cultural values and the cultivation of the specificity of cultural association: 'Under the influence of these circles, the naked prestige of "power" is unavoidably transformed into other special forms of prestige and especially into the idea of the "nation".'[71] Intellectual work as a materially abstract practice, and the nation as a form of abstract social relations are thus left to one side.

Social form in the 'age of subjectivist culture'

The determinations and limiting conditions upon the fact that Durkheim and Weber do not develop more than *en passant* theories of the nation, and that by contrast they do have somewhat more to say about the nation-*state*, are multifarious and many-layered. So far the chapter has focused upon the constraints suggested by particular approaches to method and to value orientation. There are, of course, other ways of approaching the question. For example, Lewis Coser in elaborating Kenneth Burke's aphorism that 'a way of

68. Weber, in *Weber: Selections*, (1895–1920) 1978, p. 203.
69. Ibid.
70. Weber, in *From Max Weber* (essays from 1904–20), 1968, p. 176.
71. Ibid., p. 172.

seeing is always a way of not seeing', chooses to centre upon Durkheim's conservatism. Coser's emphasis is a quite defensible way of taking up a particular aspect of content. However, I would like to embed analysis of content in questions of form. In a couple of provocative but undeveloped paragraphs Coser provides us with a suggestive way of doing just that, confirming a theme which has been running through the present chapter:

> What has perhaps not been sufficiently discussed is the curiously abstract character of [Durkheim's] patriotism and his religion of society. Here it would seem appropriate to introduce a consideration of Durkheim's background.
>
> It is customary to find evidence in most patriotic writings of an attachment to particular localities or regions, to particular historical or linguistic traditions. Not so with Durkheim [or Weber]. We encounter in his writings a highly rational, non-emotional attachment to *la patrie*. This intellectualized and abstract relation to his country may well have had its source in his social origin. When this son of a rabbi from the eastern fringes of France came to Paris to develop into one of the guiding spirits of the Third Republic, he did not feel bound to any one subgroup, class, stratum, or region. His loyalty went to France, which became for him the prototype of *the* society. His attachment was not mediated through tradition and history, but was, so to speak, abstractly intellectual.[72]

Coser makes an important point even if, in an overall sense, he over-accentuates the unmediated, single-level dominance of abstract intellectuality. His position does not evidence a notion of the contradictory subjectivity of intellectuals. In terms of the metaphor of levels-in-intersection, intellectuals have a 'double' ontology: however abstracted across time and space they may be in the practice of their work, they remain constrained simultaneously as mortal, embodied subjects. They experience the cultural contradictions which arise out of being, at one level, intellectuals *qua* intellectuals conversing via the medium of print across space and time, while at another level being bound, as Durkheim would acknowledge, by the fact of being born into specific relations of blood, in a particular locale, at a particular time. It is indicative that both Weber and Durkheim allowed the passions of war to overcome partially the intellectual face of their abstract detachment. So while Coser isolates a salient, even dominant, level of their being, given that intellectual pursuits dominated their lives, it is a level beset by cultural contradictions. Weber, for example, followed in the intellectual cavalcade from Dante and Petrarch to Montesquieu and de Tocqueville (mentioned in the previous chapter) for whom travel was a significant aspect of this lifting out. Weber's mental breakdown, attributable to attempting to resolve a manifold of contradictions,[73] was followed by years of almost continual

72. Coser, 'Durkheim's Conservatism', 1964, p. 223. As Benedict Anderson points out (personal communication), Coser misses the importance of Durkheim's Jewishness: 'All over Europe Jews looked to the state to protect them from "society".'

73. Edward B. Portis (*Max Weber and Political Commitment*, 1986) picks up on the antinomy of overt political action and the social scientist's objectivity, but he is unconvincing in making it the central motif of Weber's life. Arthur Mitzman's attempt in *The Iron Cage* (1969) to make Weber's resolutions of oedipal conflict the key to understanding is equally one-dimensional.

European travelling. Later the war became Weber's 'great trip, serving the same therapeutic functions as his earlier travels. Although well aware of its horrors, having lost a brother, a brother-in-law and several friends, he nevertheless on a number of occasions referred to the war as "great and wonderful".'[74]

Weber's words are those of someone who, at least at one level of their being, stands in a highly abstract relation to death and 'the shell-pocked leagues of shit'[75] that were given the heroic names of Verdun, Somme and Passchendaele. He faces a similar contradiction to Ulrich, the central character in Robert Musil's novel *The Man Without Qualities*. Musil claims that the 'Man Without Qualities' has less probability of experiencing the remarkable things of life than reading of them in the newspaper: 'In other words [says Musil's narrator], it is in the realm of the abstract that the more important things happen in these times, and it is the unimportant that happens in real life.'[76]

The sad irony is that to the extent Weber abstractly glorifies war he does so as an attempt to reclaim what abstract reflection and self-conscious historicity tend to dismantle. In this Weber was not so different from the ethnocentric nationalist Maurice Barrès. According to Philip Ouston, Barrès was critical of the tendency for political visionaries, 'by hypertrophy of one of its constituents, abstraction, at the expense of the other, sensation, to lose contact altogether with the world of concrete and particular facts'. The hero of Barrès's *Un Homme Libre* finds 'that his unbridled imagination has carried him into a finally uninhabitable void of pure subjectivity'. Nevertheless Barrès wants to find a way to move through 'Le passage du local à l'universel'.[77] Wassily Kandinsky (1866–1944), the first painter to create non-representational 'abstract art', similarly described the dilemma of pursuing the abstract to find the really real. He distinguished two processes in modernism:

> 1. Disintegration of the soulless, materialistic life of the nineteenth century, i.e. the collapse of the material supports that were considered the only solid ones and the decay and dissolution of the various parts.
> 2. Construction of the spiritual and intellectual life of the twentieth century that we experience and that is already manifested and embodied in strong, expressive, and distinct forms.[78]

These are examples of what was discussed at the end of Chapter 2 under the rubric of the recalling of the concrete. They are attempts to reclaim the more concrete sense-of-being, in Weber's case framed by a 'community unto

74. Portis, *Political Commitment*, p. 146. On the importance of travel see also pp. 49–50, 90, 92.

75. Thomas Pynchon cited by Paul Fussell, *The Great War and Modern Memory*, 1977, p. 330.

76. Robert Musil (1880–1942), *The Man Without Qualities*, vol. 1, (1930) 1983, p. 76. Written in the early 1920s, the novel was set in 1914 as the story of the patriotic campaign to celebrate the idea of a Universal Austria.

77. Philip Ouston, *The Imagination of Barrès*, 1974, quotes from pp. 9–10, 65ff.

78. Kandinsky, cited in Steven Holtzman, *Digital Mantras: The Languages of Abstract and Virtual Worlds*, 1994, p. 70.

death'. They are attempts to reassert in the new age the spirit – though not the structural form nor social content – which pervaded the period when God was still in His Heaven and, as Tolstoy put it, meaningful death provided the basis for meaningful life.[79] This continues to be an important political project even if it is one perverted by fundamentalism, parochialism, sectarianism and racism. Unfortunately Weber has no way of theorizing how the 'abstract' can reclaim the 'concrete', no way of demarcating his position from the direction taken by the post-war theorists of fascism. He says: 'War does something to the warrior which in its concrete meaning is unique: it makes him experience a consecrated meaning of death which is characteristic only of death in war . . . [creating] a community unto death, and the greatest of its kind.'[80]

Notwithstanding the irony that Weber wrote about phenomena of such existential power while absenting himself into the realms of abstract intellectuality, by so arguing for the possibility of social life grounded in more concrete levels of association he opens for himself the possibility of a theory of ontology which is neither primordialist nor set on one plane. Like Durkheim, however, Weber fails to take this very far. Both their methodologies of social factuality and methodological individualism did not do much more than the historians of their time in describing the 'what is-ness' of the nation and nation-state.

If the period through which Karl Marx lived gave rise, for some, to the realization that all that is solid melts into air, the late nineteenth, early twentieth century underscored this sense of flux. It marked the beginning of a period when the avant-garde intellectual, whether social theorist, artist or scientist, was confronted with the necessity of at least considering that he or she had lost the ground that Marx had stood upon when so confidently analysing 'the reality' behind the chimeras and veils. In the words of Durkheim's anti-republican, nationalist contemporary Maurice Barrès, a generation of Europeans had lived through the transition 'from the absolute to the relative'.[81] 'Our thinking has no even, solid, safe basis', says one of Robert Musil's characters, 'but goes along, as it were, over holes in the ground – shutting its eyes, ceasing to exist for a moment, and yet arriving safely at the other side.'[82] Durkheim and Weber dealt with this in quite different ways. But they both, as much as the host of other *fin-de-siècle* social theorists, felt the collective melancholy that they considered to be a consequence of the disintegration and fragmentation (Durkheim) or de-personalized rationalization (Weber) of

---

79. See Weber, 'Science as a Vocation', 1918, and 'Religious Rejections of the World', 1915, in *From Max Weber* (essays from 1904–1920), 1968.

80. Ibid., p. 335.

81. Barrès, *Les Deracinés* (*The Uprooted*) published in 1897, cited in Tiryakian, 'Emile Durkheim', 1970, p. 209.

82. Robert Musil, *The Confusions of Young Törless*, (1906) 1955, p. 177.

the social bond.[83] In all of this the nation held an ambiguous place. By not having a way of directly confronting this ambiguity, Weber and Durkheim further precluded the possibility of their adequately theorizing the pre-eminent abstract community of the twentieth century and its contradictory hold upon people.

Such a theory became all the more vital as, in the mid-twentieth century, the subjectivities and institutions of the nation and nation-state consolidated around the fragmenting networks of cultural life, while, under the banner of the community unto death, the nations of the world embarked upon new wars in the context of an ever-more dangerous, rationalized, militarized 'peace'. It is to the contribution of contemporary theory that the next three chapters now turn.

---

83. Durkheim was able to document this 'melancholy' of disintegration, as he called it, in his study of suicide, but we should keep in mind the distinction between the uneven pessimism of a substantial proportion of the avant-garde and the responses of those for whom the promise of progress and the breakdown of the old system were experienced either as release and liberation, or as part of the 'civilizing process'.

PART THREE:
CONTEMPORARY THEORY

5

Nation Formation and the Janus Faces of History: A Critique of Marxism

Because it was the first, the English – later British – experience remained distinct. Because they came second, into a world where the English Revolution had already succeeded and expanded, later bourgeois societies could not repeat this early development. Their study and imitation engendered something substantially different: the truly modern doctrine of the abstract or 'impersonal' state which, because of its abstract nature, could be imitated in subsequent history.

Tom Nairn, *The Break-up of Britain*, 1981

Within both mainstream and marxist traditions of theorizing the nation there continues to be a tendency to fracture history into contradictory faces: the primordial past and the culturally invented modern period. One of the central themes of this book has been to question the terms of the primordialist–modernist split. The present chapter brings this theme to the fore, examining the way in which, even within the work of quite sophisticated theorists, the nation is pictured from mutually exclusive perspectives. Just as the old Roman god Janus had two faces, the writings of many contemporary theorists are composed of opposing views of how history is lived and reproduced: one face assumes the primordiality of its grounding forms; the other accentuates the historicity of history and emphasizes its self-conscious invented quality. Related expressions of the cleavage occur in positing distinctions between the real or given and the artificial; or between the natural and the constructed. These are representational splits with fundamental implications for historical method and for political practice.

Some social theorists and historians have tried to go beyond either simply accentuating one or other view, or implicitly accepting the terms of the cleaving. But with regards to the national question there has been not only little success but also little awareness that it is indeed a problem.

The mainstream tradition has been divided between, on the one hand, those theorists who have been labelled as primordialists, including Edward Shils and Clifford Geertz,[1] and on the other hand, a number of writers such as Ernest Gellner who stress the invented nature of national formations.[2] This second grouping was perhaps initiated with the ambiguous writings of Lord Acton, a historian discussed earlier in the context of the period in which Marx wrote. Acton's claim that the nation became artificial with the development of a self-conscious argument for the conjunction of nation and state was an anomaly in its time,[3] but the cultural inventionist position (not necessarily expressed in the way that Acton does) has gained increasing credibility for twentieth-century writers. It has certainly gained prominence since Elie Kedourie first opened his book with the now often-quoted sentence, 'Nationalism is a doctrine invented in Europe at the beginning of the nineteenth century',[4] and Kenneth Minogue concluded his with the words: 'Nationalism . . . began by describing itself as the political and historical consciousness of the nation, and came in time to the inventing of nations for which it could act.'[5]

The marxist tradition has handled the Janus faces differently. It harbours no primordialists as such. Nevertheless, the cleaving still occurs, much as it still does in those lines of liberal theory which attempt to bypass the problem. It occurs either by a particular theorist implicitly becoming divided against him or herself, as I will argue is the case with Tom Nairn, or by the setting up of an explicit and problematic distinction between the real and the artificial or invented. For example, it is possible to find unabashed Janus-faced comments in the work of someone such as Raymond Williams. Usually a methodologically careful theorist, he writes: 'All the *real* processes have been cultural and historical, and all the *artificial* processes have been political, in one after another dominative proclamation of a state and an identity'[6] (emphasis added). One of the key problems, as many marxists will readily acknowledge, is that marxism, like mainstream theory, has still to develop an adequate working approach to that cluster of phenomena – nationality, nation, nation-state and nationalism – which can synthetically escape the limitations of the present tendency towards disconnected, regionally focused, separately periodized or single-level studies.

The nation is an abstract community of strangers who cannot hope to have a face-to-face relation with each of their compatriots. And yet, as has

---

1. See for example Edward Shils, 'Primordial, Personal, Sacred and Civil Ties', 1957, pp. 130–145; Clifford Geertz, *The Interpretation of Cultures*, 1973, chs 9 and 10; Harold R. Isaacs, 'Nationality: "End of the Road"?' 1975; Richard Lynn, 'The Sociobiology of Nationalism', 1976, pp. 11–14. Clifford Geertz is more ambiguous than the conventional labelling suggests, and might also be considered a Janus-faced theorist.

2. Ernest Gellner, *Nations and Nationalism*, 1983, pp. 40, 47, 48, 56, 65.

3. See above Chapter 3; also Acton's *Essays on Freedom and Power*, (1862) 1948.

4. Elie Kedourie, *Nationalism*, (1960) 1993, p. 9.

5. Kenneth Minogue, *Nationalism*, 1967, p. 154, also p. 33.

6. Raymond Williams, *Towards 2000*, 1985, p. 194.

been discussed at length above, it is embedded in the very historical forms from which it is already abstracted. The nation is structured through quite material processes and yet by definition it exists, like a class-for-itself, by virtue of its own sense of historicity. With those particular quandaries throw in other issues such as the historically partial conjunction of the nation with the institutional level embodied in the state, and existing theories are faced with a practical and definitional imbroglio. For the most part, contemporary marxists have handled the national question by separating the theorizing of nation and national identity from nation-state and nationalism. This is an eminently defensible move except that it masks the lack of a theory of their inter-relation. Through the eyes of the first face of Janus, nationality is seen as a given, certainly an historically constituted given, but one assumed rather than attended to with more than passing attention. Through the eyes of the second, now-dominant face, the nation-state is most often viewed as an ideological–institutional arrangement serving the national market; and nationalism is considered to be a superstructural ideology, drawing upon invented or factitious traditions. Notwithstanding the generality of these premises, in the last couple of decades, debates over the theory and politics of the nation question have been raging, strong and unresolved. This chapter begins with a contextualizing review of those debates.

New nationalisms and the New Left

Through the late 1960s into the 1970s the orthodox marxist approach to the nation question was beginning to be challenged.[7] Orthodoxy was confronted directly and practically with explaining an 'inexplicable' second wave of nationalist movements. It was a wave that had at least two places of origin: post-colonial and Western. In the Third World it arose out of the struggles and transformations that marked the end of formal empire;[8] and from *within* the long-established nation-states of Europe and North America it issued

---

7. 'Orthodoxy' is here used very broadly to include both 'classical marxism' (usually specified as the position initiated by Marx and re-worked by Lenin), and 'vulgar marxism' (the reductionist hardening of classical marxism into a positivistic or scientific doctrine, associated with the writings of the Second and Third International). 'Neo-orthodoxy' is used to encompass those contemporary theorists who, in the words of Tom Nairn (*The Break-up of Britain: Crisis and Neo-Nationalism*, 1981, p. 330), believe that if we 'lend a retrospective helping hand' an adequate theory will surely emerge from 'between the lines of the classics'. There are not many blithely unreconstructed Marxist-Leninists still writing on the nation question: one example is M. Kulichenko, *Nations and Social Progress*, 1984.

8. The literature on this first area is more extensive and goes back further. The seminal early contribution is Peter Worsley's *The Third World*, (1964) 1978. From the mainstream see John Kautsky, ed., *Political Change in Underdeveloped Countries*, 1967. The revival of left interest in the nation question was marked by the 1962 *Past and Present* conference. See Alan Adamson's notes, 'Colonialism and Nationalism in Africa and Europe', 1963.

forth from partly forgotten, but apparently 'primordial', ethnic fissures.[9] The recent explosion of neo-nationalism in Eastern Europe, exacerbated by the break-up of the Soviet bloc, had not yet burst upon the scene, but there were enough examples in Western Europe alone to warrant considerable rethinking.

We can also point to a third source of nationalism. Though in retrospect it is now starting to appear obvious, a new kind of nationalism was emerging out of the globalizing pressures of late modernity which was then overlooked by marxist and liberal alike. Evidenced partly in the celebrations of bicentenaries in the USA, Australia and France,[10] the new nationalism did not fit in with any familiar analyses including the new theoretical language associated with understanding social movements. In the heartlands of the highly urbanized, Westernized nation-states, there stirred a general and 'renewing' sense of national awareness. Without generating any social movements as such, it involved the sharpening of a sensibility dulled in the cosmopolitan optimism and 'mobile privatization' of the post-war boom.[11] People sought to reconnect with older established forms and sensibilities, including a sense of national engagement, but they did so from a standpoint that was no longer comfortable with the classical modern form of nationalism. The national past was more likely to be treated as a pastiche to be selectively criticized and lauded than as a binding essential history. National culture was more likely to be understood (in postmodern terms) as an heterogeneous patchwork of fragments than as a homogeneous seamless whole.

Orthodox theory was met by a closely associated theoretical challenge. It centred on the problem of understanding the 'realm of the cultural'. This will be discussed more generally in the next chapter, but specifically in relation to marxism, economistic and reflectionist theories of the base–superstructure kind began to look as if they might be built upon corroding scaffolding. Ironically this occurred just as commentators across the political spectrum reopened the question of the force of the economic by pointing to a transformation in the mode of production from monopoly to late capitalism, or (in the language of Daniel Bell and others) from industrialism to technetronic post-industrialism. Machinofacture was acknowledged to have lost its competitive edge to robotic, computerized and information-dominated

9. The literature on this second area, though recent, is growing all the time. For example the *Canadian Review of Studies in Nationalism* was a early leader in publishing articles including: John Agnew, 'Political Regionalism and Scottish Nationalism in Gaelic Scotland', 1981; Joseph Rudolph, 'Ethnoregionalism in Contemporary Western Europe', 1981; and Phillip Rawkins, 'Nationalist Movements Within the Advanced Industrial State', 1983.

10. See John Hutchinson, *Modern Nationalisms*, 1994, ch. 6 'Pioneers of Post-Nationalism or Insecure Parvenus?'

11. The phrase 'mobile privatization' is Raymond Williams'. His work provides a telling illustration of the turnaround in marxist sensitivity toward the nation question: *Towards 2000* (1985), his reflections on the 1980s and beyond, includes a chapter on 'The Culture of Nations', whereas his creed for the 1960s, *The Long Revolution* (1961), does not once raise the nation as an explicit issue.

production. Seen narrowly and only in these terms some marxists remained convinced that there was still reason, albeit with a modicum of sprucing up, to retain the base–superstructure framework essentially unchanged. For others the challenge went deeper. The issues raised by feminism, the counter-culture, May '68 and the student movement, by the critiques of a one-dimensional culture, and by events such as the invasions of Czechoslovakia and Vietnam, required more than reasserting a new orthodoxy.

The debate between the structuralists and the cultural materialists – including the various lines of demarcation between Louis Althusser, Nicos Poulantzas, Terry Eagleton, Fredric Jameson, Raymond Williams, Edward Thompson and Lucien Goldmann – was a response to this 'rise of the cultural'. While very critical of what became known as vulgar marxism, none of these theorists intended to dismantle completely the old edifice.[12] Nevertheless, the debates shook orthodox marxism to its foundations. The 'crisis in marxism' was still a few years away from formally being announced, but with this debate, the issues around which the crisis would later erupt were coming to the fore.[13] On the one hand, the 'discovery' and translation of Antonio Gramsci's *Quaderni del Carcere*, and on the other, the consolidation of Althusser's structuralism, simply confirmed the new emphasis which marxism, and social theory more generally, was beginning to place on culture, ideology and language.[14] From the same already-present concerns there arose a 'small clamour' for an English translation of the *Grundrisse*: this series of Marx's workbooks had been available in the original German for at least two decades.

Tom Nairn: a partial break with orthodoxy

It was in this context of a change in the social form of nationalism and a theoretical upheaval giving rise to the New Left, that an article entitled 'The Three Dreams of Scottish Nationalism' appeared in *New Left Review* (1968). The article substantially, and by intonation, diverged from some received

---

12. See Richard Johnson, 'Histories of Culture/Theories of Ideology: Notes on an Impasse', 1979.

13. See the chronicling of this in Alex Callinicos, *Is there a Future for Marxism?*, 1982. Here again there was a further sleeping challenge to orthodox marxism. At that time it went substantially, or at least publicly, unacknowledged. Represented by the writings of Michel Foucault, Giles Deleuze and Félix Guattari, Jacques Derrida and others, this challenge was initially bracketed as being of the same order as that coming from Althusser, Claude Lévi-Strauss and the early Roland Barthes. In the 1970s all these French theorists were run together as 'structuralists'. In the 1990s the once callow challenger, post-structuralism, is now the front-runner.

14. Gramsci's phrase the 'national popular' was given a renewed lease of life in the 1980s as a catch-cry around which to politically connect a plurality of social movements and groupings including working-class alliances. See the articles by David Forgacs ('National-Popular: Genealogy of a Concept'); and Iain Chambers and Lidia Curti ('A Volatile Alliance') in *Formations: Of Nation and People*, 1984.

tenets of orthodoxy: it introduced, at least metaphorically, the language of psychoanalysis; it questioned, at least in the case of Scottish history, the nexus between capitalism and protestantism; and while conventional in its critique of the 'garrulous, narcissistic windbaggery' and parochialism of bourgeois nationalism, it posited the only sane alternative as being Socialist Nationalism. Its Scottish author, Tom Nairn, was at the same time part of the editorial committee of *New Left Review*, and supported the journal's expressed intention of opening the national drawbridge and importing Western Marxism from across the English Channel. Gramsci, Sartre, Althusser and Colletti were ordained to give direction to the English marxist tradition. For his part, Nairn translated Giuseppe Fiori's biography of Gramsci for New Left Books.

Few critics could make sense of a marxist who, on the one hand, felt 'inwardly wounded by the anti-Europeanism' of the Left argument against the European Community,[15] and on the other hand continues to be a vehement advocate of the break-up of Britain; who sympathizes with the bourgeois Scottish National Party (SNP), and steadfastly argues that the 'Ulster-Protestant nationality' is not a passing ethnic relic. As Nairn says in his candid, retrospective postscript to *The Break-up of Britain*, his position reflects the 'dilemma of an insecure national identity – common among Scottish intellectuals – that had reacted by over-identification with European cultures . . . hence militant Great-English parochialism was a monster threatening everything' (p. 397). If we are interested in more than a recital of the 'muscular' logic, or otherwise, of his theory then this conditioning is also important to understanding the tensions out of which his approach was developed.

'Three Dreams' was the first of a series of iconoclastic articles, which together now comprises the most frequently debated, contemporary marxist theory of the nation. The responses from the non-marxist mainstream to Nairn's approach have been contradictory. Ernest Gellner believes Nairn's 'concrete theory of nationalism . . . to be substantially correct', but is puzzled as to how Nairn could think his theory was at all compatible with marxism.[16] John Breuilly, to the contrary, says that 'Abstractly it is a plausible and impressive argument. But it does not fit the facts.[17] Whichever is the case, Nairn has become a figure of almost compulsory citation. Anthony Giddens, in his second volume of *A Contemporary Critique of Historical Materialism*, a study specifically aimed at exploring in dialogue with marxism the 'contours

---

15. Nairn, *Break-up of Britain*, 1981, quote from p. 397. All page numbers in the body of the text will henceforth refer to this book. See also his 'British Nationalism and the EEC', 1971; *The Left Against Europe?*, 1973; and *The Enchanted Glass*, 1988.

16. Ernest Gellner, 'Nationalism, or the New Confessions of a Justified Edinburgh Sinner', 1979, p. 270. Similarly Edward Tiryakian with Neil Nevitte calls Nairn's *Break-up of Britain* a 'brilliant analysis of the nationalisms of Britain'. See their 'Nationalism and Modernity', 1985, p. 59.

17. John Breuilly, *Nationalism and the State*, 1982, p. 26.

of a post-Marxist' interpretation of the nation-state, refers *only* to Nairn's work when discussing the contemporary group of approaches written within the framework of historical materialism. Giddens makes a couple of brisk criticisms but then comments that Nairn's is 'The most illuminating account of nationalism produced in recent times by an author affiliated with Marxism.'[18] It is intended as a back-handed compliment.

The very mixed responses to Nairn's approach are in part a consequence of the limitation that despite the voluminous writings which touch on the nation question, none amounts to more than 'the scantiest outline' of a theory.[19] For example, all that Horace Davis achieves in his book, ambitiously entitled *Toward a Marxist Theory of Nationalism*,[20] is to show that marxism needs to come to terms *politically* with minority and ex-colonial national cultures. A second reason for Nairn's notoriety stems from the way in which he bridges orthodoxy and the writings of those who have started to argue for its radical reconstruction. Eric Hobsbawm's critique of Nairn is an instructive instance of the neo-orthodox over-reaction to this. While Hobsbawm ostensibly professes the need for a continual rethinking of received marxist theory – 'above all because the very development of world history changes the context, the nature and the implications of "nations" and "nationalism"' – he flatly concludes that Nairn has made neither a useful nor a convincing contribution to this development.[21] Leaving aside for the moment the question as to whether this is a sustainable criticism, it is made having only discussed Nairn's overall theory in two footnotes.[22] Hobsbawm's concern, however laudable, to defend the practical politics of orthodoxy as hardly requiring serious modification, thus leaves Nairn's theoretical approach largely unexamined.[23]

It is to such an examination that I would now like to turn. After briefly outlining Nairn's theoretical position, the chapter broadens out to assess the general implications of his and other contemporary marxist contributions for the development of a workable theory of the nation.

At the centre of Nairn's theory is the concept of uneven development; the 'shambling, fighting, lop-sided, illogical, head-over-heels fact' of the uneven development of capitalism.[24] This is tied to the premise that an adequate

---

18. Anthony Giddens, *The Nation-State and Violence*, 1985, p. 213. Compare Homi Bhabha's much more sympathetic use of Nairn in 'Anxious Nations, Nervous States', 1994.

19. Nairn, *Break-up of Britain*, 1981, p. 356, in modestly describing his own work.

20. Horace Davis, *Toward a Marxist Theory of Nationalism*, 1978. Peter Worsley did this in a more interesting way over a decade earlier (*The Third World*, 1964).

21. Eric Hobsbawm, 'Some Reflections on "The Break-up of Britain"', 1977, p. 21.

22. Ibid., fn. 12 and 13.

23. Ibid., p. 21. See the similar comment by Pierre Vilar, 'On Nations and Nationalism', 1979, p. 28. Ironically, despite his tone, Nairn is closer in particular but significant ways to the orthodox base–superstructure argument than either Vilar or Hobsbawm. Cf. Eric Hobsbawm 'Some Reflections on Nationalism', 1972.

24. From 'The Modern Janus' first published in *New Left Review* in 1975, reprinted in Nairn, *Break-up of Britain*, 1981, p. 337. On uneven development see also pp. 71–72, 96ff., 104ff., 113, 134, 178, 184ff., 202ff., 220ff, 227, 229, 318ff.

theory of nationalism can only be initiated with world history as its framework of reference. Country-by-country analyses, he says, have already
succumbed to the ideology that human society essentially consists of discrete
nations. For a similar reason, Nairn, like Poulantzas, rejects as mythology the
view that nationalism is internally determined, necessitated by either the
national market-economy and its leading class, as orthodox marxism would
have it, or by the will of the *Volk*, as idealist conceptions including even
Weber's have effectively assumed.[25]

Nairn's theory unfolds as follows: in the beginning, before the conditions of
nineteenth-century uneven development, there were the 'historic'
nation-states of Western Europe: England, France, Spain and Portugal,
Sweden, Holland. The new forces of production and the military powers of
the new form of state swept the world (in Ernest Gellner's phrase) with the
devastating force of a tidal wave. They generated an imperialism of the metropolitan centres of Western Europe over the periphery: first Central and
Eastern Europe, then Latin America, and on to other continents. In the
peripheral regions, the elites were faced with overcoming their ambivalence to
this uneven process. They wanted the means of progress – factories, parlia-
ments, schools – but they quickly found that it was only possible for a
minority to enter the kingdom of 'cosmopolitan technocracy'. Nairn thus
places intellectuals and the intellectually trained in the centre of the picture.
Out of the 'regions of intermediate social change' (Hroch), from the small
towns and rural areas of disrupted but still pre-industrial Europe, came the
new intelligentsia: modern, romantic, mobile, and from the petit-bourgeoisie
(p. 119). Rather than be left behind, the members of this newly awakened
intelligentsia consciously mobilized others against foreign domination in the
formation of a self-aware, cross-class community. They did this using the
particularities of their locale, their 'nationality' (for Nairn in inverted commas), and their inherited *ethnos*. 'The new middle-class intelligentsia of
nationalism', as his now-famous phrase has it, 'had to invite the masses into
history; and the invitation had to be written in a language they understood'
(p. 340). Thus:

> Capitalism, even as it spread remorselessly over the world to unify human society
> into one more or less connected story for the first time, *also* engendered a perilous
> and convulsive new fragmentation of that society. The socio-historical cost of this
> rapid implantation of capitalism into world society was 'nationalism'. There was no
> other conceivable fashion in which the process could have occurred. (p. 341)

---

25. Ibid., pp. 332–333. These folklores of nationalism are, Nairn adds, 'not entirely wrong'.
They are as such an important set of 'clues towards whatever these forms are really about' (p.
334). Poulantzas criticizes the national market explanation as one-sided; as not explaining why
unification occurs at the level of the nation, and as expressing a 'profoundly empiricist and pos-
itivistic conception of all the elements that are supposed to constitute the nation' (*State, Power,
Socialism*, 1980, pp. 96–97). See also Juan Gòmez-Quiñones, 'Critique on the National Question,
Self-Determination and Nationalism', 1982, p. 78. Alternatively, for Weber's position see 'The
Nation' in *From Max Weber* (essays from 1904–20) 1968, pp. 171–179, cf. p. 65.

At this intermission in the argument, Nairn's critics reach for their knives. The proponents of neo-orthodoxy conclude that Nairn has put 'Marxism at the mercy of nationalism' and moved to 'change the ideology and undermine the "science"'.[26] However, they fail to take in Nairn's underlying circumspection that nationalisms do resist, but only to be transformed themselves in the terms of the dominant industrialized countries. They miss the force of his metaphor (used in a different sense than I have been employing it) that nationalism is the modern Janus, with one face looking forward along the passage to modernity but forced to endure violent upheaval, and the other face desperately glancing backwards to the reassuring remnants of past traditions. In Nairn's argument, nationalism is always ethically and politically ambiguous. Ironically, this is the dialectic by which his neo-orthodox critics also work: it calls to mind Marx's double-sided phrase that progress resembles 'that hideous pagan idol, who would not drink the nectar but from the skulls of the slain'.[27]

A further irony is that, like classical and neo-orthodox marxism, Nairn tends to treat the original formation of the 'historic' nation and nation-state as an unproblematic historical given. This is a slightly different point from Benedict Anderson's aside that there is in Nairn the 'good nationalist tendency to treat his "Scotland" as an unproblematic, primordial given'.[28] But together these points suggest that while Nairn has become relatively careful not to repeat Marx's mistake of assuming the always-imminent death of the nation-state in general, he still has not moved to emend the limitations of Marx's approach to the birth of the nation.

Contrary to the accusations of his neo-orthodox critics, Nairn is very critical of national*ism* (that is, as distinct from nationality or nationhood). He is in fact critical to the point that his analysis is overly wrapped up in the metaphoric manner of diagnosing national*ism* as a pathology involving irrationality, sublimation, neurosis, split personality, and cultural schizophrenia.[29] The use of psychologisms is not a major problem in itself;[30] as we shall see, his friendly *bête noire*, Ernest Gellner, similarly engages in what can be overlooked largely as excesses of style effected for literary or political impact.

26. Hobsbawm, 'Reflections on "The Break-up of Britain"', 1977, p. 22. Also J.M. Blaut, 'Nationalism as an Autonomous Force', 1982.

27. Karl Marx, *On Colonialism*, (1850–88) 1976, p. 87.

28. Benedict Anderson, *Imagined Communities*, 1983, p. 85.

29. For example see Nairn, *Break-up of Britain*, 1981, pp. 101, 129, 153, 154–167, 169, 172, 177, 242, 288; and Nairn, *Enchanted Glass*, 1988, pp. 11, 87, 113, 128–129, 175 and so on. Michael Löwy, among others, also slips into the language of nationalism as pathology. See his 'Marxists and the National Question', 1976, p. 99.

30. Although cf. Sami Zubaida, 'Theories of Nationalism', 1978, p. 69. He says, I think overcritically, that Nairn shares with others like Perry Anderson and Immanuel Wallerstein a general historicist teleology: '"Nations" seem to be historical super-subjects with the attributes of agency and action: they "mobilise", "aspire", "propel themselves forward", "react", and they even have atavistic, irrational "ids" seething with traumas which explode periodically.' See also, Ronaldo Munck, *The Difficult Dialogue*, 1986, pp. 145–146.

However, in Nairn's case it is a problem in that by giving the impression of a thorough-going psychoanalytic theory of the subjective it glosses over significant gaps in his argument. In particular we find a lack of attention to the original formation of nations and nationality; a very narrowly conceived discussion of social or ideological integration; evidence of the limitations of the orthodox base–superstructure framework in theorizing the subjective and explaining the centrality of the intelligentsia; and the absence of other than a practical argument for assuming that 'ethically demarcated territorial statehood continues to be inescapable, as the political structure of all foreseeable development' and implicitly of all alternative politics (p. 371). Discussion of these issues will be opened up in the next section by considering the first Janus face that assumes rather than theorizes the primordiality of the grounding forms of human political association. Nairn is not alone in assuming the category of historic nations. We should recall from earlier discussion that Marx and Engels used the word nation to apply to polities, from the Phoenician tribes to the still-to-be-unified land of imperially connected principalities, landgraviates and bishoprics called Germany. This will lead into the issues of essentialism and primordialism. The following section takes up the second face of historiography and the issues of modernity and cultural invention. A further section, 'Past and Present', discusses the importance of a synthesis of the two faces, and the chapter concludes with an interlude on Nairn's use of the concrete–abstract distinction.

The original formation of nationality and nation

The search for Nairn's theory of nationality and nation has to begin between the lines of his discussion of the 'original' nation-states. As was earlier outlined, in the beginning before the conditions of uneven development there were the historic nation-states in Western Europe. To use the language he sometimes prefers, they were State-nations, in which nationality had played a role quite distinct from what it would assume in 'nationalism proper'. What I think he means is that pre-nineteenth century nationality was submerged below the general possibility of being politically divisive or self-consciously held.[31] Nairn says: 'Put at its most simple: they were in fact multi-ethnic assemblages in which, through lengthy processes of conquest and absorption, one or other nationality had established ascendancy (normally in late-feudal times, through the machinery of absolute monarchy)' (p. 178).

While nationality is not here the primary subject of his concern, it is evident that Nairn believes that although dominant polities prior to the nineteenth century were states over and above being nations, at the same time nationality was then already present as a primordial form of social

31. With qualifications this interpretation is borne out by Anthony D. Smith in his *The Ethnic Revival*, 1981, ch. 4. However, Smith's definition of ethnic communities as a social group with a sense of common origins and destiny appears to cut against it. Either way the notion of submerged identity is dubious.

relation.[32] So that, for example, in his words, England was 'a country of ancient and settled nationality' (p. 262) and the United Kingdom 'was the first state-form of an industrialized nation' (p. 14). If we add to this, and read backwards from another instructive comment – namely: 'Nationalism, unlike nationality or ethnic variety, cannot be considered a "natural" phenomenon' (p. 99) – it becomes clear that he considers nationality to be 'natural' in inverted commas. It is 'natural' in the sense that the 'deeply given' presents itself as natural with such force that only the inverted commas serve to remind us that it is nevertheless historical.

Does this mean, just as Althusser once accused most of his marxist confrères, and post-marxism now accuses everybody including Althusser, that lurking in Nairn's theory of the nation is that most insidious of methodological flaws – essentialism?[33] The problem of essentialism is important to our theme of the primordialist–modernist divide, and needs to be raised here directly, if only because the emerging academic dominance of post-structuralist methodology threatens to rule out any discussion of the deep historical roots of all social forms including those which ground the modern nation. Armed with an overly exuberant, post-structuralist suspicion of any form of Grand Theory it is all too easy to find the problem of essentialism in Nairn. For instance, from the questionable premise that all who seek a common socio-historical process to explain such a highly variable phenomenon effectively surrender 'to the conceptual terms of the nationalist problematic of the national "essence"',[34] Sami Zubaida throws a blanket of criticism over all theorists from Nairn to Gellner. Zubaida's position is open to easy counter-critique.[35] Nevertheless, in the midst of his uneven comments on Grand Theory, he manages to throw up a telling question which continues to confront both marxism and conventional theory: how without assuming the presence of essential nations could nationality be said to constitute the fault lines crossing the ancient social formations?[36] Nicos Poulantzas poses the question the other way round: 'What makes it possible for these seemingly transhistorical elements to be articulated at the focal point of the modern nation?'[37] Ernest Gellner wisely (and evasively) prefers to talk of entropy-resistant cultural markers rather then pre-existent national or even ethnic traits.[38] Tom Nairn's move to say that the nation is 'natural', that is, natural in inverted commas, is a similar but less effective evasion.

32. See also Nairn, *Enchanted Glass*, 1988, pp. 170–171, 177, 182, 213, 236, 307.

33. For a new turn of the screw see Norman Geras's discussion, 'Post-Marxism', 1987, pp. 40–82, which turns the essentialist critique back against 'left' post-structuralists.

34. Zubaida, 'Theories of Nationalism', 1978, p. 69.

35. In weakly acknowledging that the ideologies of nationalism 'share a common ideological field', the stridency of his disavowal of the possibility or necessity of broad theoretical work thus rebounds upon itself. Nairn could ask what explains the commonality of this 'ideological field'?

36. Zubaida, 'Theories of Nationalism', 1978, p. 69.

37. Poulantzas, *State, Power, Socialism*, 1980, p. 97. On this question see also John Ehrenreich, 'Socialism, Nationalism and Capitalist Development', 1983; and Smith, *The Ethnic Revival*, 1981, pp. 39–40.

38. See *Nations and Nationalism*, 1983, ch. 6.

While Nairn has no developed answer to the post-structuralist inquisition, but rather than indicating an inevitable essentialism it attests to the fact that he has yet to emphasize the political relevance of developing a theory of those social formations of early modern history such as the monarchical *patria* or the divisions of *natio* in the medieval universities and monasteries, formations based on forms of association from which the nation later emerged.[39] As Konstantin Symmons-Symonolewicz notes, there are only a few brief disquisitions into this shadowy area.[40] The levels argument is an attempt to express in a non-essentialist way the dialectic of continuity and dis-continuity of prior social forms into the modern period. All that we need to say at this stage in relation to Nairn is that his approach is limited to a (par-tial) theory of national*ism* and to a standpoint from which to assess the institutional politics of the modern nation-state.[41] But the broader problem remains. And, while firstly the marxist emphasis on material conditions and social being continues to be salutary, and secondly concepts such as mode of production continue to be centrally useful, the orthodox base–superstructure framework can offer us little help.

From the historic nation to nationalism as culturally invented?

Part of the problem is that although the national form is historically deter-mined it not only appears to be natural, basic and primordial, but in an unexplained way crosses changing modes of production, specifically feudal-ism to capitalism. Within mainstream sociology this has given rise to a primordialist tradition where nationality and ethnicity are treated as cultur-ally natural, or even biologically grounded associations. Within the marxist tradition it has been considered sufficient to say that the nation is located in history. (It is important to remember here that we are still talking about nationality and nation rather than nation-state.) Stalin initially bypassed the problem by distinguishing the nation as a historically constituted category from the tribe as an ethnographic category (though why this should be the case is itself not explained). But he then slips into treating nationality as a pre-national phenomenon and the problem asserts itself.[42] Otto Bauer attempted a more synthetic approach. However, his definition of the nation as a cultural community bound in common fate was derided as heresy, partly because in trying to go a step further to specify how the nation was grounded historically

---

39. We need to take seriously the research of writers such as G.G. Coulton, 'Nationalism in the Middle Ages', 1935; and Hans Kohn, *The Idea of Nationalism*, 1944. Despite their tendency to see ideas as the motor of history, the best contemporary writings on this are John Armstrong, *Nations Before Nationalism*, 1982; and Anthony D. Smith, *The Ethnic Origins of Nations*, 1986.

40. 'National Consciousness in Medieval Europe: Some Theoretical Problems', 1981.

41. This is close to the conclusions of Andrew Orridge, while leaving out his belief that Ernest Gellner adequately provides the other half of the story. See Orridge, 'Uneven Development and Nationalism: 2', 1982, pp. 181–190.

42. See Joseph Stalin, *Marxism and the National and Colonial Question*, (1913–34) 1947, p. 13.

he failed among other things to emphasize the by-then sloganized dictum that the proletariat have no country.[43]

More recently culture has become central to the debates. In the next chapter this will be given considerable attention; for the moment it is confined to the notion of cultural invention. Despite the rise of considerable interest in cultural questions, and for quite new reasons, culture continues to be treated by many marxists as effectively epiphenomenal. This includes theorists who decry the earlier stages of economic reductionism. In the new sense of the word, culture is lifted onto a pedestal of recognition and yet in the same elevation it is reduced to the arbitrary construction of instrumentally managed processes.[44] A number of contemporary marxists have with misplaced alacrity embraced the argument that ideologies which project a national historical antiquity are simply fabrications invented in the present.[45] This parallels the ascendancy of the language of cultural invention underwritten by post-structuralism[46] and also, in an odd congruence, by the line of conservative sociology from Acton to Kedourie and Gellner.

It is in fact possible and, in the terms of the present text, crucial to hold together both the historically grounded and culturally invented conceptions of the nation. An example drawn from Hobsbawm and Ranger's book, *The Invention of Tradition*, should make the issue clearer. There is little doubt that the tartan kilt was first designed by an English Quaker industrialist well after the Union of 1707, and that it was devised not to embellish the Highland tradition but to facilitate the transformation into industrial work. Furthermore there is substantial evidence that clan differentiation by tartan pattern began with the formation by the British government in the mid-eighteenth century of Highland regiments enlisted to fight in the imperial wars.[47] However, all this does not indicate that clan culture was an English or Lowland aristocratic invention. It suggests that the forms of association around which it was meaningful to 'invent' a new means of symbolizing Highland and clan differentiation were already existent.[48] Certainly intellectuals from clerics to poets contributed to giving clan culture a new level of meaning; however, even

43. Marx and Engels' phrase from the *Communist Manifesto*; on Bauer see Ronaldo Munck, 'Otto Bauer: Towards a Marxist Theory of Nationalism', 1985.

44. This applies even to Philip Corrigan and Derek Sayer's impressive study, *The Great Arch*, 1985. While they argue that a revolution in cultural forms grounds the reformation of the state, they also assert that the nation 'epitomizes the fictive community' (pp. 4ff., 118, 195).

45. See for example Eric Hobsbawm and Terence Ranger, eds, *The Invention of Tradition*, 1983. The language permeates Nairn's latest book, *The Enchanted Glass* (1988, pp. 108, 111, 126, 168, 172, 173, 184, 187 and so on).

46. See for example Gilles Deleuze and Félix Guattari, *Nomadology: The War Machine*, 1986; and going back to Friedrich Nietzsche, see pp. 49, 61–62, 160–163 in *The Portable Nietzsche*, 1985.

47. Hugh Trevor-Roper, 'The Invention of Tradition: The Highland Tradition of Scotland', 1983. On pre-1707 nationalism see Keith Webb, *The Growth of Nationalism in Scotland*, 1978, ch. 2.

48. On the reconstitution of clan and kinship in the eighteenth century see Eric Cregeen, 'The Changing Role of the House of Argyll in the Scottish Highlands', 1970.

here the 'invention of culture' argument is qualified by the long-run historical consciousness of Scottish identity. In 1320 'Scottish' royal officials wrote
to the Pope arguing that baronial loyalty was owed not primarily to the King
of Scotland, but to the *patria* itself. As Susan Reynolds comments, the
Declaration of Arbroath has been received by contemporary scholars with

> curious historical cynicism – almost a sort of inverted naïveté – which is determined
> not to take any statement of feeling or principle at face value. But a work of pro-
> paganda, as this was, must have been intended to appeal to values and emotions
> current at the time: the Scottish royal officials who drafted the letter presumably
> thought that ideas of collective political independence based on a single collective
> identity would seem convincing both to the barons in whose name it was drafted,
> and to the pope to whom it was addressed.[49]

Similarly in the late eighteenth century the Macphersons may have rewritten
'Scottish' history by treating 'Irish' ballads as if they were indigenous to
Scotland, but the question remains why the 'fabrication' was perpetrated. If
the primordialist face of Janus can hardly admit such fabrications, the second
face rarely bothers to ask that kind of question, and has no adequate way of
providing an answer.

Past and present

It is possible to synthesize the historically grounded and culturally invented
faces of history, but not as Nairn does by retaining both at the same time
without rewriting the terms of their synthesis.[50] When made explicit, a position such as Nairn's faces the danger of succumbing to the dichotomy of
essentializing the distant past and fictionalizing the present (and modern
past). The pre-modern past becomes that different country where people did
real things, had concrete relations and made unself-conscious history. The
present becomes a shallow layer of constructed artifice where all social action
is directed to accruing cultural capital. (There is also, as will be further discussed in Chapter 7, the opposite danger that in synthesizing the historically
grounded and culturally invented faces of history, quite different forms of
human association are treated as a narrative, discontinuous or otherwise,
unfolding on a single plane with a relatively unchanging ontology.)

   Like all half-truths the dichotomy of the faces of Janus has the ideological
force to take down even the most subtle theorist. The late Raymond Williams,
the Welsh-born writer who has been in the forefront of rethinking questions
of the determination of culture and the problems of the base–superstructure

---

49. Susan Reynolds, 'Medieval *Origines Gentium* and the Community of the Realm', 1983, pp.
385–386.
   50. So that Nairn can say that 'Many new "nations" had to think away millennia of oblivion,
and invent almost entirely fictitious pasts' (p. 105). He can write, 'Europe invented *nationalism*',
and a paragraph later say that, 'This original formation of nationalism took many centuries. It
is a process deeply rooted in Europe's history' (*Break-up of Britain*, 1981, p. 310). For Nairn on
nationalism as invention see also pp. 121, 141, 166, 168, 174, 215, 228, 301, 304, 310, 323.

framework, is a surprising victim. He argues that face-to-face relations and those relationships formed in local or even regionally placeable bonding are *real* (he does not simply forget to put in the mandatory inverted commas all through this discussion). They are 'of quite fundamental human and natural importance' whereas 'the modern nation-state is entirely artificial', an imposed form initiated as a 'ruling-class operation', 'a willed and selected superstructure':

> It is capitalism, especially in its most developed stages, which is the main source of all the contemporary confusions about peoples and nations and their *necessary* loyalties and bonds. Moreover it is, in the modern epoch, capitalism which has disrupted and overridden *natural* communities, and imposed artificial orders. It is then a savage irony that capitalist states have again and again succeeded in mobilising patriotic feelings in their own forms and interests.[51] (emphasis added)

Apart from being imbued with essentialist nostalgia for older modes of community the real/artifice distinction (like the 'natural'/invented distinction) repeats the problem of the unresolved faces of Janus. At the very least it does not explain how an artificial imposition has so much power. As Patrick Wright says, 'If the culture of the nation is only so much wool, then the eyes over which it is pulled must belong to sheep.'[52] There are sound reasons for agreeing with Raymond Williams that an alternative politics should reject the ideologies of race and nation as they are projected currently. Furthermore – and this is the key issue – we should reject them, as Williams suggests, 'in favour of lived and formed identities either of a settled kind, if available, or of a possible kind where dislocation and relocation require new formation'.[53] However, valorizing face-to-face relations as in themselves more real than other forms of abstract community will not achieve this desirable politics.

A theory of social forms which posited levels of social integration – from face-to-face embodied associations connected through kinship and reciprocal exchange, through to the more abstract extensions of community made possible by such means of integration as administrative apparatuses or the mass media – could with Williams criticize the subordination of locale and place to the more abstract politics of the nation-state. But it would do so without essentializing the past, or fictionalizing the present; without sacralizing the local, or demonizing the global. The claim that the form of the contemporary nation is grounded in long-run historical forms does not imply that Indonesia, India or even France or England can be said to have consolidated until quite recently as nation-states. By the same reasoning it is understandable why the early nineteenth-century Javanese prince Diponegoro could have no conception of the Indonesians or Dutch as a

51. Williams, *Towards 2000*, 1985, p. 184 with earlier quotes from pp. 180–181, 191. Cf. his novel *Loyalties* where in one brief passage he cuts through the intellectual nostalgia for the 'real life' of the Welsh valley (1985, p. 247). See also Francis Mulhern's sympathetic but forceful critique of Williams in 'Towards 2000, or News from You-Know-Where', 1984.
52. Patrick Wright, *On Living in an Old Country*, 1985, p. 5.
53. Williams, *Towards 2000*, 1985, p. 196.

collectivity. It is also explicable why this prince who intended to conquer Java, *not* liberate it, from the Dutch, is now elevated as a national hero.[54]

Nairn, despite his attachment to Scotland, has little to say about such questions of ontological grounding. Perhaps it is indicative that other than the preface to *The Break-up of Britain* the body of the text was written in chosen 'exile' from the land of his birth. Eric Hobsbawm similarly has until recently tended to direct his attention elsewhere.[55] He readily admits of himself: 'I . . . belong to a people of refugees [born in Egypt to an Austrian mother] whose experience has been such as to make me still vaguely uneasy if I don't possess a valid passport and enough cash to transport me to the nearest suitable country at short notice.'[56] On the other hand, Régis Debray has at least broached the question of the ontological history out of which the mode of association we call the 'nation' emerged. But he has taken this as a reason for asserting the priority of the national as if the nation *embodies* the levels of association from which, by its form, it is already abstracted. It has worrying consequences for Debray's political logic. He says, 'I can conceive of no hope for Europe save under the hegemony of a revolutionary France',[57] and later, heads off as President Mitterand's envoy to explain to the 'loyal French' subjects of the Pacific why they should accept nuclear detonations on their islands. Ethical questions aside, it suggests that the Imperial Nation dies hard. Between 1975 and 1991, 124 tests were conducted in the Pacific; in 1995 and against world opinion the new conservative president, Jacques Chirac, presided over the resumption of nuclear testing. In the context of the possibilities for joint research and computer-simulated testing it was very clear that what was at stake was old-fashioned national pride rather than military security.

What seems like just a theoretical question can thus very quickly be shown to have important political implications. A theory and politics of the question of human association has to confront centrally this issue of how the two faces of Janus can be integrated. Otherwise the one-sided accentuation of the grounding historical forms of the nation can lead to a sophisticated version of 'my country, right or wrong' . . . 'my nation, good or bad'. Alternatively emphasizing the modernity of the nation-state and the self-consciousness of its invented traditions can lead to a politics cast only at the level of asking what are the *institutional* requirements of an alternative political practice and how are the oppressive, homogenizing directions of the contemporary

---

54. Cited in Anderson, *Imagined Communities*, 1983, p. 19. Here he rightly says the very concept 'Indonesia' is a twentieth-century 'invention'. See also his other uses of the concept of invention and the (somewhat unresolved) qualifications of the term, pp. 15, 122, 129, 142, 143. Le Bras and Todd's work (*L'Invention de la France* written in 1981) is an example of taking the inventionist thesis past the point of usefulness: 'by rights,' they say, 'France should not exist'. It was 'invented'. Discussed in Fernand Braudel, *The Identity of France*, 1988, pp. 103ff., cited on p. 109.
   55. Cf. his latest book *Nations and Nationalism since 1780*, 1990.
   56. Eric Hobsbawm, 'The Limits of Nationalism', 1969.
   57. Régis Debray, 'Marxism and the National Question', 1977, p. 41.

bureaucratic state to be mitigated. It is this second emphasis which as I said has become the front runner in theories of the nation and nation-state. Unless we take this theorizing a stage further, the next generation, if it is still around, will look back in frustration and repeat Nairn's words, that the theory of nationalism represents our great historical failure. They will attend computer-mediated conferences on this issue, plug into the extended means of communication offered to the well-to-do of the meta-national global village, and muse nostalgically about the relative richness and concrete solidity of the past while bemoaning the continuing neo-national violence as atavism that will soon fade away.

An interlude on Nairn's concrete–abstract distinction

Before concluding this chapter, I would like briefly to comment on Tom Nairn's use of the terms abstract and concrete. They are obviously central concepts in the present work, but I have not included a fuller discussion of Nairn's use of them because, at least in his writings directly on the national question, they are only touched upon in a couple of passing references. Drawing upon Marx's notion of the abstract individuals of capitalism and J.H. Shennan's phrase, the abstract state, Nairn writes of 'the truly modern doctrine of the abstract or "impersonal" state which, because of its abstract nature, could be imitated in subsequent history' (p. 17). It is too brief a reference to draw out anything conclusive, though it does seem somewhat problematic. It appears to be imbued with an implicit diffusionism (that is, that ideas can be more readily diffused merely by virtue of their abstraction as ideas), and it is followed a couple of pages later by an overly functionalist view of class practice in the suggestion that the 'abstract political order' was a mechanism invented by the bourgeoisie to overcome the chaos of competitive anarchy, just as it 'generated the cohesive power of nationalism to hold itself together' (pp. 24–25). I would have left these fragments to lie unnoticed except that in his more recent book, *The Enchanted Glass*, the abstract–concrete distinction becomes a recurrent motif. Again, the theoretical status or import of the terms is not made explicit, but this time they pervade his argument.[58]

In *The Enchanted Glass* Nairn sets out to explain how the contemporary British monarchy has maintained the 'neo-tribal loyalty' of the people of Ukania (his name for the 'spirit-essence' of the United Kingdom). 'A personalized and totemic symbolism,' he says, 'was needed to maintain the a-national nationalism of a multinational (and for long imperial) entity; and "the Crown" could effectively translate identity onto that "higher plane".'[59]

---

58. See Nairn, *Enchanted Glass*, 1988, pp. 30, 48, 58, 63, 69, 90, 94, 97, 106, 117, 138, 139, 140, 141, 144, 160, 188, 205, 209, 212, 216, 229, 233, 273, 275, 278, 287, 288, 298, 314, 316, 355, 357, 360; all references to this sense of the abstract.

59. Ibid., p. 11.

What Nairn faces in attempting an explanation is an entity which accrues its power as much through the disembodied realm of the mass media (recall the cry of the Scottish crofter cited earlier) as out of the longer-run institutions of agency-extension; an entity which moreover relies upon recurrent traces of face-to-face contact: the Touch; the Intimate Wander through adoring crowds; the elusive ordinariness of the Royal Family; the face-to-camera-to-face addresses of the Queen broadcasting from her own home; in short, 'the human presence of Royalty with its concrete familial guarantee of all being well in the longer run'.[60] In the language of the present text, royalty thus gains its power through the same historical processes as does the nation – that is, constituted in a contradictory intersection of levels of abstraction – except that the cultural power of royalty manifestly focuses upon particular persons as *the* concrete embodiment of abstracted power. That is its strength and its weakness.

Nairn too connects royalty and nation, but he reduces the Ukanian obsession with royalty to an aspect of a unique Anglo-British national identity. He writes:

> What the theatre of Royal obsession sustains is not (real) personality, therefore, in the ordinary sense of individuality or idiosyncrasy. It projects perfectly *abstract* ideas of 'personality', which are received and revered as some kind of emblem. In other words it is an abstract cult *of* the concrete – an ideology of the (supposedly) nonideological . . . deeply and recognizably English . . . a quite decipherable and quite important aspect of national identity.[61]

Phrases such as the 'abstract cult *of* the concrete' reverberate in exciting ways back into the constitutive abstraction thesis, but there are important differences between our respective positions which, if clarified, might also serve to clarify what the present text is *not* doing. A few more illustrations of Nairn's use of the concept of abstraction will make this task easier. The following passages are taken from *The Enchanted Glass*:

1

> For Top People, clearly, the Monarch *is* an 'institution' – close indeed to being *the* institution when questions of soul and national essence arise. Under threat, it is not just the individuals but what they *mean* that counts: the abstract, sacred thing somewhere in the background.

2

> Though quite true to say [that the British state] centres on a sense of 'State' grandeur and continuity, this has never been the abstract or impersonal apparatus which post-Absolutist Republicanism fostered in Europe . . . Its awesomeness and 'near hypnotic impact' depend upon this ostensible identification of State with society: what one could also call . . . the metaphoric family unity of a Shakespearian (or pre-modern) *nationalism*.

---

60. Ibid., p. 215.
61. Ibid., p. 48. See also p. 10: the underlying structures of 'the Royal passion-play . . . are (in my view) merely the structures of nationalism'.

3

The whole development of nationalism since the 18th century has tended towards the fusion of two generally recognized levels of nationality: the personal [concrete?] or 'ethnic' identification on the one hand and formal [abstract] or passport citizenship on the other. But in the British Isles (itself a piece of phoney geography) such coalescence is impossible.

4

An anti-abstract ideology (or non-theoretical theory) is compelled to focus upon the ultra-concrete: visible things (or persons) radioactive with an otherwise ineffable significance. This poetry of national existence – intuitive decency; 'our way of doing things' – contrasts automatically and quite naturally with the foreign, the modern, the extreme, the impersonal and the noxiously abstract.

5

Analysis of pathologically concretized or anti-abstract customs and ideology has taken off from what that order itself has consecrated as 'reality': fetishized 'experience' as the incarnation of the human.[62]

The differences between the present text and Nairn's *Enchanted Glass* are methodological rather than political. They can be summarized as follows.

1   In using the levels of abstraction metaphor, *Nation Formation* attempts to overcome the problem of dichotomizing the concrete and the abstract.
2   It seeks to avoid treating the concrete as that which is palpable, material or real, over and against the abstract as that which is artificial and impersonal, is structured as ideas or is a phantom somewhere in the background.
3   Similarly, though the present text distinguishes between historical forms of nationality, it does not set up that comparison as a distinction between pre-modern, '*real* nationality'[63] and modern national*ism* – with the British case posited as fitting somewhere in between as either 'pseudo-rationalism'[64] or a metaphoric unity which draws upon the (ethnic) pre-modern and yet, via the persons of Royalty, fosters community from above.
4   Without denying the possibility of self-conscious artifice, the present text avoids the dichotomous distinction between the real and the phoney, the invented, the pseudo and so on.
5   Rather than accede to Nairn's version of the novelty of the British situation (except in the sense that *all* nation-states have unique histories) *Nation Formation* attempts to show how nation-states in general depend for their naturalized, concrete awesomeness upon intersecting levels of integration, framed by the most abstract level but never in a way that can resolve the contradictions of that intersection.

62. Quotes from ibid., p. 58, 90, 174, 94, 216.
63. Ibid., p. 176.
64. Ibid., p. 183.

With Nairn as the focus, the present chapter has examined some of the problems inherent in contemporary marxist approaches to theorizing, firstly, the original development of nationality and national formation, and, secondly, the emergence of nationalism and the nation-state. The confusions which surround the theorizing of the emergence of national formations stem in part from the lack of a non-essentialist theory of trans-epochal or trans-mode-of-production levels of social integration. Such a theory would, it is hoped, allow us to say that while nations do not come into being until they are lived *as such* (or at least abstractly recognized *as such*, usually in the first instance by intellectuals or persons lifted out of the face-to-face) the social forms which ground national formation are already lived prior to the generalization of this new sense of historicity.

In these terms, England is in no way 'a country of ancient and settled nationality'. It is rather a land which particularly after the Norman conquest had a remarkably continuous history of (relatively) settled institutional unity. The possibility of looking back over this 'unity' and framing it as a *national* unity entails, according to this argument, an abstraction of time and space, of history and territory, and thus a constitutively different subjectivity. Unfortunately, in theorizing this relation between the objective and subjective, marxist theories of the nation continue to be plagued by the limitations of the base–superstructure framework. Furthermore, the other side of the argument can be reasserted: the processes of abstraction do not simply involve inventing the past; culture is not an epiphenomenon of processes of social construction. Certainly people give the past meaning in terms of contemporary sensibilities. But to talk of this projection as fabrication or invention is to miss that it too is bound by (or rather constituted by) the conditions and subjectivities of its time – as is the ideology of cultural invention. It is not just by chance that there are lines within conservative and liberal sociology, orthodox and neo-marxism, structuralism and post-structuralism, all drawing upon similar conceptions of the invention of culture. The next chapter will attempt to take this argument a step further: it begins by introducing the concept of the 'rise of the cultural' and ends by criticizing the way that some contemporary theorists from Ernest Gellner to Fredric Jameson have asserted the emergent dominance of the cultural.

6

Nation Formation and the 'Rise of the Cultural': A Critique of Liberal Sociology

At the very same time that men [and presumably women] become fully and nervously aware of their culture and its vital relevance to their vital interests they also lose much of the capacity to revere their society through the mystical symbolism of a religion. So there is both a push and a pull towards revering a shared culture *directly*, unmediated in its own terms: culture is now clearly visible, and access to it has become man's most precious asset. Yet the religious symbols through which, if Durkheim is to be believed, it was worshipped, ceased to be serviceable. So – let culture be worshipped directly in its own name. That is nationalism.

Ernest Gellner, *Culture, Identity and Politics*, 1987

It did not however fail to produce those social conditions which lead to nationalism, i.e. to the identification of men with a High Culture which defines a large, mobile, anonymous mass of people, who however visualize that abstract society in the imagery of a concrete community.

Ernest Gellner, *Encounters with Nationalism*, 1994

While the nation continues to be an ontological formation of central, though changing, importance, it is currently beset by a two-fold development in the poverty of theory. On the one hand, a growing number of theorists are talking as if the nation-state is now an anachronistic carry-over from the modern past, fast becoming irrelevant in their version of the postmodern, post-sovereign, borderless world. On the other hand, for many people the nation is taken for granted, disappearing into its commonsense obviousness: outside the *cognoscenti*, the concepts of the nation, *this* society, and *this* community are often used as coterminous. Note how the definite article works in all those cases. When I tell acquaintances and colleagues, including academic colleagues, that I am doing some work on the nation it is invariably assumed that I am referring to some aspect or other of '*this* country of ours'. Both tendencies militate against adequately explaining the consolidation *and* transformations of the national formation. Studying the nation has engendered the submergence of theory under empirical or ideological verities, rather than the coherent integration of historical particulars and political arguments into an approach which links social form and social subjectivity.[1]

In one important way, as the previous chapter began to document, this is changing. The 1980s and 1990s have seen a new wave of attention being given to the national question.[2] It coincides with the heralding by some theorists of what will be called here the rise of the cultural. The phrase will be used with a trilateral reference: firstly, in connection with theoretical practice, it refers to the way in which questions of human subjectivity and human existence – from the new emphasis on the body and sexual difference to the recent taking apart of the constitutive notion of reality – are being pushed by social commentators into the glare of unremitting examination. It suggests the emergence of a social form which 'insists' upon its grounding conditions being theorized. It is expressive of this emergence that one feels compelled to place 'reality' in inverted commas.[3] Secondly, in relation to political practice, the phrase refers to the increasing grounding of politics in the affirmation of subjectivity:[4] hence the maxim, 'the personal is political'. Thirdly, it concerns the way in which, within late capitalism, social life is more and more *experienced* by people as being relatively fluid and 'cultural'. If Weber's phrase, the 'age of subjectivist culture', or Marx's, 'all that is solid melts into air', discussed earlier, were once the prognoses of abstracted intellectuals, they now have hit 'the person in the street' with a vengeance. The contemporary sensitivity to material and social constraints on lifestyle is the obverse side of this same process, and quite distinct from the way in which cultural boundaries were once historically lived as God-given or socially natural.

As a sign of the changing times recent studies commonly acknowledge the difficulty and unresolved nature of the national question. However, Tom Nairn's oft-quoted statement that, 'the theory of nationalism represents Marxism's great historical failure',[5] or Ralph Miliband's that, 'in no other

1. See Anthony D. Smith, 'Nationalism and Classical Social Theory', 1983; and '"Ideas" and "Structure" in the Formation of Independence Ideals', 1973.

2. Significant contributions include those of Benedict Anderson, Homi Bhabha, John Breuilly, Partha Chatterjee, Walker Connor, Ernest Gellner, Anthony Giddens, Liah Greenfeld, Eric Hobsbawm, John Hutchinson, Jim MacLaughlin, Ronaldo Munck, Tom Nairn, Cornelia Navari, Ephraim Nimni, Hugh Seton-Watson, Anthony Smith and Leonard Tivey amongst many others.

3. On 'reality' see Jean Baudrillard, 'The Precession of Simulacra', 1983, pp. 3–47; and Gerry Gill's critique of that position in 'Post-Structuralism as Ideology', 1984. The 'rise of the cultural' can also actually have the opposite effect from that of generating new ways of theorizing what remain substantive questions: in being pushed into relief, categories like the nation can appear to dissolve into relief, categories like the nation can appear to dissolve into pure invention. However insightful the post-structuralists may be, setting up the nation as a phantom meta-narrative will not take us very far. To take an example close to 'home', Andrew Lohrey's 'Australian Nationalism as Myth', 1984, provides one of the earliest examples in Australia of the limitations of this approach.

4. Russell Jacoby, *Social Amnesia*, 1975, ch. v, 'The Politics of Subjectivity'; Anthony Giddens, *Modernity and Self-Identity*, 1991; Seyla Benhabib, *Situating the Self*, 1992.

5. Tom Nairn, *The Break-up of Britain: Crisis and Neo-Nationalism*, 1981, p. 329.

area of the human sciences has the neglect been so marked',[6] cannot be taken at face value. They are now more indicative of the fundamental inadequacies of approaches to a theory of the nation than of a simple neglect. We should perhaps recall Poulantzas' comment, cited in Chapter 3, about our under-estimation of the difficulty of theorizing the nation. Eric Hobsbawm's decades-old comment is still relevant: 'Nationalism is probably the most powerful political phenomena of our century . . . but analysis has found it remarkably hard to come to grips with.'[7]

While the rise of the cultural starkly confronts many writers with the importance of understanding the nation-state and nationalism, it certainly has not forced the abandonment of narrow empiricism. To the contrary, the unimaginable complexity of the question, among other considerations, has paradoxically sent the majority of studies in the direction of sequestering the possibilities of a general social theory. The mainstream journal *Canadian Review of Studies in Nationalism*,[8] first published in 1974, carries a plethora of reviews of recently written, narrowly focused books. One of the *Canadian Review's* frequent contributors and himself author of several books on nationalism, Boyd Shafer, entitled one such article, 'If only we knew more about Nationalism'.[9] It begins by extending upon the tradition of Rupert Emerson's comment that, 'what we do not know or have taken for granted without adequate evidence adds up to an impressive body of ignorance and uncertainty which is all the more dismaying because of the frequent failure to face up to the limitations of our knowledge'.[10] Shafer says that despite his own 'incomplete' bibliography of thousands of writings he remains quite ignorant. While laudably modest his is still predominantly a statement of empirical gaps and an empiricist call for verifying research.

The other tendency in responding to the complexity of the national question is to fall back on a kind of volitional subjectivism without explaining the constitution of that subjectivity. To take an example from the mainstream, one writer who has achieved almost compulsory citation in the bibliographical procession, Hugh Seton-Watson, is 'driven to the [Weberian] conclusion that no "scientific definition" of a nation can be devised; yet the phenomenon has existed and exists'. He is reduced to the tautology: 'All that I can find to

6. Ralph Miliband cited in Horace B. Davis, *Toward a Marxist Theory of Nationalism*, 1978, p. 1. A non-marxist who has made a similar claim is Ernest Gellner: 'Nationalism is notoriously one of the most powerful forces of the modern world, but oddly enough one which has received relatively little systematic treatment by sociologists.' See also his 'Nationalism', 1981, p. 753.

7. Eric Hobsbawm, 'Some Reflections on Nationalism', 1972.

8. Other journals specifically in the area include *Nationalities Papers*, published semi-annually by the Association for the Study of the Nationalities (USSR and East Europe); *Europa Ethica: Problems of Nationalities* (Vienna); and the recently established *Nationalism and Ethnic Politics* (vol. 1, no. 1 was published in 1995). Compare these to the *New Nation*, first published in January 1891 in the United States, edited by Edward Bellamy. It 'aimed to bring about the economic equality of citizens, which is known as nationalism' (31 January, 1891).

9. Boyd Shafer, 'If Only We Knew More about Nationalism', 1980.

10. Rupert Emerson, *From Empire to Nation*, 1960, pp. 89–90, and cited in Shafer, ibid., p. 197.

say is that a nation exists when a significant number of people in a community consider themselves to form a nation, or behave as if they formed one.'[11] It is an inadequate subjectivist definition with a long heritage.[12]

The fact that Seton-Watson joins a long parade of others emphasizing the willed character of national identity is however, significant. In 1882 Ernest Renan gave his noted lecture at the Sorbonne, 'Qu'est-ce qu'une Nation?', in which he said: 'A nation is a great solidarity, created by the sentiments of the sacrifices which have been made and of those which one is disposed to make in the future. It presupposes a past; but it resumes itself in the present by a tangible fact: the consent, the clearly expressed desire to continue life in common.'[13] Despite clear transformations in thinking through the nineteenth to the twentieth centuries, Renan's conception reflects a common view held by a tradition of nationalists and theorists alike.[14] Certainly some went further. Johann Bluntschli's massive *Allgemeine Statslehre* (1852) defined the nation-state as a morally organized, masculine personality: 'History ascribes to the State a personality which, having spirit and body, possesses and manifests a will of its own.'[15] In contemporary writings it seems to be more a fall-back position than an assertion.[16] The limitations of the line from Renan to Seton-Watson, embodied emphatically, practically, in nationalist writings from, say, Jules Michelet or Giuseppe Mazzini to late twentieth-century figures as diverse as Mishima Yukio or Fidel Castro, underscores the necessity for a materialist, social relational account, but one which instates the centrality of the subjective. In short, we need to keep to the fore the theme of the subject–object relation. To put it more graphically, we need to take seriously the fact that people are prepared to die for their nation, and not simply because of a willed national spirit or a deluding ideology.

In partially recognizing the limitations of one-sided subjectivism, most

11. Hugh Seton-Watson, *Nations and States*, 1977, p. 5.

12. In the thirteenth century, long before nation-states were even envisaged, Marsilius of Padua argues that *states* were united by common will, rather than, as most of his contemporaries suggested, by a naturally occurring unitary form (*per formam aliquam unicam naturalem*). Discussed in Susan Reynolds, 'Medieval *Origines Gentium* and the Community of the Realm', 1983.

13. Ernest Renan, 'What is a Nation?', 1882, reproduced in Hans Kohn, *Nationalism: Its Meaning and History*, 1965, p. 139; also in Homi Bhabha, *Nation and Narration*, 1990.

14. Hans Kohn writes: 'The most essential element [in the formation of nations] is a living and active corporate will. Nationality is formed by the decision to form a nationality'. See his *The Idea of Nationalism*, (1944) 1956, p. 15.

15. Johann K. Bluntschli, *The Theory of State*, (1852) 1895, p. 22. The notion of the state as having a 'personality' is more abstract than the feudal view of the *regnum* or *patria* as having an abstract 'body'. Otto von Gierke (*Political Theories of the Middle Age*, 1900, pp. 67–73) shows how the idea of personality is missing from medieval political theories of the body politic. Moreover in doing so the preconceptions of the late nineteenth century speak from between the lines of von Gierke's analysis: his implicit point is that the medieval theorists should have been able to give to an abstract 'Fictitious Person' a distinct personality and will.

16. The phrase 'a fall-back position' is deployed with ironical allusion to its use by Elie Kedourie (*Nationalism*, (1960) 1993, p. 75). In the context of criticizing the way nationalists fall back on the concept of 'individual will' he goes on to affirm Renan's definition cited above.

contemporary writers retire like Seton-Watson into working their way through problems of definition, into devising classificatory schemes of different types of nations or national movements, or into documenting particular nationalist uprisings and national histories. Seton-Watson's grand survey is one of the more encyclopedic. While those types of studies remain important, we might want to say, reworking Emerson's comment, that our body of ignorance is passing from impressive to overwhelming. It has been consequently the assumption of this book that a theory of the nation requires as integral to its *starting* point an adequate theory of social formations and associated subjectivities. Social formation, as previously discussed, is taken here to have various possible levels of definition. At one level of theoretical abstraction it has been defined as the broad, structured conjuncture of social relations of a particular society conditioned and integrated through the means and relations of communication, production, organization and exchange, practised in and across its boundaries. However, the emphasis of the present discussion has been on a more abstractly conceived definition: social formation as an intersection-in-dominance of levels of integration. As a way of going further into the problem I propose to spend some time looking at the work of someone within the Weberian–Durkheimian lineage who as part of the new wave of attention has attempted a comprehensive and direct contribution to a theory of the nation. First, let me summarize a couple of the assumptions of this sociological tradition.

Out of the traditions of Weber and Durkheim

Contemporary theorists who work out of the lineage of Max Weber and Emile Durkheim start from the basic distinction between Traditional and Modern societies. It has been called the Great Divide and is relevant to one of the continuing themes of the book, the primordiality–modernity question. While the present discussion calls into question all dichotomous or ideal-type theorizing, it is important to acknowledge that the Weberian–Durkheimian lineage has thrown up a number of irreducible issues concerning the difference between social formations.

To briefly recapitulate: Durkheim distinguished between mechanical and organic forms of solidarity, while Weber's ideal-type methodology distinguished three relationships of political organization – traditional, charismatic (always a transitional phase) and rational–legal (the modern side of the Great Divide). Expressions of this same broad tradition can in turn be located in a series of typological contrasts written by those living through what Polanyi has called the Great Transformation:[17] Otto von Gierke's contrast between *Genossenschaft* and *Herrschaft*; Henry Maine's status/contract distinction; and Ferdinand Tönnies' writings on *Gemeinschaft und Gesellschaft* (1887)

17. Karl Polanyi, *The Great Transformation: The Political and Economic Origins of Our Time*, (1944) 1957.

are amongst the most prominent discussions of the Great Divide. As Robert Nisbet points out, Marx was the only writer of this period who dissented significantly from the value implications of the contrast.[18]

Drawing on these classical theorists, mainstream sociology posits the existence of three stages of the modernization process: tradition, transition, modernity. (Notice that this model still assumes a basic dichotomy.[19]) Nationalism and the nation as a way of organizing the relations between people is seen as an outcome of the 'transitional phase'. Similarly, nationalists, like Daniel Lerner's archetypal character 'the grocer of Balgat' are transitionals, persons in mental and physical motion. As Anthony Smith concludes of one line out of this complex lineage of theorists:

> The functionalist perspective on modernisation starts . . . from the suggestions in Rousseau, draws heavily on Durkheim's analysis of complex society, and ends by echoing Weber. The key to the argument is the idea of the 'imperatives' of a community of tradition . . . To survive painful dislocation, societies must institutionalize new modes of fulfilling the principles and performing the functions with which earlier structures can no longer cope. To merit the title *a new 'society' must reconstitute itself in the image of the old.*[20] (emphasis added)

Reconstitution in this 'image of the old' and the harking back to traditional myths refers in the functionalist argument to an adaptive process undergone by new societies because of legitimation crisis.[21] It is not as evocative a phrase as it first promises. Accordingly, the ideology of nationalism is theorized as that ideology which is best suited to bridging the tradition by adapting primordial ties to modern complexities, to use Edward Shils' influential phrase. In the language of Talcott Parsons, it unites particularistic with universal orientations. Clifford Geertz gives a similar but less functionalist account of what he calls the integrative revolution.[22] However, to go into any more detail at this stage would not add significantly to ground already cov-

18. Robert A. Nisbet, *The Sociological Tradition*, (1966) 1970, p. 48. See his discussion of the various conceptions of community versus society in ch. 3; also in his *The Quest for Community*, (1953) 1971.

19. The three stage model still maintains the dichotomy of traditional/modern: simple/complex, despite the broad implications of the later work of Durkheim and his pupil and colleague, Marcel Mauss, particularly Mauss' *The Gift: Forms and Functions of Exchange in Archaic Societies*, (1925) 1974. This dichotomy still pertains to approaches which expanded upon the concept of transition; take for example Walt Rostow who, in *Stages of Economic Growth: A Non-Communist Manifesto*, 1960, suggested an ideologically value-laden, five-stage evolutionary scheme: (1) traditional; (2) preconditioning; (3) take-off; (4) the drive to maturity; (5) the age of mass-consumption.

20. Anthony D. Smith, *Theories of Nationalism*, 1983, pp. 49–50.

21. This limited perspective on the reconstitution of the old is common to the so-called conventional development theorists. One of the more interesting embellishers of the structural–functional framework is Daniel Lerner, *The Passing of Traditional Society*, 1958. See also Lucien Pye, *Politics, Personality and Nation Building*, 1962. The big contemporary name in the 'theory of adaptation' is James Rosenau. See his *The Study of Political Adaptation*, 1981.

22. Talcott Parsons, *The Social System*, 1951; Edward Shils, 'Primordial, Personal, Sacred and Civil Ties', 1957; Clifford Geertz, *The Interpretation of Cultures*, 1973, chs 9 and 10.

ered by Smith's excellent critical discussion of structural functionalism, the 'mass society' model and related approaches to modernization theory in his *Theories of Nationalism* (1983). Moreover, a theory of the nation is hardly the central preoccupation of such approaches. Smith's commendable capacity to wring relevant theoretical substance out of them gives a misleading impression as to the level of formulation and direct application to a theory of the nation they had reached. It reflects more his original aim in the first edition of 1971 to 'demonstrate the close links between nationalism and "modernisation"'.[23]

Until recently, with some notable exceptions, the question of the basis for the constitution of the nation was not in itself taken up within this tradition as a pressing problem. In many ways it could quite legitimately be argued that it would be solved when the problems of social integration and social change were dispensed with. On the other hand, I would suggest, merely echoing many other critics, that the functionalists' way of dealing with social integration and social change is part of the problem, thoroughly impairing any subsequent attempts to develop a theory of the nation.

There is one writer out of the Weberian–Durkheimian lineage who has done more than any other to rethink the categories of the theory of nation. It is probably of no coincidence that he is of Jewish-Czech background and has spent most of his life lifted out of his *natus* into cultural 'exile'. I am referring to the well-known European philosopher, social anthropologist, social theorist, historian of ideas and *doyen terrible*, Ernest Gellner.[24] Gale Stokes maintains that, 'of all the writers on nationalism, Gellner is the only one who has produced a full-scale theory'.[25] She may be right, but this chapter will argue less fulsomely that although his writings are insightful they remain paradigmatic of the limitations of liberal orthodoxy. It will argue that his approach is predicated upon an ultimately unsustainable theory of the history of societal forms.[26]

Ernest Gellner: a partial break with orthodoxy

For the most part Gellner's work has been well received even when criticized. The radical Weberian, Anthony Smith, calls it 'one of the most complex and original attempts to come to grips with the ubiquitous phenomenon of nationalism', while Gavin Kitching's review in the marxist journal *Capital and Class* sympathetically describes *Nations and Nationalism* as a fine book of

---

23. Smith, *Theories of Nationalism*, 'Preface to the Second Edition', 1983, p. ix.

24. For a general discussion of Gellner see John A. Hall, 'Ernest Gellner', ch. 6 of his *Diagnoses of Our Time*, 1981; and Perry Anderson, *A Zone of Engagement*, 1992, ch. 9. (With the publication of *The Ethnic Origins of Nations*, 1986, the work of Anthony Smith must be considered to be of comparable importance to that of Gellner.)

25. Gale Stokes, 'The Underdeveloped Theory of Nationalism', 1978, p. 154.

26. Gellner is more interested in societal forms – tribal society, agrarian society, industrial society – than in particular social formations.

trenchant clarity.[27] Tom Nairn, who is himself probably the most influential contemporary marxist theorist of the nation (Benedict Anderson and Anthony Giddens are qualified in their relation to any marxist lineage) calls Gellner's 1964 chapter 'Nationalism', 'the most important and influential recent study in English'. Except for the undeveloped and only passingly relevant criticism of Gellner for engaging in 'a sort of compromise between historical materialism and commonsense' – and thus not asserting the moral ambiguity of nationalism – Nairn, like Michael Hechter, John Hall, Andrew Orridge and T.V. Sathyamurthy, uncritically incorporates some of the central tenets of Gellner's thesis into his own position.[28] Ironically both the Durkheimian–Weberian and the New Left marxist (discussed in the previous chapter) fail to deal adequately with a related dilemma: both fail, for different reasons, to put together the nation as an objectively constituted social form/social subjectivity.

From 'savage' to 'cultivated' cultures?[29]

The suggestive strength of Ernest Gellner's position arises out of its broad theoretical sweep. In other words, in having a social theoretical attitude he has more to say than the safer, perhaps more accurate, empirical studies, and as such his position is thoroughly taken apart. Before turning to a detailed critique I will try to summarize his argument. History for Gellner has three fundamental stages or ideal types of social formation: the hunting-gathering, the agrarian and the industrial.[30] Because it is a necessary condition for the development of a nation that the state has a taken-for-granted existence it is

27. Smith, *Theories of Nationalism*, 1983, p. 109; Gavin Kitching, 'Nationalism: The Instrumental Passion', 1985. By way of comparison see also Boyd Shafer's 1984 'Review of Gellner's *Nations and Nationalism*, where he comments that 'This one might be a beginning of an overall [theory of nationalism], though I am never quite certain of what Gellner's explanation explains' (pp. 141–142). For a series of criticisms aimed as shots in the dark see Partha Chatterjee, *Nationalist Thought and the Colonial World*, 1986.

28. Nairn, *Break-up of Britain*, 1981, pp. 96 and 342. Also pp. 99, 133, 317, 338, 358. Gellner is only backhandedly kind to Nairn. Gellner's 'Nationalism, or the New Confessions of a Justified Edinburgh Sinner', 1979, see Nairn's work as admirable in so far as it farewells marxism. For the uncritical use of Gellner see Michael Hechter, *Internal Colonialism*, 1975, pp. 36–43; John A. Hall, *Powers and Liberties*, 1986; A.W. Orridge, 'Uneven Development and Nationalism: 2', 1982. T.V. Sathyamurthy, *Nationalism in the Contemporary World*, 1983.

29. These terms are taken from Ernest Gellner's extended botanical metaphor: culture as savage, wild, low, spontaneous; distinguished from culture as cultivated, garden, high, nourished and national. See his *Nations and Nationalism*, 1983, p. 50.

30. These are his 'three great stages of man' (ibid., p. 114). Gellner assiduously manages to avoid the use of terms like 'feudalism' and 'capitalism'. At one point in critique of the marxist position he refers to 'capitalism' as 'an overrated category' (ibid., p. 90). In *Thought and Change*, 1964, Gellner, for example, prefers to use Walt Rostow's normatively deployed phrase, the stage of high mass-consumption (p. 166). While the subtitle of that writer's book proclaims its anti-marxist stance, Gellner's writings, at least up until the past few years, have been a series of non-marxist manifestos. With *Encounters with Nationalism*, 1994, his stance softened.

by definition not possible to talk of the emergence of the nation in pre-agrarian or tribal, hunting-gathering societies. By the middle or agrarian age the state is optional.[31] Coevally with this possibility for political centralization, a new class of specialized, literate clerics effect a cultural–cognitive centralization. Thus according to Gellner, restricted literacy causes a split between the 'great' and the 'little' traditions. At the level of the 'little' or vernacular-based tradition, the 'petty communities of the lay members of the society' are laterally differentiated and culturally drifting.[32] It follows that in the agrarian age the determinants of political boundaries are distinct from those of cultural boundaries. Given Gellner's argument that the nation comes into being with fusion of the taken-for-granted state apparatus with a relatively homogeneous culture, then, even if nationalism had 'been *invented* in such a period its prospects of general acceptance would have been slender indeed'[33] (emphasis added). With industrialization comes a new division of labour. This is related to a number of developments, but most crucially to the mobility of persons across the old, context-bound 'little' communities through, firstly, the 'functional requirement' of a mobile work-force, and secondly, the (abstracting) tendency towards universalized literacy in a generalizable language. A homogeneous 'high culture' comes to pervade and dominate social life, sustained primarily through a national education and communication system. It can only be held together, he says, by the nation-state.

Even when described at such a high level of generality the strengths and weaknesses of Gellner's position start to become apparent. For present purposes, discussion will centre predominantly on problems and shortcomings.

Discussion of Gellner's first fundamental stage of human history, the pre-agrarian, need only be brief for his own treatment of it, particularly in *Nations and Nationalism*, is perfunctory. However, it is integral to his argument that the development of nations would be impossible during the pre-agrarian epoch. So that while the notion of the pre-agrarian appears only analytically relevant in its use as a starting point for comparison to later 'enriched' cultural stages, it actually has to carry a heavy theoretical superstructure. It is relevant for us because it is indicative right from the very beginning of weakness in this type of approach to a theory of social integration. When Gellner says that:

---

31. *Nations and Nationalism*, 1983, p. 5. Gellner has a tendency to use either anthropomorphic and/or voluntaristic terms in describing cultural–structural connections. As he acknowledges in attempting to define the 'idea of the nation' his approach has two elements: (1) the 'cultural'; namely the necessity of a shared culture; and (2) the 'voluntaristic'; namely, that 'nations are the artefacts of men's convictions and loyalties and solidarities' (p. 7). With regard to the use of anthropomorphisms, Gellner continues the practice for literary effect while reluctantly and gently acknowledging that it should be avoided. See ibid., p. 51.

32. Ibid. Gellner is not altogether consistent on this. Compare his comments on participatory communities: 'they may have their local accent and customs, but these tend to be but variants of a wider inter-communicating culture containing many other similar communities' (p. 14).

33. Ibid., p. 11. The notion of 'invention' will be taken up later.

> Cultures, like plants, can be divided into savage and cultivated varieties. The savage kinds are produced and reproduce themselves spontaneously, as parts of the life of men [*sic*] . . . wild systems of this kind (in other words, cultures) reproduce themselves from generation to generation without conscious design, supervision, surveillance or special nutrition . . .[34]

or, when he compares the elaborated communications code of the industrial age to the restricted 'context-bound grunts and nods'[35] of 'backward savages', it could be concluded that he is producing, despite attempts to the contrary, an ethnocentric, elitist, teleological, functionalist and idealist version of the Great Divide. Numerous passages could be marshalled in support of such an assessment, but it is a misplaced conclusion. It misses out on the ironical style and provocative richness of Gellner's approach.

Leaving aside excesses of style there are still, none the less, substantive reasons for concluding that Gellner's work lacks an adequate account of social integration, both with regard to tribal or reciprocal exchange societies and 'modern' or late-capitalist societies. The pre-agrarian is portrayed in *Nations and Nationalism* as a form of social life in its most natural and spontaneous state: 'wild systems', he says, can be compared with 'a natural species which can survive in the natural environment'.[36] Although it may appear that Gellner here is relying upon a Janus faced dualism between the 'natural' and the 'artificially produced' (his terms), other aspects of his approach suggest a modernist anti-primordialism. There is a pervading Durkheimian ghost in the Gellnerian schema which rejects the notion of natural, primordial spontaneity. Tribal societies, integrated in mechanical solidarity, are in these terms seen as highly structured, closed systems. To see whether Gellner can elude this tension in his work we have initially to return to his earlier writing.

Structure, culture and the new subjectivity

In *Thought and Change*, Gellner makes the conventional, indeed necessary, analytic distinction between structure and culture. His next move is however

---

34. Ibid., p. 50. The notion of society-at-large as a wilderness which required cultivation merged incidentally alongside the use of the verb 'to civilize' in the seventeenth and eighteenth centuries. In the 1760s *Les philosophes* preached about the human act of civilizing 'as the method to transform the savage wilderness of society into a designed, orderly formal garden'. See Zygmunt Bauman, 'On the Origins of Civilization: A Historical Note', 1985. For more detailed parallels to Gellner's language see Lucien Febvre, *A New Kind of History*, 1973, pp. 219–257.

35. Gellner, *Nations and Nationalism,* 1983, p. 51. See also p. 33. Here, in making the distinction between 'elaborate' and 'restricted' codes, Gellner is drawing on a historically specific and oversimplified version of Basil Bernstein's distinction between linguistic codes. One could imagine Gellner approvingly quoting Bernstein when the latter says that, 'the type of social solidarity realized through a restricted code points towards mechanical solidarity whereas the type of solidarity realized through elaborated codes points towards organic solidarity. (Bernstein, *Class, Codes and Control*, 1974, p. 147 and *passim*).

36. Gellner, *Nations and Nationalism,* 1983, p. 51.

quite dubious.[37] It is related to our object–subject theme and has crucial significance for his theory of the nation. In face-to-face societies, structure,
narrowly conceived by Gellner as the social positions, roles and relationships, is theorized as primary. Structure is the 'substance' which is merely
reinforced by culture, the latter being defined as the style of being and expression or the manner in which one communicates.[38] Shared culture, he
maintains, 'is not [in face-to-face societies] a precondition of effective communication'. (There is little to be gained from pausing to ponder how culture
can be simultaneously the manner of communication and not necessary for
communication – it is possible because of a sliding definition, but more critically it arises out of problems we will have to come back to later.) In modern
societies, on the other hand, Gellner argues that the relative importance of
structure and culture reverses: 'In modern societies, culture does not so much
underline structure: rather, it replaces it!'[39] He is thus heralding the rise of the
cultural and a new emphasis on subjectivity.

Through these analytic moves Gellner is attempting, even if unsuccess-
fully, to deal with major issues implicit in classical and contemporary
accounts of social integration: that is, how to theorize various social formations as being constitutively different. There is strong reason to argue
that there is a qualitative difference between those societies constituted primarily in the face-to-face (where persons are, to use Gellner's phrase, set in
place by a frame of fairly stable relationships), and those societies in which
face-to-face contact can no longer be said to be the dominant constitutive
level of social integration.[40] In the latter setting, social relations at the level

37. Sathyamurthy argues to the contrary that it is a move that 'is absolutely crucial to a successful analytic examination of the concept of nationalism' (*Contemporary World*, 1983, p. 72).
Similarly, John Breuilly, despite his extensive criticisms of Gellner for other failings, treats the
move as Gellner's most significant contribution to theorizing the nation. See Breuilly's
'Reflections on Nationalism', 1985. Phillip Rawkins uncritically uses Gellner's structure/culture
distinction as the 'platform' for his article, 'Nationalist Movements within the Advanced
Industrial State: The Significance of Culture', 1983.

38. Gellner, *Thought and Change*, 1964, pp. 154, 155. See also *Nations and Nationalism*, where
in trying to bypass the problem of his initial definition of culture as 'a system of ideas and signs
and associations and ways of behaving and communicating' by suggesting that we look primarily 'at what culture does' (1983, p. 7), he falls into the trap of reifying culture as an acting
medium in itself. Later, after leaving the concept 'deliberately undefined', he says reductively that
'an at least provisionally acceptable criterion of culture might be language' (p. 43).

39. *Thought and Change*, 1964, p. 155. In one way *Nations and Nationalism* replicates this
argument. For example Gellner writes: 'Culture is no longer [in industrial society] merely the
adornment, confirmation and legitimation of a social order which was also sustained by harsher
and coercive constraints; culture is now the necessary shared medium, the life-blood or perhaps
rather the minimal shared atmosphere, within which alone the members of the society can breathe
and survive and produce' (1983, pp. 37–38). But in another way it contradicts it: 'The roots of
nationalism in the distinctive structural requirements of industrial society are very deep indeed'
(p. 35).

40. This statement of a qualitative difference is not the same as setting up a dichotomous view
of history. See Anthony Giddens, *Power, Property and State*, 1981, pp. 157–168 on the methodological distinction. The issue of qualitative difference between different forms of society is
relatively uncontroversial, but for a dissenting view see Mary Douglas, *Natural Symbols*, 1970.

of the face-to-face *are* fragmented and constituted more abstractly. The subjects of a nation are not held together because they will all at some time meet each other. But whether or not the more abstract form of integration underpinning the national formation is less structured is quite a different question.

While this is not the place to attempt a full-blown discussion of the form of the new relation, a few comments are needed to contextualize the problem with which Gellner is dealing and to highlight the extent to which he falls short of an adequate explanation. An explanation couched in terms of levels of integration arguably provides some insights into the national question which overcome the problems of the culture/structure inversion. To summarize the earlier exposition, it was argued that the nation came into being with the intersection of a number of distinguishable levels of social integration: the relatively 'concrete' face-to-face, clearly a necessary dimension of any conceivable society; the agency-extended – where apparatuses such as religious 'bureaucracies', and later, predominantly state bureaucracies, schools, military forces etc., and their agents such as postal workers or census collectors, connect people across increasing extensions of time and space; and the disembodied – namely the more abstract extensions of social relations possible with, for example, the initially agency-bound circulation of commodities and capital across a mass market, or as Benedict Anderson has emphasized, the new means of communication beginning with print and reaching unprecedented heights with the contemporary mass-communication industry. As the first two levels historically have become reconstituted in relation to the dominance of the third, most abstract level, people subjectively have experienced a relative 'liberation' from many of the bounded limitations of face-to-face association, and *apparently* a liberation from structure *per se*. Structure in this sense has not been replaced by culture; rather the cultural–structural form has changed.

It is partly understandable that Gellner takes the line he does. With the emerging dominance of relations of disembodied extension, a universalizing form of interchange 'presents itself' as post-structural. Nevertheless, writers such as Benedict Anderson, Geoff Sharp and Anthony Giddens[41] have in more fruitful ways begun to theorize this abstraction of social relations and its structure of apparent structurelessness. They point to the new means of abstraction and distantiation such as the mass media as being simultaneously the structural means of social extension and integration, a structure which constitutes subjects in a way that forces us to be increasingly self-active in constructing our identities. Gellner by contrast, even in his most recent writings, *Encounters with Nationalism* (1994), hardly alludes to the information revolution. In a sense, theorists such as Anderson, Sharp and Giddens

41. Giddens, *Power, Property and State*, 1981 and his *The Nation-State and Violence*, 1985; Benedict Anderson, *Imagined Communities*, 1991; and Geoff Sharp, 'Constitutive Abstraction and Social Practice', 1985.

emphasize with Gellner the breakdown and fragmentation (or rather, and this is an important restatement of Gellner's terms, the reconstitution of prior modes) of social integration. But none of them makes the mistake of trying to theorize the transformation between different forms of social relations by an analytic inversion.[42]

Problems flow through from this methodological standpoint of Gellner's. If structure is defined as that which determines one's relationship to others – for example, kinship is structural in societies he calls 'primitive' – then why are not the new determinants of social relations in contemporary societies also structural? Moreover, Gellner says at one point in his essay 'Nationalism' in *Thought and Change*, that: 'Modern societies are not quite as lacking in structure as they are sometimes depicted. Bureaucracy is the kinship of modern man.'[43] This is strange given the overall argument of that essay, but his subsequent qualification of this leads to even more confusion. Gellner writes that unlike in a kinship network, in modern societies persons can divest themselves of their ascribed roles 'as of an overcoat: the wider society lacks either legal or *ritual* sanctions for enforcing them'[44] (emphasis added). He will have to yet again qualify this last evocative statement, but before he does it is worth pointing to its immediate implications. The statement implicitly reinstates culture – previously defined by him as 'manner, conduct, ritual, dress and so forth', and which you'll remember was earlier said to be a dispensable appendage to structure within primitive societies – back into a necessary relationship to the structure of those societies. His next qualification in the same paragraph contradicts the overcoat metaphor. He says: 'The rigid ascription of roles takes place within organizations ['the kinship of modern man'], but men are fairly free to choose and change their organizations.'[45] And even here Gellner notes economic constraints to choice.

It takes a while to think through why Gellner would argue for such a problematic device as the structure/culture inversion. But the first step of a possible explanation is relatively simple: the terms, culture and structure, are for Gellner descriptive as well as (or even prior to being) theoretical concepts. Therefore, in Gellner's gender-specific language, when the structured ascription of roles breaks down to the point where 'a man is a man' then, *ipso facto*, the cultural has replaced structure as the basis of social integration.

42. Anton Zijderveld (*The Abstract Society*, 1974) gets himself into a parallel but opposite position to Gellner. Theoretically he argues for the replacement of '*cultural integration* based on "mechanical solidarity"' by '*structural integration* based upon "organic solidarity"' (p. 69) but then a few pages later he contradicts himself, arguing that 'Such uniform realities as castle, estate, or class, which give a society a strict structure, are conspicuously absent in pluralist society' (p. 72).

43. Gellner, *Thought and Change*, 1964, p. 154.

44. Ibid., p. 155. Cf. Zijderveld, *Abstract Society*, 1974, who writes that 'Moving between the institutional sectors, the modern individual is compelled to change roles like the jackets of his wardrobe' (p. 71).

45. Gellner, *Thought and Change*, 1964.

Recent theories of the 'subject' have criticized the assertion that the new individuality heralds in the person as person as overly simplifying.[46]

To pursue that line now would be to lose track of the issue of social integration. Besides, Gellner is doing his argument a disservice. It is part of his unnecessary sententiousness. When he says modern society turns everyone into a cleric of the high culture, it is as misleading as Donald Horne's claim that we are all intellectuals.[47] Nevertheless, to the extent that both point to the reconstitution of the form of subjectivity and central importance of intellectual training, they cannot just be dismissed.

For Gellner, when a society appears to be unstructured, it is necessarily held together by a common culture:

> If a man is not firmly set in a social niche, whose relationship as it were endows him with his identity, he is obliged to carry his identity with him, in his whole style of conduct and expression: in other words, his 'culture' becomes his identity. And the classification of men by 'culture' is of course the classification by nationality.[48]

Gellner is here only describing the phenomenal, the appearances of the change. Certainly the seeming paradox of the nation arising in conjunction with the individuation of person is *analytically* resolved, but it is also too neatly bypassed. It does appear on the face that the contemporary modern individual is not structured into society and from this comes Gellner's (initially) bold analytic inversion.

In his latest writings Gellner has implicitly revised the basis of his position. He seems to have finally drawn back from positing an inversion when he says: 'The national and often nationalist state, is a precise example of . . . [the] replacement of one structure by another; and that it cannot be explained by invoking historical events alone, but only by highlighting the difference between the two contrasted structures.'[49] On the face of it this is a major emendation. It appears to dull the force of the foregoing critique. My argument, in positing constitutive structural levels, would now it seems only want to qualify Gellner's statement by suggesting that while the social form is qualitatively different the change involves not the replacement of one structure by another, but the reconstitution of 'prior' levels and the emerging

46. Such theories range across the methodological spectrum. Louis Althusser, *Lenin and Philosophy*, 1971; Rosalind Coward and John Ellis, *Language and Materialism*, 1977, chs 5 and 6; Anthony Giddens, *Central Problems in Social Theory*, 1979, ch. 1; Julian Henriques et al., *Changing the Subject*, 1984; Benhabib, *Situating the Self*, 1992. On the other hand, for an example of a statement of the same quality as Gellner's, though this time with the added problem of being ahistorical, see Graham Little, *Political Ensembles*, 1985, p. 14. He says, 'There is a third form of social relations, the Ensemble, in which freedom and authority are reconciled because people interact with other people *as people*' (original emphasis).

47. Donald Horne, *The Public Culture*, 1986. A theory of the significance and changed subjectivity of intellectual groupings is crucial to a theory of the nation. For a Weberian position see Anthony D. Smith, *The Ethnic Revival*, 1981, ch. 6; and for a marxist position see Nonie Sharp, 'Nationalism and Cultural Politics', 1976.

48. Gellner, *Thought and Change*, 1964, p. 157.

49. From 'Nationalism and the Two Forms of Cohesion in Complex Societies', in his *Culture, Identity and Politics*, 1987, pp. 12–13.

dominance of a new structural level. When examined more closely, however, Gellner's position has become more theoretically confused. Given that structure is defined by him as the 'relatively stable system of roles and positions',[50] and, secondly, given that he argues that social position (i.e. structure) in modern society is fluid and mobile, he is either effectively contradicting himself – viz. structure is replaced by 'a structure' where structure is breaking down – or he is employing two quite different definitions of structure, one of which is never made explicit. Gellner still wants to argue for the rise of culture, and while this is often described in compelling ways, it is increasingly apparent that he requires a new theoretical basis for sustaining his description.

When Gellner then attempts to elucidate the positive determinants of the changed mode of integration further problems emerge: firstly his approach tends at times to be empirically misleading (I will give an example in a moment), and overall, at least when he tries to summarize his argument, it tends to be empirically reductive. Gellner's narrative is laced with insightful generalizations but it is reductive in so far as it conceives of two basic predominant carriers of change: the transition to industrialism through a persistently changing division of labour, and the subsequent development of an all-embracing education system. Although industrialism is adduced to be fundamental for the change to the national formation, Gellner's recent writing has come to acknowledge the qualifications of the Czech researcher, Miroslav Hroch. In a study of Eastern and Northern Europe, Hroch found that the original development of nationalist movements was in areas in which industrialization was *not* of direct importance.[51]

Gellner is right to conclude that, 'This finding does not destroy the theory linking nationalism and industrialisation',[52] however the problem is that he fails to incorporate this insight into the body of his theory. At times Gellner acknowledges the relevance of other factors such as the mass media and commodity circulation, but they are left as additions to the structure of his argument. This leads to empirically misleading claims such as his suggestion that the minimum size for a viable unit which can, to use his words, manufacture its subjects, is determined by the minimum size of an independently viable education system. For it not to be tautology the concept of viability has to be theorized.

A rationale for Gellner's contradictory portrayal of pre-agrarian social life as both spontaneously reproduced, and as highly integrated in a mechanical solidarity can now be suggested. The former characterization refers to cultural life and the latter to structural. But this is hardly satisfactory. And since the question was first asked as to whether Gellner could elude the contradiction the problems have compounded. These criticisms, I think, cast in doubt the very foundations of Gellner's theory.

50. Ibid.
51. Gellner, *Encounters*, 1994, ch. 14. See the discussion of the significance of Hroch's research in Eric Hobsbawm, 'Reflections on Nationalism', 1972.
52. Gellner, *Culture, Identity and Politics*, 1987, p. 25.

The following section delves further into the issue of social integration and the problem of understanding differentiation within a social whole. It leads into a discussion of Gellner's argument for a single epistemological space in industrial societies. A subsequent section, 'Uneven Development and the Cultural Boundary', discusses boundary demarcation as an aspect of our theme of the changing ontology of space and time. Each of these sections is set within the broader theme of the relation between the structure of the lifeworld (Habermas' phrase) and the subjectivity of national being (namely the object–subject theme).

Gesellschaft as mass society and culturally bounded

To return initially to old ground, despite Gellner's threefold theory of stages a basic (neo-Durkheimian) distinction is being made between traditional and modern societies: both the pre-agrarian (simple) and the agrarian (complex) come under the heading of traditional societies; the movement then within this category is from simple to complex. The influence on Gellner's theory of the Durkheimian understanding of the transformation of mechanical to organic solidarity or Tönnies' *Gemeinschaft* to *Gesellschaft* is apparent here. As Gellner approving says, the Durkheimian approach posits that society develops in the general direction of increasing complexity, differentiation and thus interdependence and functional complementarity.[53]

But we have to add a complicating dimension. Gellner is equally drawn to the 'mass society' thesis, which, he maintains, asserts that contrary to the differentiation thesis our society tends towards increased 'standardization, conformity, uniformity, in brief, a mass society'. He thus asks, 'How can two theories, which assert such diametrically opposed propositions, both appear so plausible and so illuminating?'[54] It is a question which, at least on the surface, affords for his position an easy analytic synthesis.

Most certainly Gellner is here referring to the Weberian routinization of society argument and the approach running through Ortega y Gasset to William Kornhauser,[55] rather than, say, to the Frankfurt school contributions to the 'mass society' debate. That is, he is engaged in putting together the two sides within the Durkheimian–Weberian paradigm. This is said not to damn it: despite the apparently easy amalgam of Durkheim and Weber in mainstream sociology (particularly in structural-functionalism), their coming together still entails tensions. Moreover the tension is not limited to that tradition. From a quite different perspective, Jean-François Lyotard is grappling

53. Gellner, 'Scale and Nation', 1974, p. 142. See p. 148 for an example of the positing of a clear dichotomy of traditional and modern. He does however criticize Durkheim for grouping 'advanced industrial civilizations' and 'industrial' society together under the heading of organic solidarity without making a distinction within this wider category. See *Nations and Nationalism*, 1983, p. 27.

54. Gellner, 'Scale and Nation', 1974.

55. See William Kornhauser, *The Politics of Mass Society*, (1959) 1965, *passim*; Daniel Bell, *The End of Ideology*, (1960) 1965, ch. 1; and Smith, *Ethnic Revival*, 1981, pp. 58–64.

with an analogous problem when he is careful to pre-empt objections to his analysis of the '"atomization" of the social into flexible networks' as seeming to be 'far removed from the modern reality, which is depicted, on the contrary, as afflicted with bureaucratic paralysis'.[56] Marxism has dealt with the problem by conceiving of societies as structured in contradiction. Thus Raymond Williams' concept of mobile privatization,[57] for example, actively embraces the contradiction of differentiation or atomization within standardization and conformity. Gellner's argument takes a different route. It begins by making a series of contrasts.

Gellner maintains that in the contrast between pre-agrarian society (small and therefore poor [*sic*]) and modern society (large and therefore likely to be rich), the most apparent and salient difference is that the former is constituted in the similarity of its parts, vertically as well as horizontally, and the latter is constituted in differentiation. However, he says, we can set up a differently contrasting dichotomy; that is, between agrarian and modern. In this comparison Gellner suggests that modern society indisputably comes out as standardized and 'drearily homogenous'. We are witnessing the end of 'character, individuality, uniqueness'.[58] Leaving aside both the way in which it contradicts other statements of his about a new (subjectivity of) individuality, and the dubious manner in which the contrast is made, it allows him another flourish before coming to the core of his position.

Gellner dismisses, with good reason, one possible synthesis of the 'incompatible' descriptions. It posits that the path from 'simple tribal societies to complex civilizations' includes an initial movement towards greater differentiation which then at a particular conjuncture reverses that direction. He says rather that diversification has increased all along this evolutionary pathway, and, crucially, that it has become different in kind. Society has become diversified over both space and time. This proposition is illuminating but unfortunately more limited than it sounds. It does not allude to the multiple levels of the reconstitution of time and space such as discussed by Anderson, Giddens, Lyotard, Sharp, or Alfred Sohn-Rethel, nor to the insights for history or geography method offered by, for example, Wolfram Eberhard, Norbert Elias or Fernand Braudel, Robert Sack or R.J. Johnston.[59] Gellner is

56. Jean-François Lyotard, *The Postmodern Condition*, 1984, p. 17.

57. He has used the terms in various places including: Raymond Williams, *Television: Technology and Cultural Form*, 1974, pp. 19–31; and 'Problems of the Coming Period', 1983.

58. Gellner, 'Scale and Nation', 1974, p. 142. Compare this position with approaches which emphasize a new level of individuality and a relative fluidity of identity such as Lasch's *The Minimal Self*, 1985. However, again Gellner's is more pertinently a rhetorical statement to accentuate the contrast, for ironically he could agree with much of Lasch's argument.

59. To the works of writers already cited can be added the bibliographical details of others: Alfred Sohn-Rethel, *Intellectual and Manual Labour: A Critique of Epistemology*, 1978; Fernand Braudel, 'Divisions of Time and Space in Europe', section I of *The Perspective of the World*, 1984; Robert Sack, *Conceptions of Space in Social Thought*, 1980; R.J. Johnston, *Geography and the State*, 1982; John Urry and Derek Gregory, eds, *Social Relations and Spatial Structures*, 1985; and David Landes, *Revolution in Time*, 1983; David Hooson, ed., *Geography and National Identity*, 1994.

saying that the new division of labour entails not only a spreading out of different skills and specializations (over space), but also that it requires that people flexibly adjust to changing employment needs (a mobility of persons over space and time). One is reminded of the evidence put forward in Vance Packard's descriptive work *A Nation of Strangers*, and of the subverting of International Business Machines' acronym, IBM, to mean 'I've Been Moved'. Gellner is making an important point in linking these changes to the formation of national subjectivity but at this stage in his writing it is still a limited theoretical proposition.

A homogenized cultural space?

In *Nations and Nationalism*, Gellner takes the analysis further to refer to an epistemological reformation of social space in industrial societies: 'By the common or single conceptual currency I mean that all facts are located within a single continuous space.'[60] At one level this might be accurate; in a more comprehensive sense it is misleading. That is, while it may be correct that a dominant culture of meaning reaches across a national space, to imply that knowledge becomes located on one continuous coherent plane leads to insurmountable problems of accounting for what this book has described in terms of the various levels of social life.[61] Elsewhere Gellner contradicts his argument for a single continuous space when he talks of an epistemological split between the ironic cultures of the lifeworld and the world of scientific and philosophical enquiry.[62] But even this does not seem sufficient to allow for the full complexity of knowledges either across particular national cultures or held in the practical and reflexive consciousness of any particular individual. Rather than following Gellner's notion of an epistemological split the present text has used the language of levels in (contradictory) intersection to evoke this complexity. As was argued earlier, face-to-face relations are a relatively irreducible level of social existence contributing to a complexity of social meaning which cannot be explained simply by reference to the dominant culture: this is so, even as face-to-face interaction is overlaid and reconstituted in the context of more abstract levels of integration.

60. Gellner, *Nations and Nationalism*, 1983, p. 21. Compare this with Lyotard's discussion of the transition from customary knowledge as condensed, timeless, narrative through scientific knowledge to a third phase, the plurality of 'language games' in postmodernity (*Postmodern Condition*, 1984). Gellner's position is closer to Claude Lévi-Strauss' two phase contrast between 'bricolage' and 'science' (*The Savage Mind*, (1962) trans. 1966), yet Gellner's view of scientific knowledge and practice at times approaches Lyotard's description of the third phase: science is the 'mode of cognition of industrial society'; 'It offers no guarantee of stability, it is morally meaningless and respects no hierarchies' (*Thought and Change*, 1964, p. 179).
    61. This point alludes to a similar discussion in Sharp, 'Constitutive Abstraction', 1985, pp. 59–61. On the question of the dominant culture see for example Raymond Williams, *Marxism and Literature*, 1977, particularly section II, chs 1, 6–9.
    62. Ernest Gellner, *Legitimation of Belief*, 1974, pp. 191–200.

Gellner's approach also flattens social structure conceived of in classing rather than epistemological or integrationist terms: for example, he writes class out of the history of late capitalism. Keeping class in the picture is important but does not solve the first problem. Some world systems theorists, who from a different perspective (marxist and aware of class contradictions) similarly emphasize a generalized division of labour, unfortunately also tend to collapse ontological–structural levels. In world systems theory it is capitalism rather than Gellner's modernization that sweeps all behind it.[63]

Gellner is characteristically half-aware that there is more to it than positing a single cultural space.[64] The metaphor does not suggest the complexity of life within that space, but he handles the issue by making an additional remark (discussed in a moment) which is in an unexplained tension with the first. None the less, it is crucial that the original proposition is carried, for he ultimately wants to say that 'the unification of [peoples'] ideas in continuous and unitary systems is connected with their re-grouping in *internally fluid*, culturally continuous communities',[65] namely, nations (emphasis added). It is crucial to Gellner being able to handle the notion of the boundary as the locus of identification for the new subjectivity. It is critical to initiating an explanation of how it is possible to conceive of the mobile division of labour as being partially bound within the edges of the nation-state (that is, one aspect of what the present text has referred to as an extension or, more generally, an abstraction in time and space).

His theory cannot, however, adequately handle the problems that flow from his very perceptive insights. It is starkly shown up in relation to traditional societies. On concurrent pages we find the following assertions:

1

In a traditional social order, the languages of the hunt, of harvesting, of various rituals, of the council room, of the kitchen or harem, all form autonomous systems: to conjoin statements drawn from these various fields, to probe for inconsistencies between them, to try to unify them all, this would be social solecism or worse, probably blasphemy or impiety, and the very endeavour would be unintelligible.

63. To anticipate their rejoinder, it is not sufficient to rely on the concept of 'uneven development' to explain complexity as do both world systems theory and Gellner's form of modernization theory. See Roger Dale, 'Nation State and International System: The World-System Perspective', 1984. For an interesting yet still inadequately voluntaristic attempt to 'account for the trajectories of globalization in a multi-dimensional fashion' see Roland Robertson and Frank Lechner, 'Modernization, Globalization, and the Problem of Culture in World-Systems Theory', 1985. They approvingly refer to Gellner's work as pointing to the modern state as 'heavily involved in the production of a "high" culture', and thus as implying the necessity of theorizing a world system which 'requires' cultural divisions (p. 110).

64. For a Gellnerian attempt to handle this problem – an attempt which also eclectically draws on 'cultural' marxists such as E.P. Thompson and Raymond Williams – see Phillip Rawkins, 'Minority Nationalism and its Limits: A Weberian Perspective on Cultural Change', 1984.

65. Gellner, *Nations and Nationalism*, 1983, p. 22; also *Encounters*, 1994, ch. 3.

2

> It is precisely by binding things together that traditional visions perpetuate them-
> selves and the prejudgments contained within them.[66]

As it is these statements are contradictory. Gellner is quite right to reject the
widely held view that a common culture united feudal society.[67] But even if
they respectively refer to the two parts of the split in traditional agrarian societies we passed over earlier – between (1) the 'little' traditions, and (2) the
'great' or 'high cultural' traditions – it still leaves Gellner unable to theorize
the reach and legitimation across the ruling classes of traditional *'visions'*
(or cultures) of structure such as the Great Chain of Being.[68] Moreover he
cannot acknowledge the examples (admittedly isolated examples) of what
Anthony Smith calls vertical *ethnie*, where a dominant ethnic culture does
permeate in varying degrees beyond the clerical and scribal strata.[69]

Given the culture/structure-in-dominance argument the problem is just
turned on its head in relation to modern societies. A second proposition is
added to that of the single cultural space. He says that the homogenization of
cultural facts is accompanied by a 'refusal to countenance conceptual package deals': people analyse and dissect the components of their
held-in-common High Culture.[70] In effect he is saying that a homogeneous
cultural space entails a rejection of cultural homogeneity. It is a leaning in the
direction of asking, as we asked earlier, why are people more conscious, or
conscious in a different way, of cultural questions. It means that with Gellner
we can reject Elie Kedourie's claim that nationalism imposes homogeneity.
But whether on the other hand we would want to straightforwardly accept the
functionalist overtones in Gellner's reversal, that 'it is the objective need for
homogeneity which is reflected in nationalism', is doubtful.[71]

Furthermore, even if there is something to Gellner's argument, the relationship between the homogeneous cultural space and the rejection of
conceptual package deals remains unexplained. The notion of a homogenized cultural space relies on a spatial metaphor which will be used to assert
the *closed*, boundedness of the nation. On the other hand the shift to an *openness* to interminable exploration (particularly affected by the 'programme' of

66. *Nations and Nationalism,* 1983, p. 21 and p. 22.

67. For a striking critique of the 'common culture thesis' see Nicholas Abercrombie, Stephen
Hill and Bryan S. Turner, *The Dominant Ideology Thesis,* 1984, ch. 2, and on feudalism, ch. 3.
However, for academic effect they tend to overstate the divide between elite and popular culture.
Michael Mullett (*Popular Culture and Popular Protest in Late Medieval and Early Modern
Europe,* 1987) provides a more balanced account.

68. Arthur Lovejoy, *The Great Chain of Being,* (1936) 1964. Further, compare quote 1 in the
present text to Gellner's statement of p. 31 of *Nations and Nationalism* (1983) that intellectuals
or clerks in agrarian society 'are both part of a society, and claim to be a voice of the whole of
it'.

69. Anthony D. Smith, *The Ethnic Origins of Nations,* 1986.

70. Gellner, *Nations and Nationalism,* 1983, p. 22. Also Gellner's *Legitimation of Belief,* 1974
and defined in Gellner, *Encounters,* 1994, p. 26.

71. Gellner, *Nations and Nationalism,* 1983, p. 46.

the intellectually trained) which Gellner will develop in terms of an uneven, interdependent 'cognitive and economic growth' is not subsumable within the single-level spatial metaphor. Another way of making the connection has to be conceived, and Gellner has no way of doing it.

There are two questions that still need to be asked: what gives rise to the single cultural space; and how does this relate to the new division of labour? They can be half answered in the context of a discussion of the issue of determination. The determinants of industrial society are most often cast by Gellner in functional relationships. He is explicit in referring to its 'functional prerequisites': industrial society 'wills itself to be mobile'! The division of labour over time and space 'requires' (Gellner uses the term hazily and ambiguously, but most strongly in terms of requiring as a prior condition, and only secondarily as requiring as a consequence) a new kind of person, a clerk, located in the spirit of rationality. His next proposition that this '*in turn* implies' (emphasis added) a basic shift from folk-familial imbued, low cultures to a universalized high-culture transmitted by a homogeneous education system,[72] again vaguely expresses a logical if not determinant relationship. Thus in an implicit rewriting of Weber, Gellner says that at the 'base of the modern social order stands not the executioner but the professor'.[73]

Here, with important differences, Gellner unintentionally strikes some parallels with Althusser's famous notes on the overdetermination of subjectivity through the ideological state apparatuses (ISAs) with the educational ISA as primary in training citizens.[74] However, in using the marxist language of base/superstructure it is turned upside-down. The 'base' is the educational system with its substantially common generic training. Any fashionable suggestions of openness, of criticizing common curriculum, which have become forcefully voiced in contemporary education debates would according to Gellner be merely a 'manifest function' masking its real basis. On this is forged the new superstructural division of labour. If we can ignore the opposite direction of determination contained in the concepts 'requires' and 'implies' discussed just a moment ago, this conception of the base suggests that the generic intellectual training through the educational sphere is the basis of the homogeneous cultural space. But the single cultural space is also part of the base because it 'underlies' the rational spirit (regularity and efficiency) carried by the division of labour.

Perhaps we are expecting too much of Gellner to be consistent on questions of determination: after all he makes no claims to be able to establish what he calls the 'aetiology of industrialism'. All the same, problems of methodological inconsistency suggest Gellner has managed to develop not so much an adequate theory of the nation as to emphasize some important processes in national formation. The following passage from Gellner at least summarizes his descriptive position:

72. Gellner, 'Scale and Nation', 1974, pp. 146–149.
73. Gellner, *Nations and Nationalism*, 1983, p. 34.
74. Althusser, *Lenin and Philosophy*, 1971.

Thus, in brief, the complex nature of modern technology and the high-powered training it presupposes, in conjunction with rapid mobility and the requirement of job-switches within one lifetime and between generations, ensure that modern society is both more homogeneous and more diversified that those which preceded it. It is more homogeneous in that it presupposes a shared universal basic training of a very serious nature, and at the same time, on the basis of this shared foundation, a rapidly changing superstructure is erected, which contains far more and more profoundly diversified elements than were found even in the more complex traditional societies . . . It is possible, on a basis of those very simple but pregnant premises, to construct a theory of nationalism.[75]

Uneven development and the cultural boundary

Some of the dimensions pointed to by Gellner's analysis as so far discussed, such as the erosion of differentiated agrarian communities and of local all-embracing structures, and the development of a generic system of intellectual training linked to the state, enable him to go some distance toward describing factors in the formation of the boundary of the nation. However, it cannot yet explain why boundaries become so important, or take the form that they do. Why can not they be overlapping? Why are boundaries so precisely demarcated; so passionately contested? Along what lines are these boundaries drawn: why this boundary rather than that? Why did not the internationalizing logic of industrialization immediately chase what Gellner calls the 'curiously abstracted loyalties' of nationalism to a further level of abstraction, that is, towards cosmopolitanism, world communalism or 'emanationalism'.[76] Or to put the same question with a historical emphasis, why are national boundaries more precisely demarcated than those of the universalizing sodalities of Christendom, Islamic society, or the Middle Kingdom? It cannot explain how the cultural boundaries of nations are maintained while being interpenetrated by inter-national allegiances and identities: 'the West', Europe, the pan-Islamic community, and so on.

It is at this point that Gellner draws upon the concept of uneven development, the uneven timing of the arrival of industrialism and the new division of labour. It is a concept he wrests out of the arms of the marxist tradition.[77] As we saw in the previous chapter the concept was reclaimed for marxism but in doing so Nairn had to acknowledge the significance of Gellner's contribution.

75. Gellner, 'Scale and Nation' 1974, p. 149. Similarly stated in *Encounters*, 1994, p. 46.

76. See variously: William Irwin Thompson's mystical book *From Nation to Emanation*, 1982; the chapters by Peter Butler, 'The Individual and International Relations', Zdenek Kavan, 'Human Rights and International Community', Michael Donelan, 'A Community of Mankind', Moorehead Wright, 'An Ethic of Responsibility', and Alan Pleydell, 'Language, Culture and the Concept of International Political Community', in James Mayall, ed., *The Community of States*, 1982; Tony Honore, 'The Human Community and the Principle of Majority Rule', 1982.

77. It was central to Lenin's theory of imperialism as one of the 'fundamental inevitable conditions and constitute premises of [the capitalist] mode of production'. V.I. Lenin, *Imperialism, the Highest Stage of Capitalism*, (1917) 1978, p. 60.

Gellner posits two principles of modern boundary demarcation. The first paradoxically occurs through the tendency in the early stages of industrialization for existing barriers to communication to be re-formed and extended. In the process 'low' cultural–linguistic groups of the old order are unevenly drawn into the new dominant culture. Later entrants into the new culture, or those whose dialect is more distant from the educationally mediated, bureaucratic and commercialized idiom, are profoundly disadvantaged. This is not to say that some individuals of the outlying cultural group don't become intellectually trained in the new order, but the training has its own repercussions. In the course of time, either the outlying group becomes incorporated into the dominant idiom, or some of its new intellectuals come to express the discontents of that group in terms of a putative version of the old folk culture/dialect. In other words, the new disenfranchised intellectuals came to reassert old boundaries, but on the basis of a more abstract conception of those boundaries. Gellner thus places intellectuals at the centre of the new movements. A nationalism emerges propelled in the first instance by a disenfranchised intelligentsia, affirming the folk culture as it supplants it.[78]

In one way Gellner barely develops this point about the re-forming (and abstraction) of linguistic/cultural boundaries. In another sense he takes it too far. While he gives valuable body to the old functionalist dictum that 'a new "society" must reconstitute itself in the image of the old' (quoted at the beginning of the chapter), and starts to address the issue of the masking of this process by the form that the reconstitution takes, this leads him into an excessively cultural inventionist stance. Ignoring much evidence to the contrary he claims that 'Dead languages can be revived, traditions invented, quite fictitious pristine purities restored'.[79] It seems that the force of the structuralist/post-structuralist emphasis on the 'arbitrariness of the sign' has insinuated its way into even this stalwart of mainstream theory. The shrinking *Gaeltacht* (Irish-speaking area) in Ireland at a time of national self-consciousness, the fitful sagas of Manx, Cornish, Welsh and Scots Gaelic are all examples which qualify any suggestion that cultural invention or revival is an easily managed process. The European Bureau of Lesser Languages, set up under the rationale that after 1992, Europe will find unity by fostering linguistic diversity, has commissioned the first Cornish-English dictionary since 1955, but whether this in itself will revive Cornish is questionable. Even Hebrew which appears to be one of the few successful revivals of a language was *never* a dead language.[80]

The second principle of boundary demarcation refers to the 'inhibitors of

---

78. Gellner, *Nations and Nationalism*, 1983, pp. 57–62. An example of the centrality of intellectuals to cultural nationalism is the influence in Africa of French speaking black intellectuals like Leopold Sedar Senghor. See Abiola Irele, 'Negritude or Black Cultural Nationalism', 1965. It is clear however that industrialization is not the key to the process.

79. Gellner, ibid., p. 56.

80. John Edwards, *Language, Society and Identity*, 1985, ch. 3. I use Edwards' discussion because ironically he sees himself in complete agreement with Gellner's point that nationalism becomes important precisely when folklore and folk dialect become 'artificial' (p. 94).

social entropy', or those classifications of identity which resist over time their even dispersal through the whole society, be they genetic or deep-cultural. Gellner avoids this definition being circular or primordialist by saying that 'Physical traits which [like red hair], though genetic, have no strong historic or geographic associations tend to be entropic'.[81] But in doing so he has effectively to base his theory of fissure generation upon cultural differences, and particularly upon differences which are a 'genuine prior barrier' both to mobility in the new fluid totality and to equality in this society of egalitarian expectations. This is the stage of the neo-nationalisms. But why is it the *deep*-cultural differences emerging from pre-industrial society which become important if, as Gellner claims, it was structural differences which were the key to understanding pre-national society? This takes us back yet again to the problem of arguing for the rise of the nation through the transition from society mediated by structure to one set in a fluid, single-level culture.

The rise of the cultural?

I would like to round off by generalizing the discussion to its broadest implications and exploring the assertion that the cultural is now in dominance. It should be emphasized that it is not the analytic separation of culture and structure which is being rejected out of hand.[82] What is being questioned is the way Gellner has handled the separation, and secondly the *status* of the suggestion that we are witnessing the rise of the cultural. The contemporary period, the age of subjectivist culture, has certainly brought the issues of cultural processes to the fore, but to say that is of a different status to arguing for the predominance of culture over structure. As the second version of Gellner's argument acknowledges, culture/structure are always in relationship. An adequate theory of the nation requires an account of the different structural–cultural (and object–subject) forms, the levels within them, and the internal relationship of those levels. And it is here that Gellner's position continues to fall short.

Ernest Gellner is not alone in suggesting the movement of culture into predominance. For some marxist-influenced theorists the limitations of the base–superstructure metaphor have been variously resolved in terms of the affirmative character of culture (Herbert Marcuse); the relative autonomy of the superstructural (Louis Althusser); by conceiving of a duality mediated (Theodor Adorno); or a duality in homology (Lucien Goldmann); and so on. With the recognition of a contemporary historical shift – called variously postmodernity, the third wave (Alvin Toffler, 1981) the media cycle (Régis Debray, 1981), the society of the spectacle (Guy Debord, 1967), and the

81. Gellner, Nations and Nationalism, 1983, p. 70.
82. Its opposite, the collapsing of the two, leads to what Zygmunt Bauman criticizes in structural–functionalism and phenomenology as 'a view of social structure as "typified": and so a monotonous sediment of normative cultural patterns'. See Zygmunt Bauman, *Culture as Praxis*, 1973, p. 84. Relevant to this whole discussion is section 2 'Culture as Structure'.

information society – that is the recognition, in Fredric Jameson's words, of a 'fundamental mutation of the sphere of culture' in late capitalism, the debate has been reopened.[83] The lengthy passage from Jameson about to be quoted expresses this. It has surprising parallels with the earlier version of Gellner's 'culture/structure in predominance' argument, but it also opens up a number of related problems relevant both to a critique of Gellner's continuing position and to any discussion on the transformations of the form of the nation. Jameson writes:

> What we must ask ourselves is whether it is not precisely this 'semi-autonomy' of the cultural sphere which has been destroyed by the logic of late capitalism. Yet to argue that culture is today no longer endowed with the relative autonomy it once enjoyed as one level among others in earlier moments of capitalism (let alone in pre-capitalist societies), is not necessarily to imply its disappearance or extinction. On the contrary: we must go on to affirm that the dissolution of an autonomous sphere of culture is rather to be imagined in terms of an explosion: a prodigious expansion of culture throughout the social realm, to the point at which everything in our social life – from economic value and state power to practices and to the very structure of the psyche itself – can be said to have become 'cultural' in some original and as yet untheorized sense. This perhaps startling proposition is, however, substantively quite consistent with the previous diagnosis of a society of the image or the simulacrum, and a transformation of the 'real' into so many pseudo-events.[84]

Rather than getting into a lengthy critique of this statement at this point I want just to raise a couple of problems and some questions, then to speculate upon a common and underlying basis to the inadequacy of both the prodigious-expansion-of-culture argument or the structure/culture-in-dominance position. To these positions can be added others which encounter similar problems. Christopher Lasch comes close to both and fully agrees with neither when he says:

> Identity has become uncertain and problematic not because people no longer occupy fixed social stations – commonplace explanation that unthinkingly incorporates the modern equation of identity and social role – but because they no longer inhabit a world that exists independently of themselves.[85]

Firstly, in relation to Jameson most particularly, it should be asked, what does it mean to talk of a 'prodigious expansion of culture' as occurring in the present? Does it suggest that Jameson's definition of culture is dependent on implicit phenomenological assumptions, as, indeed, is Gellner's? Is Jameson implying that in 'earlier' social formations people were not as thoroughly culturally constituted as in the present? What are the implications of setting up a Janus-faced distinction between the 'real' and the pseudo-real as both Jameson and Lasch wish to maintain? This then relates to an aspect of

83. Fredric Jameson, in one of the most often cited articles in the debates on postmodernity over the last decade and a half, 'Postmodernism, or the Cultural Logic of Late Capitalism', 1984, p. 86. The references cited here are Alvin Toffler, *The Third Wave*, 1981; Régis Debray, *Teachers, Writers, Celebrities*, 1981; Guy Debord, *Society of the Spectacle*, (1967) 1983.

84. Jameson, 'Postmodernism', p. 87.

85. Lasch, *The Minimal Self*, 1985, p. 32.

Gellner's continuing emphasis and to an issue that has been raised throughout this book (particularly Chapter 5): namely, what are the implications of
talking of culture as invention, or culture as simulacrum as it has become
more fashionable to do lately? Nationalism, in Gellner's aphoristic language
'invents nations where they do not exist', or as Donald Horne would have it
'their "reality" must be "invented"'.[86] Further to this, the problem of how to
conceive of a historical shift in the form of social integration within the para-
meters of the orthodox marxist metaphor of base–superstructure is apparent
in this passage from Jameson, but it also relates to a Weberian–Durkheimian
like Gellner who would reject any such notion of base–superstructure yet is at
least partly concerned with the question of determination.

To argue that we now (self-actively) form our identity in the cultural sphere,
or that culture has now exploded into every level of social life suggests an
acute awareness of *phenomenal* changes (in both senses of the word): from the
globalization of commodified culture and the penetration of international
popular culture into hitherto parochial or relatively closed settings; the
increasing fragmentation of those settings which grounded and even bound
the extent to which questions about identity and ontology could be explored;
to the galloping emphasis on personal, autonomous identity construction
and the realm of the unconscious.[87] However, the attempt to theorize these
developments in terms of a prodigious-expansion-of-culture or a
culture/structure inversion effectively hypostatizes the realms which have been
analytically separated and confuses substantive changes in the form of the
culture and social structure for a changed relationship between those *theoretical* realms. Gellner's earlier use of the theoretical concepts of structure and
culture as descriptive terms to be posited as the alternative webbing of social
integration certainly made this mistake. In Jameson's case he seems to be
confusing what has been described here as the processes of the extension and
abstraction in time and space of a practised-in-common level of culture
(occurring particularly throughout Western capitalist societies) with social life
becoming cultural in a more generalized way.

This can be pushed a step further through asking why social theorists are
putting more emphasis on the cultural, and why many people are more conscious, or conscious in a different way, of cultural questions. A response
would also tie in with an implied connection made in the introduction to this
chapter: namely, the new meta-interest in cultural questions is relevant to
explaining the latest wave of attention given to explaining the formation and
hold of the nation.

---

86. Gellner, *Thought and Change*, 1964, p. 168; Donald Horne, *The Public Culture*, 1986,
p. 109. See also Gellner, *Nations and Nationalism*, 1983, pp. 48–49, 55–56; Anderson, *Imagined
Communities*, 1983, pp. 15–16, 122; Richard White, *Inventing Australia*, 1981; Gary Wills,
Inventing America, 1979; E. Hobsbawm and T. Ranger, eds, *The Invention of Tradition*, 1983;
Edwards, *Language*, 1985; Edmund S. Morgan, *Inventing the People*, 1988.

87. Amongst the massive body of literature on this last development see Ernest Gellner's
own *The Psychoanalytic Movement*, 1985.

To expand this outwards, whereas the tendency towards a relative sup-
pression of theorizing the cultural by the classical positions, including even
Marx's, almost closed off the possibility through that period of theorizing the
nation, the contemporary interest in the rise of the cultural (Giddens and
Beck use the term 'reflexive modernization'[88]) is a condition for a new stage
of theorizing. But it has its own pitfalls. The expansion-of-culture position
and both versions of the culture-in-dominance argument replace an analysis
of the rise of the cultural with a description of it. They thus have restricted
insight into the possibilities of their own theorizing. This development suggests that we need to be able to theorize the broad sweep of change which
heightens in inter-relation both a new epistemology and a new self-consciousness of an ontological shakiness which previously only philosophers
built into castles in the air. It raises questions about the fundamental reconstitution of the nation in the postmodern, late-capitalist setting and how
nationality (including some of its modern forms) as one 'primordial essence'
of individual identity will continue to have force. With the emerging dominance of a new mode of integration in late capitalism and the reconstitution
of the old form of the nation, new ways of thinking about the old are coming
into prominence. In some ways a theorist like Jameson is better equipped to
deal with these questions.[89] Given the boundaries of Gellner's theory we are
restrained to focus on the formations of the 'classical nation' rather than its
subsequent transformations. Gellner's vigorous critique of the philosophy of
postmodernism[90] (much of which I agree with) blinds him to the possibility
that postmodernity may already be upon us as a material process, as an ontological formation framing without replacing tradition and modernity.

I have tried in this chapter to show how Gellner's theory of the nation rests
upon a deeply flawed theory of societal forms. Gellner leaves us with a series
of evocative and inspired, but unsustained insights. Gavin Kitching gener-
ously writes that:

> Gellner rather like Max Weber in fact, is a much better comparative historian than
> he is a theorist, and indeed his capacity for astute historical generalization tends to
> triumph *despite* the ponderous and static conceptual apparatus in which it is
> enthralled.[91]

Gellner in fact set himself a more far-reaching task: unobtrusively to loosen
habitual theoretical associations, to set up new principles which are evident
from the context in which they are developed 'until at last the context has
been set up in which an assertion can be made which is simple, and yet not a

---

88. Ulrich Beck, Anthony Giddens and Scott Lash, *Reflexive Modernization: Politics,
Tradition and Aesthetics in the Modern Social Order*, 1994.
    89. Even so, see Dan Latimer's critique in 'Jameson and Post-Modernism', 1984.
    90. Ernest Gellner, *Postmodernism, Reason and Religion*, 1992. For an excellent riposte to
Gellner see Bryan S. Turner, *Orientalism, Postmodernism, and Globalism*, 1994.
    91. Kitching, 'Instrumental Passion', 1985, p. 107.

trite repetition of the old wisdom'.[92] So far, despite his considerable rearrangements of the terms within the Durkheimian–Weberian approach, particularly the traditional/modern distinction, Gellner has not managed to carry the opening forays of classical social theory into an approach which escapes the considerable problems associated with the hardening of that tradition into an iron cage of orthodoxy. The next chapter examines a social theorist who, by drawing the Durkheimian-Weberian tradition into an unusual synthesis with insights from marxism, does escape some of the limitations of orthodoxy. However, the chapter will question whether or not this radical synthesis by Anthony Giddens is any more successful than Ernest Gellner's reworkings.

92. Gellner, *Nations and Nationalism*, 1983, p. 136.

7

Nation Formation and the Instituting State: A Critique of Structuration

What has made the nation-state apparently irresistible as a political form from the early nineteenth century to the present-day? From the state system that was once one of the peculiarities of Europe there has developed a system of nation-states covering the globe in a network of national communities . . .

In outline, it is not difficult to explain the universal scope of the nation-state in the modern world. There are three main types of factors involved, only one of which is intrinsically connected with the spread of industrial capitalism. The first is the combination of industrial and military power originally developed in the European nation-state. Rather than promoting peaceful economic advance, industrialism was from the beginning married to the arts of war. No state that did not possess military forces able to use the new organizational forms and the new weaponry could hope to withstand external attack from those that could muster such forces. The second factor is the vast expansion of the administrative power of the state, which I have argued is one of the main definitive features of the nation-state. Only with such extension of authoritative resources does it become possible to concentrate the allocative resources upon which a flourishing modern economy depends. The heightened administrative power of the state is necessary not only to consolidate resources internally, but to cope with the vast international political network of relations in which all modern states are involved with others. The third influence, or rather, set of influences, concerns a series of contingent historical developments that cannot be derived from general traits attributed to nation-states, but which nonetheless decisively influenced the trajectory of development of the modern world.

Anthony Giddens, *The Nation-State and Violence* 1985

Anthony Giddens is not alone in thinking that the existing traditions of Western social and political thought are in need of renewal and rethinking. Into this setting have stepped a proliferation of new social theories attempting to provide new means of understanding the world. However, of all those post-classical theories, theories which in a generalized way purport substantially to break with or forge a novel synthesis between the traditions of marxism and those of Weber and Durkheim, Giddens' theory of structuration is the only one that stands out as paying direct and sustained attention to the nation-state. This lacuna in avant-garde theory is surprising. It is unexpected, not the least because the nation-state has consolidated in this century as *the* predominant form of abstract community. Despite the escalated crossing of national boundaries by a flow of international capital and extended forms of cultural interchange, the nation-state continues to bind people in relations of intense, if increasingly fragile and contradictory, loyalty.

Such issues remain largely outside the preserve of contemporary, particularly postmodern, social theory. In the pantheon of big names in contemporary avant-garde, theory only Julia Kristeva has devoted more than passing paragraphs to the nation-state. Michel Foucault concentrates on institutions of power, discipline and sequestration within the state boundary. Jacques Derrida is taken by his own special expression of the cultural inventionist standpoint, to the extent that when he writes an isolated essay on the American Declaration of Independence his central interest is in deconstructing the 'patriotic' document as a fictional moment which invents its signatories in their act of signing. Giles Deleuze and Félix Guattari in occasional cryptic comments reduce the nation-state to a locus of artificial territorialization. Cornelius Castoriadis reduces the nation-state to an exemplification of his thesis that society is instituted as an act of the imaginary.[1] The list could go on. The point is that across the range of contemporary social theory, Giddens is notable in bringing his general theoretical approach to bear upon the national question. His analysis of the nation-state in the context of his overall theory is thus the subject of this chapter. Moreover, as a synthesizer of the theoretical traditions of Marx, Durkheim and Weber, discussed in earlier chapters, Anthony Giddens provides us with a doubly relevant body of work through which to draw this present work towards a conclusion.

Continuing the primordiality–modernity theme the following discussion critically elaborates upon Giddens' theory of the original formation of the nation-state. Secondly, as a continuation of the subject–object theme, the chapter examines his contribution to understanding the subjectivity and social relations of the nation and nation-state: it asks why it is that within a broader theory that makes significant strides in interpreting the relation between objective forms of social relations and modes of individual and social subjectivity, his more specific theory of the nation-state leaves this objective–subjective relation as an *ad hoc* connection. Why does Giddens retain a strict dualism of subject (nationalism) and object (nation-state) when a central rationale for the theory of structuration is overcoming such dualisms?

---

1. Michel Foucault, *Discipline and Punish*, (1975) 1982; Jacques Derrida, 'Declarations of Independence', 1986, and see also his *The Other Heading*, 1992; Felix Guattari, *Molecular Revolution*, 1984; Cornelius Castoriadis, *The Imaginary Institution of Society*, 1987. Julia Kristeva is an exception with the publication of three of her essays under the title *Nations without Nationalism*, 1993, but the book is written as a political and philosophical argument not as political theory. The one field in which the nation is given sustained attention is post-colonial theory. See for example Partha Chatterjee, *The Nation and its Fragments*, 1993.

Giddens' theory of nation-state formation

For Giddens the nation-state is a bordered power-container. It contains power through storing and extending the possibilities of time–space distantiation, for example through storing information relevant to the direct supervision of its subject population. By virtue of this reflexively monitored containment, the nation-state is quite distinct from the polities of earlier agrarian class-divided societies. This is a different point than that made by Michael Mann when he overstretches his salutary criticism of theories which conceive of societies as discrete, monolithic or unitary formations. Mann implies, I think wrongly, that across the transformations of world history, societies became more bounded and separated out from each other as state powers were increased.[2] Giddens' traditional–modern distinction which he makes specific to a comparison of state formations is more easily sustained. He argues that in contrast to the contemporary (more abstract) state, which through a rationalized network of agencies attempts to cast a relatively homogeneous shadow over its territory, traditional states did not have the administrative power to contain, pacify and monitor space in other than an uneven way. Their power decreased unevenly across the widening circles of distance from their administrative centres. (See Chapter 1 on the distinction between frontiers and borders.) While Giddens may underestimate the concern in the traditional states for precisely demarcating their frontiers,[3] his argument that traditional states did not have borders but frontiers accords with current research. Giddens thus begins, as he says, with a typological and comparative concern generically to contrast modern and traditional states.[4] Although the absolutist state is taken as marking the transition to the modern state, it is in his terms still a traditional state.[5]

Giddens highlights three political characteristics of the transition: (1) the centralization and extension of administrative power; (2) the development of more abstract practices and codes of law whereby statutes began to be drawn distinguishing between private property and the public domain, and the legal sanctions of state agencies began to replace customary sanctions; and (3) changes to the forms of managing money, in particular, the institution of large-scale tax systems to underwrite the constant military confrontations between the emerging European states (pp. 93–103). Further to these changes,

2. Michael Mann, *The Sources of Social Power*, vol. 1, 1986, *passim*. Chris Wickham (in 'Historical Materialism, Historical Sociology', 1988) draws the same implication, but he agrees with Mann's conclusion. By using the levels-in-intersection metaphor it is possible to allow for the way in which the processes of bounding work in different ways across varying extensions of space and time. See Chapter 1 above.

3. See John Armstrong, *Nations before Nationalism*, 1982, ch. 2.

4. Anthony Giddens, *The Nation-State and Violence*, 1985, p. 83. All ensuing page references in the body of the text will refer to this book.

5. Ibid., p. 93. At another point (p. 4) the distinction is not made so clearly. He says: 'In the absolutist state we discover a breakaway from traditional state forms.' It is only a minor issue, but it indicates a problem with the concept of the traditional–modern divide.

Giddens associates the rise of the absolutist state and the later nation-state with certain military developments. Firstly, he suggests that technological developments in armaments, crucially the industrial–military harnessing of gunpowder in the sixteenth century, changed the nature of war and separated defence from the fortification of cities. Secondly, the amplification of administrative power within the military and the creation of standing armies owing direct allegiance to prince and *patria* favoured the predominance of larger states and principalities over smaller ones, of unified kingdoms over what Gianfranco Poggi calls *ständestaatum*. Thirdly, Giddens singles out the importance of naval power as contributing to the rise of the English, Dutch and French states, and to the further interconnecting of the world (pp. 105–116). These factors, I suggest, are all changes in social form discussed predominantly at the ontological level of agency-extension (the administration of agents and agencies) and at the epistemological level of empirical generalization. This point will be developed and become central to a critique of Giddens' theory as being set on one plane. However, there is a lot of groundwork to be done before this criticism can be directly sustained.

Much of Anthony Giddens' writing on the national question is expressed in a comparative listing-of-factors manner. The historical description is well supported by notable contemporary research such as that conducted by Charles Tilly and his associates.[6] However, the limitations of his overall framework can begin to be exposed through an examination of some instances where Giddens moves to draw conclusions from his comparative generalizations. He says:

> The European state system was not simply the 'political environment' in which the absolutist state and nation-state developed. It was the condition, and in substantial degree the very source, of that development. It was war, and preparations for war, that provided the most potent energizing stimulus for the concentration of administrative resources and fiscal reorganization that characterized the rise of absolutism. Technological changes affecting warfare were more important than changes in techniques of production. (p. 112)

Underpinning this statement and running through his analysis are a number of propositions which are open to qualification. They warrant extensive comment. To begin with, we can question the status of the repeated assertion that the absolutist state and nation-state are European in source and origin.[7] That question becomes the subject of the following section. There is no doubting the importance, indeed overt centrality, of developments occurring in Europe; however, Giddens can be criticized along with other writers as diverse as Hans Kohn and V.G. Kiernan for being overly anxious to attest to this centrality.[8] Giddens' analysis gives the impression of a single-trajectory

6. Charles Tilly, ed., *The Formation of National States in Western Europe*, 1975.
7. See also Anthony Giddens, 'Nation-States and Violence', in *Social Theory and Modern Sociology*, 1987, pp. 170, 177, 179 and his *Power, Property and State*, 1981, p. 186.
8. Hans Kohn, *The Idea of Nationalism*, (1944) 1956; V.G. Kiernan, 'State and Nation in Western Europe', 1965, pp. 20–38.

pathway from European absolution to the nation-state. He leaves out the complication that developments of the *form* that he isolates in Europe were, *albeit with quite different cultural content*, proceeding elsewhere. Seventeenth-century Japan was for example more bureaucratic, more precisely surveyed and more intensively administered than late-feudal Europe.[9] The subsequent section takes up the question of the relation between the state and war and capitalism. The present chapter thus initially allows the structure of Giddens' own approach to set the structure of a critical response while beginning to interleave suggestions as to how the constitutive levels method presents different ways of understanding.

Europe as the source and origin?

Giddens defines the absolutist state as 'a political order dominated by a sovereign ruler, monarch or prince, *in whose person* are invested ultimate *political* authority and sanctions, including control of the means of violence'[10] (emphasis added). In contrast to Giddens' substantive analysis which overemphasizes the level of the agency-extended, this definition goes in the opposite direction to overemphasize a still-present but increasingly subordinate aspect of this form of state, namely the centring of power on the person of the prince. Given that with absolutism, face-to-face relations were already overlaid by post-patrimonial relations of agency-extension, and in Gianfranco Poggi's words, power had become 'more unitary and abstract', detaching 'itself conceptually from the physical person of the ruler', the definition is doubly misleading.[11] Furthermore, whether by this definition or a more fully considered version, it is not so clearly the case that the emergence of administrations of absolutist control depended directly upon the European setting. Ironically, it could be argued that the emergence of capitalism in Europe rather than in the 'Far East' was testimony to the far greater political and economic control that the Chinese and Japanese polities had over market relations, the movement of capital, and its private accumulation.

It would seem that Giddens is also on shaky ground when he says that traditional rulers outside of Europe had not 'incorporated the state within their own person; they sat at the pinnacle of it' (p. 93). This is not to question his insightful comment that doctrines of divine right were traditional accoutrements to something very new; it is rather to challenge the modernist and Eurocentric way in which this point is developed. There are unspoken modernist assumptions permeating Giddens' treatment of kingship as an administrative accretion upon the body politic. As Reinhard Bendix has

---

9. Joseph R. Strayer, 'The Tokugawa Period and Japanese Feudalism', and other chapters in John W. Hall and Marius B. Jansen, eds, *Studies in the Institutional History of Early Modern Japan*, 1968.

10. Giddens, *Power, Property and State*, 1981, p. 186, repeated in 'Nation-States and Violence', 1987, pp. 170–171.

11. See Gianfranco Poggi, *The Development of the Modern State*, 1978, p. 74 and ch. 4.

argued, kingship was an ambiguous institution having its roots in *kin*-group associations.[12]

There is a Eurocentrism in both the treatment of kingship and absolutism. Just to raise one example in relation to absolutism, the succession of Tokugawa shoguns who maintained a kind of Absolutist control of Japan from the seventeenth century well into the nineteenth century did so during a period of conscious insulation from most European contact. Nevertheless, they were part of a reconstitution of the traditional. Giddens might counter that the Tokugawa shogunate symbolically deferred to the sacred pre-eminence of the emperor, but it must be recognized how they controlled and isolated his power. Initially through a revival of the neo-Confucian philosophy of Chu Hsi and later through a 'proto-national' doctrine known as the 'Way of Japan as the Way of the Gods', they drew upon the emperor's status (though not as a completely self-conscious instrumental procedure) to assume political, administrative and military authority.[13] And, if Herman Ooms is right, beginning in the early Tokugawa period, as the shogun confirmed their power they 'dissolved the historical, contingent dimension of their persons, and inserted them into a Shinto scheme of the sacred'.[14]

The same question of Europe as *the* birthplace of the abstraction of the state can be raised in relation to the rise of the nation-state. Certainly Europe was central to the emergent system of capitalist exchange relations which through imperial expansion effected fundamental changes in the societies of the 'periphery'. But it is not as Giddens puts it that processes decisive to state formation, such as administrative control 'sustained primarily through the disciplinary power of surveillance', first consolidated to become an inherent feature of the European nation-state system, '*then* started to become diffused across the world'[15] (emphasis added). It can be expressed quite

12. Reinhard Bendix, *Kings or People*, 1978, ch. 1.

13. Even when emphasizing the uniqueness of Japanese development, both Bendix (*Kings or People*, 1978, ch. 12) and Johann Arnason ('The Modern Constellation and the Japanese Enigma: Part 1', 1987) draw out the structural affinities of the Tokugawa shogunate with European absolutism. Manchu China might also be drawn into the comparison: see Theda Skocpol, *States and Social Revolutions: A Comparative Analysis of France, Russia and China*, 1979. Perry Anderson appears to be in agreement with Giddens when Anderson says, quite categorically, that 'Far Eastern feudalism never passed over into Absolutism' (*Lineages of the Absolutist State*, 1986, p. 428). However, his basis for that claim is opposed to Giddens' definition: 'one basic characteristic . . . divided the Absolute monarchies of Europe from all the myriad other types . . . controlled by a personal sovereign . . . [It] was also simultaneously the age in which private property was progressively consolidated' (*Nation-State and Violence*, 1985, p. 429).

14. Herman Ooms, 'Neo-Confucianism and the Formation of Early Tokugawa Ideology', 1984. I find much of Ooms' description illuminating even though I substantially disagree with his overly instrumental, overly constructivist view of ideology. On early Japanese and Korean political unification see also Joji Watanuki, 'Nation-Building at the Edge of an Old Empire: Japan and Korea', 1973.

15. Giddens, 'Nation-States and Violence', 1987, pp. 176 and 177. For a critique of diffusionism see James Blaut, *The National Question*, 1987, pp. 10–11, 29–32, 38–39, 76–100, 172–175. While most of his criticisms are blunted by an unremitting class-reductionism, he still has instructive points to make.

differently and in ways not necessarily discordant with other emphases of Giddens' narrative. The gradual and uneven consolidation in Europe and elsewhere of developments (some discussed earlier) which conditioned the transition from the imperial or monarchical state to the abstract state contributed to a changed world time, a changed constitutive setting in which across the globe, and bearing back upon Europe, states and peoples began to assert their political and cultural identity.

Examples which qualify Giddens' focus on European absolutism as the proximate source of the nation-state are not hard to find. The Thirteen States in North America had instituted the internal pacification of its indigenous inhabitants; they had fought a war of independence against a European power which brandished absolutist doctrines of the indivisibility of sovereignty (1775–83); they had worked out a system for parcelling, commodifying and administering the 'empty' frontier territories; and, in the name of the People of the United States, had ratified a unifying constitution (1789) – all before the August Days of 1789 saw Louis XVI's *ancien régime* brought to an end by his erstwhile royal subjects.[16]

If we travel south to the colonies of Spanish America, Benedict Anderson asks: 'Why was it precisely *creole* communities that developed so early conceptions of their nation-ness – *well before most of Europe?*'[17] The apparent anachronism cannot be explained through a straightforward diffusionist argument. Giddens could respond to Anderson's question in terms of his separation between the nation-state and nationalism (that is, leaving aside problems with the way this necessary separation is made). However, this is complicated by the way Giddens goes on to bind himself in a minor analytic knot. He gives the title of 'colonial nation-states' or 'state-nations' to those former colonies who 'achieved their statehood by fighting wars of *national* liberation against the metropolitan powers' (p. 271, emphasis added). Given the force of his definition that the nation-state is a set of governing institutions maintaining exclusive power over a precisely demarcated territory, a definition which supposedly 'holds for all variants' (p. 121), the discussion of colonial nation-states belies his emphasis on the extensive reach and homogenizing administrative control of nation-state apparatuses. Implicitly, by his discussion, the USA (1781), Santo Domingo (1791), Haiti (1804), Venezuela (1811), Chile (1817), the Republic of Gran Colombia (1821), Mexico (1824), and the short-lived republic of the United Provinces of Central America (1838)[18] emerged as nation-states simultaneously with the first of the nation-states in Europe (and long before most). As an adjacent point, we can

16. Daniel Boorstin concludes that 'The whole American situation led them to expect more from large organized political units, the states and the federal government, than did their contemporaries in the Old World' (*The Americans*, vol. 2, 1969, p. 316). On the ideological and economic bearing of the American War of Independence *back upon* the later French Revolution, see E.N. Williams, *The Ancien Regime in Europe*, (1972) 1983, pp. 239–240.

17. Benedict Anderson, *Imagined Communities*, 1991, p. 50. See also Victor Alba, *Nationalists Without Nations*, 1968.

18. From Hugh Seton-Watson, *Nations and States*, 1977, ch. 5.

also ask why the term state-nation gets introduced to emphasize that in 'most post-colonial nation-states there is no sense in which a "nation" precedes the emergence of the state' (p. 272, cf. p. 251), when, by his definition, a nation cannot exist prior to its unification within state boundaries anyway.

The criticisms around the issues of Eurocentrism, diffusionism, and an unsustained linearity of change expressed over the foregoing pages are bruising rather than knock-down blows, but in conjunction with the next issue to be raised they start to add up to the conclusion that Anthony Giddens' historical synthesis of existing research is not as impressive or sophisticated as it first promises. These shortcomings cannot be separated from a major analytic preclusion that will be drawn out more explicitly as we proceed. I will argue that Giddens reduces the nation-state to an administrative structure of political and military power, and that in the process he defines away the possibility of having a theory of the nation.

Means of violence and mode of production

For the moment there is a second proposition in the earlier passage cited from Giddens, part of a group of issues, which also needs to be critically explored. He suggests that in the rise of absolutism, and thus prefiguring the transition to the nation-state, 'technological changes affecting warfare were more important than changes in techniques of production'.[19] It is indicative of a recurrent theme throughout the appropriately entitled *The Nation-State and Violence*. The task of the present section is not so much to examine the empirical evidence for such a statement as to use it to introduce a discussion of the way in which Giddens relates internal and external violence (aspects of administrative power) to the forces and relations of production.

Contemporary scholarship tends to support Giddens' emphasis upon the relevance of war to the emergence of the state and nation-state. Along with writers such as Michael Mann, he brings renewed vigour to an area which has been underplayed in certain theoretical traditions, particularly in structural–functionalist theories of nation-building which accentuate consensual integration.[20] But the above statement cannot be convincingly sustained even by reference to the historical sources upon which it is reliant. Giddens' conclusion overlooks evidence indicating for example that military developments in Western Europe (which had come after 1500 to surpass even those of China), did not achieve this advance simply because of technical advances in the military sphere as such. As William McNeill documents, in the centuries immediately after AD 1000, Chinese industry and armaments manufacture had anticipated European developments by

19. Cf. Giddens, *The Nation-State and Violence*, 1985, p. 255, where in a more tempered statement he says, 'industrialism was from the beginning married to the arts of war'.

20. For an indication of the renewed interest in the area, see Michael Howard, 'War and the Nation-State', 1979; Ronald Cohen, 'Warfare and State Formation', 1984; Michael Mann, *States, War and Capitalism*, 1988.

several hundred years. European predominance in the technology of war emerged hand in hand with, or dependent upon, other developments: the development of artillery for example drew upon metal-casting techniques emanating from the prior craft of church-bell making; it depended upon improved hard-rock mining and ore-refining techniques, and upon the relatively unabated extension of merchant capital and market relations facilitating the assemblage of raw materials. To give determinant priority to the technology of war – even if it is, as he says, 'substantially separate' from the main core of feudal production – is to ignore for analytic effect the interdependence of means of warfare with the means of exacting feudal surplus, as well as with an overdetermining, emergent set of commodity production and exchange relations.[21]

Giddens' related claim is that advances in military technology favoured larger states (p. 108). Other work suggests that in a very limited and carefully qualified sense, and with obvious exceptions, this is possibly so.[22] However, a much stronger case can be made for the importance of the changing logistics of war, the mass expansion during the seventeenth and eighteenth centuries of the numbers of men under arms, the development of standing military forces, and the effect this had upon the means and intensity of tax collection.[23] But even here we have to be careful. The Roman Empire gave way in the fourth century to a patchwork of smaller political, religious and tribal associations and entities, that is despite the imperial maintenance of a more extensive taxation system and a much larger proportion of professional soldiers to population than existed a millennium later.[24]

Why then does Giddens make such large claims for the determinative influence and autonomy (presumably relative) of the instruments and organization of war? He is not a technological determinist. Part of the answer lies in the *way* he separates authoritative and allocative resources. The problematic implications of Giddens' use of these terms will be discussed in a later section, but for the moment it will suffice to begin with some definitions and to link these terms to an issue which came up in the chapters on Ernest Gellner and Tom Nairn, namely the relation between the nation-state, capitalism and industrialism. The concept of allocative resources refers to what marxists would call the means of material production deriving from dominion over nature; authoritative resources refers in an elaboration of the Weberian sense to the means of

21. William McNeill, *The Pursuit of Power*, 1983, chs 2 and 3.

22. See Richard Bean, 'War and the Birth of the Nation-State', 1973. However, see also the very critical comments of David Ringrose, 'Comment', 1973 and Richard Roehl, 'Comment', 1973. As Benedict Anderson points out, 'The first "great" powers of Europe-in-the-world were tiny Portugal, tiny Holland, and not very big England' (personal communication).

23. Samuel Finer, 'State- and Nation-Building in Europe: The Role of the Military', 1975. For an interesting empirical discussion of the intersection between the financial effects of war and the rise of entrepreneurial capitalism, see Christopher Friedrichs, *Urban Society in an Age of War*, 1979.

24. J.B. Campbell, *The Emperor and the Roman Army 31 BC–AD 235*, 1984; Peter Garnsey and Richard Saller, *The Roman Empire*, 1987, particularly ch. 2.

dominion over human beings themselves.[25] Military power, in its capacity to extend and intensify the possibilities of applying sanctions, is treated along with the possibilities of surveillance, administration, and ideological formation as one of the four factors which create authoritative resources (pp. 14–17). It seems that the logic of Giddens' broader argument that prior to the emergence of capitalism authorization had primacy over allocation,[26] leads him to extrapolate analytically the undoubtedly important influence of military power upon pre-capitalist state formation beyond what the evidence can support.

Given, firstly, that the state did emerge prior to the consolidation of capitalism, secondly, that the nation-state is defined as an administrative power container, and thirdly, that the nation-state is theorized as arising directly out of the heightening and centralizing of administrative power, then Giddens' emphasis on authoritative resources could have been developed as a closed circle of *a priori* logic. This is part of the problem. Characteristically. however, Giddens always recognizes that there is more than a single determinative force. The '*characteristics*' of the (European) nation-state-form depend, he says, not only upon certain administrative apparatuses but also the conjunctions of capitalism and industrialism: together they constitute three, distinct '*organizational* clusters' (p. 141, emphasis added). The crucial question, apart from why they are seen in organizational terms, concerns the relationship between these clusters.

Giddens is, I would contend, more successful in discussing the relation between capitalism and industrialism than that between industrial capitalism and the nation-state. By arguing for the logical distinction between, and yet uneven historical conjunction of, industrialism and capitalism, his position is able to contrast modern and traditional state forms without following Ernest Gellner in a rewriting of the Great Divide between the agrarian and the industrial age. While Gellner is more evocative on the ontological changes impelled by a complex division of labour, Giddens' theory of history is in the end more successful in that he avoids both Gellner's disinclination to discuss the implications of capitalism and his tendency to give industrialism an inherent dynamic over and above being a particular form of productive activity.

Giddens' discussion of the relation between capitalism and the nation-state is not so successful partly because the ground is less secure.[27] Still, by implication at least, his contribution avoids many of the problems in Tom Nairn's

25. See Giddens, *Nation-State and Violence*, 1985, pp. 7–17; and *The Constitution of Society*, 1984, pp. 258–262.

26. Anthony Giddens, *Central Problems in Social Theory*, 1979, p. 162, also pp. 92–94, 100–101, 162–164. This is toned down in his *Constitution of Society* (1984, pp. 258–262), and qualified substantially in *Nation-State and Violence* (1985, pp. 7–22), but the original argument still lingers on, at least in his discussion of the state. What are we to make of his suggestion that 'capitalist society' is 'the first and only form of society in history of which it might be said with some plausibility that it both "has" and "is" a mode of production' (ibid., pp. 134–135)?

27. See for example Philip Corrigan, ed., *Capitalism, State Formation and Marxist Theory*, 1980; Gale Stokes, 'How is Nationalism Related to Capitalism?', 1986; and perhaps the best attempt, Etienne Balibar and Immmanuel Wallerstein, *Race, Nation, Class*, 1991. For a specific empirical investigation of the relation see Jim MacLaughlin, 'Industrial Capitalism, Ulster Unionism and Orangeism', 1980, or the slightly broader work of Michael Hechter, *Internal Colonialism*, 1975.

thesis that nationalism first developed in the periphery as the uneven, exploitative and remorseless nature of capitalist diffusion engendered a new fragmentation there along the fault-lines (often ethnic lines) of an earlier stage of history (see Chapter 5). And although it is much less elegant than Benedict Anderson's examination of the relevance of print capitalism to the imagined community – mostly because as I will argue below it sequesters questions of ontology, subjectivity and culture – Giddens' analysis provides us with another direct if underdeveloped avenue into considering the relevance of the changes wrought through the objective structures of capitalism. Before following this avenue, let me note its limitations.

For the most part, Giddens treats industrialism, capitalism and the formation of state administrative apparatuses as distinct organizational clusters providing the backdrop to the nation-state, but this becomes confused when it is remembered that the nation-state *is* by his narrow definition a state administrative apparatus. Hence at times it seems that Giddens' contribution is not to a theory of nation-state formation, but to the way in which an existent nation-state administrative apparatus frames industrial capitalism. Take the following examples from *The Nation-State and Violence*:

1
The maturation of capitalism involves a commodification of land and products, on the one hand, and of labour-power, on the other. While these do not proceed wholly independently of each other, the former is intertwined mainly with the development of the absolutist state. The latter – or so I shall argue – *depends for its large-scale extension* upon the formation of the nation-state (p. 148, emphasis added).

2
The centralization of state power was *the necessary condition* for the formation of commodity money (p. 154, emphasis added).

3
The early development of capitalism was indeed *predicated upon* an insulation of the political and the economic not only internal but external to the territorially bounded [therefore, nation-]state (p. 170, emphasis added).

4
The existence of such states ['already distinctively different from traditional state forms'] supplied certain *preconditions* for the early development of capitalism (p. 288, emphasis added).

These comments imply that the nation-state was a necessary *pre*-condition for the extension of capitalism. Indeed, the third and fourth passages suggest an anachronistic back-dating of the territorially bound nation-state to the period of early capitalism, usually designated as around the sixteenth century. It is a move which goes against all that Giddens has been arguing. He blocks off any other interpretation of these passages by his single-trajectory pathway from absolutism, a traditional form of state, to the nation-state, a modern form.

Elsewhere, however, Giddens writes in ways which suggest that the relation between industrial capitalism and the nation-state was more complicated than these passages indicate. The connection, he says, is to be looked for not in the relation between the nature of capitalistic enterprise and the centralization of state power, but in the social transformations wrought by capitalism.[28] Here he is referring to two key processes. The first is the eradication of the institution of the city as a distinct social form and as the dominant power container: it is symbolized by the disappearance of city walls.[29] This is a strange and misleading way of arguing what Giddens himself has better expressed as the increasing commodification of space including the transformation of the city–country relation, or what Marx has called metaphorically the 'urbanization of the countryside'.[30]

A second transformation wrought by capitalism is the abstraction of labour-power, part of a generalized abstraction and commodification of time. In examining its connection to the nation-state Giddens emphasizes one aspect of this transformation, 'the extrusion of control of the means of violence' from class relations.[31] In contrast to pre-capitalist class societies – that is, societies Giddens terms class-divided – capitalist production brings the classes into close and ongoing interaction around the workplace. The modern workplace allows for an expansion of regularized surveillance and thus for the consolidation of control by other means than direct violence. Obviously the labour contract does not end inter-class violence. However, in conjunction with the ideological commitment of the bourgeoisie to the liberal rights including 'freedom of contract', the monopoly of the means of violence was gradually passed over to public authorities. Giddens, like Nicos Poulantzas,[32] rightly suggests that this passing over did not mean that the state became a passive instrument of the ruling classes. It was as much an outcome of the working-class struggle for economic, civil and political rights as it was of the bourgeois struggle against the feudal aristocracy. A meshing of the effects of the modes of surveillance occurred as the state set up or oversaw the new institutions of sequestration (here Giddens draws upon Michel Foucault's notion of disciplinary power). 'Hospitals', prisons and poorhouses took up the handling of the large numbers of dispossessed people cut loose from the structures of feudal production. Giddens' argument is that the doubling-up of these forms of power made possible the new means of internal pacification. They became central to the administrative co-ordination which characterized the transition from the absolutist to the nation-state.

28. Giddens, *Power, Property and State*, 1981, p. 188.

29. Ibid., p. 148.

30. It is strange in that Giddens also wants to argue for the increasing centralization of power. Moreover, surely Jane Jacobs has a point when she says that in the modern period, cities have been confirmed as the predominant centres of economic power. See her *Cities and the Wealth of Nations*, 1986.

31. Giddens, 'Nation-States and Violence', 1987, pp. 173–174; also *Nation-State and Violence*, 1985, p. 160.

32. Nicos Poulantzas, *State, Power, Socialism*, 1980. It is peculiar, given the sub-title of Giddens' 1981 book, Volume 2 of *A Contemporary Critique of Historical Materialism*, that he does not mention that Poulantzas has very similar concerns to his own.

The material abstraction of social relations

There are other dimensions of this transformation, issues which Giddens does not discuss despite his eloquent and broadly conceived statement that industrial capitalism helped 'finally to dissolve the segmental character of class-divided societies' (p. 160). In the restricted space available, I will sketch the outlines of just one issue. It is an issue which bears upon one aspect of the material abstraction of social relations underpinning the interconnection of a nation of strangers. In a quite unexpected way it bears upon the theme of the intersection between the subjectivities of face-to-face relations and those formed across more abstract levels of integration.

In the early period of industrial capitalism, each labourer entered into what was (if only considered at the level of the face-to-face) an individualized contract for the sale of his or her labour. It seemed that in this noisy sphere of Freedom, Equality, Property and Bentham, the buyers and sellers of labour-power were constrained only by their own free will and perhaps by their self-interest.[33] However, as Marx shows so well, this process of the commodification of labour and its abstraction as labour-value depended upon definite historical conditions, in particular where products assume the form of commodities by being sold for exchange-value, and where for the first time the owners of the means of production and the labourers meet as free agents through the relations of the commodity market:

> The labour of the individual asserts itself as a part of the labour of society, only by means of the relations which the act of exchange establishes directly between the products, and indirectly, through them, between the producers. To the latter, therefore, the relations connecting the labour of one individual with that of the rest appear not as direct social relations between individuals at work, but as what they really are, material relations between persons and social relations between things.[34]

In short, the labour abstraction was formed as a social relation. It was a materially abstract relation in the sense that the commodification of labour did not occur only in the realm of ideas. The value of each labourer's work was mediated at various levels of lived relations. Localized struggles over wages within various industries continued to be important, but by the late nineteenth century even the most parochial struggles tended to be mediated by institutions of agency extension such as (national) unions and employer federations.[35] More importantly for the purposes of the present argument, and occurring from a much earlier period, the value of labour was mediated through the exchange of commodities and money in a context where each labourer was thus related to a market of other labourers who were largely unknown and geographically distant, a market of abstracted strangers. Any

33. Karl Marx, *Capital*, vol. 1, (1867) 1977, p. 172.
34. Ibid., p. 78.
35. For a discussion relevant to the intersections between face-to-face and agency-mediated labour solidarity, between artisanal and manufacturing industry in late nineteenth-century France, see Michael Hanagan, *The Logic of Solidarity*, 1980.

sense that labour was bound by the constraints of the face-to-face and a rec-iprocity of exchange relations was thoroughly subordinated. It was this process of abstract interconnection through the changing mode of exchange, the capitalist market and commodity exchange, that contributed to the con-stitution of the nation-state, itself an abstract community of strangers who needed never actually to meet to feel ties of commonality.

Certainly the relation between the nation-state and the processes of labour abstraction was not one of co-extension. A nexus of contributions to labour-value crossed the state boundaries by which nations tended to become delimited.[36] And within the national market, subjectivities of compatriotism were qualified by cleavages of class consciousness. Nevertheless, along with other processes of extension and abstraction, the abstraction of labour-value contributed to national formation by overlaying and reconstituting the iden-tity-forming predominance of networks of kinship and reciprocal exchange. It did so in a way and on a scale that seignorial feudalism and the absolutist state could never have effected. So long as the identity of large segments of a populace remained bound primarily by relations of the face-to-face, as in different ways European, Asian and South American 'feudal' peasants were, then the relations of agency-extension such as those instituted by the state were more likely to be received as outside intrusions than as integral with even the most extended reaches of the villagers' imagined communities. The labour and commodity abstractions contributed to both the changed form of these communities and to their inhabitants' changed subjectivities. This theme is part of the larger argument that the nation-state is a materially abstract com-munity of a particular kind, constituted in the changing, uneven and contradictory intersection of modes of integration and modes of practice.

Such a discussion, while only scratching the surface, is indicative of the inextricable meshing of social relations and social subjectivity. However, at least in his writings on the nation-state, Anthony Giddens separates off ques-tions of structured practices and changing forms of ontology and identity. It is hard to see how a discussion of the subjective implications of the labour abstraction could be subsumed under his central distinction between author-itative and allocative resources. This is part of a more general problem which relates to his overall conceptual apparatus: this can now be spelt out more explicitly.

If the nation-state is a management structure, what is the nation?

As has become obvious from the foregoing discussion of Anthony Giddens' theory of nation-state formation, his focus (with the brief exception of a foray into a theory of nationalism, reviewed in the next section) is on the form of administrative structuring. Giddens writes about the emergence of the

36. See for example Glenn Morgan, 'From West to East and Back Again: Capitalist Expansion and Class Formation in the Nineteenth Century', 1985.

nation-state from the absolutist state as a process of territorial bounding and concentration of allocative and authoritative resources by a particular kind of state apparatus. He thus qualifies Marx by Weber: as noted earlier, the concept of allocative resources refers to the means of production; the term authoritative resources refers to the means of dominion over human beings themselves, what I have been calling the means of organization. Giddens' argument is that the connection made by orthodox historical materialism between capitalism as a mode of production and the development (and predicted ossification) of the nation-state is one-sided and reductive. Like Weber, he wants to treat the mode of organization as an independent institutional clustering equally implicated in the exertion of power and the structuration of the nation-state.

Actually, in the act of redressing the balance, Giddens leans too heavily in the direction taken by Max Weber and Otto Hintze. He goes further than he may have originally intended. With the reclamation of the importance of authoritative resources, such means of power become not just built into but effectively encompass the core of his definition of the nation-state. This is at the heart of an explanation of some of the over-emphases in Giddens' theory of nation-state formation discussed earlier, such as the overemphasis on the importance of military technology and on the administrative apparatus of European absolutism. For Giddens the nation-state is a particular kind of locale, a setting of interaction circumscribed as an arena generating administrative power. It is, in short, a power container, an administrative power container. In contrast to his admonitions of the contemporary Nietzschean tendency to enthrone power as the primary basis of all social practices, as 'a mysterious phenomenon that hovers everywhere, and underlies everything',[37] at times Giddens heads along the same path. He is careful to go repeatedly back to his original point that power containers – that is, arenas generating *administrative* power – generate power through the concentration of both allocative and authoritative resources. However, this is confused by lack of clarity. At one point, administrative power is defined as the marshalling of authoritative resources (p. 19). Further on, it is suggested that: 'In all societies, traditional and modern, administrative power is the core of domination *generated by* authoritative resources, although it is not the only such resource that exists (*there is, in addition*, power deriving from control of sanctions and from ideology)' (p. 46, emphasis added). In these passages it is not clear whether administrative power is itself an authoritative resource or an outcome generated by authoritative resources, or both, if that is possible.

Much more importantly, the privileging of administrative power limits the reach of his analysis. Because, firstly, he uses the terms authoritative and administrative as definitional cohorts,[38] and given, secondly, that he cuts a sharp division between subjectivity and institutional arrangements, the

---

37. *Profiles and Critiques in Social Theory*, 1982, p. 226. Also see his *Nation-State and Violence*, 1985, pp. 29–30.
38. See for example Giddens, ibid., pp. 13–14.

nation-state is logically reduced to a particular form of structure for the administration of political and military power. He concludes:

> Drawing together the implications of the foregoing observations, we can arrive at the following concept of the nation-state, which holds for all variants and is not intrinsically bound to any particular characterization of nationalism . . . 'The nation-state, which exists in a complex of other nation-states, is a set of institutional forms of governance maintaining monopoly over a territory with demarcated boundaries (borders), its rule being sanctioned by law and direct control of the means of internal and external violence.' (p. 121)

There is nothing in this definition, or in the overall structuring of Giddens' argument discussed earlier, about the form of subjectivity constituted by (and constitutive of) this new form of institutionally regulated association.[39] Giddens thus reduces the nation-state to one form of social practice – the institutional – and to the overriding predominance of one level of social integration–agency-extension. He clearly recognizes the capacity of the state to reach beyond agency-extension to draw upon more abstracting means of organization, means of disembodied extension crossing time and space such as electronic communication and information storage. And he perceptively connects this to the formation of nation-state apparatus:

> The 'externalized' character of information traces inevitably severs communication from its intrinsic connection with the body and the face. But electronic communication for the first time in history separates 'immediate' communication from presence, thereby initiating developments in modern culture that . . . are basic to the emergence and consolidation of the nation-state. (p. 14)

However, just as with his discussion of the labour abstraction, the relevance of this process of the abstraction of organization, communication and exchange for the development of an ontologically novel subjectivity goes largely unnoticed, at least in the sense that it is basic to living as a nation of strangers.

The reduction of the nation-state to a form of administration is related to a major elision. The question of the nation as a materially abstracted relation between strangers disappears into the untheorized space between the territorialization of the state and the management of the ideology of nationalism. Despite his detailed, historically illustrated study of the nation-*state* – and despite the irony that he asks why is it that from classical to contemporary social theory, little systematic attention has been given to examining the nature of the nationally bounded unity that theorists call society – Anthony Giddens does not have more than a few words to say about the *nation* as a form of social relations. The nation is treated as if it were always made in the image of the state boundary. This screening out of the nation as an objective/subjective community of persons is partly due to the definitional stricture

39. In another context he explicitly says that, 'What makes the "nation" integral to the nation-state in this definition is not the existence of sentiments of nationalism but the unification of an administrative apparatus over precisely defined territorial bounds.' See his 'Nation-States and Violence', 1987, p. 172.

he places on the meaning of the term, nation. A nation, he says, 'only exists when a state has a unified administrative reach over the territory over which its sovereignty is claimed' (p. 119). The definition has parallels with Eric Hobsbawm's premise that the nation 'is a social entity only insofar as it relates to a certain kind of modern territorial state'.[40] In Giddens' case definitional stricture not only reinforces the methodological elision, it flows on into his theory of nationalism.

Nationalism as political ideology and personal psychology

Anthony Giddens' discussion of nationalism is summarized in the following paragraph:

> Nationalism [he says] is in substantial part a psychological phenomenon, involving felt needs and dispositions, in contrast to the nation-state which is an institutional one. I believe that one can formulate an approach to a theory of nationalism against the backdrop of the time–space transformations by means of which the 'created environment becomes the habitat of individuals in capitalist societies, and the nation-state the dominant 'power container'. Nationalism, I have suggested, feeds upon, or represents an attenuated form of those 'primordial sentiments' ['"primordial sentiments" writ large, and stripped of their association with communities of high presence-availability'] of which Geertz speaks in tribal societies or village communities.[41]

As represented in this passage there are three dimensions to Giddens' approach to understanding nationalism: firstly, the phenomenon is said to be primarily psychological (p. 116); secondly, it is attendant upon modern structural developments, in particular, co-ordination of the means of organization within the nation-state (p. 219); thirdly, it is an attenuated form of primordial sentiment.

Let me work back through these, beginning with the confusing and difficult issue of reconstituted primordiality (the primordiality–modernity theme). There is a dilemma here, invoked on occasions in earlier chapters under the label of continuity-in-discontinuity.[42] Ernest Gellner handles it by emphasizing the way in which nationalism, despite being uniquely modern, draws upon the *content* of the past: nationalism invents nations in the reworking or fabrication of pre-existing historical and cultural inheritances. Tom Nairn avoids acknowledging the dilemma by separating its terms into Janus faces: national*ism* as the ideological outcome of the uneven spread of capitalism and, alternatively, *national*ism, an untheorized basis of identity which arises out of an 'old pre-history of nationality'. Giddens is very critical of both Nairn and Gellner. However, while in the lengthy passage just cited he seems

---

40. Eric Hobsbawm, *Nations and Nationalism since 1780*, 1990, p. 9.

41. Giddens, *Power, Property and State*, 1981, p. 193.

42. Anthony Smith (*The Ethnic Origins of Nations*, 1986) draws a kindred though less abstract paradox in relation to ethnicity: 'its mutability in persistence, and its persistence through change' (p. 32).

to be pushing hard against the problems of theorizing issues relating to the continuities and discontinuities of social forms, Giddens' writing does not achieve as much as it promises. When examined more closely his theory of nationalism reduces to a couple of important but undeveloped insights and a few rhetorical gestures.

The concept of primordial attachments as derived from Clifford Geertz refers to attachments and sentiments which stem from 'givens'. In Geertz's words they are '"givens" – or more precisely, as culture is inevitably involved in such matters, the assumed "givens" – of social existence: immediate contiguity and kin connection . . . congruities of blood, speech, custom, and so on'.[43] Giddens' use of the concept as a sentiment based on contiguity and yet 'writ large' is, in terms of his spatial metaphor, a contradiction in terms – close and yet far. His theoretical apparatus of time–space distantiation meets its limits here. If employed (and it is not) it would go some way to elucidating the processes of extension by which subjectivities grounded in relations of contiguity still have meaning when abstracted across time and space. However, it remains limited by being a spatial metaphor cast on one plane. By contrast the metaphor of levels in intersection developed in the present book from Geoff Sharp's work enables analysis to proceed at least to a working analytic description (and a historical specification) of the level at which relations grounded in contiguity continue to have ontological force, even while being overlaid, reconstituted and stretched across time and space.[44] This entails the recognition of ontologically changing forms of subjectivity: for example, identifying oneself as being of the Pintupi people is fundamentally different from identifying as (Aboriginal) Australian, even though *at one level* there are similarities of form. It is an issue which, as argued in the next section, cannot be adequately handled by Giddens' overall analysis. Certainly his first and second dimensions for explaining nationalism – the fragile psychology of post-traditional routinization or the co-ordination of administrative power by the nation-*state* – cannot explain these processes. Perhaps this is why in Giddens' later writings the Geertzian terminology is dropped.

In *The Nation-State and Violence*, Giddens draws a deep divide between nationalism and pre-existing forms of group identity, this time drawing on Fredrik Barth's argument about boundary marking and exclusionary sentiments (pp. 116ff.). However, he thus appears to open himself to criticisms made by Anthony Smith of all Barthian-influenced writers for overemphasizing the role of the boundary at the expense of theorizing social relations

43. Clifford Geertz, *The Interpretation of Cultures*, 1973, p. 259. Geertz may call upon the concept of primordialism, but this does not automatically make him an essentialist or idealist. He treats the two themes of 'essentialism' and 'epochalism' (that is, the modernist sense of historicity) as being fought out not simply as doctrinal disputes, 'but much more importantly in the material transformations that the social structures of all the new states are undergoing' (p. 243).

44. Hence I disagree with Giddens' pronouncement that 'In the modern state, existential contradiction [an aspect of what I have been calling ontological contradiction] is almost completely expunged by structural contradiction' (*Nation-State and Violence*, 1985, p. 196).

within the boundary.[45] This impression is more a product of Giddens' eclectic style than representative of the totality of his view; nevertheless it indicates the fragmented way in which his argument proceeds.

The second dimension – the co-ordination of the means of organization – has been discussed in considerable detail already. The basic weakness of tacking on questions of subjectivity to an analysis which all but ignores these questions and reduces relations of national identity to a concomitant of state-bounding should already be obvious from the preceding discussion. What is less obvious is yet another unexplained tension in Giddens' analysis. How is it possible that nationalism is the 'concomitant of the co-ordination of administrative power within the bounded nation-state' (p. 219), that there can be 'no nationalism, in its modern form at least, without the formation of nations' (p. 116),[46] when as Giddens acknowledges, 'it was mainly in the *non-unified* states and principalities of central and northern Europe that modern conceptions of nationalism have their origin'?[47] (p. 119, emphasis added). On a more positive note it is worth recording one of his 'important but undeveloped insights':

> More deeply layered ideological implications are to be traced to the fact that the conditions involved in the reflexive monitoring of the modern state, as a surveillance apparatus, are the same as those that help generate nationalism. Since the discursive capabilities involved in monitoring social reproduction become of essential importance to the state, it is around the intersection between discursive consciousness and 'lived experience' that the ideological consequences of nationalism will cluster. (p. 220)

This brings us to the 'primary' dimension of psychology. Here too, important points are made, but by drawing a line between nationalism as a psychological phenomenon and the nation-state as an administrative institution, Giddens leaves himself unable to account for the overt expressions of nationality except via the problem-ridden Freud/Le Bon theory of crowd suggestibility and identification with authority figures.[48] For someone who, even if eclectic in sourcing their arguments, is usually circumspect about taking on board the unwanted baggage of other theorists, this is a particularly counterproductive move. His accompanying step of attempting to revive Max Weber's best-forgotten theory of charismatic leadership has a similar quality. While Weber and Freud have made significant contributions in other areas, on this question they are not especially illuminating.[49]

45. Anthony Smith, 'History and Liberty', 1986.

46. This of course is the opposite of Gellner's provocative point that nationalists contribute to bringing nations into being.

47. Further to this, given Giddens' definition of nationalism (*Nation-State and Violence*, 1985, p. 116) as 'the affiliation of individuals to a set of symbols and beliefs emphasizing communality among members of a political order', the sentiment goes back much further than his suggested post-eighteenth-century beginnings.

48. See Giddens, *Power, Property and State*, 1981, pp. 13 and 195; *Nation-State and Violence*, 1985, pp. 219 and 305; 'Nation-States and Violence', 1987, p. 179.

49. See for example, Sigmund Freud, *Civilization and its Discontents*, 1975, on the role of Eros in combining individuals into nations (p. 59). J.G. Merquior, who is in other ways sympathetic to Weber, criticizes the theory of charisma for its 'endemic lack of sociological depth' (*Rousseau and Weber*, 1980, pp. 181ff.). See also Chapter 4 above.

Having examined Giddens' separation of the objective (nation-state) and the subjective (nationalism) the following pages broaden out, taking this theme into a discussion of his general theory of social relations and social subjectivity.

Subject and object, person and society

In *The Constitution of Society*, a volume presented as a summation of his theory of structuration, Giddens organizes the discussion beginning with the individual, and then later goes on to accent social structure. The problem with this is not that he is open to the orthodox charge of methodological individualism, of which, incidentally, he provides as developed a critique as found anywhere. Rather it is that from whichever side of the dichotomy he begins he has consequently set up an organizing principle which makes it seem sufficient that person and society are put back together on a single ontological plane. Giddens in effect privileges the constitutional form of modern individual, the self-active agent making history 'knowledgeably' and 'autonomously'. Despite its title, *The Constitution of Society* is not about the way in which different social forms are constitutive of, and through, different modalities of subjectivity. To put person and society back together, Giddens depends largely on a theory of contextuality and regionalization. That is, people are located in overlaying clusters of relations of time and space, thus avoiding, as he says, the assumption that societies are homogeneous, unified systems.

People are thus left as active agents (which indeed they are, but in qualitatively different ways in different societies). They are understood as 'positioned' in relation to each other rather than theorized as constituted in the very form of their agency.[50] This is a different category of criticism from those usually, and I think ineffectually, made of Giddens. Various critics have made the easily countered point that his view of structure as both enabling and constraining does not sufficiently emphasize the degree of constraint upon the actor.[51]

Persons in reciprocal tribal groups are for Giddens reflective agents in the same way as individuals in late-capitalist nations. We are all social theorists, he says: the difference is to be found in the settings (stages) or locales in which we move. It is propositions of this sort which need to be carefully taken apart. Giddens wants to 'disclose features of co-presence [that is, of

50. For an interesting recent attempt to theorize the relation between person and society by one of Giddens' critics see Alex Callinicos, *Making History*, 1989, particularly ch. 1.

51. See for example John Thompson, 'The Theory of Structuration: An Assessment of the Contribution of Anthony Giddens' in his *Studies in the Theory of Ideology*, 1984. For general discussions of Giddens' work see Mike Gane, 'Anthony Giddens and the Crisis of Social Theory', 1983; Erik Olin Wright, 'Giddens's Critique of Marxism', 1983; Gregor McLennan, 'Critical or Positive Theory?', 1984; Alex Callinicos, 'Anthony Giddens: A Contemporary Critique', 1985; and, the best of these discussions, Richard Bernstein, 'Structuration as Critical Theory', 1986.

people in face-to-face relations] that are found in all societies'.[52] The problem with this is, as I will argue in more detail in a moment, that he treats co-presence ahistorically.

Face-to-face relations are certainly a primary constitutive level of human interaction. And as Giddens maintains, the level of the face-to-face continues to be basic, even when the predominant form of societal integration is extended beyond 'high presence-availability' and across time and space through such means as the media of storage and relay of information. However, his approach significantly underplays the way in which face-to-face relations, like the form of personhood, is reconstituted at different levels (in his terminology) of time–space distantiation. It is this which gives rise to the impression that Giddens' theory treats people as psychologically complex but otherwise empty shells, interacting on theatrical stages. These stages seem to be bounded by sets which if removed would only reveal to the actors that they are located on yet larger stages. The nation-*state*, at least as Giddens has defined it, is reduced to one of those stage sets.[53]

Discussion of the implications of treating co-presence ahistorically can be extended through introducing Giddens' notions of routine and actor. They work to link the objective and subjective but remain two sides of an over-generalized relation. A crucial part of understanding why Giddens treats co-presence as a world form of social interchange is the centrality he affords to the practice of routine in day-to-day life:

> The term 'day-to-day' encapsulates exactly the routinized character which social life has as it stretches across time–space. The repetitiveness of activities which are undertaken in like manner day after day is the material grounding of what I call the recursive nature of social life. (By its recursive nature I mean that the structured properties of social activity – via the duality of structure – are constantly recreated out of the very resources which constitute them.) Routinization is vital to the psychological mechanisms whereby a sense of trust or ontological security is sustained in the daily activities of social life. Carried primarily in practical consciousness, routine drives a wedge between the potentially explosive content of the unconscious and the reflexive monitoring of action which agents display.[54]

Thus the discussion of how we are to understand the constitution of persons and the nature of face-to-face integration – what he calls social integration to distinguish it from societal or system integration which occurs across time and space beyond the limitations of the face-to-face – is located in a notion of how we know as practical consciousness the ways to 'go on' in

52. Giddens, *Constitution of Society*, 1984, p. 69. He passingly acknowledges that in *The Constitution of Society* he concentrated upon material relevant to modern society (p. xvii) but this does not qualify the point.

53. Here I am agreeing (impressionistically) with Ian Craib when he says 'Giddens often talks about different levels of social organisation as if the social world possessed a depth . . . However, in the course of his bridge-building he loses sight of this depth.' See Craib's 'Back to Utopia: Anthony Giddens and Modern Social Theory', 1986, p. 17.

54. Giddens, *Constitution of Society*, 1984, p. xxiii. The 'duality of structure' as referred to here is in turn defined as: 'Structure as the medium and outcome of the conduct it recursively organizes' (p. 374).

habitual routine. (As mentioned earlier, it is the modern fragility of routine which for Giddens gives rise to nationalist identifications.)

There is, however, a tension here in Giddens' approach which will become apparent if we shift focus for a moment from social integration to look at a schematic representation of his view of the principal forms of societal integration[55] (see Figure 7.1).

Although routinization of day-to-day life is posited as transhistorical when Giddens refers to the forms of societal integration, 'routinization' only enters the schema with class society. This Weberian concept is not explained in *The Constitution of Society* and only partly addressed in his earlier book, *A Contemporary Critique of Historical Materialism*. There he says that in tribal and class-divided society routinization is normatively embedded in tradition. The ontological security of tradition, which he is rightly careful to say is not wholly positive, is radically undercut by a series of related transformations: the commodification of labour, the breaking of normative connections between work and private life, and the clear demarcation of nature and culture, particularly as lived in the manufactured environment of the city, the same processes which underpin the nation-state.[56] Thus: 'The dissolution of the foundation of society in relations of presence substantially replaces the grounding of those primordial sentiments in tradition and kinship by a *more* routinised, habitual round of "everyday life"'[57] (emphasis added). In this setting, as Giddens suggests, the sense of national community provides one strand contributing to the maintenance of ontological security. However, in *Central Problems in Social Theory* he argues that the disavowal of tradition is 'the most profound potential source of deroutinisation'.[58] In short, although he has never put it this way explicitly, the passing of tradition leads to more routinization even as it is deroutinizing. Such a position is sustainable, but not in the contradictory way in which Giddens presents it.

A related example of a terminological difficulty, one this time which Giddens does in fact recognize, is contained in the term actor. He says: 'It is precisely because there is a deep, although generalized, affective involvement in the routines of daily life that actors (agents) do not ordinarily feel themselves to be actors (players).[59] It is a passing acknowledgement. It is not adequately taken up as an indication of the different forms of subjectivity. So far as I understand his approach, he consequently does not have an adequate way of explaining why the Discovery of the Individual is a relatively recent phenomenon in world history.[60] As Agnes Heller's detailed examination of the

55. Ibid. pp. 181–182 and elaborated in Giddens, *Power, Property and State*, 1981, p. 159 and *passim*.

56. *Power, Property and State*, 1981, pp. 150–154.

57. Ibid. p. 193.

58. Giddens, *Central Problems*, 1979, p. 221.

59. Giddens, *Constitution of Society*, 1984, p. 125.

60. The term is used by Nicholas Abercrombie, Stephen Hill and Bryan S. Turner in *The Dominant Ideology Thesis*, 1984, taken from the book by Colin Morris (*The Discovery of the Individual 1050–1200*), but it is becoming a common enough theme.

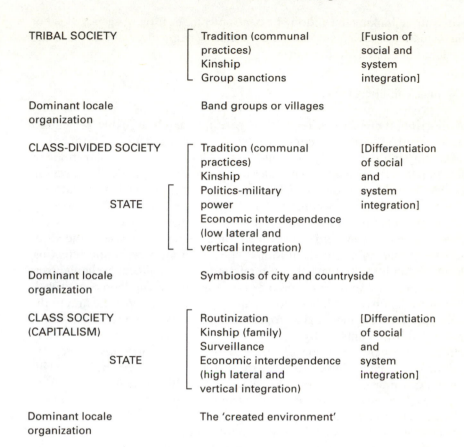

| TRIBAL SOCIETY | Tradition (communal practices) Kinship Group sanctions | [Fusion of social and system integration] |

Dominant locale organization — Band groups or villages

| CLASS-DIVIDED SOCIETY STATE | Tradition (communal practices) Kinship Politics-military power Economic interdependence (low lateral and vertical integration) | [Differentiation of social and system integration] |

Dominant locale organization — Symbiosis of city and countryside

| CLASS SOCIETY (CAPITALISM) STATE | Routinization Kinship (family) Surveillance Economic interdependence (high lateral and vertical integration) | [Differentiation of social and system integration] |

Dominant locale organization — The 'created environment'

Figure 7.1   *Societal Integration*

(Source: Anthony Giddens, *A Contemporary Critique of Historic Materialism*, second edition, 1995, reproduced with the permission of Macmillan Press Ltd.)

historical shift of the form of personhood from feudal to renaissance life indicates, it is an anachronism to generalize the metaphor of self as actor until at least the sixteenth century: 'In feudal society a [person] did not "play a role"; a [person] *was* what [s/he] had been born to be.'[61] And even thereafter the concept of self-as-actor both changes in time,[62] and can be distinguished according to intellectual training and class.

In one sense it seems petty to concentrate on the shifting of terms such as actor or routine. But there is a more important point to make. There are enormous difficulties in attempting to theorize a discontinuity of social forms

61. Agnes Heller, *Renaissance Man*, 1981, p. 206.
62. See Richard Sennett, *The Fall of Public Man*, 1977, p. 206.

while not rethinking the notion of a continuity in the form of agency. It is not just a matter of saying as Giddens does that there are divergent forms of the structuration of day-to-day life.

Continuity-in-discontinuity

A description couched in terms of constitutive levels arguably provides a more fruitful way of conceptualizing this particular instance of continuity-in-discontinuity. It would be to say that as a particular mode of integration is supplanted *in dominance* by a more abstract mode of integration (as has tended to happen through history) the routine of the day-to-day continues even as it is reconstituted. So as tribal societies constituted predominantly in the face-to-face are drawn as specific locales into a wider relationship of a new kind – one which for example in the case of the absolutist state separates out institutional spheres in an overarching religious, legal, and military system – kinship relations and reciprocal exchange continue at one level to be basic, even as they are fundamentally reconstituted. Kinship relations are still basic to feudal society as they were (and are) to the tribal person,[63] but in feudal Europe kinship was overlaid by and eventually re-formed within universalistic juridical categories. These categories were, in effect, part of the condition of routinizing what was previously taken for granted (or what could be called the routine of a prior dominant level). This helps explain the apparent paradox that, as Marc Bloch records, it was from the twelfth century onwards as kinship groups began to break down or rather change in form that family names first appeared: 'Thus in Europe, long after the demise of feudal society, the permanent family name, which today is held in common by [people] often devoid of any feeling of solidarity, was the creation not of the spirit of kinship, but of the institution most fundamentally opposed to that spirit – the sovereign state.'[64]

Here we see the intersection of two forms of social–societal integration. With changing social relations, including changing modes of production and exchange, the more abstract level assumes (an uneven) constitutive dominance and becomes the setting for reformulating something as basic as how we name ourselves.

In one way, Giddens does in fact have a conception of levels built into his analysis. The 'positioning of actors' occurs within a series of intersecting regions embedded in widening reaches of time and space. These are levels of time–space distantiation. But he misleadingly says that in tribal societies where social integration (co-presence) and system integration are effectively

---

63. This is to qualify Giddens' statement that 'traditional societies of all types have become more or less completely dissolved' (*Nation-State and Violence*, p. 34).

64. Marc Bloch, *Feudal Society*, vol. 1, 1961, p. 141. See also Giddens on the abstraction of law (*Nation-State and Violence*, pp. 98–101) as well as Gianfranco Poggi, *Modern State*, 1978, pp. 60–116.

coextensive, 'positioning is *only* thinly "layered"'[65] (emphasis added). It would be better described as the integrative levels being highly condensed. This would allow for a double point to follow: through such media as writing and print, practices which facilitate the storage and retrieval of information, relations between people can be extended (and secondly, to make a political point, they are thus attenuated across time and space). In other words, through practices of disembodied extension the possibilities of abstract communities are enhanced while at the same time relations are thinned out. Furthermore, as I have been concerned to stress, the notion of extension carries only half the picture. Having your breakfast companion read you the lead story from the morning's nationally distributed newspaper is qualitatively different to listening to a story which confirms your being as of the Red Macaw totem.[66] There is a difference that makes it only partly relevant that these interactions are both instances of face-to-face interaction.

Giddens recognizes that writing contributes to a constitutively different sense of history: in the extending of time–space relations people are afforded a consciousness of historicity, 'tradition becomes visible *as* "tradition" . . . no longer a time-honoured basis of custom but a discursive phenomenon open to interrogation'.[67] As Paul Ricoeur puts it, texts 'project new ways of being'.[68] But it does not seem to matter how many times Giddens concurs that what 'the "individual" is cannot be taken as obvious'; the full implications of this as a facet of the way in which the discontinuities between the forms of face-to-face interaction are as important as the continuities do not sink into his theory of the nation-state. This is ironical given his claim in the discussion of the nation-state to be writing a discontinuist history. Rectifying the problem would entail, as I have argued, substantially qualifying the emphasis he places on the transhistorical reflexivity of social agents. In the terms I was drawing on earlier to restate Giddens' argument, the heightening of reflexivity and the generation of a sense of national historicity is only possible as the subject is lifted into an abstract relationship to tradition-as-lived. Here time itself is constitutively more abstract *as well as* distantiated.[69]

The distinction Giddens draws between social and societal integration is used as an apparent but ineffective way out of some of these difficulties. It allows him for instance to recognize that the media of time–space distantiation

65. Giddens, *Constitution of Society*, 1984, p. 85.

66. On story telling see Jean-François Lyotard, *The Postmodern Condition*, 1984, pp. 20–23 and Robert Darnton, 'Peasants Tell Tales' in his *The Great Cat Massacre*, 1985. On the newspaper as part of a new mode of apprehending the world see Benedict Anderson, *Imagined Communities*, 1991, chs 2 and 3: 'The very conception of the newspaper implies the refraction of even "world events" into a specific imagined world of vernacular readers; and [is] also . . . important to that imagined community [as] an idea of steady, solid simultaneity through time' (p. 63).

67. Giddens, *Constitution of Society*, 1984, p. 201.

68. Ricoeur quoted in Giddens, *Nation-State and Violence*, 1985, p. 42.

69. The argument about constitutive abstraction also allows for an escape from implicitly leaving time and space as privileged categories. This is a tendency because of the use of conventional self-referring metaphors – time being distantiated turns time upon a spatial metaphor.

(which are acknowledged in a cryptic phrase to be simultaneously the means of societal integration)[70] perforce extend time and space by an '"alienation" of communication in circumstances of co-presence'.[71] However, the social–societal integration distinction is part of the problem to the extent that it bypasses the necessity of thinking of the dominant level of societal integration as itself constitutive of and constituted by the *form* of personal subjectivity. In his latest series of books, including *Modernity and Self-Identity*, Giddens has moved a significant distance in rethinking his previous conclusions about agency and identity: 'abstract systems', he says 'become centrally involved not only in the institutional order of modernity but also in the formation and continuity of the self',[72] but in his writings of the 1990s, national identity, the subjectivity of being part of a nation, gets less rather than more attention than before. It is ironical that at the very time that his theory is elaborated to the point that it could provide us with new insights into the abstraction and passion of national identity, his focus turns outward to the processes of globalism and inward to life-style politics.

In late-capitalist globalizing societies, integrated as abstract communities through the circulation of information and commodities, with kinship relegated to an aspect of an individual's personal history, and with institutionally bounded role designations such as one's job less secure and no longer as basic to personal identity, we are increasingly forced to be self-active in constructing our place in the world. When Australian Airlines advertise themselves as essential when you need to 'say "I love you", face-to-face' it is not just that the context has changed. Facing one's much-loved, occasionally visited grandparents to hear nostalgic stories of a disappearing past has a different *ontological* meaning from facing the village story-teller. As various *Arena* writers have suggested, it is that the dominant form of subjectivity has undergone a number of transformations, now in Western late capitalism heightening the ideological practice that we 'are' autonomous authors of own identity. The avant-garde and the intellectual must most intensely live the paradox that we experience multiple difference within a common constitutive form.

Giddens' theoretical attempt to offset the anti-humanist, structuralist decentring of the subject through emphasizing the self-reflexive agency of people is fraught with difficulties. It is just as likely to reinforce the current ideological practice of autonomous individualism as serve as a critique of it.[73] In other words: the predominant form of individualism in Western, late-capitalist societies (leaving aside the many ways of its expression) is lived

70. Giddens, *Power, Property and State*, 1981, p. 157.
71. Giddens, *Constitution of Society*, 1984, p. 203.
72. Giddens, *Modernity and Self-Identity*, 1991, p. 33.
73. For an elaboration of the concept of the ideology of autonomy see Geoff Sharp, 'Constitutive Abstraction and Social Practice', 1985. Also, from a quite different standpoint but arguing for changing forms of individualism, see Nicholas Abercrombie, Stephen Hill and Bryan S. Turner, *Sovereign Individuals of Capitalism*, 1986; and Seyla Benhabib, *Situating the Self*, 1992.

firstly in terms of the assumed, though of course unequally realized, belief in natural rights espoused in nineteenth-century liberal individualism. Changing social relations have brought a more recent overlay. This emergent new level based in the extended relations of the information society is expressed in the extolling of freedom from constraint. We *experience* ourselves as agents of our own destiny, 'inventors' of our identity, 'autonomously' choosing our lifestyles and privatized personal associations in a manner which takes an ontological step beyond the era when the 'possessive individual' first claimed commodity rights. In this setting, theorizing the contradictions of national formation entails a rigorous examination of the relation between theory and the constitutive milieu from which theorists take their dearest assumptions. Giddens writes for example about the way in which Machiavelli's theorems about state power became 'reflections about phenomena which they have helped to constitute'. To turn Giddens against himself, we can conclude by asking the question, is he related to the ideology of autonomy in a manner parallel to the way in which Machiavelli was implicated in the ideology of the state?

Ernest Gellner set himself the laudable task of re-working the Durkheimian–Weberian tradition, to loosen habitual theoretical associations, to set up new principles 'until at last the context has been set up in which an assertion can be made which is simple, and yet not a trite repetition of the old wisdom'. Anthony Giddens' self-imposed task is even more extraordinary. His is an attempted re-working and syncretism of the traditions of both con-ventional sociology *and* historical materialism. His work has many strengths. However, the preceding discussion suggests that Giddens' theoretical and historical analysis of the social relations and subjectivities of the nation-state is beset by problems. They arise not only out of the limitations of his histor-ical conclusions, the tensions of definitional and analytic inconsistency, the overdetermined preclusion of a theory of the nation (that is, except as couched in terms of state-bounding), but they also arise out of continuing problems which are at the heart of his overall theory of society and person. This is not to say that anyone else has done a lot better. But with the rise of cultural (ontological) questions into the glare of unremitting examination our demands on what a theory need do have become increasingly compre-hensive.

While acknowledging that social theory has many problems to overcome, the present work has been based on a rejection of the position that says because social theory cannot meet our inordinate demands then any attempt at general theory should be abandoned. Over the course of the book, existing theories of national formation have been extensively criticized, but there has been no suggestion that such theories have not made important contributions.

In an illuminating discussion of Anthony Giddens' theory of structuration Richard Bernstein explains how 'Giddens's approach reflects a point which has been forcefully made in the post-empiricist philosophy of science, i.e., we can judge the adequacy of a theory . . . by its ability to explain what is valid and invalid in rival theories'.[74] Over the preceding chapters the book has attempted something akin to just that. It has attempted to test the usefulness of the constitutive levels argument against what are generally regarded as the most thorough-going theories of the nation and nation-state deriving from the divergent traditions of Durkheimian, Weberian and marxist social theory. It has worked back and forth between examining the weaknesses (and strengths) of existing theory and developing the thesis that the nation is a materially abstract community of strangers formed in the changing intersection of levels of integration. The argument remains rudimentary in all too many ways, but at least it allows some sensitivity both to the ontological complexity of history and to the mysteries of that contradictory association we call the nation. The next, and concluding, chapter draws together a few of the themes which have been woven through the discussion.

74. Richard Bernstein, 'Social Theory as Critique', 1989, p. 23.

8

Themes for a Theory of the Nation

To speak of the renewal of community within the terms of co-operation and sharing is scarcely conceivable within the mould of the national state. That social form is radically identified with the homogenization of cultures and the increasing predominance of instrumental forms of abstract power.

Geoff Sharp, 'Constitutive Abstraction and Social Practice', 1985

One can deconstruct the constructions of others, or deconstruct the deconstructions of others, or deconstruct one's own prior deconstructions. But by having no theory (or ethics) of how or when the moment of deconstructive seeing through should be reintegrated into shared collective practices and meanings, the dictum that 'there is nothing outside the text', when extended to social interpretation, places one in abstraction from (and in that sense outside) that society. Texts are amenable to endless interpretations; but of life – we have only one.

Gerry Gill, 'Post-Structuralism as Ideology', 1984

Richard Bernstein's comment cited at the end of the previous chapter bears repeating in its full generality: 'We can judge the adequacy of a theory . . . by its ability to explain what is valid and invalid in rival theories.' Although the present text has not elaborated anything like a comprehensive alternative to the theories it has examined, it can nevertheless be assessed by how adequately it has drawn upon its central thesis of the nation as an abstract community to work through the limitations of existing theories.

The surface narrative was in this sense intended as a straightforward, historically organized and critical exegesis of significant theoretical positions. However, the material itself quickly suggested that the discussion needed to be more complicated and layered. It became apparent that from a contemporary perspective on what a theory is expected to do – or at least from the perspectives of what various latter-day theorists, for instance Nairn, Gellner or Giddens, might expect of a theory – the classical social theorists did not actually achieve theories of the nation. Certainly Marx, Durkheim and Weber were heedful of the politics of nationality and the conflicts of nation-states and national minorities. However, while they made significant contributions to political theory, when it came to elaborating theories of the constitutive practices through which older forms of community and polity became nations and nation-states, they left a relatively unmapped nether-region. Notwithstanding their intellectual urgency to both abstract from particular events and to rend the veil of social taken-for-grantedness, they failed to realize (in the sense of failed to address theoretically) the contradictory implications of their insights that social life rather than being naturally evolving or God-given is constituted in and by human practice. However brilliantly their general theories opened up new possibilities of understanding, the classical theorists made no direct attempt to explain the conjunctures of material relations and subjectivities which grounded national formation. The nation came to be conceived of as 'natural' – that is, 'natural in inverted commas'. And the nation-state came to be seen as an institutional arrangement of space which either would melt into air (Marx) or was the most developed expression of the world as it 'is' (Weber).

Two questions were posed: why, in the historical period that the intersection of nation and state was beginning to consolidate as a dominant social form, did Marx effectively dismiss the nation-state as a transitory form of association, dead before it could ossify? And how, at the same time, could he implicitly take the nation for granted as a primordial category of social relations? The first question was about the nation-state, the second about the nation: it is the second question which continues to be relevant to a discussion of later theorists including Durkheim and Weber. And it is this second question which remains the hardest to answer. Indeed the difficulty is intensified by the way in which now, a century later, both contemporary marxism and mainstream sociology are divided between those who continue to treat the nation, in an untheorized way, as a deeply embedded historical formation, and those who over-emphasize its culturally invented modernity. Nor is the situation improved by those who attempt to hold these two extremes within the one approach. Tom Nairn's position exemplifies how, by sharply dividing the categories of nation and nation-state, of nationalism and national*ism*, the Janus perspectives of primordialism and modernism can be simultaneously held in an unsatisfactory dual focus.

Parallel tensions between primordialism and modernism in Marx's position were masked partly by his political consistency, and partly by the forms of social relations he was describing. As an acute observer of his times, he recognized the phenomenal surge of late nineteenth-century internationalization, but without recourse to something like an analytic metaphor of constitutive levels, he overemphasized its one-dimensional, flattening force. Changes were occurring that could not be adequately handled within the terms of a base–superstructure framework. The rapid development of the means and relations of disembodied extension including the newspaper and telegraph were, in intersection with expanded commodity circulation and the transport revolution, contributing to connecting the globe at a more abstract level of integration. These changes in the mode of integration also became part of the transfiguration of hometown society *and* the uneven consolidation of the nation-state – hence the overlap or coincidence of apparently antithetical subjectivities, from romantic longings for the blood and soil attachments of the village, and commonsense assumptions about the primordiality of the nation, to cosmopolitan desires for a 'brotherhood of mankind'. Moreover, despite the way in which a dominant level of integration was reconstituting prior forms, it was an uneven process occurring more as the intersection-in-dominance of different forms of integration than the supplanting or complete dissolution of the old. Resistance to the modernizing tidal wave of capitalism and nation-state was common in the late nineteenth century, even if para-doxically the act of resistance itself also contributed to the reconstitution of older ways of life.

Marx was formed by his time, and yet as an intellectual who, *qua* intellec-tual, worked in the abstracting medium of the written and printed word, he was doubly sensitive to the dissolution of old certainties and the abstraction of prior forms of social life. He was driven to 'discover' abstract categories of social relations such as class which provided a new conception of unity-in-dis-unity. These analytic categories helped to deconstruct *and* to put back together a world which could no longer be explained so comfortably in terms of natural communities, natural rights and theories of social contract. However, national formation held an ambiguous place in this new schema. The nation remained, in Marx's vocabulary, unself-consciously and quies-cently, an effective representation of the real ties of the past (his phrase), while by contrast the nation-state came to be viewed as an illusory sovereignty producing persons as '*fictitious* phenomena' (his emphasis), and as a repre-sentation of the artificial veils of the present which would eventually drop away to reveal the real conditions of existence.

Weber and Durkheim also wrote of themselves as working through the methodology of abstraction, finding generalities from out of the disarray of particulars, and seeing through the veils of the immediately apparent. But, writing a generation or so after Marx, they could no longer be so sure that the nation-state would dissolve into globalism. World War I was a war of dis-solving empires and consolidating nation-states, a war confirming the death of the old absolutist states. Moreover, the classical theorists faced the uneasy possibility that nothing lay behind the veils and chimeras of the phenomenal world. In this age of subjectivist culture (Weber) the early twentieth-century theorists responded by concluding that politics could only be derived from what 'is'. For Durkheim, 'the fatherland *in abstracto*' thus had to be seen as 'the normal and indispensable milieu of human life'. The nation-state was the highest existent 'embodiment of the idea of humanity'. For Weber, the nation-state was the most obvious existent source of meaning in the struggle against the iron cage of rationalization.

Nation Formation provides only partial answers to the question of why theorists of the late nineteenth and early twentieth centuries did not develop more than implicit theories of the nation and nation-state. And the method-ology of constitutive levels provides only a tentative means of entry into understanding the classical theorists, not an automatic or *a priori* grid against which to map the emphases and aporias of their work. Nevertheless, it enables the beginnings of an approach which takes seriously the relationship between theory and the world time in which, and for which, theory is written. The classical theorists were products of their time and place, but not in the simple sense that an orthodox base–superstructure position would have it. Their ideas did not simply derive from the dominant mode of production, nor did they express the dominant episteme of discourses. Neither can it be said that their ideas floated free as the ponderings of unique (charismatic) individuals. By positing an intersection of analytically distinguishable, ontologically inharmonious levels, the abstraction thesis attempts to allow for the complexity of the object–subject relation. Secondly, it attempts to allow for the different conclusions reached by divergent thinkers, while giving some sense of the commonalities of the avant-gardist thrust. And thirdly, it accents the contradictory modes of being of the theorists themselves.

Marx, Durkheim and Weber may have been contributors to an incipient stage of what was discussed as the rise of the cultural. This push to deconstruct taken-for-granted categories of social ontology had precedents, of a kind, going back to the late-medieval period and the poets of the vernacular such as Petrarch and Dante – but when taken in comparison with the urgency of debate in the late twentieth century, the depth of the deconstructive project even in *fin-de-siècle* Europe was relatively contained. Issues of the contingency of human nature and sexual difference, the arbitrariness of linguistic meaning, and the modernity of national formation, to mention only a few, waited well into the twentieth century before eliciting the direct, sustained attention of social theorists.

When I first began reading through the work of Nairn, Gellner and Giddens I assumed that they all had fairly comprehensive theories of the nation and nation-state. While each expressed his theoretical method in quite different ways, they all had a broad interest in relating structures and relations of production, exchange and communication, and linking issues of social form (object relations) with recurrent patterns of sensibility and subjectivity (subject relations). They managed to sustain a rejection of orthodox primordialism with analyses which qualified one-dimensional modernism by ranging across contemporary to early modern history, probing the centuries prior to the nineteenth century, and thus giving consideration to the long-run transformations which frame the relatively recent conjunction of nation and state. However, in the course of unfolding a critical description of their general theories it became clear that their explanatory insight was much more oriented towards understanding the nation-*state* rather than towards analysing the long-run integration of the nation. In so far as they implicitly accept that nations existed (and exist) which were not bound by the agency-extension of state apparatuses, their theories left the nation floating in ambiguity, as an independent social form yet one entirely dependent upon its framing by the state.

It was Tom Nairn who wrote the words that 'the theory of nationalism represents Marxism's great historical failure'. His own work goes some distance towards ameliorating that situation; however, as argued, Nairn tends to treat the original formation of the 'historic' nation as an unproblematic historical given. His theorizing begins with the effect on the periphery of the nineteenth-century tidal wave of forces of production and military power emanating out of the metropolitan centres of Europe. This generated what he called nationalism proper (a curious phrase suggesting a kind of teleology). Against this, Nairn implicitly uses a concept of the 'natural' or 'historic nation' – always effectively used in inverted commas. It allows him simultaneously to avoid the critique of essentialism or primordialism, and yet continue to view the 'historic nation' through the first face of Janus, that of deep or primordial history. As an evasive tactic it almost works: as an unacknowledged theoretical assumption it carries the cost of avoiding the issue of how complex social forms such as the nation generate complex ontological contradictions. Amongst these we might include the contradictions that although the nation is an abstract community, a community which extends far beyond the boundaries of kinship relations or attachment to a perceptible place, it continually recalls 'concrete' images of blood and soil; that although it is a paradigmatically modern social formation it is materially grounded in historically long-run social forms; and that although it is imagined as territorially contained and culturally bounded, the persons who most strongly asserted those 'theories' were, in its early stages, intellectuals who were just as likely to be cosmopolitan in orientation as nationalists.

On the face of it Anthony Giddens presents us with a more comprehensive theory and history of the nation and nation-state than that attempted by Tom Nairn. Giddens' contribution is crucial as a launching point for any discussion of theories for an alternative theory of the nation. However, in the final analysis, he too bypasses the necessity of theorizing the cultural contradictions of national formation. Built into his definition of the nation-state is the assertion that the nation 'only exists when a state has a unified administrative reach over the territory over which its sovereignty is claimed'. It is, I suggest, an aspect of his Weberian overemphasis upon the changing forms of administration which structure political and military power, and his displacement of a broader discussion of the forms of social relations and subjectivities into a narrower focus on nationalism as ideology or psychology. Hence, despite some exceptional passages of writing Giddens tends to reduce the nation to one level of social practice – the institutional – and to the over-riding predominance of one level of social integration – the agency-extended. Questions associated with understanding the nation as a materially extended (in his term, time–space distantiated) and abstracted relation between strangers are left unaddressed. They sit alongside other ontological questions about the subjectivity of national formations in the relatively untheorized space between his analyses of the territorialization of the state, and the state management of the ideology of nationalism.

Of the three contemporary writers studied in detail, Ernest Gellner has the strongest interest in systematically analysing the kinds of cultural changes associated with national formation. He examines such themes as the (abstracting) tendency of the move towards universal literacy, the break with parochially context-dependent communication, and an increasing cultural homogeneity ushered in as a new level of cultural integration or what he calls a single, continuous conceptual space. However, in positing this 'high cultural', nationally framed, conceptual space it seems that Gellner, as much as Tom Nairn or Anthony Giddens, is unable to account for the tensions, contradictions and differences (and yet interpenetration) between the cosmopolitan, the national and 'residual' pockets of parochialism, between the dominant culture and subordinate or emergent cultures, and between the realms of the public and the private. The nation appears to be given the appearance of having a homogeneous constitutive force. Thus, a paradoxical issue such as the febrile fragility of the postmodern nation cannot be handled adequately within his particular way of theorizing the rise of the cultural. This is so even though he recognizes that *within* the boundaries of the new formations culture has a new fluidity and persons are increasingly mobile.

How then might a constitutive abstraction argument begin to handle some of these problems? After a resumé of the central thesis, the rest of these concluding remarks will be devoted to drawing out some of the problems which continue to beset even the most ambitious interpretative approaches to national questions.

The central thesis connecting the book is that the nation is an abstract community which only becomes possible within a social formation constituted through the emerging dominance of relations of disembodied extension. It is not a proposition which I have attempted to prove, though there is no doubt that even on non-empiricist grounds the approach would benefit from a further volume of historical exploration. Rather, it has been presented here as a working proposition infused with historical examples and embedded in a matrix of methodological premises and definitions. Those premises and definitions can be summarized as follows.

1   The concept of *abstraction* has been stretched beyond its normal usage to refer to a process that occurs both in thought and practice. The most obvious examples of abstraction as a material process are the commodity and labour abstractions and the abstraction of time and space that occurs in the practices of writing and literacy, in particular in the work of intellectuals. In each of these, the process depends upon a confluence of modes of thinking and acting, though not upon any active cognizance of its generalizing implications by the persons who nevertheless actively participate in the structuring of social life beyond face-to-face interaction.

2   The term *community* is used in a way which underlines an important aspect of its richness as a concept, namely as direct relations of mutuality and commonality: the 'contrasts, increasingly expressed in C19, between, the more direct, more total and therefore more significant relations of *community* and the more formal, more abstract, and more instrumental relationships of *state*, or of *society* in its modern sense . . .'[1] This meaning is counterposed to its much looser (often more abstract) use in contemporary parlance. In the present we do not baulk at using the term to describe associations of complete strangers or abstract entities such as the global community, or persons who happen to have an incidental commonality, including the community of

1. Raymond Williams, *Keywords*, 1976, p. 66.

American Express card-users or travellers with Singapore Airlines. While the nation of strangers is based upon more than an incidental commonality, conjoining the terms abstract and community emphasizes this tension of meanings. It creates an oxymoron that hints at the issue of what has been called ontological contradiction.

3   An *ontological contradiction* reaches into the more concrete grounding conditions of social practice and social subjectivity, and yet depends upon the abstraction of those conditions in the context of more abstract levels of social integration. Numerous examples have been used here throughout, from the dilemma of the king's two bodies to the way a national cenotaph, quite empty of particular human remains, calls upon us to remember fallen compatriots as both actually dead and abstractly representative of a spirit that lives on. In terms of the abstraction thesis the discussion of contradiction entails no implicit Hegelian or even orthodox marxist assumptions about the evolution of history, or a teleology of outcomes. An ontological contradiction is defined as a manifold of opposing modalities formed in the intersection of levels of social integration.

4   The term *social integration* is intended to be used without any connotations of social life being inherently either a consensual or conflictual process. It is not the opposite of social fragmentation. For example, it is possible, as in the setting of the postmodern nation, to argue that there has occurred a privatization and fragmentation of social life at the level of face-to-face relations, while also suggesting that the nation is constituted and held together in the dominance of a more abstract level of integration.

5   To speak of constitutive *levels* is only to invoke an analytic and abstract word-picture. According to this methodological metaphor the complexities of a particular social formation can be analysed usefully in terms of levels of social integration intersecting in dominance. In one way it is no more than a methodological way of avoiding certain problems such as treating social life as if it were constituted on one plane, that is, as one dimensional, evenly changing, consensual, or merely bounded by a grid of time–space pathways traceable on a social theorist's map. In another way, certain political implications flow from an elaboration of the levels metaphor. These are implications that have barely been touched upon, but that will be taken up in a brief coda before we close.

6   The concept of 'treating social life as if it were *constituted on one plane*' is used as a shorthand way of criticizing those theories which reduce the complexity of a social formation or even of all social formations to a single dominant ontology. There may still be a recognition by those same theorists that social life is conducted along different time–space extensions, from face-to-face *interactions* to more disembodied *interactions* mediated through the electronic media, but the actuality of constitutively different human natures formed across different societies, and the possibility of contradictory subjectivities formed within the same society or the same person, are often either disregarded or relegated to the realm of psychoanalysis.

Three sub-themes amongst others were continually emerging as issues around which to elaborate the central theme of the nation as an abstract community and to develop the methodology of constitutive levels. They can now be expressed with inflexions towards existing theory.

1

The subject–object theme: the problem of understanding the relation between subjectivity and (objective) social relations, and between ways of thinking and the structures of social practice, without setting up a theoretical chasm between ideologies of nationalism and structures of the nation-state.

2

The primordiality–modernity theme: the problem of theorizing the modernity of the intersection of nation and state, and the recent emergence of nationality as a generalized form of social relations, without losing sight of the way in which social forms constitutive of the nation have long-run continuities such as are exemplified in the medieval *natio*.

3

The theme of intellectual practice: the problem of holding together the contradictory being of one of the central groupings in the story of nations, that is, the role of intellectuals and later the intellectually trained as, on the one hand, crucial in articulating the connections of the early *natio*, providing points of reference and gathering archives for emergent national cultures, staffing the new bureaucracies of agency-extension, leading oppositional nationalist movements, or instrumentally managing cultural campaigns to legitimize the dominant state, and, on the other hand, as 'free personalities' (Meinecke) most open to the call of cosmopolitanism or post-national disdain for the boundaries of place.

As much as it is possible to separate out these themes they will be taken up one by one.

The subject of nationalism and the object of enquiry

There can be no pretence that the venerable old question of the relation between subject and object will be brought to a satisfactory resolution over the next few paragraphs. At its broadest it covers the relation between the person (as subject) and the social structures of human relations, the recursive practices lived across various levels of abstraction. More narrowly it concerns the relation between ideas and structures. A full response to the question requires a theory of the subject far beyond the resources of this book. There are, however, problems within this theme of more specific relevance to a theory of the nation around which we can draw some tentative conclusions.

What is the relation between the subjectivities of nationalism and national identity and the (objective) structures of the nation and nation-state? In what sense is the nation a cultural invention? And how far do such questions take us?

One of the apparent strengths of the contemporary theorists whom we discussed is their common quest to theorize the constitutive milieu in which ideas of nationalism arose, and to relate nationalism to the material conditions of nationhood and state formation without collapsing nationalist ideas into a derivative relation to specifically national structures. However, each in his own way fails to achieve this balance. Anthony Giddens falls to one side with his claim that nationalism is the 'concomitant of the co-ordination of administrative power within the bounded nation-state';[2] and Ernest Gellner falls to the other side in effectively arguing that nationalisms bring nations into being: 'Nationalism . . . sometimes takes pre-existing cultures and turns them into nations, sometimes invents them, and often obliterates pre-existing cultures.'[3] Tom Nairn takes it in both directions at once. On the one hand, he says that 'Many new "nations" had to think away millennia of oblivion, and invent almost entirely fictitious pasts'.[4] On the other hand, he says (as indeed would Gellner when pressed and Giddens given certain qualifications) that 'Nationalism in the real sense is never an historical accident, or a mere invention. It reflects the latest fracture-lines of human society under strain.'[5] The tension between these two positions does not amount to an insurmountable contradiction; nevertheless it requires explanation beyond the rise of the notion of invention.

None of the theorists we discussed would hold the modernist, cultural inventionist thesis to its reductive and idealist end, but to the extent that they 'stress the element of artefact, invention and social engineering which enters into the making of nations',[6] they undermine the way in which their theories purport to be theories-of-the-constitutive. In other words, they need to develop an argument as to why, and under what conditions, cultural invention arises as an historical practice. Cultural invention might be better described as an emergent ontological relation to time and space based on a sense of historicity which turns the past into a source of authenticity. Under conditions which break the nexus of time with kinship or the sacred, that is, in empty time, the past becomes a source of artefacts and condensed meanings available for displaying in the present, and a series of calendrical reference points which mark the passage of progress. As the subjectivity of persons came to be constituted in an overlay of more abstract extensions of time and space it became meaningful (and possible given developing techniques and technologies of information storage and transmittal) to dredge the past for the roots of the present. In the process, historical practices and

---

2. Anthony Giddens, *The Nation-State and Violence*, 1985, p. 219.

3. Ernest Gellner, *Nations and Nationalism*, 1983, p. 49.

4. Tom Nairn, *The Break-up of Britain: Crisis and Neo-Nationalism*, 1981, p. 105.

5. Ibid., p. 323.

6. These words of Eric Hobsbawm's express the stress he too wants to place on the element of cultural invention (*Nations and Nationalism since 1780*, 1990, p. 10). Further down the page Hobsbawm agues that nations are 'constructed essentially from above'. His proviso that at the same time they should be analysed from below is, I suggest, inadequate to analysing the complexity of intersecting constitutive levels. Brilliant historians do not necessarily make brilliant social theorists.

meanings are thoroughly reworked and relatively new practices and rituals become historicized. But whether the ascriptions of self-conscious knowledgeability implied in the term cultural invention provide an appropriate description of these contradictory reworkings is doubtful. It is true that cultural management was important to development of a generalized national consciousness, indeed it has become even more important in the age of postmodern image-politics, but cultural management was itself made possible within larger social changes. In the same way, nationalism did not invent the nation: and the nation-state was not a necessary setting for the invention of the doctrine of nationalism. Both emerged, I have argued, with the historically uneven abstraction of community and polity.

A theory of constitutive abstraction developed by such theorists as Geoff Sharp may not be the best way to proceed to a better understanding of the subjectivity and objective relations of national formation, but it does help to overcome some of the problems of existing theory. It is partly that the notion of abstraction, in its modified meaning adopted here, carries a sense of a process pertaining both to ideas and material relations, but, more than that, it is helped by the way the levels metaphor relates forms of subjectivity to particular social formations without reducing the former to the latter. This can be restated in a brief example.

The emotional evocation by the late-medieval poet Petrarch of an abstract place called *Italia* was expressed long before Italy was politically unified. It is tempting to call this sentiment patriotism, but it was neither an attachment to the *patria* in the more concrete sense of an allegiance to the patriarchal monarch nor in the more abstract sense which developed in the eighteenth century of an allegiance to the sovereign state. Petrarch's evocation was possible centuries before the various factors identified by Nairn, Gellner and Giddens as central to the nation, including the development of industrialism or expansionist capitalism or post-patrimonial administrative apparatus, had developed any purchase on the subjective being of the populace of the Apennine peninsula.

Because Nairn, Gellner and Giddens in their different ways locate the idea and subjectivity of nationality in periodized, and what might be called factorial, analyses of national formation,[7] they are unable for example to take hold of the possibility of materially grounded subjectivities which long before the nation-state came into being could abstract a territorial or cultural connection between strangers. Clearly, *Italia* was not then a nation in the modern sense of the term, but what Petrarch expressed, along with other individuals and groupings from out of the strata of intellectuals, merchants and clerics (particularly those exiled, on legatine missions, or in some way deracinated),

---

7. I am not rejecting the possibility of any form of periodizing so much as the way in which the periodizing comes to dominate the possibility of recognizing 'continuous' social forms which (analytically at least) can be said to run across particular social formations. Similarly I am not rejecting the documentation of factors central to national formation but rather objecting to the way in which different levels of analysis are conflated.

was a sense of attachment to place much more akin to that of classical nationalism than our contemporary theorists are prepared to allow.

Contemporary theorists respond in two ways. They either preclude the relevance of an exploration of the conditions grounding this subjectivity because of a (well-founded) aversion to the implicit primordialism found in the bevy of pre-1960s discussions of 'medieval nationalism', or, like Tom Nairn, they consign such phenomena to an untheorized black box labelled 'historic nations'. By using the levels metaphor it becomes possible to argue that through a manifold of quite material processes – writing and reading, transacting inter-regional financial deals based on the abstraction of money, living in exile from one's *natus*, and so on – certain individuals and groupings in late-medieval *Italia* were lifted, in one capacity of their being, on to a level that enabled them to abstract a community of strangers, or at least to conceive of an 'abstract place' disembodied from the particularizing attachments which hitherto gave it meaning. They were able to do so even though the dominant levels of integration on the Apennine peninsula were such that most of their compatriots could not have thought of, let alone lived by, that same conception.

The levels metaphor also bears back upon the theory itself. Developing the theory of national formation further and adequately broadening out the scope of explanation to include such modes of subjectivity as evinced in Petrarch's evocation, I have argued, entails working both at a more abstract level of theorizing and at a more concrete level of detailed research. The present text has tended in its methodological discussions (as distinct from its historical discussions) to emphasize the most abstract kind of form analysis, but a fully fledged approach would have to relate to a meta-theory, sitting in the background, which indicated how the theory itself could be cast at different epistemological levels of abstraction: from a form analysis of different modes of social integration and subjectivity (hence, the levels of social integration argument); through an analysis of particular social formations which incorporates comparative discussions of the dominant modes of production, exchange, communication, organization and enquiry; to more concretely couched examinations of particular conjunctures and settings, regional differences and personal including psychological histories.

Rather than being too self-conscious about this point, the present book has left it largely implicit, allowing the analysis to shift between the various levels of *theoretical* abstraction without signalling those shifts. Indeed, it would be unnecessarily distracting and awkward to do so. A fully fledged approach in bringing together various theoretical levels could incorporate, without too much methodological declaiming, some of the theory and much of the content of explanation engaged in by Tom Nairn in emphasizing the uneven spread of capitalism; by Ernest Gellner in emphasizing the processes of industrialization and the development of a new education-sanctioned subjectivity; or by Anthony Giddens in emphasizing the binding of subjectivities within the formation of military–capitalist states.

At the centre of that critical reflection, and relevant to the subject–object relation, has been a concern to avoid the problem of treating subjectivity either as split along the Great Divide between traditional and modern societies or conversely as continuing across history in a relatively homogeneous way. Anthony Giddens, despite occasional passages to the contrary, tends towards the latter by privileging the constitutional form of the modern individual, that is, the self-active subject making history knowledgeably. He attempts to avoid the problem by treating social action as constrained or enabled within quite different time–space settings, but this still tends to leave social life as different kinds of practices set on one transhistorical ontological plane.[8] Ernest Gellner, by contrast, theorizes a manifest ontological transformation in the transition from agrarian to industrial societies, but his position tends towards setting up a Great Divide in so far as his description of industrial society separates it entirely from 'prior' subjectivities. Ideas and identities are framed in Gellner's industrial society by a monolithic, homogenizing culture-polity. He thus avoids the problem of setting up a homogeneous subjectivity-in-general which crosses history, only to reduce the subjectivity of industrial society to a single, historically specific, ontological plane.[9] Tom Nairn appears to get around both of these problems, but only by leaving the fractured faces of social life unresolved.

Discussion of the Great Divide takes us into the second theme of primordiality and modernity.

Nation formation as both primordial and modern?

Implicit throughout the last section were questions relevant to the area of primordialism and modernism. They either came up as a series of overlapping tensions – the historically embedded or the culturally invented, the authentic or the artificial, the historical or the historicized, and the traditional or the modern – or they were expressed as metaphors of cleavage: the Janus-faced, and the Great Divide. To avoid being repetitive this section concentrates on the concept of continuity-in-discontinuity.

The reasons elaborated by contemporary theorists in so rigorously disparaging primordialist arguments have tended to be well founded. Essentialism, idealism, a tendency to treat social phenomena as if they cut across history oblivious to the reproductive structures of contemporary social life, functionalist assertions of basic human needs such as the need to belong, and the positing of a primal human nature, are all possible pitfalls along the primordialist path. It is possible to avoid these problems by treating human history as completely discontinuous and theorizing the nation as pertaining

---

8. Giddens could avoid this criticism by making the claim for 'self-active subjectivity' as an expressly abstract methodological point and then, on a less abstract 'theoretical level', distinguishing different *forms* of 'self-active subjectivity'.

9. Gellner could avoid this criticism by arguing for a dominant but not exclusive level of subjectivity, rather than for a single cultural space of meaning.

only to the period of modernity (and postmodernity), but this pathway is beset by another series of pitfalls summarized in the critique of theories as set on one plane. The concept of continuity-in-discontinuity is part of an attempt to find a third way.

This alternative rests upon distinctions being made between more concrete conjunctural description (Level I), comparative analysis of social formations (Level II), and the more abstract ways of analysing social form (Levels III and IV). The distinction is only an analytic one. Nevertheless, what the distinction allows, amongst other things, is a way of distinguishing between levels of continuity and discontinuity. At the more concrete level of analysis of social formations and specific conjunctures a *discontinuous* history of national associations and political administrations can be quickly sketched:[10]

- The late-medieval development of associations called *nationes* (single, *natio*) and the emergence for some of an abstract sense of place.[11]
- The early modern abstraction of state apparatuses, though within the patrimonial political form of the kingdom or empire.
- The post-sixteenth-century politicization of the concept of the nation, although with the predominant political structure remaining that of kingdom or empire.
- The emergence of explicitly nationalist movements from around the early nineteenth century.
- The rise of a public sphere in association with ideologies of public sovereignty and national citizenship.
- The uneasy nineteenth-century conjunction of national citizenry and abstract state, forming in some cases what has been called the classical modern nation-state.
- The late twentieth-century postmodern nation, associated both with the rise of the new and neo-nationalisms and with the overpassing of national borders by an increasingly globalized flow of culture, capital and persons.

The past is a thoroughly unfamiliar place; in ways that contemporary sensibilities tend to block out, the extent of this discontinuity with the present is subjectively confronting. However, from a more abstract vantage point it is possible to conceive of continuities in the discontinuity of social formations and practices in a way which does not succumb to the contemporary, nostalgic tendency to flatten the past into a rustic or undeveloped version of the present. This abstracted view of continuity is exemplified in a comparison of two quite different types of association set within two completely disparate kinds of social formation.

The late-medieval *nationes* at the University of Bologna were small communities of scholars formed within a loosely connected system of city-states

---

10. This sketch obviously is neither sufficiently comprehensive nor detailed enough to give any sense of regional differences.

11. My argument here does not depend upon this being the first such emergence.

and kingdoms, whereas the contemporary Australian nation is a much more extended multicultural community, largely built out of pan-continental migration, bound by state borders, and set within a global system of other nation-states. Social theorists in Australia are beginning to describe it as a postmodern nation. In short, at this level of description the *nationes* of Bologna and the nation-state of Australia are fundamentally different. Yet they both are part of a continuity of social forms. Both, I suggest, are abstract communities where the social practices and subjectivities which integrate them as communities are formed in an overlay of relations of disembodied extension (even if that overlay is set within quite different configurations of less abstract, intersecting levels of integration). Both communities, drawing upon practices constituted at a disembodied level of abstraction, 'call upon' less abstract levels to give their association a depth of meaning. Both communities connect strangers in terms of affiliations expressed through a continuing but subordinate level of face-to-face integration.

This argument needs far more historical filling out than is possible here (a second volume will be necessary to do this), but it should be made clear that the argument only suggests that there are *some* continuities of social *form*, not that the *practices* and *means* of disembodied extension are the same. In the case of contemporary Australia, it is the mass media which most prominently provide a means of disembodied extension between people who at the level of the face-to-face may or may not have fleeting visual contact, probably will not have any interaction, and except for immediate kin most certainly will not be bound by very full ties of face-to-face integration.[12] It is by learning of their (national) history and culture through generic intellectual training in a state-based education system, by reading books and newspapers, and by watching television broadcasts, replays and re-enactments of significant 'events' that contemporary Australians will most frequently reinforce both their sense of simultaneity with their eighteen million living compatriots and their connection to those who came before them. In the case of the late-medieval *natio*, community is formed, and divisions are generated, through the held-in-common experience of at one level being lifted out of the more parochial constraints of place while at another level still subjectively having one's identity constituted by those constraints. The practices which lift the medieval cleric out of the parochial, range from simply travelling to Bologna or Paris or Oxford and facing strangers of a different *natus*, to the possibilities of translocating in time and space principally through the activities of reading and writing. In other words, social forms which have a recognizable continuity can be constituted through practices with markedly different content and set at a different point in world time.[13] Hence, in terms

12. Throughout, the terms 'contact', 'interaction' and 'integration' have been used to designate progressively higher degrees of mutuality in face-to-face relations.

13. This is not to disagree with Benedict Anderson's point that 'The world-historical era in which each nationalism is born probably has a significant impact on its scope.' See *Imagined Communities*, 1991, p. 63.

of the speculative thesis presented here that national association only becomes possible within social formations constituted in the contradictory dominance-in-intersection of relations of disembodied extension, the *natio* is different from but continuous with the modern nation.

Intellectual practice and the abstraction of community

The relevance of intellectual practice to the national question suggested itself for a number of reasons. Firstly, it is integral to any reflexive study of the nation and its theorizers. Theorists of the nation are by definition engaged in intellectual practice, and even such an apparently politically disengaged practice as writing about national formation bears back upon the lived reality of nationhood. In a work that attempts to understand some of the underpinnings of the theorizing process and how those same social forms and practices which ground the nation rebound upon the practices and assumptions of theorists, the theme of the practice of intellectuals could not be avoided. Secondly, it was relevant because intellectuals and the intellectually trained have been in the forefront of both oppositional nationalist movements and the official nationalisms of the old and new empires and states. Thirdly, intellectual training, via state-education systems, became after the late nineteenth century one of the central reproducers of a form of culture which was both inseparable from the practical and imaginative lives of national citizens as well as indispensable to their administration by the centralized state: this 'dual' process was crucial to the intersection of relations of agency-extension and disembodied extension.

While Anthony Giddens makes no direct statement on the role of intellectuals and the intellectually trained in the development of nations and nation-states it remains, in effect, an unacknowledged ellipsis connecting his argument. The growth of a public sphere of textually mediated state administration is at the centre of his theory. Yet the ellipsis marks the question, 'who are the actors in this sphere?' He leaves aside the issues of how such apparatuses are dependent upon new kinds of intellectual training, and what happens to clerics as their relationship to the prince is systematically abstracted – that is, becomes increasingly post-patrimonial, depersonalized, desanctified, rationalized, centralized and dependent upon the storage of information over time and space. Giddens passes over questions about the subjective practice and contradictory (or liminal) position of the intellectually trained, a move which, as writers such as Benedict Anderson and Anthony Smith indicate, is to miss out on an important aspect of national integration.

By contrast, Tom Nairn and Ernest Gellner place these themes of intellectuals and intellectual training more explicitly within their theoretical pictures (at least in the second and third senses as used above). For Tom Nairn, intellectuals and the intellectually trained, or what he fuses together as the new intelligentsia, provide the medium through which nationalism is refracted into a given society: 'spreading from the top downwards' the intelligentsia is pivotal to the diffusion of the idea, even if it is compelled to put nationalist concerns into the language of the 'popular mass still located upon an anterior level of development . . . upon a level of (almost literally) "prehistoric" diversity'.[14] While this argument has some force, it tends to concentrate upon nationalism as an idea: one simply diffused by a certain class of persons. The relation of intellectuals to the subjectivity of nationalism becomes reduced to the ideologically couched self-interest of that class, albeit a constrained self-interest, in mobilizing a cross-class alliance against outside intrusions.

Here Ernest Gellner's approach ironically is more thoroughgoing than Nairn's historical materialism in exploring the material conditions of the relation between intellectual training and nationhood. Gellner's theory has parallels with Tom Nairn's in emphasizing 'active cleavages of interest' which arise in the uneven process of modernization, cleavages which throw intellectuals back upon the traditional markings of cultural identity to legitimize both themselves and a new integrative (national) culture. However, Gellner puts this process in the context of the breakdown of prior regional cultures and the subsequent *cultural* importance of state-sponsored education systems. This, he says, takes us '*some* of the way towards a schematic explanation of nationalisms: these factors explain why in general (abstracting from local complications) modern loyalties are centred on political units'.[15]

There is a nice ambiguity in Gellner's phrase 'abstracting from local complications' which unintentionally accords with the theoretical approach taken by this book. Clearly what Gellner means is that he, Ernest Gellner, is abstracting from the particular in making the generalizations he does. The present text goes further again. It has generalized from issues of epistemology and methodology to suggest that the process of abstraction is crucial to the possibility of intellectual work. Those processes which were discussed as being most relevant to the relation between intellectual practice and the formation of nations were the abstractions of time and space carried by the techniques and technologies of information storage. From these steps in the argument we are able to reflect upon intellectual practice, attempting to understand some of the underpinnings of the theorizing process and how those same social forms and practices which ground the nation rebound upon the practices and assumptions of the theorists of national formation.

As intellectuals *qua* intellectuals, Marx, Weber and Durkheim worked in a medium which materially transcended the dominant modalities of time and space pertaining during their lifetimes. They interrogated dead authors, made comparisons to long-disappeared communities, and projected the possibilities of current political trajectories into future worlds. At the same time, as embodied human beings they not only consciously experienced the contradictory constraints of time and place, but also were formed in ways which slipped under the intellectual guard of self-conscious reflexivity, and, more deeply, which constituted their very subjectivity. For example, Weber's dispassionate/

14. Nairn, *Break-up of Britain*, 1981, pp. 100, 101.
15. Ernest Gellner, 'Nationalism', 1981, p. 163.

passionate glorification of the community unto death carried the contradictions of the conjunction of intellectual rationalism and subjective 'need'. Weber was logically and subjectively led to the glorification of war. Distinguishing the *forms* of social relations (the rich, condensed intersection of face-to-face and more abstract bonds forged in war), from the blind stupidity, degrading patriotism and senseless carnage of war did not seem to be a pressing consideration in his schema of things. Whether the classical social theorists chose a politics of internationalism or of abstract nationalism, the cultural (and theoretical) means were not yet available for them to take apart the grounds of that choice. The classical theorists simply took for granted rather than felt the need to theorize the fact that they lived and worked in the medium of homogeneous empty time and (national) historicity rather than Messianic time; in a milieu dominated by territorially bounded (national) space rather than by the ritually overdetermined condensations of place; and in a period when the phrase the body politic had become a dead metaphor, no longer evoking the philosophical conundrums of Hobbes' 'Mortall God' and the doctrine of the King's Two Bodies.

If, as I have argued, national formation and subjectivity require as a necessary-though-not-sufficient condition the abstraction of social relations integrated in the emerging dominance of disembodied extension, then it comes as no surprise that intellectuals and the intellectually trained are in the forefront of imagining and enacting the nation. Such persons work in the medium of disembodied extension. They have in this capacity played a significant part in the complex of basic changes in world history, changes which have brought us to the stage when the nation is deeply embedded yet deeply contradictory.

A political coda

Theoretical arguments, however abstract, can never be divorced from history or be without political implications. The present book, written during a time of considerable change in the configurations of international and domestic politics, is no exception. What does it mean that the political question commonly posed in this area, namely 'Is national identity a good or a bad thing?', has not been explicitly raised? In fact the question seems to be bypassed. Given that Tom Nairn first used the metaphor of the nation as Janus-faced in relation to the ambiguous ethical quality of nationalism, the move made earlier to rework the metaphor in terms of the contradictory ontology of nationality confirms this impression. In the current climate with the call of nations into the Gulf War, with the crises in Eastern Europe and the Baltic States, and with continual assertions of neo-nationalisms around the globe the question remains vexing. However, it is I think the wrong focus around which to frame a politics.

It is telling that the contemporary academic consensus on the question of the ethical virtue of nationalism or national identity has tended towards responding ambivalently: 'it is and it is not'. The response, with its account-ing-styled adding up of historical examples on either side of a ledger, indicates the unhelpful nature of the question. Asking whether nationality is good or bad moves the focus excessively on to the moral *content* of political practice rather than allowing for an examination of the constitutive *form* which grounds (and is instantiated in) that practice. A focus on form can arguably allow for a more thoroughgoing political ethics.

In developing a response to the coming period there are decisions which go beyond asking whether we will support the national framework, or opt for inter-nationalism, post-nationalism, cosmopolitanism, a return to the vil-lage, or some other alternative. As Michael Ignatieff writes, 'If patriotism, Samuel Johnson remarked is the refuge of the scoundrel, so post-nationalism and its accompanying disdain for the nationalist emotions of others, may be the last refuge of the cosmopolitan.'[16] A deeper choice is faced. Is the onto-logical thinning out of social life through the constitutive dominance of the most abstract levels of social relations an acceptable development? Or might it not be preferable to work towards a form of social relations in which the various constitutive levels are held in a rich, complex and mutually qualifying manifold? This latter possibility would in practice throw up its own contra-dictions, particularly as the level of the face-to-face came to impose significant constraints upon the 'openness', ephemerality and speed of post-modern life. It would mean that identification with the nation-state was reduced to a subordinated aspect of a social relations of reciprocity and social co-operation between persons living as members of less abstracted commu-nities.

This is not to advocate a return to the boundaries of the parochial village, even if it ever existed as the pastoral ideal suggested. It is rather to hope for a new politics of human cooperation which does not reduce us to homeless minds. It is to argue for a form of ontological socialism which does not reduce politics either to wars of position in the public sphere or to struggles for state control of the mode of production. It is to advocate a new kind of local-regional-global social relations, reaching across the boundaries of place but in a way which does not reduce others to objects of our romantic or abstract internationalism.

In all of this the nation will continue to have some relevance. By recogniz-ing that the nation-state will continue for the foreseeable future to be an influential form of polity-community, albeit one caught between globalism and localism, we can begin to avoid the potentially dangerous pulls of each. We can begin to *re*construct the nation-state as a culturally based institution that qualifies the ravages of globalism while being open to cultural diversity within its borders; which works across and beyond the limitations of parochial localism while protecting the rights of minorities. It seems ironical now, as the modern nation-state falls from grace as the dominant centre of

16. Michael Ignatieff, *Blood and Belonging*, 1994, p. 11.

social relations, that it should offer the possibility of positively mediating the local and the global. But then we live in different times. The openings are there for a new kind of nation-state: a polity-community which, for example, on the one hand writes into its constitution specific obligations to support financially and politically the needs of strangers across the globe and, on the other hand, sets up the legal and social conditions for local regions and face-to-face communities to take over more of the responsibility for managing their own futures. In this kind of future the intermeshing extensions of locality, nationality and globality (and the contradictory intersections of more and less abstract ways of relating to others) could work to qualify and enhance each other rather than, as the prophets of globalism would have it, be subsumed under the latest wave of rationalizing, commodifying, information-charged development.

This, however, is to begin another story, a story which as one nineteenth-century philosopher put it, needs to be worked out in practice rather than just wrapped up in theory.

Appendix
Levels of Theoretical Abstraction

The overall argument is that a comprehensive theory of social relations and subjectivities has to work across a manifold of levels of theoretical abstraction. Below is set out one possible way of conceiving such a manifold.

I   Empirical generalization

(a)   In particular

e.g. ● Biographies of particular persons.
       ● Histories of particular polities such as 'post-settlement' Australia.
       ● Descriptions of particular institutions, fields of activity of discourses.

(b)   In general
Drawing on particular accounts and studies, analysis at this level attempts to be more comparative and to survey the longer term.

e.g. ● Histories of the practices of 'personhood', gender relations, class-based lifeworlds.
       ● Comparative histories of a political form such as 'the nation-state'.
       ● Descriptions of an institution-in-general such as 'bureaucracy', fields such as 'the law', or discourses such as 'social democracy'.

At this level, analysis that does not reach for more abstract ways of understanding, runs the risk – however detailed its description – of superficiality or empiricism. Nevertheless, empirical generalization remains a basic level of analysis necessary to any approach in order to avoid abstract theoreticism.

II   Analysis of modes of practice

(a) In particular
Analysis at this level of theoretical abstraction proceeds by resolution of particular *modes of practice*. The present approach complicates 'classical historical materialism' by analytically distinguishing at least five primary modes.

1   Production (dominant and subordinate).
2   Exchange (dominant and subordinate).
3   Communication (dominant and subordinate).

4   Organization (dominant and subordinate).
5   Enquiry (dominant and subordinate).

In practice, no *mode of practice* exists as a separate, autonomous form. The rationale for this five-fold classification is that it avoids some of the reductionism of a classical 'mode of production' approach without becoming too unwieldy.

(b) In general
Drawing on analyses of particular modes of practice, analysis at this level attempts to describe conjunctures between such modes. Generalizations are made about the structural connections between dominant modes of practice, thus allowing for the short-hand designation of *formations of practice*:

e.g. ● (Reciprocal) tribalism
     ● (Absolutist) feudalism
     ● (Industrial) capitalism
     ● (Information) capitalism
     ● (Command economy) socialism.

These designations, as with all concepts of all classifying schemes, can only be used as working appellations not reified entities. In practice, social formations tend to be defined in terms of the dominant *formation of practice*, but this is not to rule out subordinate formations.

III Analysis of modes of integration

(a) In particular
Analysis proceeds by resolution of *levels of social integration* (and differentiation). While in theory one could distinguish any number of levels of integration, the present approach sets out three such levels:

1   Face-to-face integration
2   Agency-extended integration
3   Disembodied integration.

In practice, no *level of integration* exists as a separate, autonomous form.

(b) In general
Drawing on analyses of levels of integration, generalizations can be made, firstly, about the *intersections* between these (ontological) levels – for example, charting the emergence of ontological contradictions – and, secondly, about the complexities of social life as summarized at less and more abstract (epistemological) *levels of theoretical abstraction*. Following the second path, generalizations can be made which further enrich and contextualize our understanding of particular life histories, fields and discourses (Level I),

modes and formations of practice (II) and the ontological categories and formations of social life (IV).

e.g. • Modern (industrial) capitalism
     • Postmodern (information) capitalism
     • Autonomous individualism
     • Homogeneous disembodied time.

IV Categorical analysis

At this level, analysis works by reflexively 'deconstructing' categories of social ontology. It attempts to take nothing for granted, including the epistemological and ontological assumptions of its own approach (especially the tendency of some deconstructive projects to give priority to the so-argued 'liberatory' potentialities of practices of deconstruction).

(a) In particular
Structural archaeologies (as distinct from 'classical' histories or descriptions – see I(a) above) of particular categories of existence such as:

• Time and space
• Culture and nature
• Gender
• Embodiment
• Knowledge, language, theory.

(b) In general
Drawing on discussions of particular ontological categories, generalizations can be made about different forms of ontological formation, for example:

• Traditionalism
• Patriarchy
• Modernity
• Postmodernity.

As with all other concepts in the present approach to 'levels of theoretical abstraction' they remain provisional concepts, provisional as tested against the criterion 'Are they useful for understanding the complexities of social life?' At this level, analysis which is not tied back into more concrete political–ethical considerations is in danger of abstracted irrelevance, utopianism without a subject, or empty spiritualism.

Bibliography

There are thousands of relevant sources on the national question. To make this bibliography manageable it was necessary to list only references actually cited in the footnotes. This has meant leaving out countless important writings from E.H. Carr's *Nationalism and After* and Karl Deutsch's *Tides Among Nations* to Aijaz Ahmad's *In Theory: Classes, Nations, Literatures*, many of which were read or consulted. For further reading there are numerous bibliographical monographs which can be consulted: the *Canadian Review of Studies in Nationalism* has published more than a dozen volumes of its specialized annotated bibliography.

Abercrombie, Nicholas, Hill, Stephen and Turner, Bryan S. *The Dominant Ideology Thesis*, London, George Allen and Unwin, 1984.

Abercrombie, Nicholas, Hill, Stephen and Turner, Bryan S. *Sovereign Individuals of Capitalism*, London, Allen and Unwin, 1986.

Achebe, Chinua *Things Fall Apart*, London, Heinemann, (1958) 1974.

Acton, John Dalberg *Essays on Freedom and Power*, Glencoe, Free Press, (1862) 1948.

Adamson, Alan 'Colonialism and Nationalism in Africa and Europe' (a report on the fifth *Past and Present* conference), *Past and Present*, 24, 1963, pp. 65–74.

Agassi, J. 'Methodological Individualism', *British Journal of Sociology*, 11, 1960, pp. 244–270.

Agnew, John A. 'Political Regionalism and Scottish Nationalism in Gaelic Scotland', *Canadian Review of Studies in Nationalism*, 8, 1, 1981, pp. 115–129.

Alba, Victor *Nationalists Without Nations: The Oligarchy Versus the People in Latin America*, New York, Frederick A. Praeger, 1968.

Allott, Kenneth *Jules Verne*, London, Cresset, (n.d.) c.1940.

Alomes, Stephen *A Nation at Last? The Changing Nature of Australian Nationalism 1880–1988*, North Ryde, Angus and Robertson, 1988.

Althusser, Louis *For Marx*, London, Verso, (1965) 1979.

Althusser, Louis *Lenin and Philosophy, and other Essays*, New York, Monthly Review Press, 1971.

Anderson, Benedict *Imagined Communities: Reflections on the Origin and Spread of Nationalism*, London, Verso, 1983; second edition 1991.

Anderson, Perry *Lineages of the Absolutist State*, London, Verso, (1974) 1986.

Anderson, Perry *A Zone of Engagement*, London, Verso, 1992.

Ariès, Philippe *The Hour of Our Death*, Harmondsworth, Penguin, 1981.

Armstrong, John *Nations before Nationalism*, Chapel Hill, University of North Carolina Press, 1982.

Arnason, Johann 'The Modern Constellation and the Japanese Enigma: Part 1', *Thesis 11*, 17, 1987, pp. 4–39.

Auerbach, Erich *Literary Language and its Public in Late Latin Antiquity and in the Middle Ages*, New York, Bollingen, 1965.

Avineri, Shlomo *Hegel's Theory of the Modern State*, London, Cambridge University Press, 1972.

Aylmer, G.E. *The King's Servants: The Civil Service of Charles I, 1625–1642*, London, Routledge and Kegan Paul, 1961.

Aylmer, G.E. *The State's Servants: The Civil Service of the English Republic, 1649–1660*, London, Routledge and Kegan Paul, 1973.

Balibar, Etienne and Wallerstein, Immanuel *Race, Nation, Class*, London, Verso, 1991.

Barnard, F.M. 'National Culture and Political Legitimacy: Herder and Rousseau', *Journal of the History of Ideas*, 44, 2, 1983, pp. 231–253.

Barrett, William *Irrational Man*, New York, Doubleday, 1962.

Bartlett, John *Familiar Quotations*, London, Macmillan, (1882), fourteenth edition 1977.

Baudrillard, Jean 'The Precession of Simulacra', *Art and Text*, 11, 1983, pp. 3–47.

Bauman, Zygmunt *Culture as Praxis*, London, Routledge and Kegan Paul, 1973.

Bauman, Zygmunt 'On the Origins of Civilization: A Historical Note', *Theory, Culture and Society*, 2, 3, 1985, pp. 7–14.

Bauman, Zygmunt *Modernity and Ambivalence*, Cambridge, Polity Press, 1991.

Baumann, Gerd *National Integration and Local Integrity: The Miri of the Nuba Mountains in the Sudan*, Oxford, Clarendon Press, 1987.

Bean, Richard 'War and the Birth of the Nation-State', *Journal of Economic History*, 33, 1, 1973, pp. 203–221.

Beck, Ulrich, Giddens, Anthony and Lash, Scott *Reflexive Modernization: Politics, Tradition and Aesthetics in the Modern Social Order*, Cambridge, Polity Press, 1994.

Bell, Daniel *The End of Ideology*, New York, Free Press, (1960) 1965.

Bendix, Reinhard *Kings or People: Power and the Mandate to Rule*, Berkeley, CA, University of California Press, 1978.

Benhabib, Seyla *Situating the Self: Gender, Community and Postmodernism in Contemporary Ethics*, Cambridge, Polity Press, 1992.

Benjamin, Walter *Charles Baudelaire: Lyric Poet in the Era of High Capitalism*, London, New Left Books, 1973.

Bennett, Tony, Buckridge, Pat, Carter, David and Mercer, Colin, eds.

Celebrating the Nation: A Critical Study of Australia's Bicentenary, Sydney, Allen and Unwin, 1992.

Berger, Peter *Facing up to Modernity*, Harmondsworth, Penguin, 1979.

Berman, Marshall *All that is Solid Melts into Air: The Experience of Modernity*, London, Verso, 1983.

Bernstein, Basil *Class, Codes and Control: Theoretical Studies Towards a Sociology of Language*, New York, Schocken Books, 1971, revised edition 1974.

Bernstein, Richard J. 'Structuration as Critical Theory', *Praxis International*, 6, 2, 1986, pp. 235–249.

Bernstein, Richard J. 'Social Theory as Critique' in David Held and John B. Thompson, eds, *Social Theory of Modern Societies: Anthony Giddens and his Critics*, Cambridge, Cambridge University Press, 1989.

Bhabha, Homi, ed. *Nation and Narration*, London, Routledge, 1990.

Bhabha, Homi, 'Anxious Nations, Nervous States', in Joan Copjec, ed., *Supposing the Subject*, London, Verso, 1994.

Biddiss, Michael *The Age of the Masses: Ideas and Society in Europe Since 1870*, New York, Harper and Row, 1978.

Binkley, Robert C. *Realism and Nationalism: 1852–1871*, New York, Harper and Row, (1935) 1963.

Birch, Anthony H. 'Minority Nationalist Movements and Theories of Political Integration', *World Politics*, 30, 3, 1978, pp. 325–344.

Blaut, James, M. 'Nationalism as an Autonomous Force', *Science and Society*, 46, 1, 1982, pp. 1–23.

Blaut, James, M. *The National Question: Decolonizing the Theory of Nationalism*, London, Zed Books, 1987.

Bloch, Marc *Feudal Society*, vols 1 and 2, Chicago, University of Chicago Press, (1940) translated 1961.

Bloom, Solomon F. *The World of Nations: A Study of the National Implications in the Work of Karl Marx*, New York, Columbia University Press, 1941.

Bluntschli, Johann Kaspar *The Theory of the State*, Oxford, Clarendon Press, (1852) 1895.

Boersner, Demetrio *The Bolsheviks and the National and Colonial Question*, Westport, CT, Hyperion, (1957), 1981.

Boorstin, Daniel J. *The Americans*, vol. 2: *The National Experience*, Harmondsworth, Penguin, 1969.

Borst, Arno *The Ordering of Time*, Cambridge, Polity Press, 1993.

Bottomore, Tom 'Sociology', in David McLellan, ed., *Marx: The First Hundred Years*, Oxford, Fontana, 1983.

Bourdieu, Pierre *The Logic of Practice*, Cambridge, Polity Press, 1990.

Braudel, Fernand *The Wheels of Commerce*, vol. 2: *Civilization and Capitalism 15th–18th Century*, London, Fontana, (1979) 1985.

Braudel, Fernand *The Perspective of the World*, vol. 3: *Civilization and Capitalism 15th–18th Century*, London, Collins, 1984.

Braudel, Fernand *The Identity of France*, vol. 1: *History and Environment*, London, Collins, 1988.

Breuilly, John *Nationalism and the State*, Chicago, Chicago University Press, 1982; second edition 1994.

Breuilly, John 'Reflections on Nationalism', *Philosophy of the Social Sciences*, 15, 1985, pp. 65–75.

Bukharin, Nikolai *Historical Materialism*, New York, International Publishers, (1921) 1925.

Burke, Peter *Sociology and History*, London, George Allen and Unwin, 1980.

Buthman, William Curt *The Rise of Integral Nationalism in France: With Special Reference to the Ideas and Activities of Charles Maurras*, New York, Octagon, 1970.

Butler, Peter 'The Individual and International Relations' in James Mayall, ed., *The Community of States*, London, George Allen and Unwin, 1982.

Bynack, V.P. 'Noah Webster's Linguistic Thought and the Idea of an American National Culture', *Journal of the History of Ideas*, 45, 1, 1984, pp. 99–114.

Cahm, Eric and Fisera, Vladimir Claude *Socialism and Nationalism*, vol. 1, Nottingham, Spokesman, 1978.

Callinicos, Alex *Is there a Future for Marxism?*, London, Macmillan, 1982.

Callinicos, Alex 'Anthony Giddens: A Contemporary Critique', *Theory and Society*, 14, 2, 1985, pp. 133–166.

Callinicos, Alex *Making History: Agency, Structure and Change in Social Theory*, Cambridge, Polity Press, 1989.

Campbell, J.B. *The Emperor and the Roman Army 31BC–AD235*, Oxford, Clarendon Press, 1984.

Cannadine, David 'The Context, Performance and Meaning of Ritual: The British Monarchy and the "Invention of Tradition", c.1820–1977', in Eric Hobsbawm and Terence Ranger, eds, *The Invention of Tradition*, Cambridge, Cambridge University Press, 1983.

Caraman, Philip *University of the Nations: The Story of the Gregorian University of Rome from 1551 to Vatican II*, New York, Paulist Press, 1981.

Cardiff, David and Scannell, Paddy 'Broadcasting and National Unity', in James Curran, Anthony Smith and Pauline Wingate, eds, *Impacts and Influences: Essays on Media Power in the Twentieth Century*, London, Methuen, 1987.

Castles, Stephen, Cope, Bill, Kalantzis, Mary and Morrissey, Michael *Mistaken Identity: Multiculturalism and the Demise of Nationalism in Australia*, Sydney, Pluto Press, 1988.

Castoriadis, Cornelius *The Imaginary Institution of Society*, Cambridge, Polity Press, 1987.

Catto, J.I., ed. *The History of the University of Oxford*, Oxford, Clarendon Press, 1984.

Chamberlin, E.R. *Preserving the Past*, London, J.M. Dent, 1979.

Chambers, Iain and Curti, Lidia 'A Volatile Alliance: Culture, Popular Culture and the Italian Left', *Formations: Of Nation and People*, London, Routledge and Kegan Paul, 1984.

Chatterjee, Partha *Nationalist Thought and the Colonial World: A Derivative Discourse*, London, Zed Books, 1986.

Chatterjee, Partha *The Nation and its Fragments: Colonial and Postcolonial Histories*, Princeton, NJ, Princeton University Press, 1993.

Chesneaux, Jean *The Political and Social Ideas of Jules Verne*, London, Thames and Hudson, 1972.

Chesneaux, Jean 'Information Society as Civic Mutation', *Arena*, 81, 1987, pp. 26–34.

Chickering, Roger *We Men Who Feel Most German: A Cultural Study of the Pan-German League, 1886–1914*, Boston, MA, George Allen and Unwin, 1984.

Clanchy, M.T. *From Memory to Written Record: England 1066–1307*, London, Edward Arnold, 1979.

Clift, Dominique *Quebec Nationalism in Crisis*, Kingston and Montreal, McGill-Queen's University Press, 1982.

Cohen, Ronald 'Warfare and State Formation: Wars Make States and States Make Wars', in R. Brian Ferguson, ed., *Warfare, Culture and Environment*, Orlando, FL, Academic Press, 1984.

Cohler, Anne M. *Rousseau and Nationalism*, New York, Basic Books, 1970.

Connor, Walker 'The Politics of Ethnonationalism', *Journal of International Affairs*, 27, 1, 1973, pp. 1–21.

Connor, Walker *The National Question in Marxist–Leninist Theory and Strategy*, Princeton, NJ, Princeton University Press, 1984.

Connor, Walker *Ethnonationalism: The Quest for Understanding*, Princeton, NJ, Princeton University Press, 1994.

Corrigan, Philip, ed. *Capitalism, State Formation and Marxist Theory*, London, Quartet, 1980.

Corrigan, Philip, and Sayer, Derek *The Great Arch: English State Formation as Cultural Revolution*, Oxford, Basil Blackwell, 1985.

Coser, Lewis 'Durkheim's Conservatism and its Implications for his Sociological Theory', in Kurt Wolff, ed., *Emile Durkheim et al.: Essays on Sociology and Philosophy*, New York, Harper and Row, 1964.

Cottle, Basil *The Triumph of English 1350–1400*, London, Blandford Press, 1969.

Coulton, G.G. 'Nationalism in the Middle Ages', *Cambridge Historical Journal*, 5, 1935, pp. 15–40.

Coward, Rosalind and Ellis, John *Language and Materialism: Developments in Semiology and the Theory of the Subject*, Boston, MA, Routledge and Kegan Paul, 1977.

Craib, Ian *Modern Social Theory: From Parsons to Habermas*, Brighton, Wheatsheaf, 1984.

Craib, Ian 'Back to Utopia: Anthony Giddens and Modern Social Theory', *Radical Philosophy*, 43, 1986, pp. 17–21.

Crankshaw, Edward *Bismarck*, London, Macmillan, 1981.

Cregeen, Eric 'The Changing Role of the House of Argyll in the Scottish Highlands', in N.T. Phillipson and Rosalind Mitchison, eds, *Scotland in the Age of Improvement*, Edinburgh, Edinburgh University Press, 1970.

Cummins, Ian *Marx, Engels and National Movements*, London, Croom Helm, 1980.

Cummins, Ian 'Marx, Engels, and the Springtime of Peoples', in Roland Sussex and J.C. Eade, eds, *Culture and Nationalism in Nineteenth-Century Eastern Europe*, Columbus, Slavica, 1985.

Dale, Roger 'Nation State and International System: The World-System Perspective', in Gregor McLennan, David Held and Stuart Hall, eds, *The Idea of the Modern State*, Milton Keynes, Open University Press, 1984.

Dandeker, Christopher *Surveillance, Power and Modernity*, Cambridge, Polity Press, 1994.

Darnton, Robert *The Great Cat Massacre*, Harmondsworth, Penguin, 1985.

Davis, Horace B. *Nationalism and Socialism: Marxist and Labor Theories of Nationalism to 1917*, New York, Monthly Review Press, 1967.

Davis, Horace B. *Toward a Marxist Theory of Nationalism*, New York, Monthly Review Press, 1978.

Debord, Guy *Society of the Spectacle*, Detroit, Black and Red, (1967) 1983.

Debray, Régis 'Marxism and the National Question', *New Left Review*, 105, 1977, pp. 25–41.

Debray, Régis *Teachers, Writers, Celebrities: The Intellectuals of Modern France*, London, Verso, 1981.

Deleuze, Gilles and Guattari, Félix *Nomadology: The War Machine*, New York, Semiotext(e), 1986.

Derrida, Jacques 'Declarations of Independence', *New Political Science*, 15, 1986, pp. 7–15.

Derrida, Jacques *The Other Heading*, Bloomington, IN, Indiana University Press, 1992.

Dickens, A.G. *The German Nation and Martin Luther*, London, Edward Arnold, 1974.

Dodgshon, Robert A. *The European Past: Social Evolution and Spatial Order*, London, Macmillan, 1987.

Donelan, Michael 'A Community of Mankind', in James Mayall, ed., *The Community of States*, London, George Allen and Unwin, 1982.

Douglas, Mary *Natural Symbols: Explorations in Cosmology*, Harmondsworth, Penguin (1970) 1978.

Draper, Hall *The Marx–Engels Chronicle*, New York, Schocken, 1985.

Dunn, Michael 'Marxism and the National Question', *Arena*, 40, 1975, pp. 29–41.

DuPlessis, Robert S. 'The Partial Transition to World Systems Analysis in Early Modern European History', *Radical History Review*, 39, 1987, pp. 11–27.

Dupré, Louis *Marx's Social Critique of Culture*, New Haven, CT, Yale University Press, 1983.

Durkheim, Emile *Professional Ethics and Civil Morals*, London, Routledge and Kegan Paul, (1890–1900) 1957.

Durkheim, Emile *Montesquieu and Rousseau: Forerunners of Sociology*,

Michigan, University of Michigan Press, (1892, published posthumously 1918) 1965.

Durkheim, Emile *The Division of Labour in Society* (with an introduction by George Simpson), New York, Macmillan, (1893) translated 1933.

Durkheim, Emile *The Rules of Sociological Method*, New York, Free Press, (1895) 1966.

Durkheim, Emile *Socialism and Saint-Simon*, London, Routledge and Kegan Paul, (1896, published posthumously 1928) 1959.

Durkheim, Emile *Moral Education: A Study in the Theory and Application of the Sociology of Education*, New York, Free Press, (1902–3, published posthumously 1925) 1973.

Durkheim, Emile *The Evolution of Educational Thought: Lectures on the Formation and Development of Secondary Education in France*, London, Routledge and Kegan Paul, (1904–5, published posthumously 1938) 1977.

Durkheim, Emile *The Elementary Forms of Religious Life*, London, George Allen and Unwin (1912) 1976.

Durkheim, Emile *'Germany Above All': German Mentality and the War*, Paris, Armand Colin, 1915.

Durkheim, Emile and Dennis, E. *Who Wanted War? The Origin of the War according to Diplomatic Documents*, Paris, Armand Colin, 1915.

Dyson, Kenneth *The State Tradition in Western Europe*, Oxford, Martin Robertson, 1980.

Eagleton, Terry *Criticism and Ideology: A Study in Marxist Literary Theory*, London, Verso, 1978.

Eberhard, Wolfram *Conquerors and Rulers: Social Forces in Medieval China*, Leiden, E.J. Brill, revised edition 1965.

Eccleston, Bernard 'The State and Modernisation in Japan', in James Anderson, ed., *The Rise of the Modern State*, Sussex, Wheatsheaf, 1986.

Eco, Umberto *Travels in Hyper-Reality*, London, Pan, 1987.

Edwards, John *Language, Society and Identity*, Oxford, Basil Blackwell, 1985.

Ehrenreich, John H. 'The Theory of Nationalism: A Case of Underdevelopment', *Monthly Review*, 27, 1, 1975, pp. 57–61.

Ehrenreich, John H. 'Socialism, Nationalism and Capitalist Development', *Review of Radical Political Economics*, 15, 1, 1983, pp. 1–42.

Eisenstein, Elizabeth *The Printing Revolution in Early Modern Europe*, Cambridge, Cambridge University Press, 1983.

Eley, Geoff 'Nationalism and Social History', *Social History*, 6, 1, 1981, pp. 83–107.

Eley, Geoff 'State Formation, Nationalism and Political Culture in Nineteenth-Century Germany', in Raphael Samuel and Gareth Stedman Jones, eds, *Culture, Ideology and Politics*, London, Routledge and Kegan Paul, 1982.

Elias, Norbert *The Civilizing Process*, vol. 2: *State Formation and Civilization*, London, Basil Blackwell, (1939) translated 1982.

Elias, Norbert *Time: An Essay*, Oxford, Blackwell, 1992.

Emerson, Rupert *From Empire to Nation*, Boston, MA, Beacon Press, 1960.

Engels, Friedrich *The Origin of the Family, Private Property and the State*, Harmondsworth, Penguin, (1884) 1985.

d'Entrèves, Alexander Passerin *The Notion of the State: An Introduction to Political Theory*, London, Oxford University Press, 1969.

Eyerman, Ron, Svensson, Lennart G. and Sederqvist, Thomas, eds, *Intellectuals, Universities and the State in Western Modern Societies*, Berkeley, CA, University of California Press, 1987.

Febvre, Lucien *A New Kind of History* (edited by Peter Burke), London, Routledge and Kegan Paul, translated 1973.

Fernández-Armesto, Felipe, ed. *The Peoples of Europe*, London, Times Books, 1994.

Finer, Samuel 'State- and Nation-Building in Europe: The Role of the Military', in Charles Tilly, ed., *The Formation of National States in Western Europe*, Princeton, NJ, Princeton University Press, 1975.

Forgacs, David 'National-Popular: Genealogy of a Concept', in Formations Editorial Collective, eds., *Formations: Of Nation and People*, London, Routledge and Kegan Paul, 1984.

Foucault, Michel *Discipline and Punish: The Birth of the Prison*, Harmondsworth, Peregrine, (1975) 1982.

Frazer, Elizabeth and Lacey, Nicola, eds, *The Politics of Community*, London, Harvester Wheatsheaf, 1993.

Freud, Sigmund 'Thoughts for the Times on War and Death' (1915), in *Collected Papers*, vol. 4, London, Hogarth Press, 1934.

Freud, Sigmund *Civilization and its Discontents*, London, Hogarth Press, (1929) 1975.

Friedman, Jonathan 'Culture, Identity, and World Process', *Review*, 12, 1, 1989, pp. 51–69.

Friedrichs, Christopher R. *Urban Society in an Age of War: Nordlinger, 1580–1720*, Princeton, NJ, Princeton University Press, 1979.

Fussell, Paul *The Great War and Modern Memory*, Oxford, Oxford University Press, 1977.

Gane, Mike 'Anthony Giddens and the Crisis of Social Theory', *Economy and Society*, 12, 1983, pp. 368–398.

Garnsey, Peter and Saller, Richard *The Roman Empire*, London, Duckworth, 1987.

Geertz, Clifford *The Interpretation of Cultures*, (particularly ch. 9, 'After the Revolution: The Fate of Nationalism in the New States' and ch. 10, 'The Integrative Revolution: Primordial Sentiments and Civil Politics in the New States'), New York, Basic Books, 1973.

Gellner, Ernest *Thought and Change*, London, Weidenfeld and Nicolson, 1964.

Gellner, Ernest 'Scale and Nation', in his *Contemporary Thought and Politics*, London, Routledge and Kegan Paul, 1974.

Gellner, Ernest *Legitimation of Belief*, London, Cambridge University Press, 1974.

Gellner, Ernest 'Nationalism, or the New Confessions of a Justified Edinburgh Sinner', in his *Spectacles and Predicaments: Essays in Social Theory*, Cambridge, Cambridge University Press, 1979.

Gellner, Ernest 'Nationalism', *Theory and Society*, 10, 6, 1981, pp. 753–776.

Gellner, Ernest *Nations and Nationalism*, London, Basil Blackwell, 1983.

Gellner, Ernest *The Psychoanalytic Movement: Or the Coming of Unreason*, London, Paladin, 1985.

Gellner, Ernest *Culture, Identity and Politics*, Cambridge, Cambridge University Press, 1987.

Gellner, Ernest *Postmodernism, Reason and Religion*, London, Routledge, 1992.

Gellner, Ernest *Encounters with Nationalism*, Oxford, Blackwell, 1994.

Geras, Norman *Marx and Human Nature: Refutation of a Legend*, London, Verso, 1983.

Geras, Norman 'Post-Marxism', *New Left Review*, 163, 1987, pp. 40–82.

Giddens, Anthony *Central Problems in Social Theory: Action, Structure and Contradiction in Social Analysis*, London, Macmillan, 1979.

Giddens, Anthony *Power, Property and State*, vol. 1: *A Contemporary Critique of Historical Materialism*, London, Macmillan, 1981.

Giddens, Anthony *Profiles and Critiques in Social Theory*, London, Macmillan, 1982.

Giddens, Anthony *The Constitution of Society*, Cambridge, Polity Press, 1984.

Giddens, Anthony *The Nation-State and Violence*, vol. 2: *A Contemporary Critique of Historical Materialism*, Cambridge, Polity Press, 1985.

Giddens, Anthony 'Nation-States and Violence', in *Social Theory and Modern Sociology*, Cambridge, Polity Press, 1987.

Giddens, Anthony *Modernity and Self-Identity*, Cambridge, Polity Press, 1991.

von Gierke, Otto *Political Theories of the Middle Age*, Cambridge, Cambridge University Press, 1900.

Gildea, Robert *Barricades and Borders: Europe 1800–1914*, Oxford, Oxford University Press, 1987.

Gill, Gerry 'Post-Structuralism as Ideology', *Arena*, 69, 1984, pp. 60–96.

Gluck, Carol *Japan's Modern Myths: Ideology in the Late Meiji Period*, Princeton, NJ, Princeton University Press, 1985.

Gòmez-Quiñones, Juan 'Critique on the National Question, Self-Determination and Nationalism', *Latin American Perspectives*, 9, 2, 1982, pp. 62–83.

Goody, Jack *The Domestication of the Savage Mind*, Cambridge, Cambridge University Press, 1977.

Goody, Jack *The Logic of Writing and the Organization of Society*, Cambridge, Cambridge University Press, 1986.

Goody, Jack *The Interface Between the Written and the Oral*, Cambridge, Cambridge University Press, 1987.

Gosden, Christopher *Social Being and Time*, Oxford, Blackwell, 1994.

Gould, Carol *Marx's Social Ontology: Individuality and Community in Marx's Theory of Reality*, Cambridge, MIT Press, 1972.

Gould, Peter and White, Rodney *Mental Maps*, Boston, MA, George Allen and Unwin, second edition 1986.

Gouldner, Alvin W. *The Future of Intellectuals and the Rise of the New Class: A Frame of Reference, Theses, Conjectures, Arguments, and an Historical Perspective on the Role of Intellectuals and Intelligentsia in the International Class Contest of the Modern Era*, New York, Seabury, 1979.

Gourevitch, Peter Alexis 'The Re-emergence of "Peripheral Nationalisms": Some Comparative Speculations on the Spatial Distribution of Political Leadership and Economic Growth', *Comparative Studies in Society and History*, 21, 1979, pp. 303–322.

Greenfield, Liah *Nationalism: Five Roads to Modernity*, Cambridge, MA, Harvard University Press, 1992.

Gregory, Derek 'Presences and Absences: Time–Space Relations and Structuration Theory', in David Held and John B. Thompson, eds, *Social Theory of Modern Societies: Anthony Giddens and his Critics*, Cambridge, Cambridge University Press, 1989.

Gregory, Derek and Urry, John, eds *Social Relations and Spatial Structures*, London, Macmillan, 1985.

Grew, Raymond 'How Success Spoiled the Risorgimento' in Eugene C. Black, ed., *European Political History 1815–1870*, New York, Harper and Row, 1967.

Gross, David 'Space, Time, and Modern Culture', *Telos*, 50, 1981–82, pp. 59–78.

Gross, David 'Temporality and the Modern State', *Theory and Society*, 14, 1, 1985, pp. 53–82.

Guattari, Félix *Molecular Revolution*, Harmondsworth, Penguin, 1984.

Guback, Thomas and Bettig, Ronald 'Translating the *Manifesto* into English; Nineteenth Century Communication, Twentieth Century Confusion', *Journal of Communication Inquiry*, 11, 2, 1987, pp. 3–16.

Guenée, Bernard *States and Rulers in Later Medieval Europe*, Oxford, Blackwell (first published in French 1971), 1988.

Habermas, Jürgen *Legitimation Crisis*, London, Heinemann, 1976.

Habermas, Jürgen *Communication and the Evolution of Society*, Boston, MA, Beacon, 1979.

Hall, John A. 'Ernest Gellner' in his *Diagnoses of Our Time: Six Views on Our Social Condition*, London, Heinemann, 1981.

Hall, John A. *Powers and Liberties: The Causes and Consequences of the Rise of the West*, Harmondsworth, Pelican, 1986.

Hall, John W. and Jansen, Marius B., eds *Studies in the Institutional History of Early Modern Japan*, Princeton, NJ, Princeton University Press, 1968.

Hanagan, Michael P. *The Logic of Solidarity: Artisans and Industrial Workers in Three French Towns, 1871–1914*, Urbana, University of Illinois Press, 1980.

Handman, Max Sylvius 'The Sentiment of Nationalism', *Political Science Quarterly*, 36, 1921, pp. 104–121.

Hayes, Carlton 'The War of Nations', *Political Science Quarterly*, 39, 4, 1914, pp. 687–707.

Hayes, Carlton *Essays on Nationalism*, New York, Russell and Russell, (1926) 1966.

Hechter, Michael *Internal Colonialism: The Celtic Fringe in British National Development, 1536–1966*, London, Routledge and Kegan Paul, 1975.

Heller, Agnes *Renaissance Man*, New York, Schocken Books, (1967, translated 1978) 1981.

Henriques, Julian, Hollway, Wendy, Urwin, Cathy, Venn, Couze and Walkerdine, Valerie *Changing the Subject: Psychology, Social Regulation and Subjectivity*, London, Methuen, 1984.

Herod, Charles C. *The Nation in the History of Marxian Thought: The Concept of Nations with History and Nations without History*, The Hague, Martinus Nijhoff, 1976.

Hertz, Frederick *Nationality in History and Politics*, London, Kegan Paul, 1944.

Hinkson, John 'Post-Lyotard: A Critique of the Information Society', *Arena*, 80, 1987, pp. 123–155.

Hinkson, John 'Postmodern Economy: Value, Self-Formation and Intellectual Practice', *Arena Journal*, new series 1, 1993, pp. 23–44.

Hirst, Paul and Woolley, Penny *Social Relations and Human Attributes*, London, Tavistock, 1982.

Hobbes, Thomas *Leviathan*, London, Dent, (1651) 1976.

Hobsbawm, Eric 'The Limits of Nationalism', *New Society*, 2 October 1969, p. 523.

Hobsbawm, Eric 'Some Reflections on Nationalism' in T.J. Nossiter, A.H. Hanson and Stein Rokkan, eds, *Imagination and Precision in the Social Sciences: Essays in Memory of Peter Nettl*, London, Faber and Faber, 1972.

Hobsbawm, Eric 'Some Reflections on "The Break-up of Britain"', *New Left Review*, 105, 1977, pp. 3–23.

Hobsbawm, Eric 'Mass-Producing Traditions: Europe 1870–1914', (1983) in Eric Hobsbawm and Terence Ranger, eds, *The Invention of Tradition*, Cambridge, Cambridge University Press, 1983.

Hobsbawm, Eric *Nations and Nationalism since 1780: Programme, Myth and Reality*, Cambridge, Cambridge University Press, 1990.

Hobsbawm, Eric and Ranger, Terence, eds *The Invention of Tradition*, Cambridge, Cambridge University Press, 1983.

Hobson, John A. 'Nationalism and Imperialism', the introductory section to *Imperialism: A Study*, London, George Allen and Unwin, (1902) 1968.

Holmes, Dave 'Marxism and the National Question' in Jon West, Dave Holmes and Gordon Adler, *Socialism or Nationalism?*, Sydney, Pathfinder, 1979.

Holtzman, Steven *Digital Mantras: The Languages of Abstract and Virtual Worlds*, Cambridge, MIT Press, 1994.

Honore, Tony 'The Human Community and the Principle of Majority Rule', in Eugene Kamenka, ed., *Community as a Social Ideal*, London, Edward Arnold, 1982.

Hooson, David *Geography and National Identity*, Oxford, Blackwell, 1994.

Horne, Donald *The Public Culture*, London, Pluto, 1986.

Howard, Michael 'War and the Nation-State', *Daedalus*, Fall 1979, pp. 101–110.

Hroch, Miroslav 'From National Movement to Fully Formed Nation', *New Left Review*, 198, March 1993, pp. 3–20.

Hubatsch, Walter *Studies in Medieval and Modern German History*, London, Macmillan, 1985.

Hudson, Wayne and Carter, David, eds, *The Republicanism Debate*, Sydney, NSW University Press, 1993.

Huizinga, Johan *Men and Ideas: History, the Middle Ages, the Renaissance* (particularly the essay 'Patriotism and Nationalism in European History'), New York, Meridian, 1959.

Hutchinson, John *Modern Nationalisms*, London, Fontana, 1994.

Ignatieff, Michael *Blood and Belonging*, London, Vintage, 1994.

Irele, Abiola 'Negritude or Black Cultural Nationalism', *Journal of Modern African Studies*, 3, 3, 1965, pp. 321–347.

Isaacs, Harold R. 'Nationality: "End of the Road?"', *Foreign Affairs*, 53, 3, 1975, pp. 432–449.

Jacobs, Jane *Cities and the Wealth of Nations*, Harmondsworth, Penguin, 1986.

Jacoby, Russell *Social Amnesia*, Boston, MA, Beacon Press, 1975.

Jameson, Fredric 'Postmodernism, or the Cultural Logic of Late Capitalism', *New Left Review*, 146, July 1984, pp. 53–92.

Jenkins, Brian and Minnerup, Günter *Citizens and Comrades*, London, Pluto, 1984.

Johnson, Richard J. 'Histories of Culture/Theories of Ideology: Notes on an Impasse', in Michelle Barratt, Philip Corrigan, Annette Kuhn, and Janet Wolff, eds, *Ideology and Cultural Production*, London, Croom Helm, 1979.

Johnston, R.J. *Geography and the State: An Essay in Political Geography*, London, Macmillan, 1982.

Kamenka, Eugene 'Political Nationalism – The Evolution of the Idea' in E. Kamenka, ed., *Nationalism: The Nature and Evolution of an Idea*, Canberra, Australian National University Press, 1973.

Kamenka, Eugene, ed. *Community as a Social Ideal*, London, Edward Arnold, 1982.

Kantorowicz, Ernst '*Pro Patria Mori* in Medieval Thought', *American Historical Review*, 56, 3, 1951, pp. 472–492.

Kantorowicz, Ernst *The King's Two Bodies*, Princeton, NJ, Princeton University Press, 1957.

Kautsky, John H., ed. *Political Change in Underdeveloped Countries: Nationalism and Communism*, New York, John Wiley, 1967.

Kavan, Zdenek 'Human Rights and International Community', in James Mayall, ed., *The Community of States*, London, George Allen and Unwin, 1982.

Kedourie, Elie *Nationalism*, London, Hutchinson, (1960) 1993.

Keith, Michael, and Pile, Steve, eds, *Place and the Politics of Identity*, London, Routledge, 1993.

Kelly, George Armstrong 'Mortal Man, Immortal Society? Political Metaphors in Eighteenth-Century France', *Political Theory*, 14, 1, 1986, pp. 5–29.

Kern, Stephen *The Culture of Time and Space, 1880–1918*, Cambridge, MA, Harvard University Press, 1983.

Kiernan, V.G. 'State and Nation in Western Europe', *Past and Present*, 31, 1965, pp. 20–38.

Kitching, Gavin 'Nationalism: The Instrumental Passion', *Capital and Class*, 25, 1985, pp. 98–116.

Koestler, Arthur *The Act of Creation*, London, Pan, (1964) 1977.

Kohn, Hans *The Idea of Nationalism: A Study in its Origins and Background*, New York, Macmillan, (1944) 1956.

Kohn, Hans *Nationalism: Its Meaning and History*, New York, Van Nostrand Reinhold, revised edition 1965.

Kohn, Hans *Prelude to Nation-States: The French and German Experience, 1789–1815*, Princeton, NJ, Van Nostrand, 1967.

Koht, Halvdan 'The Dawn of Nationalism in Europe', *The American Historical Review*, 52, 2, 1947, pp. 265–280.

Kornhauser, William *The Politics of Mass Society*, London, Routledge and Kegan Paul, (1959) 1965.

Krieger, Leonard 'Germany', in Orest Ranum, ed., *National Consciousness, History and Political Culture in Early-Modern Europe*, Baltimore, MD, Johns Hopkins University Press, 1975.

Kristeva, Julia *Nations without Nationalism*, New York, Columbia University Press, 1993.

Kulichenko, M. *Nations and Social Progress*, Moscow, Progress Publishers, 1984.

Kurauchi, Kazuta 'Durkheim's Influence on Japanese Sociology', in Kurt Wolff, ed., *Emile Durkheim et al., Essays on Sociology and Philosophy*, New York, Harper and Row, 1964.

Landau, Terry *About Faces*, New York, Doubleday, 1989.

Landes, David *Revolution in Time*, Cambridge, MA, Belknap/Harvard University Press, 1983.

Lasch, Christopher *The Minimal Self: Psychic Survival in Troubled Times*, London, Picador, 1985.

Latimer, Dan 'Jameson and Post-Modernism', *New Left Review*, 148, November 1984, pp. 116–128.

Lawson, John and Silver, Harold *A Social History of Education in England*, London, Methuen, 1973.

Le Bon, Gustave *The Psychology of the Great War*, London, Fisher Unwin, English translation 1916.

Leed, Eric '"Voice" and "Print": Master Symbols in the History of Communication', in Kathleen Woodward, ed., *The Myths of Information: Technology and Postindustrial Culture*, Madison, WI, Coda Press, 1980.

Lenin, V.I. *Imperialism, the Highest Stage of Capitalism*, Moscow, Progress Publishers, (1917) 1978.

Lerner, Daniel *The Passing of Traditional Society*, New York, Free Press, 1958.

Lévi-Strauss, Claude *The Savage Mind*, London, Weidenfeld and Nicolson, (1962) translated 1966.

Lewis, I.M., ed. *Nationalism and Self-Determination in the Horn of Africa*, London, Ithaca Press, 1983.

Little, Graham *Political Ensembles*, Melbourne, Oxford University Press, 1985.

Lockwood, David 'Social Integration and System Integration', in G.K. Zollschan and W. Hirsch, eds, *Explorations in Social Change*, London, Routledge and Kegan Paul, 1964.

Lohrey, Andrew 'Australian Nationalism as Myth', *Arena*, 68, 1984, pp. 107–123.

Longford, Elizabeth *Victoria R.I.*, London, Pan, 1966.

Lorrain, Jorge *The Concept of Ideology*, London, Hutchinson, 1979.

Lovejoy, Arthur O. *The Great Chain of Being*, Cambridge, MA, Harvard University Press, (1936) 1964.

Löwy, Michael 'Marxists and the National Question', *New Left Review*, 96, 1976, pp. 81–100.

Lunde, Erik S. 'The Ambiguity of the National Idea: The Presidential Campaign of 1872', *Canadian Review of Studies in Nationalism*, 5, 1, 1978, pp. 1–23.

Lukács, Georg *History and Class Consciousness: Studies in Marxist Dialectics*, Cambridge, MIT Press, (1922, new edition, 1967) 1976.

Lynn, Richard 'The Sociobiology of Nationalism', *New Society*, 1 July 1976, pp. 11–14.

Lyotard, Jean-François *The Postmodern Condition: A Report on Knowledge*, Manchester, Manchester University Press, 1984.

MacDougall, Hugh *Racial Myth in English History: Trojans, Teutons and Anglo-Saxons*, Montreal and Hanover, Harvest House and University Press of New England, 1982.

MacLaughlin, Jim 'Industrial Capitalism, Ulster Unionism and Orangeism: An Historical Reappraisal', *Antipode: A Radical Journal of Geography*, 12, 1, 1980, pp. 15–28.

MacLaughlin, Jim 'The Political Geography of "Nation-Building" and Nationalism in Social Sciences: Structural vs. Dialectical Accounts', *Political Geography Quarterly*, 5, 4, 1986, pp. 299–329.

MacLaughlin, Jim 'State-Centred Social Science and the Anarchist Critique: Ideology in Political Geography', *Antipode*, 18, 1, 1986, pp. 11–38.

MacLaughlin, Jim 'Nationalism as an Autonomous Social Force: A Critique of Recent Scholarship on Ethnonationalism', *Canadian Review of Studies in Nationalism*, 14, 1, 1987, pp.1–18.

MacLaughlin, Jim 'Reflections on Nations as "Imagined Communities"', *Journal of Multilingual and Multicultural Development*, 9, 5, 1988, pp. 449–457.

McLellan, David *Karl Marx: Early Texts*, Oxford, Basil Blackwell, 1972.

McLennan, Gregor 'Critical or Positive Theory? A Comment on the Status of Anthony Giddens' Social Theory', *Theory, Culture and Society*, 2, 2, 1984, pp. 123–129.

McLuhan, Marshall *Understanding Media: The Extensions of Man*, London, Abacus, 1973.

McNeil, William *The Pursuit of Power: Technology, Armed Force and Society since A.D. 1000*, Oxford, Basil Blackwell, 1983.

Mann, Michael *The Sources of Social Power*, vols 1 and 2, Cambridge, Cambridge University Press, 1986, 1993.

Mann, Michael *States, War and Capitalism: Studies in Political Sociology*, Oxford, Basil Blackwell, 1988.

Marx, Karl *On Colonialism*, Moscow, Progress Publishers, (1850–1888) 1976.

Marx, Karl *Capital*, vol. 1, Moscow, Progress Publishers, (1867) 1977.

Marx, Karl and Engels, Frederick *Collected Works*, London, Lawrence and Wishart, 1976–1985.

Marx, Karl and Engels, Frederick *Selected Works*, vols 1–3, Moscow, Progress, 1977.

Mauss, Marcel *The Gift: Forms and Functions of Exchange in Archaic Societies*, London, Routledge and Kegan Paul, (1925) 1974.

Mayall, James, ed. *The Community of States*, London, George Allen and Unwin, 1982.

Mayer, Arno J. *The Persistence of the Old Regime: Europe to the Great War*, London, Croom Helm, 1981.

Mazzini, Giuseppe *The Duties of Man and Other Essays*, London, Dent, (1844–70) 1924.

Meinecke, Friedrich *Cosmopolitanism and the Nation State*, Princeton, NJ, Princeton University Press, (1907) 1970.

Mercer, Colin 'Regular Imaginings: The Newspaper and the Nation' in Tony Bennett, Pat Buckridge, David Carter and Colin Mercer, eds, *Celebrating the Nation*, Sydney, Allen and Unwin, 1992.

Merquior, J.G. *Rousseau and Weber: Two Studies in the Theory of Legitimacy*, London, Routledge and Kegan Paul, 1980.

Meznarić, Silva 'A Neo-Marxist Approach to the Sociology of Nationalism, Doomed Nations and Doomed Schemes', *Praxis International*, 7, 1, 1987, pp. 79–89.

Michels, Robert 'Patriotism', in *First Lectures in Political Sociology*, New York, Harper and Row, (1927) 1965.

Minogue, K.R. *Nationalism*, London, Batsford, 1967.

Mitchell, M. Marion 'Emile Durkheim and the Philosophy of Nationalism', *Political Science Quarterly*, 46, 1, 1931, pp. 87–106.

Mitzman, Arthur *The Iron Cage*, New York, Grosset and Dunlop, 1969.

de Montmorency, J.E.G. *State Intervention in English Education*, Cambridge, Cambridge University Press, 1902.

Moore, G.E. 'A Defense of Common Sense', *Contemporary British Philosophy*, 2, 1925, pp. 193–223.

Morgan, Edmund S. *Inventing the People: The Rise of Popular Sovereignty in England and America*, New York, W.W. Norton, 1988.

Morgan, Glenn 'From West to East and Back Again: Capitalist Expansion and Class Formation in the Nineteenth Century', in Howard Newby, Janet

Buyra, Paul Littlewood, Gareth Rees and Teresa L. Rees, eds, *Restructuring Capital: Recession and Reorganization in Industrial Society*, Houndmills, Macmillan, 1985.

Morgenthau, Hans J. *Politics Among Nations: The Struggle for Power and Peace*, New York, (1948) fifth edition 1976.

Morris, Richard B. *Basic Documents in American History*, New York, Van Nostrand, 1965.

Mosca, Gaetano *The Ruling Class/Elementi di Scienza Politica*, New York, McGraw Hill, (1896, 1923 edition) 1965, p. 482.

Moses, John A. *The Politics of Illusion: The Fischer Controversy in German Historiography*, London, George Prior, 1975.

Muir, Ramsay *Nationalism and Internationalism: The Culmination of Modern History*, London, Constable, 1916.

Mulhern, Francis 'Towards 2000, or News from You-Know-Where', *New Left Review*, 148, 1984, pp. 5–30.

Mullett, Michael *Popular Culture and Popular Protest in Late Medieval and Early Modern Europe*, London, Croom Helm, 1987.

Munck, Ronaldo 'Otto Bauer: Towards a Marxist Theory of Nationalism', *Capital and Class*, 25, Spring 1985, pp. 84–97.

Munck, Ronaldo *The Difficult Dialogue: Marxism and Nationalism*, London, Zed Books, 1986.

Musil, Robert *The Confessions of Young Törless*, London, Picador (1906) 1955.

Musil, Robert *The Man Without Qualities*, vol. 1, London, Picador (1930), 1983.

Myers, Fred *Pintupi Country, Pintupi Self: Sentiment, Place, and Politics among Western Desert Aborigines*, Washington and Canberra, Smithsonian Institute Press and Australian Institute of Aboriginal Studies, 1986.

Nairn, Tom 'The Three Dreams of Scottish Nationalism', *New Left Review*, 49, 1968, pp. 3–18.

Nairn, Tom 'British Nationalism and the EEC', *New Left Review*, 69, 1971, pp. 3–28.

Nairn, Tom 'The Left Against Europe?', *New Left Review*, 75, 1972, pp. 5–20 (later published as *The Left Against Europe?*), Harmondsworth, Penguin, 1973).

Nairn, Tom *The Break-up of Britain: Crisis and Neo-Nationalism*, London, Verso, 1977, second edition 1981.

Nairn, Tom *The Enchanted Glass: Britain and its Monarchy*, London, Radius, 1988.

Navari, Cornelia 'The Origins of the Nation-State', in Leonard Tivey, ed., *The Nation-State*, Oxford, Martin Robertson, 1981.

Nietzsche, Friedrich *Thus Spake Zarathustra* (1891–92), and other writings (1865-1889) in Walter Kaufmann, ed., *The Portable Nietzsche*, Harmondsworth, Penguin, 1985.

Nimni, Ephraim 'Great Historical Failure: Marxist Theories of Nationalism',

Capital and Class, 25, 1985, pp. 58–83. A longer version appears in Martin Shaw, ed., *Marxist Sociology Revisited: Critical Assessments*, London, Macmillan, 1985.

Nimni, Ephraim 'Marx, Engels and the National Question', *Science and Society*, 53, 3, 1989, pp. 297–326.

Nimni, Ephraim *Marxism and Nationalism*, London, Pluto, 1991.

Nisbet, Robert A. *The Quest for Community*, London, Oxford, (1953) 1971.

Nisbet, Robert A. *The Sociological Tradition*, London, Heinemann, (1966) 1970.

Oakesmith, John *Race and Nationality*, London, Heinemann, 1919.

Ooms, Herman 'Neo-Confucianism and the Formation of Early Tokugawa Ideology', in Peter Nosca, ed., *Confucianism and Tokugawa Culture*, Princeton, NJ, Princeton University Press, 1984.

Orridge, A.W. 'Uneven Development and Nationalism: 1', *Political Studies*, 29, 1, 1982, pp. 1–15.

Orridge, A.W. 'Uneven Development and Nationalism: 2', *Political Studies*, 29, 2, 1982, pp. 181–190.

Ouston, Philip *The Imagination of Barrès*, Toronto, University of Toronto Press, 1974.

Packard, Vance *A Nation of Strangers*, New York, David McKay, 1972.

Parker, William N. *Europe, America, and the Wider World: Essays on the Economic History of Western Capitalism*, vol. 1: *Europe and the World Economy*, Cambridge, Cambridge University Press, 1984.

Parsons, Talcott *The Social System*, London, Routledge and Kegan Paul, 1951.

Petrus, Joseph 'Marx and Engels on the National Question', *Journal of Politics*, 33, 1971, pp. 797–824.

Peyre, Henri 'Durkheim: The Man, His Time, and His Intellectual Background', in Kurt Wolff, ed., *Emile Durkheim et al., Essays on Sociology and Philosophy*, New York, Harper and Row, 1964.

Plamenatz, John 'Two Types of Nationalism', in Eugene Kamenka, ed., *Nationalism: The Nature and Evolution of an Idea*, Canberra, Australian National University Press, 1973.

Pleydell, Alan 'Language, Culture and the Concept of International Political Community', in James Mayall, ed., *The Community of States*, London, George Allen and Unwin, 1982.

Poggi, Gianfranco *The Development of the Modern State*, London, Hutchinson, 1978.

Polanyi, Karl *The Great Transformation: The Political and Economic Origins of Our Time*, Boston, MA, Beacon Press, (1944) 1957.

Portis, Edward B. *Max Weber and Political Commitment: Science, Politics and Personality*, Philadelphia, Temple University Press, 1986.

Poster, Mark *Foucault, Marxism and History: Mode of Production versus Mode of Information*, Cambridge, Polity Press, 1984.

Poster, Mark *The Mode of Information: Poststructuralism and Social Context*, Cambridge, Polity Press, 1990.

Poulantzas, Nicos *Political Power and Social Classes*, London, New Left Books, (1968) 1973.

Poulantzas, Nicos *State, Power, Socialism*, London, Verso, (1978) 1980.

Pye, Lucien W. *Politics, Personality, and Nation Building: Burma's Search for Identity*, New Haven, CT, Yale University Press, 1962.

Rawkins, Phillip 'Nationalist Movements Within the Advanced Industrial State: The Significance of Culture', *Canadian Review of Studies in Nationalism*, 10, 2, 1983, pp. 221–233.

Rawkins, Phillip 'Minority Nationalism and its Limits: A Weberian Perspective on Cultural Change', *Canadian Review of Studies in Nationalism*, 11, 1, 1984, pp. 87–101.

Rawls, John *A Theory of Justice*, London, Oxford University Press, 1972.

Renan, Ernest 'What is a Nation?', (1882), reproduced in part in Hans Kohn, *Nationalism: Its Meaning and History*, New York, Van Nostrand Reinhold, 1965.

Reynolds, Susan 'Medieval *Origines Gentium* and the Community of the Realm', *History*, 68, 1983, pp. 375–390.

Ringrose, David R. 'Comment on Papers by Reed, de Vries, and Bean', *Journal of Economic History*, 33, 1, 1973, pp. 222–227.

Ripalda, José Maria *The Divided Nation: The Roots of a Bourgeois Thinker: G.W.F. Hegel*, Amsterdam, Van Gorcum, Assen, 1977.

Roberts, Stephen *History of Modern Europe*, Sydney, Angus and Robertson, 1950.

Robertson, Roland and Lechner, Frank 'Modernization, Globalization, and the Problem of Culture in World-Systems Theory', *Theory, Culture and Society*, 2, 3, 1985, pp. 103–117.

Rodinson, Maxime 'Le Marxisme et la Nation', *L'Homme et la Société*, 7, 1968, pp. 131–149.

Roehl, Richard 'Comment on Papers by Reed and Bean', *Journal of Economic History*, 33, 1, 1973, pp. 228–231.

Rosdolsky, Roman 'Worker and Fatherland: A Note on a Passage in the *Communist Manifesto*', *Science and Society*, 29, 1965, pp. 330–337.

Rosdolsky, Roman *Engels and the 'Nonhistoric' Peoples: The National Question in the Revolution of 1848*, (1964) translated by John-Paul Himka, in *Critique*, 18–19, 1987.

Rose, J. Holland *Nationality as a Factor in Modern History*, London, Rivingtons, 1916.

Rosenau, James N. *The Study of Political Adaptation: Essays on the Analysis of World Politics*, London and New York, Frances Pinter and Nichols, 1981.

Rostow, Walt W. *Stages of Economic Growth: A Non-Communist Manifesto*, Cambridge, Cambridge University Press, 1960.

Rudé, George *The Crowd in History: A Study of Popular Disturbances in France and England, 1730–1848*, New York, John Wiley, 1964.

Rudolph, Joseph R. 'Ethnic Sub-States and the Emergent Politics of Tri-Level Interaction in Western Europe', *Western Political Quarterly*, 30, 4, 1977, pp. 536–557.

Rudolph, Joseph R. 'Ethnoregionalism in Contemporary Western Europe:

The Potential for Political Accommodation', *Canadian Review of Studies in Nationalism*, 8, 2, 1981, pp. 323–341.

Sack, Robert David *Conceptions of Space in Social Thought*, London, Macmillan, 1980.

Sathyamurthy, T.V. *Nationalism in the Contemporary World*, London, Frances Pinter, 1983.

Sayer, Derek *The Violence of Abstraction: The Analytic Foundations of Historical Materialism*, Oxford, Basil Blackwell, 1987.

Scaff, Lawrence 'Fleeing the Iron Cage: Politics and Culture in the Thought of Max Weber', *American Political Science Review*, 81, 3, 1987, pp. 737–755.

Schivelbusch, Wolfgang 'Railroad Space and Railroad Time', *New German Critique*, 14, 1978, pp. 31–40.

Schorer, Mark 'The Structure of the Novel: Method, Metaphor and Mind', in Barbara Hardy, ed., *Middlemarch: Critical Approaches to the Novel*, London, Athlone, 1967.

Scott, Jonathan F. 'Inculcation of Nationalism in French Schools after 1870', in Louis Snyder, ed., *The Dynamics of Nationalism*, Princeton, NJ, Van Nostrand, 1964.

Seigel, Jerrold *Marx's Fate: The Shape of a Life*, Princeton, NJ, Princeton University Press, 1978.

Sennett, Richard *The Fall of Public Man*, Cambridge, Cambridge University Press, 1977.

Seton-Watson, Hugh *Nations and States: An Enquiry into the Origins of Nations and the Politics of Nationalism*, London, Methuen, 1977.

Shafer, Boyd C. *Nationalism: Myth and Reality*, London, Victor Gollancz, 1955.

Shafer, Boyd C. 'If Only We Knew More about Nationalism', *Canadian Review of Studies in Nationalism*, 7, 2, 1980, pp. 197–218.

Shafer, Boyd C. 'Review of Gellner's *Nations and Nationalism*', *Canadian Review of Studies in Nationalism*, 11, 1, 1984, pp. 141–142.

Shaheen, Samad *The Communist (Bolshevik) Theory of National Self-Determination*, The Hague, W. van Hoeve, 1956.

Sharp, Geoff 'A Revolutionary Culture', *Arena*, 16, 1968, pp. 2–11.

Sharp, Geoff 'Hollowed Out from Within', *Arena*, 63, 1983, pp. 1–2.

Sharp, Geoff 'Intellectuals in Transition', *Arena*, 65, 1983, pp. 84–95.

Sharp, Geoff 'Constitutive Abstraction and Social Practice', *Arena*, 70, 1985, pp. 48–82.

Sharp, Geoff 'Extended Forms of the Social', *Arena Journal*, new series 1, 1993, pp. 221–237.

Sharp, Geoff and White, Doug 'Features of the Intellectually Trained', *Arena*, 15, 1968, pp. 30–33.

Sharp, Nonie 'Nationalism and Cultural Politics', *Arena*, 43, 1976, pp. 58–77.

Sheffer, Gabriel, ed. *Modern Diasporas in International Politics*, London, Croom Helm, 1986.

Shennan, J.H. *The Origins of the Modern European State, 1450–1725*, London, Hutchinson, 1974.

Shils, Edward 'Primordial, Personal, Sacred and Civil Ties', *British Journal of Sociology*, 8, 1957, pp. 130–145.

Shouldice, Larry, ed. *Contemporary Quebec Criticism*, Toronto, University of Toronto Press, 1979.

Simkhovitch, Vladimir G. 'Approaches to History: 3', *Political Science Quarterly*, 47, 3, 1932, pp. 410–439.

Simmel, Georg *Conflict and the Web of Group-Affiliations*, translated by Kurt H. Wolff and Reinhard Bendix, London, Free Press, (1908) 1955.

Simmel, Georg *The Sociology of Georg Simmel*, translated, edited and with an introduction by Kurt H. Wolff, London, Free Press, 1950.

Skocpol, Theda *States and Social Revolutions: A Comparative Analysis of France, Russia and China*, Cambridge, Cambridge University Press, (1979) 1984.

Smith, Alan G.R. *The Emergence of a Nation-State: The Commonwealth of England 1529–1660*, Essex, Longman, 1984.

Smith, Anthony D. 'Ethnocentrism, Nationalism and Social Change', *International Journal of Comparative Sociology*, 13, 1972, pp. 1–20.

Smith, Anthony D. '"Ideas" and "Structure" in the Formation of Independence Ideals', *Philosophy of the Social Sciences*, 3, 1973, pp. 19–39.

Smith, Anthony D. *The Ethnic Revival*, Cambridge, Cambridge University Press, 1981.

Smith, Anthony D. *Theories of Nationalism*, London, Duckworth, (1971) second edition 1983.

Smith, Anthony D. 'Nationalism and Classical Social Theory', *The British Journal of Sociology*, 34, 1, 1983, pp. 19–38.

Smith, Anthony D. *The Ethnic Origins of Nations*, London, Basil Blackwell, 1986.

Smith, Anthony D. 'History and Liberty: Dilemmas of Loyalty in Western Democracies', *Ethnic and Racial Studies*, 9, 1, 1986, pp. 43–65.

Smith, Anthony D. *National Identity*, London, Penguin, 1991.

Snyder, Louis L. *German Nationalism: The Tragedy of a People*, New York, Kennikat Press, (1952) 1969.

Sohn-Rethel, Alfred *Intellectual and Manual Labour: A Critique of Epistemology*, London, Macmillan, 1978.

Solovyof, Vladimir 'The National Question from a Moral Point of View', chapter 5 in his *The Justification of the Good: An Essay on Moral Philosophy*, London, Constable, (1897) 1918.

Stalin, Joseph *Marxism and the National and Colonial Question: A Collection of Articles and Speeches*, London, Lawrence and Wishart, (1913–34) 1947.

Stokes, Gale 'The Underdeveloped Theory of Nationalism', *World Politics*, 31, 1978, pp. 150–160.

Stokes, Gale 'How is Nationalism Related to Capitalism?', *Comparative Studies in Society and History*, 28, 1986, pp. 591–598.

Strayer, Joseph R. 'The Tokugawa Period and Japanese Feudalism' in John W. Hall and Marius B. Jansen, eds, *Studies in the Institutional History of Early Modern Japan*, Princeton, NJ, Princeton University Press, 1968.

Symmons-Symonolewicz, Konstantin *Modern Nationalism: Towards a Consensus in Theory*, New York, Polish Institute of Arts and Sciences in America, 1968.

Symmons-Symonolewicz, Konstantin 'National Consciousness in Medieval Europe: Some Theoretical Problems', *Canadian Review of Studies in Nationalism*, 8, 1, 1981, pp. 151–166.

Tabori, Paul *The Anatomy of Exile: A Semantic and Historical Study*, London, Harrap, 1972.

Talmon, J.L. *The Myth of the Nation and the Vision of Revolution: The Origins of Ideological Polarisation in the Twentieth Century*, London, Secker and Warburg, 1981.

Thom, Martin 'Tribes within Nations: The Ancient Germans and the History of Modern France', in Homi Bhabha, ed., *Nation and Narration*, London, Routledge, 1990.

Thompson, David *Europe Since Napoleon*, Harmondsworth, Penguin, (1957) 1971.

Thompson, John B. 'Ideology and the Social Imaginary', *Theory and Society*, 11, 5, 1982, pp. 659–681.

Thompson, John B. 'The Theory of Structuration: An Assessment of the Contribution of Anthony Giddens' in *Studies in the Theory of Ideology*, Cambridge, Polity Press, 1984.

Thompson, Kenneth *Emile Durkheim*, London, Ellis Horwood and Tavistock, 1982.

Thompson, William Irwin *From Nation to Emanation: Planetary Culture and World Governance*, Findhorn Scotland, Findhorn Publications, 1982.

Tiedemann, Arthur *Modern Japan*, Princeton, NJ, Van Nostrand, 1955.

Tilly, Charles, ed. *The Formation of National States in Western Europe*, Princeton, NJ, Princeton University Press, 1975.

Tipton, C. Leon, ed. *Nationalism in the Middle Ages*, New York, Holt, Rinehart and Winston, New York, 1972.

Tiryakian, Edward 'Emile Durkheim', in Tom Bottomore and Robert Nisbet, eds, *A History of Sociological Analysis*, London, Heinemann, 1970.

Tiryakian, Edward and Nevitte, Neil 'Nationalism and Modernity', in Edward Tiryakian and Ronald Rogowski, eds, *New Nationalisms of the Developed West*, Boston, MA, Allen and Unwin, 1985.

Tiryakian, Edward and Rogowski, Ronald, eds *New Nationalisms of the Developed West: Toward Explanation*, Boston, MA, Allen and Unwin, 1985.

Toffler, Alvin *The Third Wave*, London, Pan, 1981.

Tönnies, Ferdinand *Community and Society*, New York, Harper and Row, (1887) 1963.

Trevor-Roper, Hugh 'The Invention of Tradition: The Highland Tradition of Scotland', in Eric Hobsbawm and Terence Ranger, eds, *The Invention of Tradition*, Cambridge, Cambridge University Press, 1983.

Tudjman, Franjo *Nationalism in Contemporary Europe*, Boulder, CO, East European Monographs, 1981.

Tully, R.E. 'Moore's Defense of Common Sense: a Reappraisal After Fifty Years', *Philosophy*, 51, 1976, pp. 289–306.

Tunstall, Jeremy *The Media are American: Anglo-American Media in the World*, London, Constable, 1977.

Turner, Bryan S. 'Personhood and Citizenship', *Theory, Culture and Society*, 3, 1, 1986, pp. 1–16.

Turner, Bryan S. *Orientalism, Postmodernism and Globalism*, London, Routledge, 1994.

Turner, Stephen and Factor, Regis *Max Weber and the Dispute over Reason and Value: A Study in Philosophy, Ethics, and Politics*, London, Routledge and Kegan Paul, 1984.

Urry, John and Gregory, Derek, eds *Social Relations and Spatial Structures*, London, Macmillan, 1985.

van Abbé, Derek *Image of a People: Modern German Writing in its Social Context*, London, Harrap, 1964.

Verne, Jules *A Tour of the World in Eighty Days*, New York, Burt, (1873) n.d.

Vilar, Pierre 'On Nations and Nationalism', *Marxist Perspectives*, 5, 1979, pp. 8–29.

Vincent, Andrew *Theories of the State*, Oxford, Basil Blackwell, 1987.

Virilio, Paul *Speed and Politics*, New York, Semiotext(e), 1986.

Walker, Mack *Germany and the Emigration, 1816–1885*, Cambridge, MA, Harvard University Press, 1964.

Walker, Mack *German Home Towns: Community, State and General Estate, 1648–1871*, Ithaca, NY, Cornell University Press, 1971.

Wallerstein, Immanuel *The Modern World System: Capitalist Agriculture and the Origins of the European World-Economy in the Sixteenth Century*, New York, Academic Press, 1976.

Walsh, M. Christine, ed. *Prologue: A Documentary History of Europe, 1848–1960*, Australia, Cassell, 1968.

Watanuki, Joji 'Nation-Building at the Edge of an Old Empire: Japan and Korea', in S.N. Eisenstadt and Stein Rokkan, eds, *Building States and Nations*, vol. 2: *Analyses by Region*, Beverly Hills, CA, Sage, 1973.

Webb, Keith *The Growth of Nationalism in Scotland*, Harmondsworth, Penguin, 1978.

Weber, Eugen *The Nationalist Revival in France, 1905–1914*, Berkeley, CA, University of California Press, 1968.

Weber, Eugen *Peasants into Frenchmen: The Modernization of Rural France, 1870–1914*, Stanford, CA, Stanford University Press, 1976.

Weber, Max Inaugural Lecture, Freiburg, May 1895, 'The National State and Economic Policy', *Economy and Society*, 9, 4, 1980, pp. 428–449.

Weber, Max *Weber: Selections in Translation* (edited by W.G. Runciman, translated by Eric Matthews), Cambridge, Cambridge University Press, (1895–1920) 1978.

Weber, Max *The Protestant Ethic and the Spirit of Capitalism* (translated by Talcott Parsons), New York, Charles Scribner's Sons, (1904–5 translated 1930) 1958.

Weber, Max *From Max Weber: Essays in Sociology* (essays from 1904–20 translated, edited and with an introduction by H.H. Gerth and C. Wright Mills), New York, Oxford University Press, 1968.

Weber, Max *The Theory of Social and Economic Organization* (edited with an introduction by Talcott Parsons), New York, Free Press (Part 1 of *Wirtschaft und Gesellschaft*, 1910–20, posthumously published 1921) 1945.

Weissbort, Daniel, ed. *Post-War Russian Poetry*, Harmondsworth, Penguin, 1974.

Wessell, Leonard P. *Karl Marx, Romantic Irony and the Proletariat: The Mythopoetic Origins of Marxism*, Baton Rouge, Louisiana State University Press, 1979.

White, Philip L. 'What is a Nationality', *Canadian Review of Studies in Nationalism*, 12, 1, 1985, pp. 1–23.

White, Richard *Inventing Australia: Images and Identity 1688–1980*, Sydney, George Allen and Unwin, 1981.

Wickham, Chris 'Historical Materialism, Historical Sociology', *New Left Review*, 171, 1988, pp. 63–78.

Williams, Colin 'Ethnic Resurgence in the Periphery', *Area*, 11, 4, 1979, pp. 279–283.

Williams, E.N. *The Ancien Regime in Europe*, Harmondsworth, Pelican, (1972) 1983.

Williams, Raymond *The Long Revolution*, London, Chatto and Windus, 1961.

Williams, Raymond *Television: Technology and Cultural Form*, Glasgow, Fontana Collins, 1974.

Williams, Raymond *Keywords: A Vocabulary of Culture and Society*, Glasgow, Fontana, 1976.

Williams, Raymond *Marxism and Literature*, Oxford, Oxford University Press, 1977.

Williams, Raymond *Problems in Materialism and Culture*, London, Verso, 1980.

Williams, Raymond 'Problems of the Coming Period', *New Left Review*, 140, 1983, pp. 7–18.

Williams, Raymond *Towards 2000*, Harmondsworth, Penguin, 1985.

Williams, Raymond *Loyalties*, London, Chatto and Windus, 1985.

Wills, Garry *Inventing America: Jefferson's Declaration of Independence*, New York, Vintage Books, 1979.

Wingfield-Stratford, Esmé *The Foundations of British Patriotism*, London, Right Book Club, 1940.

Wirth, Louis 'Types of Nationalism', *American Journal of Sociology*, 41, 1936, p. 723–737.

Wolf, Eric R. *Europe and the People Without History*, Berkeley, CA, University of California Press, 1982.

Worsley, Peter *The Third World*, London, Weidenfeld and Nicolson, (1964) 1978.

Wright, Erik Olin 'Giddens's Critique of Marxism', *New Left Review*, 138, 1983, pp. 11–35.

Wright, Moorhead 'An Ethic of Responsibility', in James Mayall, ed., *The Community of States*, London, George Allen and Unwin, 1982.

Wright, Patrick *On Living in an Old Country: The National Past in Contemporary Britain*, London, Verso, 1985.

Wylie, Jonathan 'The Sense of Time, the Social Construction of Reality, and the Foundations of Nationhood in Dominica and the Faroe Islands', *Comparative Studies in Society and History*, 24, 1982, pp. 438–466.

Zeitland, Irving M. *Ideology and the Development of Sociological Theory*, Englewood Cliffs, NJ, Prentice-Hall, 1968.

Zernatto, Guido 'Nation: The History of a Word', *Review of Politics*, 6, 1944, pp. 351–366.

Zijderveld, Anton C. *The Abstract Society: A Cultural Analysis of Our Time*, Harmondsworth, Penguin, 1974.

Žižek, Slavoj *For They Know Not What They Do: Enjoyment as a Political Factor*, London, Verso, 1991.

Zubaida, Sami 'Theories of Nationalism', in Gary Littlejohn, Barry Smart, John Wakefield and Nira Yuval-Davis, eds, *Power and the State*, London, Croom Helm, 1978.

Index

nation-state, *cont.*
as administrative structure 105, 158, 161, 164ff., 180, 182, 187; as artificial 117, 152, 181; and capitalism 159–161; as central to international relations xi, 151; classical nation-state 34, 191; concept of 10, 12–13, 158; conjunction of nation and state 12, 14, 40, 42, 45, 47, 57, 67, 89, 96, 104, 131, 180, 182, 185; and continuing tribal solidarities 5; 'death of' xi 37, 111, 165, 180; defined 13ff., 157, 160, 165, 166; dissolving from within 34; as European in origin 154–157; as framing people's lives xi, xv, 70, 152; 'historic' 62, 110; immutability of 83; as imposed 117; as *kokutai* 5, 65; as modern xi, xii 14, 18, 34, 46, 67, 70, 114, 118; modern nation-state 34–35, 41; monopoly over means of violence 65 *(see also* violence*)*; as nation-*state* (state-nation) 158, 166, 182; as part of system of nation-states 151; permeability of boundaries xv, 34; as power container 153, 160, 165, 167; resistance to 117, 181; as rooted in past 68; as taken for granted 90, 151; unevenly consolidating 30 fn.35, 59–60, 70, 105, 180; and *Volksgeist* 76
The Nation-State and Violence 158, 161, 168
natural, and the artificial 132, 181; *see also* nation
naturalization of citizenry xi, 16
Nietzsche, Friedrich 58, 67, 70, 73, 96, 165
Netherlands and the Dutch 37, 72, 110, 154
New Left Review 107, 108
New Zealand 34, 36
Newton, Isaac 77
Nicholas II 64
Nimni, Ephraim 50
Nisbet, Robert 128
Normandie 10
North America 105
nostalgia 44, 117, 176

Oakesmith, John 84
object-mediated integration 25
objectification (reification) 73
objective relations; *see under* subjective being
Olympics 35, 36
ontological categories, concept of xii, 21, 37, 182, 200; *see also specific categories such as* body and embodiment, time
ontological formations 21, 123, 149, 200; *see also particular formations such as* modernity
ontological levels, as collapsed into one plane 141; *see also* plane

ontological security 37, 171, 172
ontology 161; changing forms of 5, 57, 116, 160, 164, 177; and cultural depth, 35–36, 46, 92, 101, 146; defined xii; defined 148; ontological shakiness, 149; and social frame 7, 91, 118; 'what is-ness', 96, 101, 180, 181; *see also* abstraction, contradiction
Ooms, Herman 156
The Organization of the Family 54
Orridge, Andrew 130
Ortega y Gasset, José 138
Ouston, Philip 100

Packard, Vance 140
Pan-German League 52 fn.20, 85, 90
Pareto, Vilfredo 83, 85
Paris Commune 53
parochialism 101, 108, 196; penetrated from outside 148
Parsons, Talcott 128
particularistic relations 5, 6
patria (*la patrie*) 9, 28, 29–30, 40, 42, 88, 114, 116, 154, 188; *communis patria* 11, 29; *see also* fatherland, state
patrimony 27, 29, 191
patriotism (*amor patriae*) 17, 29–30, 86, 87, 88–89, 99, 188, 195; compatriotism 164; *pro patria mori* 29–30
people 11, 16, 20, 29, 41, 42, 44, 60, 110; as audience 45–46; as basic unit of analysis 55; as natural subject of history 43; 'of the United States of America' 157
perennialism 19
performing arts 68, 69, 76
Periodic Table of Elements 77, 78
persons; as abstract heroes 3, 35; abstracted xii, 29, 93, 119; as actors 171, 172–173; as autonomous authors of our own identity 176–177; fictitious or '*Artificiall person*' 28, 74; mobility of 131, 140, 144; as self-active subjects 134, 148, 170, 176, 190; theorized 48, 170ff.
Peterson, Scott 4
Petrarch, Francesco 63, 80, 99, 182, 188, 189
peuple; *see* people
Philosophes 54
Philosophiae Naturalis Principia Mathematica 77
philosophy, the discipline of 68, 69, 76, 177; as keeper of the state 79
Phoenicians 59, 112
Picardie 10
Piedmontese 61, 62